Life and Death

C000243016

'Royal Charter'

The true story of a treasure-ship wrecked on the coast of Anglesey

Chris and Lesley Holden

CALGO PUBLICATIONS

www.calgopublications.co.uk

Copyright -- Calgo Publications

All rights reserved. No part of this book may be reproduced, photocopied, stored in a retrieval system or be transmitted by any means or in any form without the previous permission of the authors, given in writing.

Disclaimer -- Every effort has been made to ensure that the information contained in this book is accurate and up to date. However, the Authors and Publisher respectively accept no responsibility or liability for any errors, omissions or alterations, or for any consequence resulting from the use of, or reliance upon, any information contained within this book.

Chris and Lesley Holden assert their moral right to be identified as authors of this book in accordance with the Copyright Designs & Patents Act 1988.

A Catalogue Record Entry for this book is available from the British Library.

ISBN: 978-0-9545066-2-9

Photographic Credits

Chris & Lesley Holden -- pages 4, 9, 18, 20, 21, 22, 24, 25, 35, 36, 38, 39, 43, 46, 47, 48, 49, 50, 52, 54, 69, 79, 90, 121, 132, 142, 143, 155, 157, 184, 196, 206, 207, 208, 242, 256, 261, 267, 269, 270, 271, 273, 274, 277, 279, 283 & 284.

Chester Sub-Aqua Club -- pages 120, 126, 243, 272, 274, 275 & 276.

Phil Brown -- page 65. Richard Bufton -- page 175. Mark Chaloner -- page 55.

Sir Neil Cossons --- page 256. John Fearon -- page 54.

Simon Fielding -- pages 37, 38, 47, 229, 274 & 278. Sam Holland -- page 183.

Ron Hurley -- page 245. Paul Kay -- pages 34, 62, 63, 73, 98 & 276.

Neil O'May -- page 118. Joyce Rigg - page 247.

Mike Round -- pages 56 & 61. Tony Tollitt -- page 9.

Ken Wainwright -- page 72. Robert Williams -- pages 219 & 262.

Engravings from the 'Illustrated London News' and similar periodicals -- pages 7, 11, 12, 16, 23, 26, 28, 30, 31, 32, 33, 41, 42, 44, 53, 100, 103, 104, 107, 109, 133, 137, 179, 193, 209, 218, 241, 250, 254, 258, 259 & 285.

Diagrams -- Chris Holden - pages 19 & 131.

Published by Calgo Publications,

CALGO

33, Meadowcroft, Higher Kinnerton, Chester CH4 9AY

United Kingdom. Telephone: 01244 660579

Website: www.calgopublications.co.uk or e-mail info@calgopublications.co.uk

Printed and bound in the United Kingdom by Amadeus Press Ltd., Cleckheaton, Yorkshire.

Introduction

"Picture this, if you can, to your imagination, and you have before you what I had before me in reality on that dreadful morning. After an hour of this, the ship parted amidships, the death warrant of hundreds; then came the dreadful work, but no wild shouts, no desponding, noisy cry, but a deep, terrible, stunning groan of 'All is lost! All hope is gone!'

It was now about half floodtide, the waves increasing in height every moment. When the ship parted, I went on the poop deck. The first thing I saw was a number of ladies struggling in the water on the poop — I rescued one. Some of them went overboard, others, as the water ran off, came round again. Then two or three tremendous waves came thundering over us, smothering everything, and drove me and the female that was in my arms away to leeward."

So wrote Samuel Edward Gapper, one of the few survivors of the wreck of the once-proud steam-clipper 'Royal Charter', whose smashed remains now lie in only a few feet of water against the rocky shore of Anglesey, North Wales. Just a few miles short of her destination at Liverpool, she was now reduced to a vast tangle of bent and twisted wrought iron, with an unknown number of human bodies trapped amongst the debris, all surrounded by a carpet of shining sovereigns, precious ingots, brilliant nuggets and sparkling gold-dust.

Having left Melbourne, Australia on the 26th of August, 1859, the 'Royal Charter' had made a rapid and almost uneventful voyage southwards into the 'Furious Fifties', that remote part of the Southern Ocean beyond Tasmania and New Zealand. Heading eastwards, she rounded Cape Horn at the tip of South America, sailed between the Falkland Islands and South Georgia, before heading northwards through the middle of the Atlantic Ocean to arrive off the port of Queenstown, Ireland, on the 24th of October. She paused here briefly while a few passengers and mail-bags were sent ashore. With only a relatively short distance to her home port, the 'Royal Charter' had almost completed her sixth circumnavigation of the world, and her commander, Captain Taylor, had assured his passengers that he expected to be in Liverpool within 24 hours. Sadly, their fate was destined to be otherwise.

The story of the disaster has been told many times before. By Charles Dickens, W.F. Peacock, A & J.K. [sic] and Frank Fowler during the reign of Queen Victoria; by E. Neil Baynes and Leslie Clow during the 1930s; and more recently by Alexander McKee in his excellent book 'The Golden Wreck', originally published in 1961. This most recent book inspired me to dive on the wreck-site in 1982, and on many subsequent occasions since that year.

But there are inconsistencies in these accounts of the wreck, and I wanted to know more about the 'Royal Charter', her place in history, the passengers and crew, her construction, and the reasons why she was wrecked. Fortunately, most of the primary sources of information from 1859 have been preserved in the various libraries and archives around the world, so this book contains many of the original newspaper articles of evidence given under oath, and of eyewitness accounts of the event.

It has been published in time for the 150th anniversary of the catastrophe.

Chris Holden

Questions raised

As mentioned, there are many previous accounts of the history of the 'Royal Charter, but some of these stories contain information that disagrees with that given by the survivors of the disaster. One book states that the clipper left Adelaide to head westward around the Cape of Good Hope, when the contemporary newspapers say that she left Melbourne for Liverpool, eastwards via Cape Horn. Other suppositions are that she was an 'iron-clad', that she was launched sideways into the River Dee in Scotland rather than the Welsh river of that name, and that her captain tried to escape in a boat when she was wrecked. Of course, the Victorian reporters may have been totally wrong, or may have embellished their stories to make them more exciting in an age when the daily and weekly periodicals were full of disasters, murders, suicides, robberies and war, so the original accounts are reproduced here with very little modification to their contents to enable you, the reader, to form your own opinion of what took place on that dreadful night of October 25th - 26th, 1859. Certainly, some of the evidence given under oath is contradictory, especially regarding the time of a particular occurrence, but that is totally understandable as people were in great danger and in no mood to check that all their pocket-watches were synchronised.

Many questions have been asked about the ship, her captain, the crew, the passengers, the Liverpool pilot service and the local people of Anglesey:

- Was the captain drunk?
- Was he in a hurry to get home in sixty days?
- Why did all the women and children die?
- Did the 'Royal Charter' pause at Holyhead instead of continuing to Liverpool?
- Why was there no pilot on-board?
- Why didn't the captain order the masts to be cut down to lessen the strain on the anchor-cables?
- Why were only two anchors deployed, when the 'Royal Charter' carried four of them?
- Did the anchors stop the vessel from drifting, and why did the anchor-cables fail?
- Finally, a personal question. Who was Tom Tyson? The name-plate shown here was recovered from the wreck in 1982, but at the time of printing, no clue has been found as to who he was. This plaque may be the identification for his luggage, or it may be the label from his cabin door. But who was he?

There are many other contentions, but hopefully you can answer some of them yourself by reading the original newspaper reports from Victorian times, and forming your own opinion about the tragic events of the 26th of October, 1859.

Contents

Acknowledgments

This book could not have been made possible without the assistance of many others, both divers and non-divers who have given support, help or advice in one form or another.

In particular, we would like to thank (in alphabetical order) -- Roger Amsden, Chris Andrews, Dave Balfour, Mike Bowyer, Richard Bufton, Mark Chaloner, Nigel Cossons, Graham Davenport, Peter Day, Pete Drurey, Brian Entwistle, Dave Ferrier, Simon Fielding, Sam Holland, Gillian Holmes, Derlwyn Hughes, Keith Hurley, Ron Hurley, Neil Isherwood, Gerald Jellicoe, Dr. Cecil Jones, Ian Jones, Paul & Lucy Kay, Martin Kidds, Carol Kirkwood, Chris Michael, Nigel and Sarah Musgrave, Geoff Oldfield, Neil O'May, Richard & Liz Owen, Joyce Rigg, Mike Round, Janet Sampson, Mike Sedgwick, Jon Shaw, Dave Stead, Peter Stone, John Stubbs, Vince Thurkettle, Tony Tollitt, Wally Waldron, Pauline Wilson, Graham Wright and Jan Wynne.

Our thanks must also go to all past and present members of Chester Sub-Aqua Club for their patience and help, as well as for the many wonderful days that we have spent diving with them. Many other sub-aqua clubs and individual divers have made us very welcome, and have freely contributed information to this book.

The staff at all the local libraries and archives have continued to provide a vast amount of help while researching the historical information on the 'Royal Charter' and the other ships described in this book.

A Perfect Hurricane.

Strictly speaking, the British Isles do not suffer from actual hurricanes, as these meteorological occurrences can only be sustained where the temperature of the sea is 26 degrees Celsius or greater, a situation not found in the waters of northern Europe. Despite this, the country is occasionally visited by hurricane-force winds that reach Force 12 on the Beaufort Scale (over 64 knots / 74 mph) to create a sea state that is officially described as 'phenomenal.'

However, the word 'hurricane' was used frequently within the newspaper reports of the 19th century, and has therefore been used by the authors to describe hurricane-force winds.

In its edition of November the 5th, 1859, the Caernarfon and Denbigh Herald described the weather conditions on the night of October 25th - 26th, as:

'a perfect hurricane.'

THE LIVERPOOL AND AUSTRALIAN STEAM NAVIGATION COMPANY'S NEW STEAM-CLIPPER "ROYAL CHARTER."

An engraving of the 'Royal Charter' from the 'Illustrated London News' of 1855.

"It must be borne in mind, too, that we are now only at two months' distance from the colonies: the *Royal Charter* has accomplished the passage in fifty-nine days. Moreover, the journey is in every respect like a pleasure-trip in a yacht. The *Royal Charter*, in which I came home, is as richly and comfortably appointed as a private hotel. Sheep, pigs, and bullocks, geese and turkeys, were slaughtered on board every day. A cow or two supplied us with milk; cool fruits and rich conserves were constantly on the table; soda-water and shaving water came together if desired.

Active stewards (there were a score of them) were always at hand; a motherly stewardess looked after the little ones; and at every remarkable point in the journey the jovial Captain gave 'Sweethearts and Wives', and exhilarated us with champagne. And then — and this must close in all — the sights and studies of the sea!

The birds dipping their restless wings in the iris-crest of the wave, and shaking the drops off haughtily in the sun like a rain of stammel diamonds; the shark gleaming, green and still, just an arm's depth below the surface; the whale blowing its foamy fountain high above the wave; the shoals of porpoises playing leap-frog under the very bows of the vessel; the shadowy ships far off against the sunsets, their suffused masts melting behind the horizon, like ribs of molten copper."

Frank Fowler.
'Southern Lights and Shadows',
published 1859

Safety

If you choose to visit the wreck-site on foot, there is a well-defined coastal-footpath from Moelfre. Maps and guides are available from local and national booksellers, but please note that the path can be steep and slippery in places, and that it runs very close to the cliff-top. The rocks where the 'Royal Charter' was wrecked are steep, sharp, slippery and partially covered in sea-weed. Take care.

For sub-aqua divers, full details and directions are given in 'The Essential Underwater Guide to North Wales - Volume Two', also by Calgo Publications.

For marine safety-information, visit the Maritime and Coastguard Agency website at www.mcga.gov.uk

Newspaper articles

This book uses many articles taken directly from the North Wales and national newspapers of the 1850s and 1860s, with much of the text being a record of the evidence given in court while the witness was under oath. Hopefully, this is a true and accurate account of the tragic events of October, 1859, rather than someone's personal opinion.

Glossary -- Nautical terms etc.

Many of the words used in the newspaper reports quoted in this book are nautical terms, and may not be familiar to the reader. An explanation of some of them is given in the glossary at the end of this book.

Currency

British currency at the time of the wreck was pounds, shillings and pence (then written as *l. s. d.*), so to clarify some of the newspaper text, the '£' sign has been substituted for the letter ' *l* ' to indicate pounds sterling.

One pound sterling = 20 shillings. 1 shilling = 12 pence.

Measurements

Throughout the Victorian era, Imperial Measures were used for distance and weight.

1 mile = 1,760 yards = 1.6 Kilometre. 1 yard = 3 feet (approximately 1 metre).

Fathoms were used for depth, where 1 fathom = 6 feet (approximately 2 metres).

Weight was measured in tons, hundredweights (cwt.) and pounds (lb.)

1 ton = 20 cwt. or 2,240 lb. 1 cwt. = 112 lb.

1 ton is approx. 1,000 kg; 1 cwt. is approx. 50 kg. 1 lb. is approx. 0.45 kg.

Inflation

To give a rough idea of what an item would be worth in the 21st century, you need to multiply the 1859 values by around 50, and in some cases perhaps by a factor of 100. To quote from the 'Illustrated London News' of January 28, 1860, *'The mass of gold impacted in the fissure is part of an ingot of the purest quality imported, worth more than £4 an ounce'.* Today's gold is worth considerably more than £4 an ounce, and currently costs well over 100 times more than it was in 1859.

Maps and Charts

The map shown on page 70 is dated 1859, those on pages 110, 216 and 248 are dated 1860, and the one on page 177 is dated 1886.

The charts used in this book were published in 1838, 1859, 1867 & 1898.

Updates and corrections

New information is bound to come to light once a book has been printed, so please visit our website - www.calgopublications.co.uk

Joseph Roger's (Rodger's) grave in Liverpool.　　William Stephen's stamp.

Spelling and grammar

Wherever you travel in the world, there may be more than one variation in the spelling of the place-names of the various cities, towns and villages.

This book mainly uses those spellings given on the latest Ordnance Survey maps and Hydrographic Office charts, but where there are quotations from old newspapers, the spelling used at that time in history is given. The most obvious variations are in the spellings of 'Moelfre' or 'Moelfra', and 'Anglesey' or 'Anglesea', all of which were used in the 1850s. The town of Caernarfon was known as 'Caernarvon' or 'Carnarvon' at various times during the past, hence the spelling of 'Carnarvon and Denbigh Herald' used for newspaper headings in this book.

Slight alterations have been made to the newspaper text. For example '&c.' has been replaced by the more modern 'etc.' as an abbreviation for the word 'etcetera'.

People's Names

Within the original newspaper reports, there are several variations of people's surnames, but the following changes have been made for consistency and to avoid confusion:

Joseph Rogers tombstone is marked as 'Rodgers', but the newspapers mostly used his name as 'Rogers', without the letter 'd'. Note that one of the ship's officers was also called 'Rogers', again without the letter 'd'.

'Stephens' has been used for the First Officer of the 'Royal Charter', as written on his personal stamp shown above. Some newspapers used 'Stevens'.

'Croome' has been substituted for 'Kroom' where the latter variation has been used.

'Hosken' has been used where the newspapers mistakenly used 'Hoskins'.

BLUE BOXES -- The story of the 'Royal Charter' has links to many other vessels and people from the middle decades of the 19th century. To clarify the narrative, the connection between these ships or persons and the 'Royal Charter' is given in blue text-boxes such as this one.

Life in the 1850s

1850
- The first reports appeared about the discovery of alluvial gold in south-eastern Australia, the news having been kept secret for 18 months.
- The 'Emily' arrived in Australia after a 118-day voyage from Plymouth, carrying 30 married couples, 62 single men, 43 single women, 18 boys and 29 girls. Three deaths and three births were recorded during the time at sea.
- Thirty-eight 'distressed needlewomen' from London set sail as emigrants on the 'Culloden' thanks to a public subscription to pay for their passage.

1851
- The Great Exhibition was opened at the Crystal Palace, Hyde Park, London.
- The Colony of Victoria was established in Australia, separate from New South Wales.
- Gold was discovered in Victoria, and in a single week, 10,220 ounces of gold were brought into Melbourne.

1852
- Australian exports of gold were 856,188 ounces, dramatically up on the 134,420 ounces of 1851.
- The 'Chowringhee' took 121 days to sail from London to Melbourne.
- With the gold-rush in full flood, 29,378 emigrants sailed from Liverpool to Port Philip.
- The Government of Victoria introduced a system of licences for gold-diggers.

1853
- The steamship 'Great Britain' took 65 days from Liverpool to Melbourne, and 62 days for the return journey.
- At Ballarat, Australia, miners found nuggets weighing 77 lb 8 oz and 69 lb 6 oz.
- The Lieutenant-Governor of Van Diemen's Land appealed to London for a supply of Free Emigrants.

1854
- Over 83,000 people left Britain for a new life in Australia and New Zealand.
- The emigrant-ship 'Tayleur' ran ashore near Dublin, Ireland, with the loss of over 300 lives. Wrecked on her maiden voyage, compass-error was partly to blame.
- Twenty-two diggers and four soldiers died in a clash at the Eureka Diggings in Australia.
- On the 14th of September, British, French and Turkish forces landed in Crimea.

1855
- The 'Guiding Star' disappeared between Liverpool and Melbourne. Lost with about 500 passengers and crew, she probably hit an iceberg.
- The Victoria Commission Report was published, highlighting the discontent and dissatisfaction of the miners at the diggings, and suggesting improvements for managing the goldfields.
- The Black Ball Line won the contract for mail to Victoria. A ship was to leave Liverpool on the 5th of each month, with a penalty for passages longer than 65 days.

1856
- The steam-clipper 'Royal Charter' left Liverpool on her maiden voyage with nearly 300 passengers. After an unplanned diversion, she took 59 days from Plymouth to Melbourne, returning with 327 passengers and around 6 tons of gold.
- The Treaty of Paris was signed at the end of March, thereby ending the war with Russia.

1857
- The wooden clipper 'Dunbar' was wrecked at Port Jackson Heads, Sydney, Australia, with just one survivor out of the 122 passengers and crew.
- In April, the 'Royal Charter' brought home 128,000 ounces of gold (including one nugget weighing 323 ounces) and 13,000 sovereigns. On her second voyage of 1857, she arrived in Liverpool with 84,000 ounces of gold and 24,000 sovereigns.
- The 'Red Jacket' arrived in Liverpool from Australia, with 126 passengers, 70,000 ounces of gold, 500 bales of wool, and a quantity of tallow, hides & wines.

1858
- The supply of labour in Victoria started to exceed demand, and there were reports of unemployed people starving in the streets.
- The 'Royal Charter' arrived in Liverpool on the 17th of July with 93,000 ounces of gold and 30,400 sovereigns. She was a month overdue, raising fears that she had foundered at sea.
- Plans were put forward to build a tunnel linking England and France.

1859
- Work began on the construction of the Suez Canal.
- On her fifth homeward-voyage, the 'Royal Charter' reached Queenstown, Ireland, in April with 27,000 ounces of gold worth £109,464, 149 passengers and 583 bales of wool.
- Nearing the end of her sixth voyage home from Melbourne, the 'Royal Charter' was totally wrecked at Moelfre, Anglesey, North Wales, less than 50 miles short of her home port of Liverpool. Hundreds of men, women and children perished.

CHAPTER ONE

The Australia Run

From a print entitled 'My Trip to Australia. The Scene On Board the Emigrant Ship'.

By the early 1850s, Australia had progressed from being a penal colony to a land of great opportunity where it was possible to become extremely rich from agriculture, from trade, or by breaking one's back in the newly-discovered goldfields of New South Wales and Victoria. The rapidly-growing city of Melbourne was the destination of thousands of hopeful emigrants from the 'Old World', setting out from English ports such as Liverpool, London and Sunderland to arrive at Port Phillip and Hobson's Bay, the gateway to Melbourne.

The Suez Canal was still only a dream, as work did not commence until the end of the decade, so the journey to Australia was long and hazardous, following a route that used the prevailing winds to speed a vessel on her way. From England, sailing ships would head southwards past the Cape Verde Islands, out across the Atlantic towards Brazil, and then head east once they picked up the 'Roaring-Forties' trade-winds that pushed them along to ports such as Melbourne and Sydney. The route home was again in an easterly direction, through the Southern Ocean past Cape Horn, and then northwards once the Atlantic Ocean had been reached. At the beginning of the decade, most emigrants travelled in slow, leaky, wooden sailing-ships, but as the 1850s progressed, timber was superseded by iron, and sail was gradually replaced by steam power, shortening the journey-time by half. Yet, for a brief period, a hybrid class of vessel emerged on the 'Australia Run', that of the iron-hulled auxiliary screw-steamship such as the 'Royal Charter'.

LARGE NUGGET OF GOLD FROM PORT PHILLIP.

Captain G. T. Brown, of the fine ship *Chowringhee*, of Sunderland, has just arrived in the East India Docks, from Port Phillip, with a large quantity of gold — 68,000 ounces — on freight alone, independently of that brought by the passengers, of whom Captain Brown had about fifty from the above colony, principally successful diggers.

The gold was deposited, in the course of last week, in the bullion office at the Bank of England. It included an immense nugget weighing 545 ounces*, which is stated to be the largest piece ever brought into this country. It was found at the White Horse Gully, Bendigo Diggings, by George Potter, one of a party of three — Robert Bennett and John Hasset being his successful partners. Potter states that the gully where the nugget was found is not more than six yards from the place where the great Victoria Nugget was discovered. It had been repeatedly turned over, and many of the holes were abandoned and full of water. The exact spot was one that had been covered up with the soil from the neighbouring holes, and the only spot of the allotment belonging to the before-named party that had not been searched by them; indeed, they were on the point of leaving for another allotment when George Potter, in turning the earth over lightly, about eighteen inches below the surface, struck his pick upon the mass embedded in the sand, etc., and the Nugget remains in the same state as when first extracted by him. Potter and his comrades are seamen, and came over in the *Chowringhee*. Among the passengers in the *Chowringhee* were some persons who went out in the *Lady Elgin*, about twelve months ago, as Government free-emigrants: they have returned with a considerable sum in gold dust — some £1,000 worth.

Illustrated London News. March 12, 1853

*545 ounces (troy) = 16.95 kg.

Make no mistake, any voyage by sea during the Victorian era was extremely dangerous, due to a wide variety of hazards. There was no way of predicting the forthcoming sea conditions other than by referring to a barometer and a thermometer, and by having a captain's nose for 'dirty weather'. Fire, disease, collision, piracy and a lack of accurate and detailed sea charts all combined to make life at sea a most perilous occupation. Disease could suddenly sweep through the accommodation, brought on board by just one unknowing or uncaring passenger, but what if this spread to the ship's crew and decimated them? With a lack of experienced hands, the ship would become unmanageable, increasing the risk of running ashore or foundering at sea. And what if the ship did sink? There was insufficient space in the lifeboats for the crew, never mind the hundreds of desperate passengers facing a certain death in the icy depths. At least the sailors were prepared for the possibility of a premature end to their lives, and sometimes had religious crosses tattooed on the soles of their feet in the belief that this would ward off the attention of any hungry sharks.

So, how could a would-be emigrant increase his or her chance of actually arriving at their destination? A good track record of the shipping company, the ship and her captain were essential, as a fast, consistent passage reduced the risk of disease breaking out aboard the vessel, and lessened the chance of running out of food and water on a prolonged journey. Steam power at sea was still in its infancy, using low-pressure, inefficient, unreliable, bulky engines and boilers that took up valuable cargo-space, but a voyage by steamship meant that there was less chance of being becalmed, when a sailing-ship could be unable to make any progress for weeks on end while her supplies of food and water ran short.

Of course, most vessels did actually arrive at their final destination, but to give an idea of the number of shipping casualties, this is just one of the many articles printed in the English newspapers listing the losses during just one week of that period.

FORTY SHIPS AND NEARLY FOUR HUNDRED LIVES LOST

During the past week no fewer than 40 total wrecks have been posted on the books at Lloyd's. Among the most calamitous were the destruction by fire of the ship *Schah Johan.* She was bound from Calcutta to the West Indies, and had on board 300 coolie emigrants. For four days, every effort was made to save the ship and the unhappy creatures on board, and ultimately three rafts, crowded by 300 souls, were set adrift, and have never since been heard of. The master, officers, and crew, about 60, were picked up in a very distressed condition, five days after, by the ship *Vasco de Gama.* The *Admella,* screw steamship, was completely wrecked near Cape Northumberland on the coast of Western Australia, and 87 lives were lost. Another heavy loss is the total wreck of the well-known American clipper ship *Sovereign of the Seas,* which took place on the pyramid shoal in the Straits of Malacca on the 6th of August. She was of 1,988 tons, and had made some of the most rapid passages on record from China. The English ship *Chinchurah,* Eastaway, from London for Calcutta, was totally lost on the Gaspar Sands; and the ship *Thomas Brassey,* from Bombay for Liverpool, was abandoned off the Cape of Good Hope; the *City of Calcutta,* from Calcutta for the Clyde, was wrecked in the river Hooghly; the *Hellespont* steamer struck on a rock on leaving Naples, and went down, but the passengers and crew were saved; the *Victoria,* of Glasgow, foundered off Anholt in the Cattegat, but all on board were preserved. There are, in addition, many vessels missing, respecting which the most painful forebodings are entertained.

Chester Chronicle. October 8, 1859

Even when a wreck had been sighted by another vessel and information had been passed to the authorities, it was by no means certain that help would be on hand to rescue and provide sustenance to any survivors. There was no requirement for a vessel to carry life-saving equipment, while shore-based lifeboats and supplies of other rescue-apparatus were scarce in the British Isles and hardly existed elsewhere in the world, especially along a remote and inhospitable coastline such as that of southern Australia.

Frightful Shipwreck. Fifty Lives Lost.

One of the most frightful shipwrecks which ever occurred on the Australian coast took place early in August, near Cape Northumberland, about thirty miles to the west of the imaginary line separating Victoria from South Australia. The sacrifice of life, although large, upwards of 50 persons having been lost, is not the most horrible part of the catastrophe. The sufferings of the unfortunate survivors exceed anything we ever read of in the history of shipwreck and disaster at sea. For seven days, they were on the wreck, during five of which they were without food of any description.

The *Admella* was a fine steamer of about six hundred tons burthen and 500-horsepower, and had been regularly trading between Adelaide and Melbourne for the last two years. She left the former post on the 5th of August, and at about half-past four the following morning, while running at full speed, struck on Carpenter's Reef.

From the evidence of the chief mate, it appears that, when the ship struck, she went into three pieces almost immediately, and about forty people continued clinging to the bow portion for two days, when they were nearly all washed off and lost. All the provisions that were saved were a small bag of almonds, 20 lbs. of cheese, half a ham, 10 lbs. of beef, eight bottles of porter, and a bottle of whiskey, with a very small quantity of water. These provisions were afterwards all washed away, and for four or five days the poor creatures were totally deprived of food. Each night carried off its victims, about 20 in one night having died from cold.

At last, two sailors managed to get on shore by means of a raft, and gave information at the nearest telegraph station, from whence the news was sent out to Melbourne and Adelaide simultaneously. Numbers of people soon visited shore, and discovered that some on the wreck were still alive. The Messrs. Henty, when the news arrived in Melbourne, ordered their ship, the *Lady Bird*, to proceed at once to the wreck, and applied to the Chief Secretary to guarantee the increased insurance, which was refused!!! The *Lady Bird* was unable to find the wreck, and had to return to Portland for information. The South Australian government exhibited a little more humanity than Victoria, and sent out the *Corio*, which reached the wreck five days after the ship struck. She sent out her lifeboat, but the sea was too heavy, and the wreck could not be reached. The seventh night closed upon the wretched survivors, now reduced to twenty-seven, and although in sight of relief, out of its reach! The *Lady Bird* again arrived at the spot, and a little steamer, the *Ant*. The seventh night passed, and with it four more of the unhappy crew, into eternity. At last the sea became calmer, and success rewarded the efforts of the various crews. The wreck was reached, and twenty-three were saved! The excitement in Melbourne and Geelong was intense, and much indignation was felt at the callousness of the government. A subscription has been set up for the sufferers and the gallant crew of the *Lady Bird*.

Caernarfon & Denbigh Herald.
October 15, 1859

Connection to the 'Royal Charter'
• The inquiry into the wreck of the 'Admella' suggested that the rivets might have failed. The 'Royal Charter' may have had a similar problem. See page 207.

Why were so many people risking their lives to escape from Britain and start a new life in Australia? As shown on the following page, there were diggers who had become fabulously wealthy in a very short period of time at the goldfields. They had won the equivalent of the jackpot in today's lottery, and they meant to enjoy their success in style. Back in North Wales, letters had appeared in the local newspapers painting a rosy picture of life in the colonies, even for those whose aspirations were more mundane than those of a gold-miner. For the Welsh-speaking emigrants from North Wales, there were even familiar church services being held in their native language.

A Letter from Australia by William Badrack Jones, dated Melbourne, Nov. 20, 1855.

"A working man here need not be afraid of being out of employment – he need not work for a few coppers a day, as in Wales; he need not be under any obligation to his employer, for he knows there is plenty of work to be had. I have been getting £10 10s. per week; and a fortnight ago, by working a little over hours, I earned £12 7s. 6d. Joiners are paid at the rate of 30 shillings a day. Bricklayers, stonemasons etc. earn 30 shillings to 36 shillings a day – time of labour from six to six – an hour being allowed for breakfast, an hour to dinner, and a quarter of an hour at eleven and four o'clock termed 'smoking time'. We leave off on Saturdays at four o'clock. We have not to work as hard here for 30 or 36 shillings as in Wales for 30 or 36 coppers a day. At this time the farmers are about finishing their haymaking. They have found it very difficult to get men. A great quantity of fruit and herbs come to town daily.

Coals are dear and scarce here; wood is generally burnt, and this is sold in Melbourne at three pounds per load. A person newly arrived would think it strange, perhaps, to go into a first-rate parlour or drawing room where there is no grate; but such is often the same, owing to the limited number of grates imported until lately. Two rows of bricks fixed edgeways, with an open space in the middle, are made to serve instead. Owing to the rapid increase of building, houses are becoming abundant, and amongst them there are a great many boarding houses. The charge for board and lodging in these places is 30s. a week and upwards, per head. I am paying £2 per week, for which I have a fine bedroom for three, and the best of everything to eat - being allowed three meals a day, and a glass of ale with dinner. I have purchased a piece of land - building allotments - for £198 18s. It is situated at Prahran, a distance of three miles from Melbourne. I intend getting a couple of wooden houses to place upon it. These may cost me four or five hundred pounds, but they will soon pay for themselves. Welsh is preached here twice every Sunday. A school-room has been engaged for the use of dissenters of various denominations. I heard a young man from Carnarvonshire preaching there. His name, I believe, was Moses Jones. I have seen a great number of Carnarvon men here.

I would advise those who come out here not to bring with them a large stock of clothing, for, owing to the competition among parties who import goods of that description, clothes are almost as cheap here as in England. Money makes money, so let the emigrant keep in his possession as much of that as he can. Guns and watches are also cheap here. An emigrant should likewise understand, when engaging with the agents at Liverpool, whether he is to be landed in Melbourne free of expense or to be left to take his chance in the bay. Myself and party had to pay about £15 for landing; also, keep a look out to see in what part of the hold your boxes are placed, so that you may get at them once a month during the passage, instead of like myself being unable to do so until I arrived in the Bay, after being three months out."

Caernarfon & Denbigh Herald.

Melbourne as depicted in the 'Illustrated London News' of November 24th, 1855.

Mr. Howitt, in his "Two Years in Victoria", lately published, gives the following scene of reckless extravagance of the successful diggers:-

You can scarcely pass Bouverie-street (a horse-dealing ground) without danger of being galloped over, for the diggers are always buying horses there, and come headlong out of the yard into the street, and gallop and rampage about the streets in a furious way. The whole street swarms with diggers and diggeresses. Men appear in slouching wide-awakes, with long untrimmed hair and beards, and like navvies in their costume. Some have heavy horse-whips in their hands, and are looking at the exploits of other diggers on horseback, with a knowing air.

Others are swearing about the doors of pot-houses, where others, again, are drinking and smoking. Others, with a couple of bundles, or a pair of huge boots, swung over their shoulders, are lighting their pipes at a candle, or sharpening digging apparatus. The whole street abounds with second-rate shops which supply tools, kettles, tin-ware, boots, clothes, and so on. You are amazed at the price of every article. These scenes are continually going on. Amid all this there were open carriages driving about crowded with diggers and their diggeresses, at the rate of £1 per hour.

Diggerdom is gloriously in the ascendancy here.

One of the diggers asked the hire of a cab for the day.

"Perhaps more than you'd like." said the Jarvie, for the digger was a very common-looking fellow.

"What is it?" asked the digger.

"Seven pounds for the day."

"There is ten." said the fellow;

"You can light your pipe with the difference."

Illustrated London News.
November 24, 1855

Such a wonderful extravagance for the lucky few, but that situation changed as more and more able-bodied men arrived at the goldfields in the expectation of making their fortunes. Friction surfaced between the various nationalities as the gold became more elusive, so the 'Illustrated London News' continued:

> This disturbance is caused by a general scarcity of gold. Some may say in reply that the present returns of gold are equal to any former return. This may be the case, but consider the increased population of the diggings, which is three times that of 1853, and yet the same amount of gold only is obtained. But Melbourne and the district is in a state of poverty: there are thousands prowling about the streets who cannot get work.

Neither was it a particularly safe place if you had been lucky enough to make your fortune:

> Four fellows, last Saturday, armed with guns and pistols, stopped successively twenty people, tied them under a tree on the most frequented highway to the next village, St. Kilda, and in the broad day, at half past three o'clock in the afternoon. This game they kept up till half-past five, or two full hours. Numbers of wealthy merchants go out that way about that time of day, and some of them were caught. There is a report that the Governor himself was on that road very nearly at that time. The fellows have finished their work, then went off towards the Dandenong ranges 'sticking up' or 'bailing up' in colonial phrase, that is stopping and robbing every one that they met. The Government has offered a reward of £2,000 for their apprehension.

Two Years in Victoria, published 1855

Although some spectacular finds of gold were still being made, the boom-years were coming to an end by 1856, leaving thousands of poverty-stricken emigrants stranded many miles away from their home countries. Meanwhile, the emigrant-laden ships were still arriving full of hopeful men, women and children who had been lured by the letters home from those who had already arrived, and by articles published in Europe and Australia. Again, there is a clue in the 'Illustrated London News' suggesting that cheap labour was needed in the colony to satisfy the needs of the growing agricultural industry.

> I do not write through interest in any way, but in pity for those poor unfortunate beings who have been so foolish as to believe the reports of some of the Australian papers, whose editors and proprietors are influenced by the squatters, whose interest it is to fill the colony with labour, for the purpose of getting shepherds and herdsmen for little or nothing except their rations.

By August 1859, many people were returning home from Australia. Some had made their fortunes in the goldfields or other mining-ventures; others from store-keeping and inn-keeping, from agriculture, shipping and even criminal activities. But alongside these were the poor, the sick, the old and the disillusioned, and as we shall see, the auxiliary steam-clipper 'Royal Charter' lay waiting at Hobson's Bay, Melbourne, waiting to take on board anyone who could afford the cost of the passage back to England.

Connection to the 'Royal Charter'
- Construction of that vessel began in 1854, at the height of the Australian gold-rush.
- In six round-the-world voyages, the 'Royal Charter' transported around 20 tons of raw gold and at least 175,000 sovereigns from Australia to Britain.

Gibbs, Bright and Company

Gibbs Bright and Co. were one of many shipping-lines that operated out of Liverpool, having started in the 1770s when George Gibbs joined with his friend Richard Bright. They were both West India merchants; the Brights owned estates in Jamaica. George's brother Anthony began trading as a wool merchant, exporting English cloth to Spain and importing Spanish fruit and wine. His business started in 1787, and became extremely successful under his sons, George and William, by obtaining a monopoly over guano from Peru. This extremely lucrative trade in fertiliser established the company of Anthony Gibbs and Sons, who eventually became a merchant bank.

A contemporary rhyme went:

'The House of Gibbs, that made their dibs, by selling the turds of foreign birds.'

In 1818, George Gibbs and his son, another George, joined Robert Bright to form a company in Bristol, where, in addition to their other trading activities, they acted as agents for the steamers 'Great Western' and 'Great Britain', and held places on the governing-board of the Great Western Railway. As the Port of Liverpool became more important, more business was transferred there, and they changed their name to Gibbs, Bright and Co. They acted as agents for the shipping lines, but around 1850, became shipowners themselves, having at least eight vessels on the Australia run. With the purchase of the clipper 'Eagle', their 'Eagle Line' was born.

For Port Phillip and Adelaide to sail the beginning of September, 1851, the beautiful, new clipper ship *Eagle*, 1,065 tons register. The accommodation has never been equalled to Australia. -- Apply to the owners, Gibbs, Bright & Co,

News of the New South Wales gold strike reached Britain in 1851, and the 'Eagle Line' ship 'Albatross' was the first to land gold at Liverpool, arriving there in August 1852. Gibbs, Bright and Co. were uniquely placed to profit from the transport of goods and people to the colony, returning to Liverpool with gold and other valuable cargoes. In anticipation of a rapidly expanding market, they purchased the steamship 'Great Britain' on the 2nd of January, 1851, as she was for sale after a recent stranding in Ireland and was capable of carrying hundreds of passengers. Paying only £18,000 for her, they began to repair and alter her to suit their needs. William Patterson, her original builder, oversaw the work, and she left Liverpool for Australia on the 21st of August, 1851.

The Australian branch, Bright Bros. and Co., was opened in 1853 as insurance, shipping and general agents. In 1881, the company was reorganised, with the Australian firm becoming Gibbs, Bright and Co., which still trades as a successful company with a wide variety of financial interests. The British end amalgamated with Anthony Gibbs and Sons, who then converted the 'Great Britain' to a sailing ship. This large financial company was taken over in 1980 by the Hong Kong and Shanghai Banking Corporation (HSBC) to form the basis of their insurance broker business in the U.K. Descendants of both the Gibbs and Bright families became prominent figures in politics and banking, owned substantial properties, and received knighthoods.

CHAPTER TWO

Ships of Iron

During the Victorian era, a wooden merchant-vessel or warship required a vast amount of timber, and one estimate states that a 74-gun man-of-war required 2,000 trees that were seventy-five years old or 250 trees that had been growing for one hundred and fifty years. It wasn't just a case of having a sufficient amount of wood - the timber had to be of the right quality and shape. This was especially true for the 'knees', the brackets that connected the vertical and horizontal timbers together. With the rapid expansion of shipbuilding, the British forests had been decimated by the middle decades of the 19th century, leading to an increase in foreign-built vessels from the timber-rich areas of North America. Many of the sailing-ships operating out of Liverpool were built by Donald McKay of Boston, whose clipper-ships were longer, leaner and faster than the run-of-the-mill cargo ships, but wood simply wasn't strong enough for the hulls of the propeller-driven steamships that were to revolutionise the shipbuilding industry.

Fortunately for the British economy, iron had been used as a suitable material for shipbuilding since around 1819, and the quality and quantity of wrought iron increased rapidly as the 19th century progressed. Metal was cheaper and more durable than wood, it allowed more cargo to be carried than in a wooden vessel of similar size, it didn't burn, and it required less maintenance than timber. Iron's disadvantages were corrosion, its effect on a ship's compass, a general lack of knowledge of the material, and the fact that barnacles easily attached themselves to an iron hull, whereas they avoided a wooden hull that had been fitted with a sheath of copper or similar metal.

Wrought iron allowed the British shipyards to regain their hold on this strategically-important industry by utilising the metal for the plates, frames and brackets that were assembled to make a ship's hull. Iron ships relied on thousands of iron rivets that were inserted whilst red-hot into holes drilled or punched in two pieces of metal. To draw the iron plates tightly together, the head of the rivet was quickly hammered over by a skilled team of men before it could cool down. Unless the rivets were correctly fastened in their holes, seawater could easily leak past a loose rivet or between the iron plates of the hull, so it was essential that the rivet-heads inside the hull were protected from damage by loose cargo rubbing against them, or even by sand-laden seawater slopping about in the bilges. The adjacent diagram (A) shows how a rivet could simply fall out to leave a hole if the head was abraded away to a significant amount, and how this problem was partially reduced by the introduction of punched holes that were slightly countersunk (B).

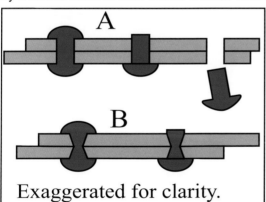

Exaggerated for clarity.

Having superseded wood as the major material for building ships, iron was used for only a relatively short period of time before steel became available. The first steel vessel was the 'Ma Roberts', constructed in 1858 at Laird's shipyard on the River Mersey in the north-west of England.

The S.S. 'Great Britain', preserved in the dry-dock at Bristol where her keel was laid in 1839.

The transition of a vessel from land to water was always going to be a recurring nightmare for any shipbuilder, and we will see just how difficult this operation could be when we come to the launch of two other iron-built ships, the 'Great Eastern' and the 'Royal Charter'. However, the 'Great Britain' had been constructed in a dry-dock, so there was no problem with getting her afloat as the builder simply flooded the dock and opened the gates to allow her out into the basin at Bristol, England. On the 19th of July 1843, thousands of people came from near and far to watch the event in the presence of Prince Albert, the husband of Queen Victoria.

Unfortunately for her designer, Isambard Kingdom Brunel, and her builder, William Patterson, their new ship was too wide to pass through the lock-gates that led into the Cumberland Basin, the gateway to the River Avon. The anticipated improvements to the gates had not been carried out in time, so their ship was now afloat, but lay confined to the freshwater-reaches of the river. At least she was free of the restrictions imposed by the dry-dock, but there were some pessimistic voices raised that she could end her days rusting away in Bristol Docks or that the whole port was going to be closed down for a month while modifications were made to the lock-gates. Fitting-out continued, and her machinery was installed as she lay alongside the quayside at Bristol, until eventually in December 1844, the locks were modified to allow her to pass into the tidal waters of the River Avon and taste the open sea of the Bristol Channel.

The steamship 'Great Britain'

Looking forwards along the upper deck.

Looking down into the hold, this photograph shows her complex construction.

Despite her keel being laid down as long ago as 1839, the steamship 'Great Britain' survives to this day in the comfort of the dry-dock where she was originally built at Bristol. This shows the durability of her wrought iron construction, the dedication of the enthusiasts who brought her back from the Falkland Islands and those who continue to preserve her today. A visit to the vessel at Bristol Docks is strongly recommended to understand the conditions that passengers and seamen endured on their voyages to and from the Antipodes.

That great innovator and engineer, Isambard Kingdom Brunel was famous for his railways and bridges, with trains running on his Great Western Railway between London and the port of Bristol by 1841. When Prince Albert came to Bristol by train for the launch of the 'Great Britain', he was pleasantly surprised to be able to leave London at 7.00 a.m., arrive in Bristol by 10.00 a.m., attend the launch of the vessel and the subsequent ceremonies before returning to Buckingham Palace by 7.15 p.m. To ensure the smooth running of the railway on such a prestigious occasion, Brunel himself acted as the train's engineer in each direction.

By December 1844, the 322-foot long, 3,675-ton 'Great Britain' was free of the confines of Bristol Docks, and began her sea-trials on the 8th of January, 1845. Having successfully completed these tests, she set out for London only to run straight into a strong north-westerly gale whilst off Lundy Island in the Bristol Channel, during which time she was struck by a heavy sea that knocked out three of her port-holes, buckled part of the deck, tore away part of her figurehead and smashed some crockery. Weathering the gale successfully, she reached the River Thames in triumph but lay there for five months, during which time she was visited by Queen Victoria. The vessel was eventually made ready for sea and able to earn her keep, so she left the River Thames for Liverpool in June, 1845, from where she made three trips to New York and back before she was laid-up for the winter.

A reconstruction of her original propeller.

These were the early days of steamship construction, and the designers of such vessels were continually gaining experience and improving their skills. By the end of her last voyage of 1845, it was clear that the efficiency of her propulsion could be improved, so her original 6-bladed propeller was replaced by a more effective 4-bladed one, and alterations were made to the air-pumps and flues for the boilers. The masts and rigging were also altered at this time to improve her sailing performance. Her subsequent trials in the Irish Sea in April, 1846, showed that these modifications had been successful, and she left Liverpool on the 9th of May, 1846, on yet another voyage to New York and back.

However, it wasn't all going to be plain-sailing for the 'Great Britain', and things went terribly wrong when she left Liverpool on the 22nd of September, 1846, again destined for New York. She was under the command of Captain Hosken, whose son was later to spend some time as Third Engineer of the 'Royal Charter'. Due to what was later described as *'the most egregious blundering'*, she ran ashore at Dundrum Bay on the east coast of Ireland where she was to remain stranded for nearly a year before Brunel was able to refloat her on the 27th of August, 1847. She was then towed to Birkenhead on the River Mersey, where she lay unwanted until January 1851, when she was purchased by Gibbs, Bright & Company for a mere £1,800. This company must have been quite forward-thinking, as news had only recently arrived in Britain of the Australia gold-strike, and Gibbs, Bright & Co. were eventually to operate both the 'Great Britain' and the 'Royal Charter' on the route between Liverpool and Melbourne.

It was immediately obvious that repairs and modifications were required before the 'Great Britain' was fit for her new role, that of carrying hundreds of passengers and tons of cargo to Melbourne and Sydney in as short a time as possible. William Patterson, her original builder, was placed in charge of the work, creating a link between himself and Gibbs, Bright & Co. that would continue with the construction of the 'Royal Charter'. A smaller, more efficient engine was supplied by John Penn & Co., new boilers were installed, a new propeller was fitted to take advantage of the new engine, and a new deck-house was built to provide additional passenger accommodation.

The first voyage under her new owners was from Liverpool to New York in May, 1852, but the sudden rush of emigrants to the Australian goldfields lead to an urgent need for passenger accommodation on the route between England and Melbourne. She then made three round trips to Australia, before the outbreak of the Crimean War in 1854 lead to her being requisitioned by the British Government for use as a troopship.

DEPARTURE OF THE "GREAT BRITAIN" FOR AUSTRALIA.

About three o'clock on Saturday afternoon, this splendid screw steamship, Captain Matthews, weighed her anchor in the Sloyne*, and steamed gently down towards the mouth of the Mersey; her passage being watched with intense interest by crowds of enthusiastic spectators, who had stationed themselves on the Liverpool side. Steam-boats and other craft, gaily dressed with flags and streamers, and filled with people, were moving about in all directions, while the ferry-boats were crammed with passengers, who preferred the Cheshire side of the river as a point of view. The deck of the *Great Britain* was crowded with passengers, to take farewell of old England. Several tug-boats hovered round the leviathan; at intervals guns were fired from the *Great Britain* herself; from the *Arctic,* which lay in the Sloyne; and from Mr. Parry's pleasure gardens at Seacombe, while an almost uninterrupted series of hearty cheers resounded from the steamer, the neighbouring boats, and the piers. At length the fort was breasted, and after firing a salute, the smaller vessels fell back, and the *Great Britain* sped on her way with upwards of 630 passengers and a very heavy mail.

The *Great Britain,* at the time she left the river, was drawing 22 feet of water. The quantity of coal taken on board is about 1400 tons, chiefly Welsh, with a small quantity of anthracite and patent fuel as an experiment. There is enough to steam the whole distance without stopping, but, lest anything should occur, she will call at the Cape of Good Hope to replenish her supply, and take in livestock. It is expected that she will reach the Cape in about twenty-five days, whither ships have been dispatched with coals to wait her arrival. After staying there two or three days, she will proceed to Melbourne and Sydney, and it is confidently expected that she will reach the former place in fifty-six days from England, whereas double that length of time is considered an average voyage for a sailing vessel. The *Great Britain* is fully equipped to resist any attempt to attack the vessel that might be made, for she is mounted with six heavy deck guns, and arms and ammunition for 100 men. The crew of the *Great Britain* consists of about 130 persons in all.

Illustrated London News. August 28, 1852

* Sloyne - part of the River Mersey at Liverpool.

The crest of the "Liverpool and Australian Navigation Co.

The 'Great Britain' was charted by the British Government during 1855 and 1856 to act as a troopship, conveying soldiers between the English ports of Liverpool and Portsmouth, and the overseas destinations of Gibraltar, Malta, Italy and Turkey. To the financial detriment of Gibbs, Bright & Company, the signing of the Treaty of Paris on the 30th of March, 1856, terminated their contract by the middle of that year, and another task was sought for their vessel.

Meanwhile, the 'Royal Charter', another of Gibbs, Bright & Company's vessels, had completed her first voyage to Melbourne, and arrived back in Liverpool in August 1856 having established the viability of an auxiliary-steamship on the route between England and Australia. An auxiliary-steamship was a vessel designed to use her sailing ability to take advantage of the trade-winds for the majority of her journey, but could use her steam engine and propeller should there be little or no wind. Gibbs, Bright & Co. operated under the title of 'The Liverpool and Australian Navigation Company', and had gained much knowledge from Captain Boyce of the 'Royal Charter', so further modifications were put in hand to alter the 'Great Britain' and make her more suitable for her new role.

The winter months of 1856 - 1857 were used to make these latest alterations to the 'Great Britain', when she was fitted with a larger deck-house that could accommodate 80 first-class passengers, and her motive power was improved to give her a single funnel, three masts, and a two-bladed propeller that could be lifted clear of the water when under sail. She then resumed her career early in 1857, with a voyage to Melbourne taking only 62 days, but needing 93 days for her return.

The screw steamship *Great Britain* has left her dock and is anchored in the Sloyne. [*Liverpool*] She will sail on the 16th for Melbourne. This vessel has undergone a thorough refit since her discharge from the transport service, and her accommodations for passengers are unsurpassed, a poop-cabin, 95 feet in length having been added. She will carry a much larger quantity of canvas than ever. The mainmast has been placed 15 feet, and the mizzenmast 6 feet, forward of their former position, and she has been fitted with a lifting screw similar to the one carried by the *Royal Charter*, and which has been proved to work admirably. Her new stern-post is an immense piece of wrought iron.

The Times. Saturday, February 14, 1857

Arriving back in Liverpool in August, 1857, The 'Great Britain' was again requisitioned by the British Government, this time to transport troops to Bombay at the time of the Indian Mutiny. Resuming her civilian career in 1858, she again made trips to New York before settling into a routine on the Australia Run, a task that was to occupy her for almost the next twenty-five years. Having spent nearly 33 years steaming and sailing the oceans of the world, her passenger-carrying days came to an end as she arrived home in Liverpool at the end of January, 1876. Rather than being scrapped, she was laid up in Birkenhead Docks, just across the River Mersey from Liverpool.

The elaborate decoration on the stern of the steamship 'Great Britain'.

In 1881, Gibbs, Bright & Company were absorbed by the London firm of Anthony Gibbs & Sons, who therefore became the owners of the 'Great Britain' and needed to find a profitable use for her. The removal of her steam engine and boilers gave her additional cargo space to produce a vessel capable of transporting bulk cargoes under sail alone, so she now spent the next two voyages taking coal to San Francisco via Cape Horn, and returning to Liverpool with a cargo of wheat. Leaving Cardiff for Panama in February 1886, she was forced to run for shelter in the Falkland Islands where it became clear that her sailing-days were over. She was then used as a storage facility in Port Stanley until 1937, when she was towed to a remote inlet called Sparrow Cove to be scuttled in shallow water. Thankfully, the 'Great Britain' was rescued from this location by a dedicated group of enthusiasts who had the foresight to raise enough funds and support to bring her back to her birthplace of the dry-dock at Bristol, arriving home in July, 1970.

Connection to the 'Royal Charter'

- Both ships were built by William Patterson.
- Now safely housed in dry-dock at Bristol, the 'Great Britain' was slightly shorter but had a greater beam than the 'Royal Charter'. She can be visited today to give an idea of what life was like aboard an emigrant-ship.
- Gibbs, Bright & Co., became owners of the 'Great Britain' in January 1851. Their subsequent experience of the route to Australia lead them to purchase and complete the partially-built framework that became the 'Royal Charter'
- In 1856/57, Gibbs, Bright & Co. fitted the 'Great Britain' with a lifting-screw similar to that of the 'Royal Charter', presumably due to the success of the latter ship.

The iron clipper-ship 'Tayleur', wrecked near Dublin on her maiden voyage.

The launch of the new iron first-class sailing vessel, built by the Bank Quay Foundry Company, on the right bank of the Mersey, at Warrington, took place yesterday. Her proportions are 2,500 tons (new measurement); length of keel and forerake, 225 feet; rake of stern-post, 5 feet; beam, 39 feet; depth of hold (from underside of the deck to the top of the flooring), 28 feet; sheer, 2 feet 6 inches. She has three decks, with saloon on the upper deck and cabins and berths for captain and principal officers. She is exceedingly strong built, being double-riveted throughout, and being divided into five water-tight compartments. The total quantity of iron in her is estimated at 780 tons. She is the property of Messrs. Charles Moore and Co., of Liverpool, and is to make her first voyage to Australia. Her commander is Captain Noble, and she will be capable of accommodating 680 passengers, besides taking a heavy cargo. She has at her head a fine full-length figure of Mr. Charles Tayleur, of the firm who have built her, and after whom she is named.

The River Mersey at Warrington is but narrow, being 36 miles above Liverpool (following the course of the stream), and the experiment of launching such a large vessel was one which, of course, excited much anxiety on the part of the builders, and all concerned. An immense number of people crowded the banks of the river to witness the launch, and as the tide rose more than usually high, overflowing the fields for a considerable distance, many of them were placed in considerable jeopardy whilst moving to higher ground. Men were seen in some places standing up to the knees in water rather than retreat, but the masses sought the higher ground in confusion, and some ludicrous scenes occurred. The nautical men present said they had never witnessed a more successful and magnificent launch. There were probably no less than 10,000 people present.

Liverpool Mercury. October 3, 1853

The sailing ship 'Tayleur'

Although our main story is that of the 'Royal Charter', we really need to look at the one and only voyage of the iron clipper 'Tayleur', launched in October 1853 by the Bank Quay Foundry Company at Warrington, on the River Mersey in North-west England. This shipyard lies only around twenty-five miles from Sandycroft on the River Dee, where Charles Moore & Company were in the process of building another ship for their fleet, the one that was destined to become the 'Royal Charter'. There was fierce competition for the Australian trade, so the 'Tayleur' had to be strongly-built and extremely seaworthy, and needed a competent captain and crew for the long voyage to Melbourne and back. The trip to Australia would take her hundreds of miles south of the Cape of Good Hope, and the homeward passage would be via Cape Horn.

The 'Tayleur' was shorter and narrower than the 'Great Britain', and lacked a steam engine so that she was driven along by the uncertainties of the wind alone. How on earth the officers, crew and six hundred and eighty passengers were supposed to live on board such a vessel for three or four months is difficult to comprehend, but those were the conditions to be expected and endured in Victorian times.

She was quickly fitted out with sails, provisions and navigation equipment such as her compasses, and left Liverpool for Australia only a few months later carrying a large complement of passengers who were aiming to start a new and prosperous life on the other side of the world. Unfortunately, their hopes were quickly dashed:

THE WRECK OF THE "TAYLEUR"

A feeling of consternation was produced in Dublin yesterday by the news received in the course of the afternoon that another fearful shipwreck had been added to the long list of those calamities, for which this coast has of late obtained so sad a notoriety. The rumours on the subject were, as might be expected, somewhat exaggerated, but the truth, as far as we have yet been able to arrive at it, is sufficiently awful without any addition to its melancholy circumstances. The *Tayleur*, Captain Noble, which sailed from Liverpool on Friday with 496 passengers, for Melbourne, and a crew, making in all about 576 adults on board, after being tossed about the channel for some thirty hours, was at an early hour yesterday morning driven on the rocks of Lambay Island, some miles to the north of Howth, and became a total wreck, only about 250 persons of her vast freight of human life being saved. The lateness of the hour at which the news reached Dublin, the difficulty of reaching the scene of the locality, owing to its distance, and the boisterous state of the bay, prevented any accurate details from yet becoming known here; but I subjoin from the morning papers such particulars as have yet been collected. *Saunder's News Letter* says:

Numerous highly influential parties in this city possessed relatives and connections who had taken their passages on this noble vessel, and the feelings of consternation with which they and the general public learned the sad tidings of her total destruction on the very day after her proud debut, can far more readily be imagined that described. The news of the disaster first reached town yesterday afternoon, between one and two o'clock, by the arrival of some of those who had been fortunate enough to escape from the wreck, and by means of a fishing boat had managed to reach the nearest portion of the coast, Rush, from whence they had been conveyed to Dublin by the Drogheda line of railway. These persons, as we ascertain from authentic sources, were three in number, and the melancholy event having been immediately communicated to Mr. Walsh, the agent of Lloyd's, steps were forthwith taken to reach the scene of disaster, and convey relief to the sufferers. For this purpose the City of Dublin Steam Packet Company's vessel *Prince*, Captain Dearl, was put into requisition – her steam

LOSS OF " THE TAYLEUR " AUSTRALIAN PACKET-SHIP, OFF LAMBAY ISLAND.

was at once got up, and she left the quay shortly after three o'clock, p.m., to bring the survivors to town. From the accounts received up to the hour at which we write – three a.m. - it would appear that about 250 persons have been saved out of the entire number in the vessel at the time she struck. Among these, rumour confidently asserts, are her commander, Captain Noble, the first mate, and ten seamen; the remainder of the vessel's numerous crew are wholly unaccounted for. It is asserted by the passengers who reached Dublin that the *Tayleur* made the land at half-past 11 o'clock p.m., on Saturday, after experiencing some heavy gales in the channel, that she struck Lambay Island at 12 o'clock at night, and that in less than half an hour afterwards she had gone down in seven fathoms, a portion of her masts alone remaining above water.

As it was the forepart of the vessel which got fast upon the rocks, it is feared that few, if any, of the cabin passengers escaped. Those who managed to reach the shore did so by means of lines running from the vessel to the rocks, and the number saved would in all probability have been much greater, had not the vessel on one occasion given a sudden lurch, by which upwards of one hundred human beings were precipitated into the sea. As soon as the *Prince* had left the quay, attention was directed to the necessity of providing accommodation for the unfortunate passengers upon their arrival, and a plentiful supply of fuel and straw for bedding was speedily procured, and placed in readiness in the capacious stores of the Waterford Steam Packet Company. At a quarter past five o'clock this morning the *Prince* steamer had not returned to the North Wall.

Thomas Kemp, one of the surviving passengers of the *Tayleur,* gives the following account of the catastrophe:-

'The *Tayleur* left Liverpool on Thursday, at noon, in tow of the steamer *Victory*, with a fine breeze from S E. She had on board as near as I could learn, 670 persons, including the crew. All went on well until about noon on Saturday. At that time, one of my fellow passengers came running into my cabin, and said that there was land on the lee bow.

I asked him how far distant; he replied, that he believed from three to four miles. I immediately went on deck, and saw the land distinctly, which appeared to me to be only about three quarters of a mile distant. From the progress the ship was making towards the land, I saw there was no hope of escape, and I prepared myself for the worst. The wind was blowing fresh from S.W., the ship being under topsails. As soon as it was known to the passengers that the land was so close they all crowded on deck, and ensued such confusion that the crew were prevented from obeying any orders that might have been conveyed to them by the officers. Both anchors were let go; but either the cables broke or the heavy sea caused to them to drag, for they did not stay the progress of the ship, and she soon struck on a rock,

which I afterwards learned was called "The Nose" of Lambay Island. After striking, she turned broadside on to the rock, and many of the passengers jumped on the shore. She remained in this position only a few minutes, when she slid off, filled rapidly, and went down stern foremost, with only the top of her mast visible above water. The survivors were mustered and counted, and it was found that there were about 250 saved; the number that perished will therefore be 420. The captain and the first and third mates were saved; the second mate, and surgeon and his lady and child perished. Only three women and two children were saved.'

The *Tayleur* was a new ship, of 2,200 tons register. She was built at Warrington, and commanded by Captain Noble.

Liverpool Mercury. January 24, 1854

Totally wrecked on her maiden voyage, the life of the 'Tayleur' was short and brutal. How on earth could a newly-built ship, constructed using the latest designs and materials, run ashore such a short period after leaving port? As was normal for any major loss of life at sea, an inquiry had to be held to ascertain the cause of the disaster, and the one held at Malahide, near Dublin, came to several conclusions including:

LIFEBELTS! LIFEBELTS! LIFEBELTS!

LOSS OF THE TAYLEUR IN DUBLIN BAY,

UPWARDS OF FOUR HUNDRED HUMAN BEINGS DROWNED.

The whole of these unfortunate persons would have saved their lives had they been provided with one of HELLEWELL'S LIFE and PROPERTY BELTS, varying in price from 7s. 6d. each. Most invaluable at sea in case of shipwreck.

That the parties were drowned by the sinking of the said ship off Lambay Island, and that this deplorable accident occurred in consequence of the highly culpable neglect of the owners in permitting the vessel to leave port without compasses properly adjusted, or a sufficient trial having taken place to learn whether she was under control of the helm or not; and we find that Captain Noble did not take sufficient precaution to ensure the safety of the vessel by rounding-to after he found the compasses were in error.

So, the 'Tayleur' was judged to have run ashore partially because her compasses gave false readings, a problem that was bound to happen when such an instrument was placed close to a large mass of iron without some sort of correction being made.
The hull of the 'Tayleur' was exactly that large mass of iron.

Connection to the 'Royal Charter'
- Charles Moore & Co., the owners of the 'Tayleur', had another iron ship under construction at George Cram's shipyard on the River Dee. Losing confidence in iron ships, they sold the incomplete hull to Gibbs, Bright & Co. at a time when Cram was in financial difficulty. This was modified to become the 'Royal Charter'
- The Liverpool Compass Committee was established the year after the 'Tayleur' was wrecked. Its task was to investigate the effect of iron on a ship's compass.

Brunel's dream-ship had her intended name 'Great Eastern' painted on her bows, but Miss Hope, the daughter of the chairman of the Great Eastern Steam Navigation Company, actually named her 'The Leviathan' at the launching ceremony.

A Monstrous Steamship.

Preparations are making at the factory of Mr. Scott Russell for the construction of a leviathan steamship. She is to be 675 feet in length, or three times the length of the *Duke of Wellington,* 88 feet in width, and 60 feet in depth from the deck to the keelson. She is to be built entirely of iron, and to be double and cellular up to the water-line, to be 23,000 tons burden, and to have stowage for 10,000 tons of coal. As she is, when finished, to sail from Milford Haven, it is expected that the coals will be put on board at cost price, and that the stock laid in will enable her to make the complete circuit of the globe, sailing all through at the rate of fifteen miles an hour, and making the whole circuit in sixty days. She will be ship-rigged, with four masts, and will accommodate 600 first class passengers, each with a separate state-room, 1,500 second-class passengers, and above 2,000 [*sic*], besides an immense cargo of goods.

North Wales Chronicle.

Saturday, July 1, 1854

The steamship 'Great Eastern'

Isambard Kingdom Brunel

As one of the most talented engineers of the mid-18th century, Isambard Kingdom Brunel was famous for his railways, bridges and tunnels, along with the steamships 'Great Western' and 'Great Britain'. However, his ambition was to create an even larger vessel that could transport passengers across the oceans in luxury, comfort and speed as had never been accomplished before, so early in 1854, the keel of his 'Leviathan' was laid at Blackwall on the River Thames, several miles downstream of London. Today, a 23,000-ton vessel is not regarded as being especially large, but this was a great leap forward from the 3,675-ton 'Great Britain', Brunel's engineering marvel of a little over a decade earlier.

Steamships no longer relied on the fickle variations of the wind and tide, and could therefore take the shortest, quickest routes to their destination, assuming that they had the capacity to carry enough fuel for the journey. Unfortunately, the low-pressure, inefficient steam engines of that period consumed a vast quantity of coal, and the smaller vessels couldn't carry enough fuel to make a long voyage without calling at one or more 'coaling stations' along the way. The early days of aviation required several refuelling stops on a long-distance flight, but now we expect our Boeing 747s and Airbus A-380s to fly non-stop from London to Sydney. Increasing the size of a ship or aircraft allows more fuel to be carried to give a greater range, but large ships need large ports, and Brunel's new venture would need a deep-water harbour with access by rail for her passengers and for the thousands of tons of coal that were needed to fill her bunkers.

The launch of the 'Great Eastern' was originally scheduled for the 3rd of November, 1857, when it was expected that the hull would slowly slide sideways into the River Thames at Blackwall. Three years had elapsed since her keel was laid, and, at that time, she was the largest vessel yet constructed anywhere in the world. Her intended name was to be 'Great Eastern', but she was actually christened 'Leviathan' by Miss Hope, the daughter of one of the directors of the Eastern Steam Navigation Company which had financed her. Perhaps being given the wrong name was an ill-omen, for she moved only a few feet before halting on the slipway, killing one workman and injuring four others in that short distance. Further attempts were made to float her on the 4th and 28th of November, as more and more immense chains and hydraulic rams were brought to Blackwall, but there was still only a slow progress towards the elusive river. By the middle of January, 1858, the huge hull had been moved around 200 feet (65 metres), and she finally floated on the River Thames at the end of January, 1858.

The hull was then towed to nearby Depford for completion. All that was now required was the installation of her engines and other fittings, but a major problem arose as the delays and extra costs of the construction and launch had drained the coffers of

"THE GREAT EASTERN" STEAM-SHIP.

Belt, braces and a piece of string -- Brunel was taking no chances, so the 'Great Eastern' was equipped with paddle-wheels, a propeller and a full set of sails.

her owners, so no progress could be made until further financial arrangements were completed. Speculation was rife as to what would happen to Brunel's creation, with the following news item being written at a time of tension with our recent ally.

The Emperor Napoleon [*of France*] is in treaty for the purchase of the *Leviathan*. The negotiations for the purchase were interrupted by his declaration that he might possibly offend the Queen of England. Her Majesty is, however, understood that the *Leviathan* was purely a commercial speculation, with which the Government had nothing to do. The negotiations were then renewed by the Emperor, who is extremely desirous to possess the big ship, which would be used as a sea battering-ram; the bows would be reinforced by stupendous iron beams and girders of immense size and strength, and sharpened so that she might cut down any ship by a collision. Thus armed, propelled by the combined forces of 2,400 horses, her broad areas of canvas spread forth to catch additional impetus from the winds, the *Sea Titan* would rush forth into the ocean in search of prey; and where is the ship that could either elude or resist a foe of such magnitude?

Liverpool Mercury. September 7, 1858

Perhaps the newspaper report was untrue, as it seems unlikely that Britain would have sold the ship to a potential adversary, but the 'Eastern Steam Navigation Company' soon went into liquidation, and the 'Great Eastern' became the property of the 'Great Ship Company', who now began to transform the bare hull into a sumptuous floating-hotel fit for the transatlantic passenger-trade.

Another year was to pass before she was ready for her sea-trials, having so far taken well over four years in her construction, yet she still wasn't fully fitted-out as a luxury liner. Finally, on the 8th of September 1859, the 'Great Eastern' steamed out of the Thames with the intention of reaching Holyhead in North Wales, but a huge explosion destroyed one funnel and killed five stokers while she was off the south coast of England.

A bow-view of the 'Great Eastern'. Note the six hawse-pipes for the anchor-chains.

The ship was still pressing onward, like a horse that had lost its rider, and at either end all was still and deserted, while in the centre all was smoke, fire, vapour and confusion. The great funnel, eight tons in weight, had been shot up as if from a mortar many feet into the air, and had returned broken in two pieces on the deck, whose immense strength had been sufficient to arrest its further downward progress. The whole centre of the ship seemed to be only one vast chasm, and from it was belching steam and dust, something that looked ominously like incipient conflagration.

North Wales Chronicle. September 17, 1859

The 'Great Eastern' was forced to put into Weymouth Harbour where the necessary repairs were made before she could continue her journey, and she finally reached Holyhead on the 10th of October, 1859, with no-one aware of the hurricane that was heading her way with the potential to destroy her. Brunel was already suffering from ill-health, and news of the explosion brought on so much additional stress that he suffered a stroke and died just a few days later.

Connection to the 'Royal Charter'
- She was also built of iron, although far larger than the 'Royal Charter'.
- Like the 'Royal Charter', she proved reluctant to take to the water.
- Both ships used anchors designed by John Trotman.
- In October, 1859, passengers on the 'Royal Charter' asked her master, Captain Taylor, to steam close to Holyhead so that they could see the 'Great Eastern'.
- She was anchored in Holyhead Harbour when the 'Royal Charter' was wrecked.
- The 'Great Eastern' was lucky to survive that dreadful night, but a reporter on board her wrote an article describing the full fury of the hurricane.

A model of the auxiliary steam-clipper 'Royal Charter', by courtesy of Oriel Ynys Môn, Isle of Anglesey County Council's Museum and Culture Service.

The dimensions of the *Royal Charter* are:-
Length overall, 336 feet; breadth of beam, 42 feet; and depth extreme, 26 feet 6 inches. Her registered burden is 2,700 tons. Viewed from the quay of the Huskisson Dock, where she is moored, she presents a pleasing picture. She possesses all the airy grace of a clipper-ship, combined with the imposing solidity and strength which iron is now universally admitted to possess. The lines of her sheer are easy and graceful, and are carried forward in an unbroken sweep until they terminate in the figure-head, which is a finely-carved full-length figure of a flying angel, in the hands of which is a wavy scroll, containing the name of the vessel. The bow is very neatly shaped, and on each side of the headboards, the name of the ship is also carved and gilded. The stern is elliptical in form, and is ornamented with beautifully-executed carved designs, richly gilded. Forward, her lines are sharp, being a medium between the "wave" and the "hollow" principle, while aft, her run is clean, yet possesses sufficient fullness to keep her buoyant and easy when bowling along with a strong breeze, under canvas alone, at the rate of sixteen knots an hour. This, we believe, she will accomplish with ease. Her great length has enabled the builder not only to give the ship a sharp entrance and a clean run, but also to preserve a long floor - a substantial body to rest upon - tending to make her comfortable to all parties on board in all weathers.

European Times. December 21, 1855.

The auxiliary steam-clipper 'Royal Charter'

The *Royal Charter* was a magnificent specimen of shipbuilding. She was some thirty feet longer than the *Great Britain*; could, without her 'auxiliary screw', sail eighteen knots an hour; and was, in matters of internal appointment, more like a West-end hotel than a ship which had to brave the seas and storms of Cape Horn. Her principal saloon was one hundred feet long, was fitted up with stained glass, rich hangings, velvet couches, candelabra, book-cases, piano, and all the other elegancies which have of late been made so much of in the reporters' descriptions of the *Great Eastern*. There were about forty cabins at the sides of the saloons, beside some twenty or thirty first-class berths on the deck immediately under. The 'intermediate' and 'steerage' accommodation was very large — capable, I should say, of receiving from four hundred and fifty to five hundred passengers — while in the forecastle and 'cock-pit' there were, when I came from Australia, about one hundred men, consisting of officers, pursers, midshipmen, crew, etc., etc. Along the main-deck, there was a row of shops — a wine-store, a grocery-store, a meat-store, and a bakery, together with two or three kitchens. (I may add here that the ship carried a score of stewards and cooks.) In the centre of the vessel, a large space was devoted to the engine and engineers' apartments, and just on one side were the cow and sheep pens. Altogether a noble craft — so noble that I never looked at it without thinking, "Great God! Will this vessel ever be swallowed by the waters!"

Frank Fowler (a former passenger of the 'Royal Charter')

Basically, the 'Royal Charter' was a fast, square-rigged, iron-built sailing ship that made the best use of the prevailing winds when heading eastwards around the world to Australia, before continuing eastwards around Cape Horn for the return home. Designated as a 'clipper', this class of ship was built for speed rather than for the bulk transport of cargo, so her hull was long, narrow and sleek. The well-established route around the world had many problems - icebergs, uncharted reefs, and areas of strong winds, but there was also the likelihood of being becalmed for days or even weeks on end. This latter problem meant that stocks of food and water could be depleted before a vessel reached her destination, increasing the risk of disease breaking out amongst the hundreds of passengers on board.

As well as her masts and sails, the 'Royal Charter' was fitted with an auxiliary steam engine that could propel her along in the absence of any suitable wind. She was not designed to steam all the way to Australia as the quantity of coal required would have been a huge financial burden on her owners, and taken up valuable accommodation and cargo space. The wind was free, whereas coal cost money.

The flag of Gibbs, Bright & Co.

As with their purchase of the 'Great Britain' in January 1851, Gibbs, Bright & Co. could see a bargain in the partially-built iron vessel that lay on the banks of the River Dee at George Cram's shipyard, close to Sandycroft near Chester, so they employed William Patterson, to complete the vessel. Patterson was an experienced builder of iron ships, having previously built the 'Great Britain' at Bristol and carried out modifications on that vessel at Liverpool for Gibbs, Bright & Co.

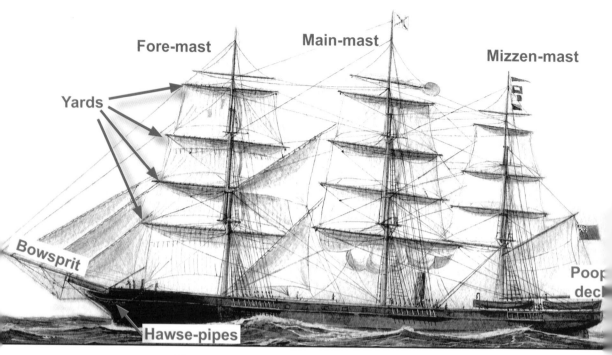

The masts and rigging of the 'Royal Charter'.

The *Royal Charter,* independent of her steam power, is a full-rigged ship, and is the first English vessel which has adopted the American plan of double topsails* on each mast. This rig gives the ship a most formidable appearance by having on each mast five yards. The difference between this and the ordinary rig consists in the lower topsail yard being secured to the cap of the topmast by a truss, and, in the absence of slings, the yard is supported in the centre from below by a crane, stepped upon the heel of the foremast. Thus, the lower top-sail is the size of a close-reefed topsail of the old rig, and sets entirely by the sheets. The upper topsail, which is managed in the ordinary manner, has its foot laced to the top of the yard below, so that no wind can escape between the two topsails. By this arrangement the ship can be reduced to close-reefed topsails at any time, by lowering the upper topsails. The lower masts and bowsprit are built of pitch pine, and hooped with iron. Her topmasts and lower yards are also of pitch pine. The spars are very strong, and, together with the substantial rigging, are fitted in a superior style. In order to convey an idea of the immense spread of canvas at command, we give the following:-
Length of mainmast from the deck, 75 feet; masthead, 18 feet; main topmast, 64 feet 6 inches; main topgallant mast, 41 feet; main royal, 24 feet. The length of the mainyard is 101 feet, lower topsail yard 92 feet, upper topsail yard 85 feet, topgallantyard 60 feet 6 inches, and royal yard 42 feet The fore and mizzen masts and yards are proportionately heavy. The total amount of her canvas will exceed 15,000 yards.

European Times.
December 21. 1855

* Howe's Close-reefing Topsail - a system of easily decreasing the amount of sail set.

The accommodation

Having thus described the outward appearance and machinery of the ship, we will endeavour to give some slight idea of her internal arrangements. Going on deck, the first object which attracts attention is a house, including, under the same roof, various compartments to be appropriated to the practical workers of the vessel. When occupied it will, indeed, present all the essentials of a busy colony. There is, for instance, the purser's room, with its numerous nooks and corners for the reception of choice wines and other pleasant liquids; the stowage room; officers' mess room; the stock house, with convenient folds for sheep, and roomy pens for the feathered tribe; the galley, with its elaborate apparatus for converting into inviting food the unconscious occupants of the stock-house, and containing capacious cooking-ranges, on the most approved design, by Messrs. Foster and Sons, with a monster oven, in which, before breakfast, a number of four-pound loaves and hot rolls can be baked, sufficient to satisfy a thousand people. If we may form any idea, from the size of this galley, and the completeness of its *cuisine* equipments, the passengers on board the *Royal Charter* would be amongst the best fed people in the world during the fifty-odd days they will occupy her spacious berths. If care is thus being taken to keep the passengers well supplied with the necessaries of life, equally satisfactory provision has been made to secure that important promoter and preserver of health, complete and frequent ablution. One of the compartments of this same house on deck is fitted up with a bath of capacious dimensions, in which, were it necessary, half a dozen people might indulge in a bracing plunge at the same time. The first-class passengers have baths of their own, so that this will be at the entire service of those occupying the intermediate berths. The poop deck is a fine promenade, upwards of 70 feet long, beneath which there is a spacious and elegant saloon, flanked on either side by the state cabins, which are spacious and well lighted and ventilated. They are divided from the saloon by a screen, placed at a uniform distance of about three feet from the cabin doors, and thus giving the passengers an opportunity of promenading the entire length without incommoding persons conversing in the saloon, or being themselves disturbed in their reveries. This screen is chastely decorated, the lower panels being painted white, surrounded by gold beadings, while the upper panels are formed of sliding windows, filled in with ground glass, bearing appropriate nautical designs, in which sea nymphs, Father Neptune, dolphins, and mermaids are variously grouped. One of these windows is placed opposite every cabin door, and may be closed or let down at pleasure. There is a peculiar advantage in this passage or lobby. By an ingenious contrivance, grateful currents of air find their way freely into every part, and thence into the cabins through the Venetian bars in the doors, and the ventilating apertures above; while the unbroken floods of light, admitted into the saloon through two spacious skylights, are equally well diffused. Each cabin is supplied with two toilet stands, with white marble tops, and two mirrors, between which will be placed, on a small mahogany stand fixed to the wall, a neat silver candlestick containing a wax taper. The beds are hung with rich French wool hangings of beautiful chintz patterns; and the floors are covered with elegant Brussels carpets. Besides a bookcase, to be stocked with an interesting collection

A candlestick from the wreck.

The ladies' boudoir of the 'Great Britain'.

of works for the use of passengers, the furnishing of the saloon includes a piano and several mirrors of large dimensions. The ladies' boudoir, which is extreme aft, is elegantly fitted, and contains a luxurious sofa, while the floor will be covered with a velvet-pile carpet. The saloon is relieved by numerous carvings of fruit and figures of every description, cut out of soft wood.

The 'tween decks are lofty, and well ventilated by means of shafts communicating with the upper decks, and admitting copious and never-failing supplies of fresh air. The height from deck to deck is between nine and ten feet; and the whole of the spacious area is well lighted. The berths for the second and third-class passengers are of a substantial and permanent nature, and, as is the case with every other part of the ship, they bear evidence of the determination of the owners to spare no expense in making all on board comfortable. Even the seamen, who are but too frequently thrust into a "cribbed, cabined, and confined" space, devoid of light and ventilation, have been well cared for, in the fore topgallant fore-castle, which is between eight and nine feet high.

European Times. December 21, 1855.

Decorative glass from the wreck-site.

The steam engine

The crest of the "Liverpool and Australian *Steam* Navigation Co.

The middle of the 19th century was a period of great innovation that provided huge leaps forward in technology. Steam engines were still massive, inefficient and costly, but advances in metallurgy and precision engineering allowed their working-pressure to be increased from the 5 psi of the original engines of the 'Great Britain' to the much higher pressure that was available to the engineers of subsequent vessels. A pressure-gauge recovered from the wreck of the 'Royal Charter' shows a maximum reading of 150 psi, but this is far greater than her working-pressure. The newly-designed trunk-engines built by John Penn & Co. were lighter and more compact than the original 'inverted-V' engines or the later 'oscillating-engines' of the 'Great Britain', and this innovative principle saved valuable cargo-space, although they required regular attention as the seals tended to wear out rather rapidly. To advertise the presence of this additional means of propulsion, the Liverpool and Australian Navigation Company now proudly incorporated the word *STEAM* in their company emblem to give us the Liverpool and Australian Steam Navigation Company. Compare this emblem to the one shown on page 24.

The auxiliary steam power [*of the Royal Charter*], which is similar to that on board of the line-of-battle ships *Duke of Wellington, Royal Albert,* etc., consists of a pair of trunk engines, direct acting, of 200 horse-power, nominal. They were constructed and fitted by Messrs. Penn, of Greenwich. The diameter of each cylinder is 50 inches; effective diameter 45 inches; diameter of trunk 21 inches; and length of stroke 27 inches. The engine-room and boilers are placed abaft the main-mast, in such a position as to keep the vessel in trim. The pitch of the screw is 13 feet, and its diameter 14 feet. The bunkers will hold 425 tons of coal, which, it is calculated, will be considerably more than will be consumed on her voyage to Australia. The screw shaft is 130 feet in length, and is carried to the stern through an alley, along the top of which is placed a perforated pipe, which permits water continually to drop to prevent heating. The shaft can be disconnected in a minute and a half, and the screw lifted out of the water in ten minutes. The engines have been worked for several hours, and proved satisfactory in every particular, all the bearings being cool. While in dock, the engines were permitted to work only up to fifty-five revolutions; but they are calculated to go as high as seventy revolutions per minute. There appears to be no doubt among practical men that, under steam alone, the *Royal Charter* will attain eight knots per hour. In other screw-steamers, the huge funnel is an unsightly object, but in this vessel that necessary appendage, which is placed a short distance abaft the mainmast, is some-what diminutive, and only slightly detracts from her shipshape and noble appearance.

European Times.
December 21, 1855.

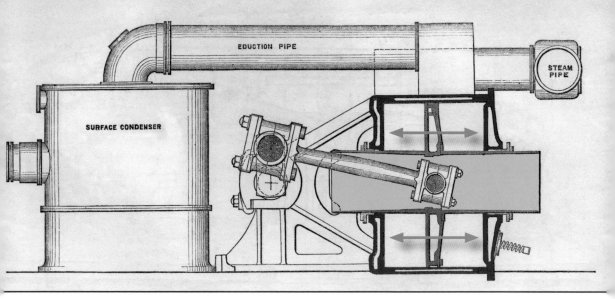

EDUCTION PIPE

STEAM PIPE

SURFACE CONDENSER

Penn's horizontal trunk-engine. From 'The Marine Steam Engine' by R. Sennett. The trunk (coloured green) slides left and right as steam is introduced into one side of the cylinder and then into the other side of the cylinder. The cylinder is coloured brown in the diagram.

This was the latest technology in marine steam engines, with one contemporary report describing Penn's creation as:

> It is a horizontal trunk-engine. In this engine, a round pipe called a trunk penetrates the piston, to which it is fixed, being in fact cast in one piece with it; and the trunk also penetrates the top and bottom of the cylinder, through which it moves, and is made tight therein by means of stuffing boxes [*i.e. seals*]. The connecting rod is attached at one end to a pin fixed in the middle of the trunk, while the other end engages the crank in the usual manner.

The advantage of these 'double-acting' engines was that the expanding steam forced the trunk one way and then the other, to increase the power without adding weight. Their disadvantage was that they needed seals, otherwise known as 'stuffing-boxes', where the trunk slid through the outer casing. These seals were difficult to keep clean, and often allowed high-pressure steam to escape into the engine-room.

Lying horizontally across the hull, Penn's latest design kept the weight of the engine low down in the hull, a feature that would considerably improve a vessel's sailing-ability. These engines ran at a higher speed than earlier designs, enabling them to operate without the massive system of chains or gears that were needed on vessels such as the 'Great Britain'. That vessel had an 'inverted-V' engine which took up a vast amount of space, but the smaller engine supplied by Penn meant that the 'Royal Charter' could carry more cargo, more passengers, and most importantly for the shipowner, she would provide more profit. Gibbs, Bright & Co. decided that it was well worth investing in the latest technology, despite the huge cost:

> Messrs. Penn and Co., of Greenwich, supplied the engines; the price paid for them was very high, £55 10s per horse-power.

If you multiply £55 10 shillings by 200 (horsepower) and then again by 50 to estimate the cost at today's prices, you get a total of around half a million pounds as the price of the steam power, a tremendous investment by Gibbs, Bright & Co. that they needed to retrieve as quickly as possible. For further details of Penn's design, including an animated diagram, visit the website of the Western Australian Museums Service who have salvaged and renovated one of these marine steam engines.

These early engines utilised only a single-expansion of the steam, leading to the high fuel-consumption reported in the 'Illustrated London News' of 1855:

> The coal to be used on board is anthracite, from which there will be no smoke; and 22 tons in the 24 hours, to produce a speed of nine knots with 76 revolutions is the estimated consumption. Reducing the quantity to nine tons, a speed of six knots and fifty revolutions could be had.

The 'European Times' article shown on page 39 suggests that her coal capacity was only 425 tons, so it was impossible for the 'Royal Charter' to steam all the way to Australia without calling somewhere along the way to refill her bunkers, a delay that would have cost time and money, and probably taken much of the profit out of the enterprise. As an *auxiliary* steam-clipper, she wasn't designed to use her engine all of the time, a fact that would have pleased her engineers and stokers as conditions were very unpleasant when the boilers were lit. The engine-room was poorly-ventilated, extremely noisy and incredibly hot, with temperatures reaching up to 130 degrees Fahrenheit (55 degrees Celsius). As previously stated, the seals between the sliding-trunk and the outer casing of the engine were prone to leak, so the atmosphere in the engine-room would have been contaminated by steam and smoke, but perhaps the only advantage of working in these conditions was the allowance of beer, porter or diluted brandy that they were given in addition to their normal rations.

Very few of Penn's trunk-engines have survived to the present day, as they were soon superseded by the far more efficient 'compound-engine', but a replica of a trunk-engine can be seen at Portsmouth in the old warship 'HMS Warrior'. Powered by both sail and steam, 'HMS Warrior' was a significant development in warship design. Launched in late 1860, she was the first iron-hulled, armoured battleship in Queen Victoria's navy, and like the 'Royal Charter', she had a lifting-screw that could be retracted when under sail. Penn's engines were a popular choice in warships of that era, as their low profile meant that they could be installed below the waterline of a man-of-war, where they would be less likely to be damaged by enemy action.

This engraving gives an idea of the massive size of the trunk-engines of 'HMS Warrior' which were far more powerful than the 200-horsepower unit fitted to the 'Royal Charter'.

The Lifting-screw

The 'Royal Charter' was primarily a sailing ship, with the steam engine being used only if light winds made progress impossible, when she was entering or leaving harbour, or in an emergency such as the hurricane of October 1859. Unfortunately, when not being driven by an engine, an immersed propeller creates a considerable drag on a vessel, slowing her down and causing an unwelcome vibration as the screw rotates due to the forward motion of the hull. A well-tried principle at this time was to disconnect the drive-shaft and lift the screw clear of the water when the ship was under sail alone, thus reducing the drag of the screw and thereby increasing the speed of the vessel. Because the screw needed to be raised into a recess in the hull without any of the blades dragging in the water, a twin-bladed propeller was the only option available to the designers, as a screw with three or four blades would have needed a

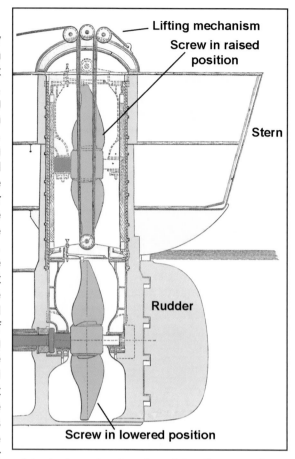

A typical mechanism for raising the propeller.

massive shaft to be cut in the stern. The diagram above shows the screw when it had been lowered to drive the ship under steam power, and also the position (in dotted-lines) where it had been raised out of the water. Despite the advantage of producing less drag, these 'screw-wells' took up valuable space around the stern and reduced the structural integrity of the hull. They also needed to be soundly constructed, as there would be a total disaster if the propeller and its frame suddenly dropped away from its retaining position to possibly tear away the whole of the rudder assembly.

The lifting-screw of the 'Royal Charter' caused some difficulty on her maiden voyage as it proved difficult to raise up out of the water, a situation that was attributed to either the mechanism being too finely machined or that it had become jammed because of corrosion. One and a half hours were initially wasted in this task, but the system appears to have worked reasonably well once the problems had been sorted out and the ship's crew became skilled at raising the propeller. One passenger described the task as *'an awkward operation on account of the capstan being placed forward instead of aft',* but Gibbs, Bright & Co. must have been satisfied with the design as they used the same principle again when they had the 'Great Britain' refitted in 1856-57 by Thomas Vernon & Son, a shipbuilder and repairer of Liverpool. See the photograph opposite.

A reconstruction of the lifting-screw and housing fitted to the 'Great Britain' in 1856-57.

Anchors and cables (chains)

Around the middle of the 19th Century, vast improvements were being made to the design of ships' anchors, with many variations being manufactured and tested. The long-established Admiralty-pattern anchor was still in use with the Royal Navy, but these were rather heavy and required considerable manpower to retrieve them from the seabed. This wasn't a major problem for a heavily-manned fighting-vessel, but hauling up a heavy anchor was hard, back-breaking work for the fewer crew-members of a merchantman, so a lighter anchor with the same holding-power was a great advantage.

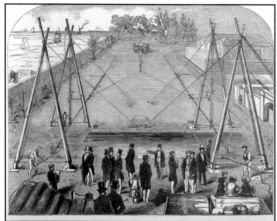

The method used to compare the anchors.

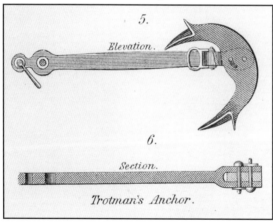

Trotman's Anchor.

In 1852 , the Lords Commissioners of the Admiralty set up an Anchor Committee *'to investigate and determine the relative merits of anchors, in compliance with a requisition from the principal Shipowners, Underwriters, etc. of the United Kingdom.'*
Trials were held at the Royal Dockyard, Sheerness, Kent, with examples of their designs being submitted by Trotman, Rodger, Mitcheson, Lenox, Honibal, Isaac and Aylen. As a result of these tests, the 'Anchor Committee' affirmed that:

Trotman's Patent Anchors were superior to all others, possessing thirty-five percent more holding-power than either Porter's or Roger's, and equivalent in all respects to ordinary anchors of 28 per cent greater weight.

John Trotman's design had won the day, so manufacturers such as Henry Wood of Saltney, Chester, began to produce a range of anchors to Trotman's design and specification. Located only a few miles upstream from George Cram's shipyard at Sandycroft, and with a railway line that ran past both sites, it would seem natural for Henry Wood to produce the anchors for the 'Royal Charter'.

Her [*the Royal Charter's*] anchors are of the most approved description (Trotman's patent) which, together with the cables, were manufactured by Henry Wood and Co., of the Liverpool and Dee Iron Works, Chester. Mr. Trotman, the patentee, has been awarded the first-class medal for anchors, at the Paris Exhibition, and Messrs. Wood have also been awarded one for their manufactures.

European Times, December 21, 1855.

Trotman's,	.	.	.	1·28,	or 28 per cent. superior to **Admiralty.**		
Rodger's,	.	.	.	1·26,	or 26	do.	do.	do.
Mitcheson's,	.	.	.	1·20,	or 20	do.	do.	do.
Lenox's,	.	.	.	1·13,	or 13	do.	do.	do.
Honibal's,	.	.	.	1·09,	or 9	do.	do.	do.
Aylen's,	.	.	.	1·09,	or 9	do.	do.	do.
Admiralty,	.	.	.	1·	the standard.			
Isaac's,	.	.	.	·73,	or 27 per cent. inferior to **Admiralty.**		

The published results of the tests are shown above, although there was some dispute as to the fairness of the outcome. One report says:

> It has also been stated that the Admiralty anchor was treated unfairly, as one was taken promiscuously out of store for the trial, whereas the other competing anchors were made specially for it.

In other words, the Admiralty-pattern anchor was a standard-issue model, whereas the others were specially made for the tests, and were probably of a higher quality than production-line models.

Henry Wood also manufactured anchor-chains, otherwise known as cables, and he supplied these to the shipyard at Sandycroft for use on the 'Royal Charter'. Each individual link of a chain needed to be welded by hand, a process that required an iron bar to be heated until red-hot, bent into shape, and then hammered while still hot to produce one complete link. This required skill, concentration and hard work in a sweltering-hot atmosphere, when one undetected bad weld could have disastrous consequences in a situation where the lives of a ship's

Chain-making at Henry Wood's factory. Flintshire Record Office (ref. PH/58/60).

crew and passengers would be totally reliant on the strength of that link. In the 1850s, there were no statutory requirements for the anchors and anchor-cables of merchant-vessels to be independently tested, although some shipbuilders did commission proving-tests similar to those insisted upon by the Royal Navy. An example of an anchor being tested for the 'Great Eastern' is shown on page 258 of this book.

As the 1859 inquiry into the loss of the 'Royal Charter' was to show, the anchors and chains fitted to that vessel were of the usual weight and strength for a merchant ship of her size, although rules for iron ships were still being formulated at the time of her construction in 1855. The anchor-cables for the 'Royal Charter' were manufactured and tested by Henry Wood & Co. to the requirements of the Mercantile Marine, but they were not independently checked by anyone else. It wasn't until the Chain Cables and Anchors Act of 1864 became law that companies such as Henry Wood were forced to have the quality of their products verified by an independent test-facility. This lead to the establishment of the Lloyd's Cambrian Chain and Anchor Public Testing Company at Boundary Road, Saltney, Chester, adjacent to Wood's factory.

"The stupendous cannon from the wreck of the 'Royal Charter' .... It should be remarked that this cannon was presented to Mrs. Williams by Captain Martin, superintendent to Messrs. Gibbs and Bright, as a trophy for several benevolent acts connected with the dire catastrophe." -- North Wales Chronicle. January 4, 1862.

Armament

During the 19th century, many passenger-vessels were defensively-armed, so the 'Royal Charter' was equipped with several cannon and a variety of small-arms. After all, she would be carrying a valuable cargo of gold worth many millions of pounds at today's prices, and this would certainly attract the attention of any rogue ship that was capable of intercepting and plundering her. The 'Illustrated London News' of 1855 contained the following report:

> We might add that the *Royal Charter* is to be well armed. She is to have eight guns -- four 18 pounders, and four 24 pounders, besides a large swivel-gun in the forecastle, and a good number of *Minié* rifles for the saloon.

Fortunately for the safety of the passengers and crew, the cannon were never used in anger. The following passage describes the ship's arrival at Melbourne in 1857 when the gun-crew's lack of proficiency caused damage to their own ship, but what would have happened in a serious fire-fight at sea?

> .. we found ourselves in Hobson's Bay. Almost immediately the mail boat (a wee little steamer) came alongside for the mails. We fired salutes and blew away part of the bulwarks.

In addition to the ship's supply of side-arms, many passengers carried weapons for their own protection, as pistols, rifles and gun-tools have been recovered from the wreck. This amount of fire-power wouldn't have been enough to fight off a man-of-war or a heavily-armed pirate ship, but the 'Royal Charter' had a turn of speed that could probably out-run most of her potential adversaries. Designed by Captain Minié, the Minié rifles were provided so that the crew and first-class passengers were sufficiently well-armed to challenge any intruders or mutineers, either in port or on the high-seas. These guns were a recent development of muzzle-loader that gave improved accuracy, range

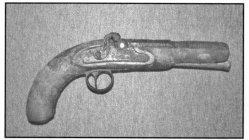
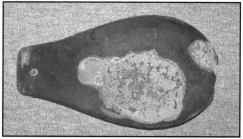
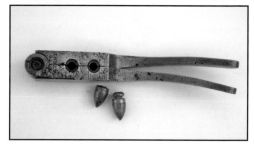

A pistol, powder-flask and bullet-mould, all recovered from the 'Royal Charter'. The bullet-mould is 0.36 calibre, and marked 'Colt's Patent', after the famous gunsmith.

and penetrating power over previous firearms, and were probably carried from lessons learned after an audacious robbery in 1852 when twenty-two men, armed with swords and pistols, rowed out to the ship 'Nelson' moored in Hobson's Bay, Melbourne.

Choosing a dark night, the intruders quietly boarded the vessel and rounded up the ship's mate, three seamen and three male passengers who were the only persons aboard with the exception of the cook. At first Henry Draper, the mate, refused to reveal where the valuables were stored, but after being shot in the side and 'pricked by a sword', he was forced to help the intruders load the gold into their boats before being locked in the hold along with the seamen and passengers. The robbers certainly chose the most opportune moment, as they successfully escaped with £30,000 in gold. That might not sound a massive amount of money at today's values, but this was a total of eight thousand, six hundred ounces of the precious metal. At a present-day price of well over £500 per ounce, there was probably the equivalent of five million pound's worth of treasure taken that night.

Unfortunately for the intruders, the ship's cook had hidden from the gang, so he released the seamen and passengers as soon as the robbers had rowed away from the ship. Once the alarm had been raised, the Lieutenant Governor of the colony offered a reward for information leading to the apprehension and conviction of the perpetrators of the robbery, while additional incentives made a total pay-out of £750 for the arrest of the gang and the recovery of the missing property. As a final incentive, a conditional pardon was offered to any convict who could provide any information that would lead to a successful conviction. Fortunately for the owners of the gold, some of the robbers were quickly recognised and captured, so Henry Draper got his revenge by giving evidence against them in court and was no doubt satisfied when they were sentenced to fifteen years hard labour on the roads and other public works, with the first three years of their punishment to be served 'in irons'. The court-case meant that Draper had to stay behind when the 'Nelson' sailed, but he was awarded £300 as compensation for his loss of earnings, and then settled in Australia where he gained employment as a pilot at Port Phillip.

Food and drink

A finely-carved, wooden napkin-ring from the dining-tables of the 'Royal Charter'.

Eating and drinking was a very important part of life on any emigrant-ship, and the 'Royal Charter' was certainly no exception. Two months or more at sea was a very long time if the meals were of poor quality, so a ship's reputation and therefore profitability could depend on the dining arrangements. Refrigeration and ice-making machines were still rare, so fresh meat was provided by sheep, pigs, bullocks, turkeys and geese that were kept alive until required, while a cow would provide fresh milk for the more affluent passengers. Certainly, the First-class and Saloon passengers ate very well, dining in elegant style while being served by stewards, after being called to the table by the dinner-bell. It didn't matter what the weather conditions were like; calm or storm, dinner was to be served as normal. The Reverend William Scoresby, a First-class passenger, wrote in his journal describing the food:

Wednesday, February 27, 1856. For the first time since our joining the *Royal Charter*, our provision at dinner-time failed us in the article of roast beef! The admirable service and provision may be worthy of some little notice. The saloon passengers, omitting children, are 54 in number, which, with four officers of the ship, makes an amount of 58 to be provided for. Two tables, separated only by the mizzen mast, run down the centre of the saloon, extending together to 50 feet in length. The dinner is served up in silver plate. The bill of fare for February 21st, which is a fair sample of the ordinary provision, ran as follows:—2 joints of roast beef; 2 roast and 1 boiled mutton; 2 roast and 2 boiled chickens; 4 dishes of mutton cutlets; 4 dishes of mutton curry; 1 ham; 2 tongues; 2 roast pork and apple sauce; 2 mutton pies. Vegetables — potatoes, carrots, rice, cabbage, etc. Pastry — 4 plum puddings, brandied; 4 rice puddings, 6 fruit tarts, 4 open tarts, 2 sago puddings. Dessert, various. For breakfast, tea and coffee, with milk from two cows; beef-steaks, mutton cutlets, Irish stew, spiced ham, cold beef or mutton, ham, sardines, rice porridge, stewed mutton, and prevailing articles; with bread, baked on board; and, generally, very capital hot rolls. At tea, on alternate days, the tea and coffee, with toast, plain bread and biscuits, has the addition of marmalade, jam, etc., in ample supply. Luncheon, in the early part of the voyage, when breakfast was at nine and dinner at four, was a respectable set out, commencing with a capital soup.

The meal was expected to be served on time, whatever the weather might throw at the vessel:

April 6, 1856. About 10 a.m. there was quite an inundation from the skylights; but the stewards again on the alert had soon baled out the body of water, and removed and replaced the hundreds of suspended glasses and other apparatus above the table, in dry, clean, and proper order. No sooner had this been accomplished and everything got right, than another sea (it being the height of the hurricane) came over the poop-deck, and again sent its large contributions to the discomfort below. Again were the men at their posts — industrious and active, as we have seen a colony of ants, when their hill structure has been damaged by

The elegant dining-room of the steamship 'Great Britain'.

the foot of a passer-by — and the same round of renovation and replacement carried into effect as before! Notwithstanding these seas and the water coming in by the forward doors or main-companion of the saloon, the arrangements of the day were little interrupted, and at 3.30 p.m., just half an hour after the usual time, we heard the dinner-bell sending forth its wonted summons. To our surprise the tables were covered as in favourable times: a dinner of considerable variety — in roast and boiled mutton, pork, cutlets, stews, curries, vegetables — with plum-pudding surrounded by brandy flame, rice puddings, tarts in variety, which in due course came on — and all served up in the ordinary handsome order. Excepting soup and an accident to the fowls, the hurricane and peril occasioned no other lack in the provisions for the table.

Basic eating for the steerage passengers.

Of course, not everybody on board could afford the more luxurious accommodation, so the passengers in steerage-class had to prepare their own food and eat it in far more basic circumstances than those of the Reverend Scoresby and his wife. As shown in this photo from the 'Great Britain', metal plates and mugs were used instead of elegantly-patterned china, with bare wooden benches for the seating arrangements.

The Dee Estuary and tidal reaches of the river, from Liverpool Bay to Chester. c.1850.

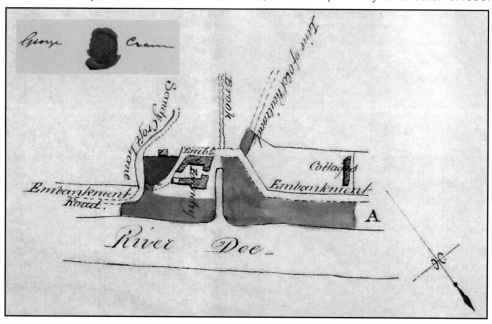

A map of George Cram's shipyard at Sandycroft, c.1854.
Reproduced with the permission of Cheshire Record Office.

CHAPTER THREE

Shipbuilding on the River Dee

Nowadays, the River Dee in North Wales seems an unlikely place for a shipbuilding industry, as it is shallow and tidal, and the Dee Estuary has ever-changing channels and sandbanks to make navigation difficult. However, despite these problems, several shipyards thrived along the southern bank of the river until well into the 20th Century, with wood, iron and steel vessels being built at several sites that included Mostyn, Bagillt, Flint, Connah's Quay, Queensferry, Sandycroft, Saltney and Chester.

By 1842, the family-firm of Rigby was running a shipyard on the south bank of the Dee at Sandycroft (near Hawarden), and this company appears to have been willing to experiment with a new method of propelling a small vessel, although their sculling steamboat doesn't appear to have made its mark in the history books. Around 1852, the shipyard was taken over by George Cram, who launched several iron vessels there, and laid down the keel of what was to become the steam-clipper 'Royal Charter'.

IMPORTANT INVENTION FOR PROPELLING STEAM BOATS.

A trial was lately made on the Liverpool river of Mr. Edward Finch's patent propeller, which was eminently successful. A small steamer called the *Lapwing*, of 45 tons burthen and 18 horsepower, has been constructed at the well-known engineering establishment of Mr. Rigby, at Hawarden, for the purpose of trying the merits of Mr. Finch's invention. We are informed that, in coming round to Liverpool, although so small a vessel, she performed some part of the trip at the rate of 12 miles per hour. After steaming in the river for some time, where she was an object of much interest to the old craftsmen and a large number of spectators, she sailed away with a number of gentlemen on board to the North-west Light-ship, and returned to Liverpool by way of the Formby Channel, between 7 and 8 in the evening. The trip gave great satisfaction to the voyagers, and convinced all parties that this novel invention will be of great importance, and when fully developed, of general application to sailing vessels, as well as to steam-packets. The day after the trial, the *Lapwing* left the port for Hawarden, where further experiments are being made to make her still more efficient; and, from the spirit shown in this experiment, we await her return with considerable interest, as it is generally considered that no improvement has taken place in propelling steam vessels since their first introduction. The invention appears a very simple contrivance. The paddle-boxes are still preserved, but, instead of paddle-wheels, two plates are applied, the broadest parts of which are at their extreme ends, fixed obliquely at an angle of about 4 degrees, one on each side of the vessel, at the end of the paddle shaft. These plates, or propellers, are made of wrought iron, and appear very strong and compact, and about 11 feet long and 3 feet 6 inches wide in the broadest parts. They are entirely out of the water twice in the revolution of the paddle-shaft, when the engine is on her centres, and have the deepest hold of the water when the engine is at half-stroke, or at its greatest power. They thus act like oars, or sculls, no back water is created, and the disagreeable beating of the paddle-boards on the water, and consequent vibration of the vessel, is avoided. On Thursday, the *Lapwing* performed a voyage of fifty miles, calling at the North-west Light-ship, and returned to Liverpool between seven and eight o'clock. The trip was a most delightful one; plentiful cheer was provided for the voyagers, and the complete success of the experiment was placed beyond doubt.

Polytechnic Journal. 1842.

The River Dee at Sandycroft.

From the various agreements between George Cram and his creditors, it appears that he was a very successful shipbuilder, but his financial affairs were not as well managed as his manufacturing capability. By April 1853 his bank-account was overdrawn by more than the agreed £5,000 limit. Determined to continue here and at his other shipyard at Chester, he still managed to negotiate a lease for extra land at Sandycroft to build a railway or tramway to the main Chester to Holyhead line. By June 1854, he had delivered two steamships to the docks for final completion, but there was a major problem about to create his downfall - as shown by these extracts from legal documents, he simply hadn't been paid!

8th of June – certain steamship 'Golden Queen' for Van Hoey Smith of the City of London .... now in Birkenhead Docks having her engines and other machinery (£4,345 6s or thereabouts owing on this ship) .... another ship 'The Mino' for Paul Yintora & Co. of Barcelona, now in Sandon Dock at Liverpool, engines being fitted.

Cram was now owed well over £5,000 for the two ships, but he needed ready-cash to survive in business. Borrowing another £677 17s 3d from his banker, Mr. Williams, Cram assigned the money that he was owed to Mr. Williams. However, these measures failed to solve the problem, as his financial woes rapidly increased --

16th of August, 16, 1854. .... Conveyance of real estate and assignment of personal estate to Messrs. Septimus Edwards (Iron Merchant) of Liverpool and Robert Roberts (Slate Merchant) of Chester. .... all and every Stock in Trade, machinery, plants, goods, wares and merchandising, books of accounts and other debts, sum and sums of money, and all securities for money, share rights and interests and all other personal Estates and Effects (except the wearing apparel for himself and his family)

This was a cruel world, as the creditors left George Cram and his family with nothing but the shirts on their backs, but there was still work in progress at Sandycroft that lead to the launch of another vessel just before Christmas, 1854.

On Thursday last at noon, a very beautiful iron ship, of 1,460 tons register, was launched from Mr. Cram's ship-yard, at Sandycroft. She belongs to Messrs. Sharples, Jones, and Co., merchants, of Liverpool, and is intended for the Australian or Indian trade. The vessel was named the *Winifred* by Miss Jenny Jones, youngest daughter of the owner. The ship glided off the ways in the most beautiful manner, and was immediately taken in tow by a steamer, and arrived in Liverpool the same evening. Nautical judges consider her of superior construction, and her lines are equal to any first-class ship afloat. She has full poop and top-gallant forecastle, and her figure-head was greatly admired. She is allowed by everyone who has seen her to be the strongest vessel ever built of iron; her dimensions are as follows: Length over all, 235 feet beam 35 feet 9 inches; depth 22 feet 6 inches. She is by far the largest vessel ever built on the River Dee. We understand there is at present on the stocks at Sandycroft a vessel of 2,600 tons, nearly as large again as the one mentioned above, which will be launched some time next spring.

Chester Chronicle. December 23, 1854

The first half of 1855 saw the construction of the 'Royal Charter', the largest ship ever built on the banks of the Dee. Originally ordered from George Cram by the owners of the 'Tayleur', the 'Royal Charter' was finally completed by Gibbs, Bright & Co. who brought in the expertise of William Patterson to complete the clipper, as they were a firm of shipowners rather than shipbuilders. Once the 'Royal Charter' had been launched, the slipway at Sandycroft was to remain idle despite the following advert:

The Sandycroft Iron Works are situated on the banks of the Dee, about one and a half miles from Hawarden, and are capable of building vessels and steam engines for them, up to 3,000 tons burthen. When in full operation, they employ upwards of 700 hands. The works are the property of Mr. Williams, banker, of Chester.

Slaters Directory for 1856

The phrase *'when in full operation'* was somewhat over-optimistic and premature, as an advert appeared in 'The Times' newspaper of the 9th of January, 1856, advertising the sale of the *"Engine Factory, Foundry, and Iron Ship Yard from which the splendid vessel 'Royal Charter' and other first-class steamships have been lately launched."* There was no immediate rush of potential buyers, but the local firm of John Taylor eventually moved there from nearby Rhydymwyn in 1862 to take advantage of the adjacent railway to transport the machines that they produced for the mining industry. By 1890, the site was known as the Sandycroft Foundry and Engine Works, which produced crushing machines (known as stamps) for mines and collieries not only in Britain but also for export to India, Brazil, South Africa, New Zealand and Australia. By 1920, competition from other companies had increased dramatically, leading to the gradual run-down and closure of production in 1925.

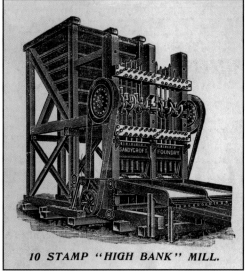

10 STAMP "HIGH BANK" MILL.

A Sandycroft-built stamping machine.

In 1925, the Dee-built ferry 'Lurgurena' endured a four-month voyage to Hobart, Tasmania. Steaming under her own power, the 15,000-mile journey took her through the Suez Canal, then via Aden, Colombo, Java and the Western Australian port of Bunbury.

The end of shipbuilding on the River Dee

The wreck of the 'Ilesha'.

Shipbuilding on the Dee continued into the 20th century, with motor-ships such as the 'Kingsholme' being built by Abdella & Mitchell at Queensferry in 1914. Renamed 'Ilesha' and powered by two Bolinder oil-engines, this 109-ton steel vessel didn't survive for long as it suffered failures of both engines during a trip to West Africa in 1915, and now provides a popular diving-site off Bardsey Island at the western tip of North Wales. James Crichton & Company had two shipyards on the river, where they built a variety of vessels that varied from motor-launches to small lightships and floating grain-elevators. The Dee was still capable of producing ships that could reach Australia under their own power, as proved by Crichton's in 1925 when they launched the 'Lurgurena'. This 200-foot (61-metre) long vehicle-ferry endured a horrendous four-month voyage to Hobart, Tasmania under her own steam. A year later, the same yard launched two more vehicle-ferries, the 'Kalang' and 'Kara Kara' to be used at Sydney Harbour while the famous bridge was under construction. These ferries also made the trip to Australia under their own steam.

Despite export-orders to Portugal, Ceylon (Sri Lanka), India, West Africa, East Africa and South America, Crichton's closed their Connah's Quay yard in 1932 and the one at Saltney in 1935. This ended major shipbuilding on the Dee, but the river is still used today as the means of transporting the massive wings of the Airbus A-380 aircraft as they make their way from the manufacturing plant at Broughton, Chester, to Toulouse in France.

The River Dee today.

Destined for an Airbus A-380, an aircraft wing passes the site of the former shipyard at Sandycroft which was located on the small promontory at the right of the photograph. Each wing is around 45 metres long, while the 'Royal Charter' was just over 97 metres (320 feet) in overall length.

The site of the former shipyard is now partially wooded. The 'Royal Charter' was launched diagonally into the river with her stern pointing upstream towards Chester (to the left of the photograph). The Dee Estuary and the open sea lies to the right.

A new screw steam-ship, intended for the Liverpool and Australian Steam Company, for whom Messrs. Gibbs, Bright, & Co. are managers, is now nearly ready for launching, and is expected to be floated next month. She is building by Mr. Cram, at Sandycroft, near Queen's Ferry.

The following are her dimensions: Length overall, 320 feet; breadth of beam, 41 feet 6 inches; depth of hold amidships, 26 feet 6 inches; burthen, 3,000 tons. She will be a full-rigged ship, with double yards on the fore and main masts to facilitate reefing. The machinery is constructing by Messrs. Penn and Son, of Greenwich, who made the last engines for the *Great Britain,* and we understand the work is nearly finished. The available power gained by large boilers will be at least 300 horses, and her screw will be lifted when circumstances require her to go by the wind alone.

Liverpool Albion,
April 30, 1855

Note that the various figures given for the weight of the 'Royal Charter' are quoted as 2,600, 2,700 or 3,000 tons *registered burthen.* This is actually a calculation based on the cargo capacity of the vessel rather than the actual weight of the materials used in her construction.

The Launch of the 'Royal Charter'.

Chester Chronicle
AND CHESHIRE AND NORTH WALES ADVERTISER
SATURDAY, AUGUST 4, 1855

Launch of the Australian Steam-ship
Royal Charter.

Despite the heavy soaking rain on Tuesday last, thousands of people assembled on the banks of the Dee, from Chester, Liverpool, and all parts of Flintshire, to witness the launch of the magnificent screw steam ship *Royal Charter,* which has been built at Sandycroft, near Queens Ferry, for the Australian Steamship Company of Liverpool. From Chester, everything that could roll was on the road, and everything that could float was on the water, with people eager for the spectacle. The cop on both sides of the river was crowded with pedestrians who urged their way resolutely, not withstanding the skyey* influences were so unpropitious, and the pathway so toilsome. Unfortunately, their expectations, which they had endured so much to realise, were doomed to disappointment, for the noble vessel did not float.

The work on her was completed some days ago, and she only waited for a sufficiently-high tide to take her off the stocks. Tuesday was appointed for this important ceremony, and everything prepared to meet the occasion. To show more clearly the difficulties attending the launch, we may explain that the River Dee is at this part much too narrow to allow the vessel to be placed across it, and she therefore had to be built and launched almost in a line with the stream, astern up the river, so as to let her take the water in the same direction as the flood tide runs.

To add to the difficulties, the Sandycroft side of the river is impeded with banks of mud and sand just above the building yard. More than a week ago, an excavation of these banks was commenced in the course of the intended launch, and the ship's 'ways' carefully laid down over it; so carefully as apparently to preclude all possibility of a mishap. At the proper time, the 'ways' were well 'soaped' as usual, so as to let the ship slip easily along them. Having thus described the locality of the intended launch, we may now allude to the efforts made on Tuesday to accomplish it.

A party of about 60 ladies and gentlemen from Liverpool went by the railway, amongst whom were Mr. Nathaniel Hawthorne**, the American consul at Liverpool, many shipbuilders, and nearly all the gentlemen from the large establishment of Messrs. Gibbs, Bright, and Co., the agents here for the company to which she belongs. The three fine boats *Rattler, Sampson* and *Pilot,* belonging to the Liverpool Steam-tug Company were in attendance to tow the vessel round to Liverpool. The steamers *Cygnet* and *Test,* numerous small boats and barges, and every description of vehicle were freighted with parties from Chester, and pedestrian spectators from all the surrounding neighbourhood lined both banks of the river, and presented a terrible array of -- umbrellas! Captain Martin, the marine superintendent of the company, Captain Boyce, of the Australian ship *Eagle,* and other practical gentlemen were present to superintend and assist in carrying out the arrangements. At one o'clock, the tide being just on the full, and everything declared in readiness, Mr. William Patterson, the builder, (who constructed the *Great Britain,* at Bristol) gave the word, -- the daggers were soon struck down, -- the lady of Mr. Samuel Bright dashed the bottle on to the bow of the ship in a spirited manner, and christened her the *Royal Charter,* -- and the noble-looking craft then began to slide slowly down the 'ways', amid the vociferous cheers

*skyey – like the sky; ethereal.

** The famous novel 'Moby Dick' was dedicated to Nathaniel Hawthorne.

of thousands. She got more speed in a few yards, but in a few yards more, she sensibly decreased her rate of progress again, and after her stern as far as about her mid-ship section had become immersed, she came to an unmistakable dead stop. The cause is attributable to the daggers not being knocked away simultaneously, one remaining fixed, notwithstanding the efforts to remove it. The consequence was the ship slewed on the launch ways, and so got jammed, so that further progress was impracticable. Efforts were made for a short time to tow her off by the steamers, but the hawsers snapped, and the attempt was abandoned. Fresh shores were rapidly put up to her sides, and, as she still rested on her 'cradle', no fears of injury were entertained. Disappointment was depicted on every countenance; and after indulging in the vain hope of seeing her afloat for nearly half an hour, the large crowd began to disperse, the heavy downfall of the rain acting as a powerful inducement to make them 'move off'. On the tide falling, it was discovered that the failure of the launch was owing to the ground having given way under the starboard 'ways', and we have much pleasure in stating that, when we left the ship at four o'clock, she was quite dry, standing perfectly upright, had not sustained an iota of injury, and was still flying the gay colours with which she had been 'dressed off' in the morning. At night, efforts were made to get her off the stocks, and again on Wednesday, but unfortunately without success. About 200 men were employed in excavating a course for her through the mud bank in which her stern got embedded, and she has been lightened of her ballast to a great extent. Mr. Alex Bisset, one of the surveyors for the Liverpool underwriters, came over to assist with his advice the arrangements for floating her, but we regret to say that the renewal of the attempts on Wednesday and Thursday's tides were unsuccessful. As the tides are now decreasing, she must remain where she is until the 30th instant, when there will be, at flood, a depth of 21 feet 7 inches when, if ever, she will float.

The *Royal Charter* is put together with great ability and carefulness so as to ensure the greatest possible strength, and comfort and safety of passengers. The outline of her hull is beautiful, her model is well proportioned, and her clipper lines must ensure great speed when she is used (as she can be) either as a sailing ship or steamer separately, or as both combined. We may repeat here, that her dimensions for tonnage are -- length, 320 feet; beam, 41½ feet; depth of hold, 26½ feet; measurements, 2,785 tons. She will be fully rigged as a ship, and will be able to spread as much canvas as the *Great Britain*, which vessel, it is well known, carries an enormous suite of sails. Her boilers and machinery will occupy about 350 tons of space. The engines, which will be of (nominally) 300 horse-power, with boilers to work up to 500 horse-power, are Messrs. Penn, and Son's patent -- direct-acting trunk cylinder, similar to those which have proved so successful in the *Himalaya**. She will have a two-bladed 'lifting screw' so that she can at any time, in ten minutes, be turned from an auxiliary screw-steamer to a complete clipper sailing-ship - a change which can never be accomplished with an ordinary screw-steamer however much canvas she may carry, for it is obvious that a vessel with a screw of any form dragging behind her cannot get the full power of her canvas. The *Royal Charter,* like a screw line-of-battle ship, will be enabled when desirable to lift her screw several feet out of the water, and slide it down in its place again when required, with like facility. This feature, indeed, is the most important one about her, and it will enable her owners to make a real test of the comparative advantages - on all points - of sailing-ships and steamers, for such long voyages as those

---

* 'Himalaya', 3,550 Tons. Launched by C. J. Mare, of Blackwall, London. in 1853 as the largest ship in the world. She belonged to the P&O Steam Navigation Company.

to the Antipodes.

The *Royal Charter* has a poop cabin nearly 100 feet long, which will be fitted up in a first-class style for about 50 passengers. There is a range of fourteen staterooms, ten feet by six feet four inches along each side, and mostly fitted with two berths each. The saloon (like all other deck houses) is 7½ feet in height, it is lighted with spacious skylights and circular port windows in each state-room, and the arrangements for ventilation are ample. There will be commodious ladies' cabins and steward's pantry attached. Further forward on this deck are a set of houses, 50 feet in length, comprising officers' berths and mess rooms, the largest and best cooking-range we have seen on board ship, and a butcher's shop in which, also, all the livestock will be kept. The forecastle forward is 62 feet in length, and includes the space for the ship's 'people', well-finished water-closets, urinals, etc. The 'tween-decks below are unrivalled by those of any other vessel. They will have a clear length of nearly 340 feet, and on each side there are 55 circular port windows, six feet apart, besides numerous deck-lights, hatchways, and ventilating shafts. In height, they are 8 feet "clear." Although, according to government measurements, this part of the ship would accommodate 635 passengers, the owners will only fit it up for 588, who will thus be accommodated with even more than their fair share of room. The vessel will carry a crew of 85 hands, 'all told' and thus, with a full complement of passengers,

her human cargo will consist of about 720 souls.

Her outward appearance is very graceful. Her bow is ornamented with a full length figure of a winged Mercury, carrying in his hand a scroll, bearing, in gilt letters, the words *Royal Charter,* in allusion to the company having been favoured by Government with a charter of limited liability. Every portion of her outfit will be of the very best description. She is provided with Trotman's patent anchors, which the Admiralty trials and previous as well as subsequent experiments have proved to be unrivalled, manufactured at the Dee Iron Works, Chester, by Messrs. Henry Wood and Company.

She is double-riveted throughout, and divided by six really water-tight bulkheads. Along her entire length runs a box keelson, 2 feet 9 inches deep, and 1 foot 9 inches wide, with a capacity for 5,500 gallons of water. The portion under the machinery, however, will be used for keeping engineers' stores. In conclusion, it may interest some to know that the *Royal Charter* was originally laid for a clipper sailing-ship, to be built by Messrs. Cram and Co., of Chester, for a Liverpool house. She was shortly afterwards purchased by Messrs. Gibbs, Bright and Co., for her present owners, and altered to a screw-steamer by Mr. Patterson, who has completed her for the company to which she belongs. She was expected to be ready for sea in October, when she will be at once placed upon her own station, if not required by government for transport purposes. *

The end of July 1855 should have seen the sleek clipper sliding gently down the slipway to rapturous applause from thousands of spectators basking in glorious summer sunshine. But the sun did not shine, and the 'Royal Charter' proved totally unwilling to take to the water no matter how many steamers were employed to pull her into her natural element. This was a very inauspicious start for the vessel, as she was going to be stuck on the slipway until at least the next spring-tide**, two weeks or even a month hence. It nearly became a very costly experience for Gibbs, Bright & Co., as she could easily have buckled her hull without the supports that were quickly put in place to take the weight of all that iron.

* This suggests that there was the possibility that the 'Royal Charter' could be requisitioned for transporting troops to the Crimean War.
** A spring-tide - when the difference between high-tide and low-tide is the greatest.

Launch of the *Royal Charter*.

We have the satisfaction of announcing that the *Royal Charter* was successfully launched from the building yard at Sandycroft, on Thursday last, about one o'clock a.m. On Monday night, and after the workmen had left the vessel, she slipped about 40 feet along the ways. On Tuesday, at noon, the attempts to extricate her were resumed, and the result was a further advance towards the water of 20 feet, where she was nearly three parts afloat, but still holding by the fore part. At night, when the highest tide of the month was at the full, the work was continued with additional progress, and on Wednesday night, with very little exertion, she floated almost of herself. Previous to her launching the numbers on the stern indicated a depth of 9 feet 3 inches, and when she was fairly afloat the indicator at the stern showed 12 feet. The launch was greeted with hearty cheers from the parties present, comprising a considerable crowd, and the event was announced by the firing of guns. On Thursday at one o'clock p.m., the time of high water, the *Royal Charter* was taken in tow by three steam tugs, and proceeded down the river on her way to Liverpool. She was gaily decorated, and as she passed Queen's Ferry and other places much cheering took place. By the time she got to Flint Castle the tide had ebbed considerably, and on passing a corner where two channels meet, she took the ground, and became safely embedded without any strain or shock. At the flood yesterday, about one a.m., she again floated, and at the turn of the tide she proceeded as far as Dawpool, where she anchored in deep water on the Dee side of Hilbre Island. From thence she would proceed to Liverpool, where, all difficulties being surmounted, we have no doubt she is safe in dock, and the riggers, joiners, etc. busily employed in fitting her for sea.

Chester Chronicle. September 1, 1855

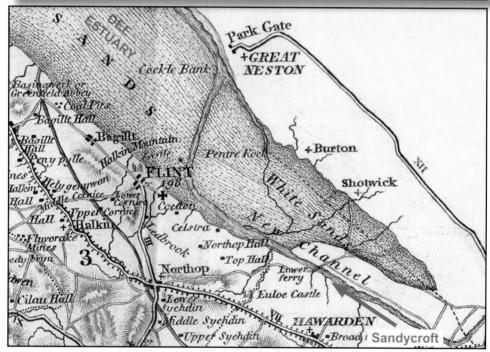

Note the sharp bend in the channel at Flint. This is where the 'Royal Charter' ran aground. The damage to her hull was not mentioned by the Chester Chronicle.

An aerial photograph of the Dee Estuary, showing the maze of channels and sandbanks.

THE "ROYAL CHARTER".

The fittings of this vessel are now rapidly proceeding. It is not known whether she will be dispatched to Australia, or be taken up by Government for the transport of troops. It is almost impossible to conceive the responsibility of releasing the *Royal Charter*. The narrowness of the stream, the short time the tides served, the rush of water while the tide avails, and the yielding ground of the bank, presented difficulties of no ordinary character. Add to this the great weight of the vessel herself, which was 1,700 tons [*sic*]. As, however, she has been safely got off, we may congratulate the Underwriters and owners on the release of their property from its perilous position, and also on the fact that they had parties in their employment competent to perform the service. To Captain Bisset, surveyor for the Liverpool Underwriters' Association, Mr. Patterson, the builder, and Captain Martin, the superintendent for the owners, this result is mainly due. They have had a herculean task, and the manner in which it has been performed reflects the highest credit upon their judgement and skill. The committee of the Town Council have closed their enquiries into the failure of the launch of the *Royal Charter* at Sandycroft on the 31st of July, and we learn that they have come to the conclusion that, not withstanding the depth of water in the river was considerably short of what it ought to have been under the River Dee Company's Acts, the vessel was not stopped in her launch by want of water, but by other causes which must have produced the same result in any other locality. She measures 2,680 tons. It appears also, that on her way down the Dee, she stuck on a sandbank near Flint, in consequence of being an hour too late on the tide.

Chester Chronicle. September 8, 1855

The hull of the 'Royal Charter' was constructed from wrought iron, but her masts and spars etc. were made of wood.

To read the Chester Chronicle of the 1st and 8th of September, 1855, it could be believed that the worries of Gibbs, Bright and Company were now over. Despite having been stuck on a sandbank, the 'Royal Charter' had reportedly arrived unscathed in Liverpool Docks, where preparations were being made to make her ready to earn her living on the high-seas. Unfortunately, that report was totally incorrect, and she actually arrived there battered, bruised and needing much work to repair her before the steam engine could be installed. Hull-plates needed to be replaced, and additional strengthening was required to make her seaworthy, as later described by the foreman in charge of the repairs.

She was brought to Liverpool, put in dock and repaired. She broke 33 or 35 flooring angle-irons. She bent her main keel amidships. It was bent two and a half inches in a distance of about twelve feet in the midship part. The midship keelson was broken. The garboard strake was bent a little. The butts of the garboard strake were strained in some places, but not broken. Four or five of the stanchions of the whole beam in the midship body of the ship were bent; some of the rivets were started in the bottom, just where the great pressure came, and no-where else. Many of the rivets there were shaken; these were replaced. Stronger plates were put in the main keelson, at the sides and top, for the space of about 40 feet. It was a very workmanlike job, and the vessel was properly repaired.

William Patterson must have shaken his head in despair at the grounding of the 'Royal Charter' as he had previous experience of such a mishap. Having launched his creation, the 'Demerara', at Bristol in November, 1851, that vessel was being towed down the winding River Avon by three tugs. On one of the curves in the river, Mr. Patterson suggested to the pilot that their speed was excessive, but they still took the bend with too much 'way' on the flotilla, and the 'Demerara' drove hard into the river-side to wedge herself across the waterway. With her bow and stern pressed firmly against the opposite banks, the ebb-tide left her high and dry as the water receded from under the hull, causing her to twist and buckle. So much damage was done that she was declared a total wreck, and her hull was sold as scrap by the underwriters.

Patterson was luckier with the 'Royal Charter', and once the damage had been rectified, the compasses could be adjusted in their final positions as the extra machinery and repairs had altered the magnetic signature of the ship. Gibbs, Bright & Co. were not about to repeat the disaster of the 'Tayleur' by allowing their new and prestigious vessel to run ashore because of defective or badly-adjusted navigation-instruments.

"Her bow is ornamented with a full length figure of a winged Mercury, carrying in his hand a scroll, bearing, in gilt letters, the words 'Royal Charter'".

Finally, several months overdue, the sea-trials of the auxiliary screw-steamer 'Royal Charter' of the 'Eagle Line' could now commence. Captain Boyce, her commander, and Tyndall Bright, one of her owners, must have breathed a huge sigh of relief.

The *Royal Charter* -- This magnificent screw-steamer made her first trial trip on Tuesday, under most favourable auspices. She steamed out of the Sandon Dock at noon, escorted by one of the Tug Company's boats, and took a "round turn" to the Rock, returning safely to anchor off the landing stage. She proceeded to sea on Wednesday, but the weather was very thick, and after cruising in the channel, the steamer anchored about four miles outside the Bell Buoy. There were about sixty guests on board, and the time was passed most pleasantly.

Dinner was served in the saloon about four o'clock, Mr. Tyndall Bright in the chair. After the cloth was withdrawn, apropos speeches were delivered by the chairman, Captain Boyce and other gentlemen. About seven o'clock on Thursday morning, the weather having cleared up and become as bright as could be desired, she steamed out in a north-westwardly direction, which course she continued for about a couple of hours, making a speed of about ten knots an hour. The screw was then disconnected, and all her plain sail was set. In this condition, with a very light breeze, she made Puffin Island at the rate of ten knots an hour. She was then tacked about, and she steadied in the most beautiful manner. She came up with a moderate breeze from the N.N.E, at the rate of from 13½ to 14 knots an hour; but it is calculated that she will be able to make at least 18 knots an hour. She passed every clipper ship in the channel and the river, running 26 miles in two hours. Altogether, the trial was of the most satisfactory character, and the company, when landing at five o'clock, expressed their highest admiration of the vessel's performance both under sail and steam.

European Times. December 21, 1855

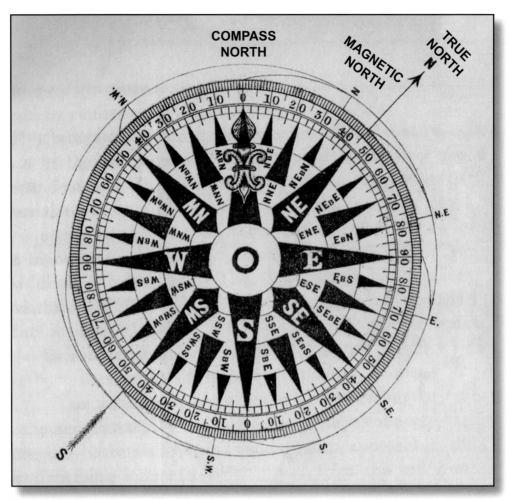

This diagram shows an uncorrected compass from the 'Royal Charter', as used as an example in 'Cameron's Azimuth & Altitude Tables' of 1859. Note the difference between Compass North, Magnetic North and True North. There was much work to be done in making sure that the compasses of an iron ship could be used with accuracy.

To fully appreciate the problems faced in navigating an iron ship by the use of a magnetic compass, it is important to understand the following:

Compass North is the direction in which the compass shows 'North', and is greatly affected by the ferrous parts of a vessel. The diagram above shows a 45 degree error.

Magnetic North is the direction that a compass will point if influenced only by the earth's magnetic field.

True North is the direction to the North Pole.

Variation is the difference (in degrees) between True North and Magnetic North. This value depends upon the location on earth, and slowly changes over a number of years.

Deviation is the error introduced into a compass by the magnetic properties of a ship. This error varies as the ship's heading alters, and should be written on a Deviation Card so that the compass error is recorded and can be allowed for.

'Swinging a ship'. This is when a ship is pulled round on a succession of different headings to record the error of a ship's compass. This is marked on the Deviation Card for each heading.

CHAPTER FOUR

The Reverend Dr. William Scoresby

The 'Scoresby Chair', made of timber recovered from the wreck of the 'Royal Charter', and presented to his widow.

William Scoresby (junior) was born on the 5th of October, 1789, at Cropton, Yorkshire, but he grew up in the Yorkshire port of Whitby and in London. His father, William Scoresby (senior) was captain of a whaling ship, and many of the father's skills were passed down to his son. Arctic explorer and surveyor, captain of the whale-ship 'Esk', botanist, scientist, vicar of Bradford, and an author; such were the many facets of the Reverend William Scoresby.

He met many famous people during his lifetime, some of whom became good friends. These included Captain Manby who was famed for designing a means of saving life from shipwreck by a mortar that fired a line out from the shore, Sir Humphrey Davy who introduced the miner's safety-lamp, Sir John Ross, another Arctic explorer, James Joule, the scientist best remembered for his work on the Mechanical Equivalent of Heat, and on a trip to Washington D.C., he even visited the White House to meet the President of the United States of America. His name appears frequently in the newspapers of the first half of the 18th century. In 1817, he recorded the greatest depth then known in the Greenland Sea, when his sounding-weight failed to hit the seabed with 7,200 feet of line hanging below the ship; the 1820s were spent exploring the Arctic seas and publishing the results of his observations; the 1830s saw him recording the results of his experiments with magnetism; and by 1849, he was involved with the investigation into the disappearance of Sir John Franklin and the crew of the 'Fox', who had attempted to find the North-west Passage in the Arctic wastes of Canada. Much scientific information was recorded by William Scoresby, but his connection with the 'Royal Charter' was because of his interest in the correct use of a ship's compass, especially the problems that were being encountered as iron replaced wood for shipbuilding.

In the summer of 1855, aged 65, Scoresby wrote to one of his friends in Liverpool to ask if anyone knew of a shipowner who could provide him with a berth on an iron-hulled ship that was about to circumnavigate the world. Scoresby was determined to carry out further experiments at sea to verify his theories on magnetism. As he put it:

I am disposed, God willing, to undertake such a voyage in order to verify and complete the investigations I have been so long in pursuing on the important object of the compass action in iron ships.

As we have seen, the 'Tayleur' was a brand-new, seaworthy ship, but she stood no chance of survival when she ran into that large immovable object called Lambay Island in January, 1854. Several reasons were attributed to the loss of that vessel, one of which was the problem of using a compass in an iron ship. Safe navigation at sea depended upon the trustworthiness of a ship's compass, and Charles Moore & Co., the Liverpool-based owners of the 'Tayleur', had totally lost confidence in the ability of a ship's captain to safely rely on the compass of such a ship, so they quickly sold their interest in another iron hull that was under construction for them at Mr. Cram's shipyard on the River Dee, at Sandycroft in North Wales. The new wonder-material of iron no longer had a place in their fleet of ships, as there were too many problems introduced by its magnetic properties. Lives had been lost, the 'Tayleur' and her cargo lay at the bottom of the Irish Sea, and there was to be no profit coming to the shipowners until the problem was resolved. At this time, two eminent people had differing opinions on how the magnetic properties of an iron vessel affected a ship's compass.

Sir George Biddell Airy believed that the influence of an iron hull could be partially counteracted by placing magnets and pieces of iron in close proximity to the ship's compass, and a 'deviation card' could be drawn to show the amount of error at each point of the compass that the ship was heading.

Meanwhile, the Reverend William Scoresby had a different theory, as he was convinced that the constant pounding of waves on a hull could change the magnetic properties of a ship, and he was to publicly argue that the 'Tayleur' was lost due to her compasses being adjusted in accordance with Airy's ideas. Scoresby believed that the way to overcome the problem was to install a 'compass aloft', to be mounted as far away as possible from any ironwork. This was a valid principle in a vessel such as the 'Royal Charter', as she had wooden masts and was rigged with ropes made of hemp, but the future lay with iron-masts and wire-rigging, further developments that would make Scoresby's methods impractical.

Who was correct - Airy or Scoresby? Could the problem be relatively easily surmounted as predicted by Airy, or was a ship likely to suddenly change its magnetic signature while at sea to cause total confusion? While history has proved that Airy was more correct than Scoresby, these two eminent and well-respected men published their ideas in a series of letters to 'The Atheneum' in the latter months of 1854 and the early months of 1855.

This difference of opinion was causing total chaos for the shipowners and underwriters. Which of these two esteemed gentlemen should they believe? George Airy held the grand title of 'Astronomer Royal', while Scoresby was a highly-experienced ship's captain and Fellow of the Royal Society who had been investigating the problems of a ship's compass for many years. Something urgently needed to be done, so the Liverpool Compass Committee was set up in 1855, in an attempt to sort out the mess.

By now, it was very clear that Scoresby's theories urgently needed to be proved or disproved before many more ships, cargoes and lives were lost due to faulty navigation. The committee needed to appoint a trustworthy person to take readings on a variety of compasses on a round-the-world voyage, and who could be more respected, trustworthy and truthful than the Reverend William Scoresby himself?

During the last few months of 1855, several factors were coming together to hopefully provide an answer to the controversy and put an end to the misery and financial losses caused by faulty compasses. The committee's task was to investigate and produce one or more reports on the problem, and all they needed was a suitable ship and a scientist to travel around the world making recordings of the various compasses during the voyage. In an ideal world, with plenty of time to make detailed experiments, a government survey-vessel would set off on an expedition lasting several years, but that would take too much time, need a vast expenditure of money, and perhaps cost hundreds of lives as vessels continued to stray off their chosen course.

The compromise taken by the Liverpool Compass Committee was as follows:

- They would accept William Scoresby's offer to further investigate the problem.
- A berth would be provided for him on the forthcoming voyage of the 'Royal Charter' to Australia and back. This ship was ideal for Scoresby's purpose, as it was constructed with an iron hull and wooden masts.

Everything was now dropping into place. The committee had their respected scientist, a berth for him on an appropriate ship, and a selection of compasses, dipping-needles, chronometers and charts. What else could go possibly wrong?

That 'what else' turned out to be William Scoresby himself, because he initially refused to share a cabin with a stranger, and the scientific venture was in great danger of failing before the 'Royal Charter' had even left the River Mersey unless the cost of the empty berth in his cabin was paid for. Fortunately, a compromise was arranged, and Mrs. Georgina Scoresby and a maid accompanied William on this, his final voyage of discovery. Scoresby was extremely pleased with the results of his voyage, believing them to be an absolute verification of all his theories and the rebuttal of those of his rival. If Scoresby was correct, then the compass at the masthead was the only way to safely navigate the oceans of the world in a vessel built of iron.

> Every principle I had asserted was completely verified. The compasses were adjusted on the very ingenious principle of the Astronomer Royal [*George Airy*], the errors being compensated by antagonistic magnets in England. Exactly as I had said before the British Association in 1846, these compasses ceased not only to be useful, but they went further wrong than any others on board. Every principle of a compass aloft, as the only means of a safe guidance, was fully established. If he cannot combat with an enemy, a general gets as far away from it as he can. In our compass aloft, we had our perfect guide and standard of reference at all times.

William and Georgina returned to England on the 'Royal Charter', arriving at Liverpool in the middle of August, 1856. He then retired to his home in Torquay to write up his journal, but died on the 21st of March, 1857, before it could be published. His book was subsequently edited and printed in 1859 by his friend and fellow researcher, Archibald Smith. The Reverend William Scoresby's body was taken to Whitby to be buried in the same grave as his father, and he is still remembered today in the Melbourne suburb that carries his name.

Connection to the 'Royal Charter'

- To obtain further information on how iron would effect a ship's compass, the Liverpool Compass Committee arranged for William Scoresby to travel on the 'Royal Charter' on her first journey around the world.
- William Scoresby wrote a detailed account of the voyage in his book 'A Journal of a Voyage to Australia and Round the World for Magnetical Research'.

CARRYING A MAIL

EAGLE LINE

STEAM TO AUSTRALIA UNDER SIXTY DAYS

 The Liverpool and Australian Navigation Company's Steam Clipper Sailing Ship

ROYAL CHARTER

of 2,719 Tons Register; 200 Horse Power;

F. BOYCE, late of the "Eagle," Commander, will be despatched for Melbourne direct on the 17th JANUARY, forwarding Passengers for Sydney, Adelaide, Hobart Town, etc.

FARES – FROM 16 to 60 GUINEAS.

Built expressly for the Company, this vessel combines all the advantages of a Steamer with those of a Clipper or Sailing Ship, and offers the only opportunity yet presented to the public of certainty in the time required for the voyage.

The Main Saloon is beautifully fitted up. The Passenger Deck is 8 feet 4 inches high, with side ports every 6 feet, exclusive of other ventilation. Baths are provided for all classes of passengers; and the arrangements for cooking and carrying livestock are perfect.

Passengers are respectfully informed that as this Steamer must be sent to sea *punctually* to her time, they must be in Liverpool not later than the 15th, their luggage being forwarded on or before the 12th; and that no Cargo will be taken after noon on the 11th January.

All Letters and Newspapers must be forwarded through the Post Office, and endorsed "Per *Royal Charter,* from Liverpool" otherwise they will not be forwarded.

Apply to GIBBS, BRIGHT, & Co., Liverpool

Parcels sent to the care of Bright, Brothers, and Co., Melbourne, will be carefully forwarded to all parts of Australia.

This advert appeared in the Chester Chronicle of December 29th, 1855. Note that Gibbs, Bright & Co. are already advertising the voyage as 'Under Sixty Days' despite the fact that the 'Royal Charter' hadn't even left Liverpool.

CHAPTER FIVE

Australia and back

The lighthouse at the mouth of the River Mersey should have been the last close-up view of land until they reached Australia. Unfortunately, this was not to be the case.

By the middle of the 1850s, Liverpool was firmly established as a major port of embarkation for those wishing to emigrate to America, Canada or Australia, and the 'Liverpool Mercury' newspaper of the 28th of December 1855 carried adverts for vessels sailing to New York, Boston, Philadelphia, Baltimore, Halifax, Gibraltar, Malta, Constantinople, Shanghai, Hong Kong and Melbourne. Competition was fierce on the route to Australia, with companies such as the 'Fox' line, the 'Black Ball' line, the 'Liverpool' line, the 'White Star' line and the 'Eagle' line of Gibbs, Bright & Co. all offering berths from £14 upwards.

A little over five months after the first attempt had been made to launch the 'Royal Charter', she was finally ready to transport her first fare-paying passengers to Australia. Her record so far had not been auspicious -- her original builder was bankrupt, her plans had been altered to lengthen her hull, she had stuck on the slipway and refused to take to the muddy waters of the River Dee, she had been badly damaged on a sandbank off Flint, necessitating an expensive delay while repairs were undertaken in dry-dock at Liverpool, but she had avoided being requisitioned as a troopship to the Crimea or beyond. Now, finally, by January 1856, she was ready to set out to circumnavigate the world by sail and by steam.

A maiden voyage was always going to be a major test of a ship, her captain and her crew, yet the advertisement shown opposite stated categorically 'Steam to Australia in Under Sixty Days'. Prospective passengers must have wondered whether there was any guarantee to that claim, but perhaps the reassuring words 'F. Boyce, late of the Eagle' were sufficient to allay any fears, as Captain Francis Boyce had sailed the Australian route for many years, and certainly knew most of the problems along the way. Or at least, the passengers hoped that he did.

As previously mentioned, the clipper was carrying the Reverend William Scoresby, his wife and her maid. At sixty-six years of age, Scoresby certainly wasn't going to Australia in order to earn his fortune in the goldfields, as his presence on the 'Royal Charter' was in order to understand the effect of the earth's magnetic field on a ship's compass by making regular notes of the bearings shown by four of these instruments located at different points around the ship.

Most importantly from a historian's point of view, the reverend gentleman kept a meticulously recorded journal of his exploits on this voyage, to be published in his 'Journal of a Voyage to Australia and Round the World for Magnetical Research'. This record of the maiden voyage of the 'Royal Charter' was printed shortly after his death, and a modern-day reprint of this book is now available from Elibron Classics.

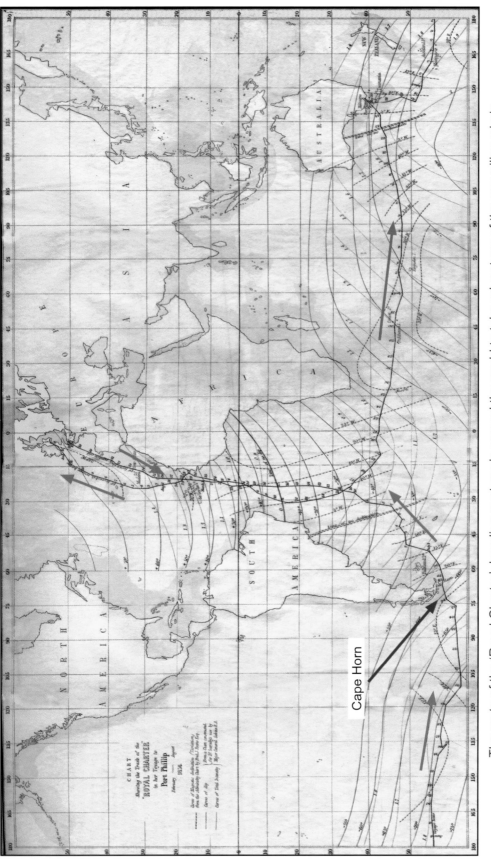

The route of the 'Royal Charter', heading eastwards around the world to take advantage of the prevailing winds.

Cape Horn

The Carnarvon & Denbigh Herald

AND NORTH AND SOUTH WALES ADVERTISER

Saturday, December 15, 1855

LIVERPOOL AND AUSTRALIAN NAVIGATION COMPANY.

On the seventeenth of January next, the *Royal Charter* will leave this port for Melbourne, and the principle of a clipper ship with auxiliary steam power will now, for the first time, be fairly tried. The Liverpool and Australian Navigation Company, having arrived at the clear conviction that it is in vain to hope that steamers relying entirely upon their engines, or sailing-vessels trusting only to their sails, can make the passage with regularity and despatch, have determined on combining the two motive powers, and giving their vessels the benefit of both.

The advantage of this is obvious. The mere steamer is either compelled to carry coal sufficient for the whole voyage and thus lose much valuable space, or it necessitates the establishment of coaling stations, and thereby loses still more valuable time, and increases vastly the expense. Its engines require so much room that the masts are crowded together, and the efficiency of the sails is materially impaired. A mere sailing-ship, on the other hand, is harassed by a bad wind and stopped by a calm, and a voyage is seldom so favourable as to be without either.

It is apparent then that the leading principle of the Liverpool and Australian Navigation Company is one of great value, and that the *Royal Charter*, which has been expressly built to carry out this principle, will solve the problem of the most expeditious passage to Australia.

The *Royal Charter* is a magnificent clipper-ship of 355 feet in length (longer than the *Himalaya*); she stretches 13,000 feet of canvas, and all her lines are adapted for speed. She is, moreover, a steamer with engine of 200 nominal horse-power, and an improved screw so-arranged that when not wanted it can be lifted out of the water, and even (if necessary) placed on deck. In fair wind, therefore, the *Royal Charter* will, like any other clipper, trust entirely to her sails; in contrary winds, or in a calm, she will lower her screw, get up her steam, and leave all her rivals far behind.

The measurement of this ship is 2,720 tons; her beam is 42 feet; depth of hold 26 feet.

The accommodation of the *Royal Charter* is excellent. The chief saloon is divided by passages (running on either side) from the first class state cabins, an arrangement most conductive to the comfort of the passengers. This saloon, which is 100 feet long, is beautifully fitted up; and the ladies' cabin, with its large poop windows and elegant furniture, has been most carefully adapted for its purpose. There are two large bath-rooms for the accommodation of the after-saloon passengers, as well as one three times the size for the use of the 'tween-deck passengers.

The main deck below is arranged for the second and third class passengers; the berths are very light and well ventilated, and three good mess-rooms will prevent the usual disagreeable arrangements of tables passing through the sleeping-places of passengers.

The cooking-galleys are said to be the best and largest of any ship afloat; the forecastle is also probably the finest ever seen.

In short, no expense and no pains have been spared to render the *Royal Charter* complete in every department, and no ship ever offered more ample accommodation, or a greater amount of comfort to those who will be her passengers.

Tall-ships still gather in the Wellington Dock.

From William Scoresby's point of view, everything was now in place for the great experiment. He had a berth on board an iron-built ship; he had his compasses; he had various other instruments such as a 'dipping-needle' which would tell him the angle of declination of the earth's magnetic field, and a pelorus to measure bearings relative to the compass heading. He had charts, a pocket chronometer, and lastly, he had the company of his wife.

However, none of his trials could begin until the 'Royal Charter' had been 'swung', the process whereby the compasses are checked for errors by slowly spinning the vessel round while noting the readings of each instrument as the ship pointed in a certain direction. This process hadn't been done by the beginning of January, 1856, and it was only by a last-minute effort that the Wellington Dock in Liverpool could be cleared of other vessels to allow the completion of this essential task.

So far, the 'Royal Charter' had failed to meet just about every deadline that had been set for her, so it wasn't too surprising that she didn't leave England on the 17th of January, 1856, but delayed overnight to steam out of the Mersey Estuary on Friday, the 18th under the guidance of a Liverpool pilot. It had been intended to disembark the pilot at Holyhead that evening, but darkness falls rapidly this far north in January, and a strong wind and tide combined to make the situation too dangerous to put him ashore. Then, at the dawn of the following day, and still with the pilot on board, the 'Royal Charter' nearly succumbed to the fate of the 'Tayleur', as the tell-tale signs of breaking waves were spotted at a distance of only three-quarters of a mile. For several minutes, her future was undecided, but she finally managed to claw her way round onto a safe course and steam away from the 'Lucifer Shoals', a dangerous reef near the Tuskar Rock off Wexford in Southern Ireland. Such a narrow escape so early in the maiden voyage must have come as a severe shock to Captain Boyce, the pilot, and to William Scoresby, the latter immediately wondering whether the ship's magnetism had suddenly changed in accordance with some of his predictions. If Scoresby's theories were right, how on earth were they going to safely navigate all the way to the Antipodes if they were having problems even before they had escaped the confines of the Irish Sea?

This wasn't going to be a fast and easy journey, as she met light and variable winds that slowed her down, immediately followed by a strong south-westerly gale that again reduced her speed considerably. Far more worrying to her captain, crew and passengers, she was much too low in the water, the result of several hundred tons of stone ballast being loaded in the expectation that this amount was needed to keep her seaworthy. Someone had miscalculated the amount of ballast that was required, with the effect that she was too deep in the water and was shipping seawater as she ploughed her way across the Bay of Biscay, the area off Western France well known for bad weather. Other problems rapidly became apparent, as a horrendous vibration erupted once the ship reached a certain speed while running under both sail and steam, and the vessel proved difficult to steer. Added to this, the passengers were having a very uncomfortable time, as water poured into the first-class, second-class and third-class accommodation through the seams of the hull, the skylights, and a variety of other places. There was too little freeboard, the fare-paying passengers were soaked through, the captain was ill, and they were still well within European waters with thousands of miles ahead of them before they reached Melbourne. By January the 24th, it was clear that the 'Royal Charter' was in no fit state to continue on her voyage, so Captain Boyce made the reluctant decision to turn round, and he chose Plymouth on the south coast of England as a suitable port where he could remove much of the ballast and repair the leaks that had

Heavy seas poured over the bows of the clipper, as she was too deep in the water.

caused such misery to everyone aboard. Arriving at Plymouth on the 26th of January, work commenced to unload 400 tons of excess ballast and to re-caulk the seams that were allowing seawater to flood into the hull. Scoresby put the whole episode down to teething troubles, remarking in his journal:

> The first putting to sea in such a ship must always be an experiment, and the adventurers on a first voyage bear the burden of the trial and testing of the various qualities and matters affecting personal comfort in a ship, of which subsequent passengers reap the benefit.

Thankfully, the work of unloading the ballast was quickly completed, allowing the ship to ride a foot higher at the stern and two feet higher at her bow, making a vast improvement to her sailing abilities and the comfort of her passengers.

Saturday the 16th of February, 1856, brought fine weather and a favourable wind, allowing the 'Royal Charter' to leave Plymouth Sound and head out into the English Channel to resume her voyage. The steam engine was briefly put into use the following day, but the screw was soon disconnected and hoisted to allow her to use her sails and speed along at between 9 and 13 knots as Scoresby began his task of recording the readings of the various compasses. But what a difference the diversion to Plymouth had made. No longer did the 'Royal Charter' flood the passengers' berths to half-drown and freeze her human cargo. Only nine days out from Plymouth, the Canary Islands were in sight, and the temperature had increased sufficiently for the wearing of summer clothes. By the 6th of March, she was at the equator, but the temperatures started to fall two weeks later as she progressed south-eastwards into the South Atlantic.

The Killing of the Albatross

Despite having spent part of his life hunting whales, Scoresby seems to have had a love of wildlife, as he wrote about the various marine animals and seabirds encountered on the voyage. He was very unimpressed by some of the so-called 'sportsmen' aboard the 'Royal Charter', as shown by this entry in his journal:

Thursday, March 20, 1856. A cruel sport, much indulged in on the previous day, was happily interrupted this morning by rain. The shooting at albatrosses, which in great numbers follow the ship, appears to be a prevalent usage in many ships of our class voyaging to Australia and other considerable southern latitudes. From half-past six until half-past eight a.m., the after-part of the poop of the *Royal Charter* was yesterday occupied with 'sportsmen' and lookers-on, who with rifles or other guns were every now and then firing at the unconscious elegant birds gracefully hovering about our rear. I fancy 50 to 100 shots were fired, happily with rare instances of their taking effect; but in one case I saw, on being induced to look astern by a general shout, a poor stricken bird struggling on the surface of the water apparently mortally wounded. This useless infliction of injury and suffering on these noble looking birds, where there was no chance of obtaining them as specimens for the museum, nor for any other use, was to my feelings, and, I believe, the feelings of many others, particularly painful. The inducement was 'sport', the object, practise in shooting. With some it was, one would earnestly hope, indulged in from want of consideration, and from example. But in attempting remonstrance, it was curious to hear the excuses for the cruelty on these confiding or unfearing creatures; 'they were savage birds'; 'they attacked their unfortunate associate, as soon as it was sufficiently clear of the ship, to prey upon it'; 'a boy who had once fallen overboard was attacked by an albatross, descending upon him with immense force, and striking him with its bill on the head, so that when a boat reached him, his face was found covered with blood, and the skull fractured' — therefore, it was inferred, 'it was proper to shoot them.' I quietly applied the argument to the case of dogs. I had known a dog attack a person and injure him dangerously; it was therefore proper to amuse ourselves as we had opportunity by shooting dogs! But the case was not admitted to be in point.

Falling nearly calm about 10 a.m., a line with a baited hook was put over the stern by one of the passengers, which before long, whilst the engine and screw were getting into action, was seized by an albatross, and the fine majestic bird hauled almost unscathed upon deck. It showed a disposition to defend itself, whilst in vain attempting to rise from the deck, and frequently drove the crowd of lookers-on before it. Captain Boyce had seen a trial of power betwixt an active terrier dog and an unfortunate albatross that had been hooked and drawn upon deck; but the bird, though but little adapted for rapid movement, soon gave the dog an impressive lesson by seizing him by the nose and biting him so severely that he ran off howling most piteously! The power in the bill, a strong gull-shaped weapon of eight inches in length, with a sharp bent point, is singularly great. It required caution, and justified the retreat of our little crowd of spectators in avoiding the huge bird in his attempts to make way through their ranks with a view to escape. Its dimensions were as follows: Spread of wings across the back, from tip to tip, exactly 10 feet. Length from the tip of the beak to end of the tail, 3 feet 7 inches. Circumference round the body and compressed wings, 2 feet 9 inches. Length of the bill (as bare of feathers), 8 inches. Web foot 7 inches long and 8 inches broad. These webs are often used for the construction of purses, by being separated betwixt the skin or web, above and below, and leaving the claws as ornaments. They are flexible, have a fine yellow surface when dry, and are considered at once curious and ornamental.

THE
ROYAL CHARTER GAZETTE

No. 1.   SATURDAY, FEBRUARY 23, 1856.   Price One Penny.

We sincerely congratulate our fellow-passengers on resuming our voyage, after a long and irksome detention in Plymouth, and fervently hope that kind providence will grant us a more favourable run than we experienced after our departure from Liverpool. The many necessary repairs and alterations our noble vessel has undergone whilst lying in Plymouth Sound, will, we trust, materially increase the comfort of all classes of passengers, and prevent a repetition of those complaints that existed.

Through the kindness of our respected commander, we are enabled to publish a copy of the ships' log. Our subscribers and friends will find each issue of the Gazette to contain a copy of the log; together with the distance run, up to the morning of each publication.

Leaving Old England at a period when she is engaged in a gigantic struggle against despotic Russia, it may not be deemed in-opportune if we briefly review the position of the powers directly engaged in the war, as well as those interested in obtaining peace. The acceptance of the Austrian propositions - without any reservation on the part of Russia, indicates a strong desire to conclude a peace as speedy as possible. The Czar is said to be heartily tired of war. Ready to accept even harder conditions than those obtained for him through the good offices of his imperial brother at Vienna, ministers were therefore appointed from the various courts to meet in Paris on or before the 20th, to discuss those propositions, and if possible obtain for Europe another respite from war and its attendant evils. It is more than probable that prior to our arrival in Australia, an honourable and a lasting peace will be concluded, giving trade and commerce a stimulant calculated to benefit not only Europe, but the whole continent of Australia.

The following information referring to the Ballarat Diggings, is extracted from the Melbourne Argus, 10th November, 1855.

We learn that the miners on Cobbler's have at last struck upon the old sand and slate bottom so well known to the deep-sinkers of Ballarat, and that the line itself is fast making for Winter's Flat. The latter is supposed to be one of the connecting-points between Ballarat and Magpie. The sinking on Cobbler's is still light, a claim being easily worked in a month, and the yield varying from £40 to £200 a man. The Eureka is progressing quietly: every day given evidence of forming a junction with the Red Hill somewhere behind Moses's store. It has about a third of a mile to run yet, the whole area being strictly shepherded. On the Gravel Pits the chief news consists of a claim having just touched the headings at 184 feet with every prospect of not bottoming at less than 190 feet; there is already a fair show of gold. Many parties have succeeded in making a little money at Magpie have since returned, to set in afresh, both on the Eureka and on the Gravel Pits. Shares are below zero, and as for half-share men they are not to be found. This last remark refers especially to the Gravel Pits.

ALL THE GOLD IN THE WORLD.

Taking a cubic yard of gold at £2,000,000, which is in round numbers, all the gold in the world at this estimate, might, if melted into ingots, be contained in a cellar 24 feet square, and 16 feet high. All our boasted wealth already obtained from California and Australia would go into an iron safe, about nine feet square and nine feet high.

GOLD SOLVENT TEST. * —To intending emigrants, and to our readers in Australia, the method of detecting and separating small quantities of gold from ore may not, perhaps, be unworth reading — nay, studying. The ore, crushed to powder, is first to be put into a mixture of muriatic [*hydrochloric*] acid, water, and chloride of lime, to the consistency of cream; after remaining together for twelve hours, three times its bulk of water is to be added, and the whole strained. This operation will dissolve out all the gold and iron from the ore. To the clear liquor which comes away we are now to add soda (washing soda) until it ceases to taste sour, or, rather until it tastes of soda. This being done, we are then to add a pair of Seidlitz powders, which cause all the iron to be deposited, leaving the gold in solution. After again straining or filtering the liquor, we must lastly add a solution of protosulphate of iron (green vitriol dissolved in water): this mixture causes all the gold to be deposited in the form of a brown powder, which, being heated and hammered, presents the usual appearance of the sought-for metal. The proper Seidlitz powder consists of (blue paper) potassio-titrate of soda, two draechm; bi-carbonate of soda, two scruples, mixed. The white paper contains half a drachm of tartaric acid. If it be inconvenient to use or procure the muriatic acid and chloride of lime, named first, to put the ore in, we can use with like effect a mixture of saltpetre, common salt, and strong vitriol. All the materials herein named are exceedingly cheap, and the principle to work upon is equally sure, for the detection of small quantities of gold in ore, to the most elaborate assays of the refiner. If the ore contain any platinum, it is dissolved with the gold, and can be precipitated from the solution by sal-ammoniac, which process hastened by the addition of spirits of wine, gin, or brandy.

NOURISHING DIET.—A returned gold-hunter from California says that he once lived for ten days on broth made from an old door-mat. It was that made him so fat.

The emigration from Europe is gradually changing the character of the vegetation in Australia. Native plants are giving way to those which have been introduced by man; and nearly 100 species are found growing wild which have been brought from Europe and the Cape.

A gold-digger entered one of the Sydney banks to deposit the sum of £3,200, the result of a few months labour. He was asked to write his name, but he could not write. A "lady" who was with him offered to sign the books for him; and this course having been assented to, they left the bank. Soon, however, it struck the digger that the "lady" could at any time she chose draw out the capital, while he, without her assistance, could not obtain a single penny. He communicated his fears to his companion. She laughed. She also had thought of it; but she refused to give up her claim unless he gave her his name. The end of the affair was that they were married.

Adventures of a Sailor Boy.

Finding my desire for sea so strong, my kind-hearted mother made interest to have me taken on board a man of war, a matter not very difficult in those times. I, on the 12th day of July, 1810, turned my back on my native village of Bladen, and my face towards scenes of music, storms, bloodshed and hunger. Need I say that, when left by my mother on the deck of the vessel, tears were mutually shed, and when the departing boat carried her from my sight, I felt like one alone in the world. On the morning following my arrival, I was put into a mess. The one to which I was attached, was composed of your genuine weather-beaten old tars. I was unfortunate enough to incur the decided hatred of one of them at the first glance he cast at me. After various delays in harbour, we were at last ready for sea, and under sailing orders, the tide and wind were both propitious; then came the cry 'make sail', the favouring breeze at once filled our sails, and the form that had lain

* This appears to be a highly dubious and dangerous process.

for weeks motionless on the waters, now bounded along the waves like a thing of life. Our frigate had orders to convey three hundred troops from Portsmouth to Lisbon, to assist the Portuguese against the French. The wind being favourable we ascended the Tagus on the ninth day. After a short stay at Lisbon we received orders to proceed to the coast of France, and assist in the blockade of Rochelle. Determined to accomplish some exploit, our captain made an attempt in cutting out some of the French small crafts that lay near the shore, accustomed to sending out our barges almost nightly, we were not long in making the necessary preparation. (To be continued.)

It is a singular fact that the genuine Yankee does not like the sea. A contributor to the Dublin University Magazine once asked an English Jack Tar on board an American ship to explain the phenomenon. "They ben't fit for hard work" was his quaint reply "they're good for nothing but peddlin an book larnin".

ANECDOTE OF ONE OF OUR CRIMEAN HEROES — One of Her Majesty's veterans, now serving in the Crimea, is a native of Monsfield Woodhouse, and when a boy in the Wesleyan school, was noted for being rather a rough, unteachable fellow. But on leaving the school, as is the custom, a Bible was presented to him, as a token of the good wishes of the governor of the institution. Some years afterwards, he enlisted into Her Majesty's service, and previous to quitting the English shores for the seat of war, he visited his native village for the purpose of taking leave of his friends, and amongst the rest called on his old Sunday School teacher who gave him many suitable lessons of advice and asked him whether he ever read the Bible he had presented to him on leaving the school. He answered in a negative, and the teacher then begged of him to promise him that he would read some portion of the sacred volume every day, when far removed from friends or home, which promise he not only gave, but appears to have kept; for one night, whilst enjoying a little relaxation from the duty of the trenches, he was engaged in pursuing the Holy Book, when a cry was raised that the enemy was coming. He bounded to his feet, slipped the volume in his pocket, and prepared to meet the foe. While so engaged he was struck by a musket ball, which entered the sacred treasure, and lodged in the Book of Psalms. Thus the long neglected bible in all probability was the happy means of saving his life.

Ale in the Moon. A rustic having gone to the Calton Hill Observatory to get a sight of the moon, after having got a glance of it, drew away his head to wipe his eyes, and, in the interval, the end of the telescope noiselessly fell down, so as, instead of pointing to the heavens, to point down to the earth. The rustic's surprise was unutterable when he again looked through, and beheld the sign of a public-house at a short distance, with the declaration "Edinburgh ale" etc. He started back and exclaimed, "Edinburgh ale in the moon! Gude preserve us, that beats awl"

ACCIDENT. Whilst the steamer *Lord Yarborough* was lying close to the quay, embarking the passengers, an accident occurred to Mrs. E. Major, which fortunately was unattended with a more serious result than receiving an involuntary cold bath.
On Sunday last, Divine Service according to the rites of the Church of England was performed in the after saloon, by the Rev. Dr. Scoresby. Considering the number of passengers on hoard, the attendance was very scanty. We were highly pleased with the very appropriate and eloquent sermon delivered by the Rev. gentleman.
All communications must be addressed to the editor and authenticated by the name of the writer, not necessarily for publication, but as a guarantee of good faith.

ADVERTISEMENTS.

The charge for inserting an advertisements in the Gazette is Two Pence per line, we beg to suggest to our friends the desirability of advertising any articles they may either want to dispose of or purchase.

ON SALE,

Apply at No. 43, Bourke street.

	s. d.		s. d.
Pickles superior assorted, per Bottle,			1 6
do. smaller size			0 9
Sardines, per Box,	1 6	&	2 0
Anchovies, per Bottle,	1 6	&	3 0
Herrings, best Yarmouth bloaters, 9 for			1 0
Marmalade, best Scotch per Jar,			1 6
Chocolate, best soluble per lb.,			1 6
do. Confection in Tablets each,			0 2
do. do. per lb.			2 0
Patent Flour, per lb.			0 6
Toilette Soap, per Cake,			0 6

N.B.—Every article supplied, warranted quality.

DANIEL DORAN,

Hair Cutter, etc.

Begs to intimate to the passengers of the "Royal Charter" that he is prepared to Shave, Cut, and dress Hair, and perform all the various operations of his calling with convenience and despatch, and at strictly moderate charges.— First and Second class passengers waited on at their cabins.   43, Bourke-street.

AUSTRALIAN GUANO — One of the most important items of intelligence lately received from Australia, is that of the existence of a large deposit of Guano in South Australia. The attention of the local government was immediately directed to a matter of so great importance, not only to the colony itself, but also to the agricultural interests of the mother country. The official report is most favourable, and strongly recommends the use of it in the colony.

MUCH THE SAME — Why is twice eleven like twice ten?

Because twice *eleven* are twenty-*two* and twice ten are twenty *too*.

The Royal Charter Gazette will be published for the future on every Wednesday and Saturday, and not as previously announced.

ROYAL CHARTER:

Printed and Published by GEORGE VAN TREIGHT, at No. 6, Hotham Square.

Saturday, February 23, 1856.

Scoresby continued to make meticulous notes of the various compass headings, despite the problems of reading the bearings from the instrument located at the top of the mizzen-mast. His 'compass aloft' could only be read from the deck by the use of an opera glass, a difficult task in bad weather, but this was preferable to having someone climb the rigging simply to read the instrument.

By the 1st of April, they were in the vicinity of Prince Edward Island, south-east of the southern tip of Africa, weathering a westerly gale in the middle of showers of hail and sleet that obscured the lookout's ability to spot that terrible danger of these southern seas, the iceberg. As nightfall approached, the incentive of a reward from the captain was enough to keep the men awake at their posts, and they managed to give adequate warning of imminent danger on three occasions within just a few hours. After passing the night without a major incident, a large iceberg came into sight off the port bow, a mass of frozen water that Scoresby estimated as being up to a quarter of a mile wide and possibly 200 feet (60 metres) in height.

The dinner-bell.

The ocean continued to be rough as they sailed eastwards towards Australia, and on the 5th of April, the ship was struck by a heavier wave than most, with the result that a large amount of seawater poured into the dining-room just as the breakfast table was being set. Scoresby noted that this was the first time since leaving Plymouth that the first meal of the day was late, although there was only a five-minute delay before the hot rolls, eggs and ham, porridge and various other dishes were ready to be served. As the wind rose to hurricane-force, Howe's system was used to reduce the amount of sail in use without having to send men aloft to carry out that dangerous task. Then more huge seas washed over the decks, cascading into the saloon to delay the ringing of the dinner-bell, this time necessitating a delay of half-an-hour before the meal of roast and boiled mutton, pork cutlets, stews, curries and vegetables was ready to eat. Thankfully, the gales began to abate by the 9th of April, by which time they were south of Western Australia, and running at a disappointing eight knots. The calm weather gave Scoresby an opportunity to check the magnetic polarity of the various features of the ship, with his verdict being that their polarity had been reversed due to the earth's magnetic field.

Wednesday the 16th of April brought their first sight of Australia, so, fifty-nine and a half days after leaving Plymouth, they picked up a pilot and transferred some of the British mail to other boats, before the 'Royal Charter' finally steamed into Port Phillip. As they entered the bay, the saloon passengers thanked Captain Boyce for their safe delivery to the colony, and presented him with a purse of sovereigns, despite the protracted journey-time. Scoresby spent his first few days ashore by viewing the City of Melbourne and paying visits to Government House, but his real priority was to further his studies of ship's magnetism. With this in mind, he obtained the co-operation of Captain Thomas Taylor, an employee of Gibbs, Bright & Co. who had travelled to Australia on the 'Royal Charter', and who was eventually to take command of her. With assistance from the crew of 'H.M.S. Electra', the ship was again 'swung' so that Scoresby could complete the first half of his project on May 1st, leaving him with three weeks to socialise amongst the colony's merchants, lawyers and officials.

The Return Voyage - May to August, 1856

Surprisingly, the troubles of the outward voyage of the 'Royal Charter' seem to have been quickly forgotten, so Gibbs, Bright & Co. would have been very pleased if they had read the entry in Scoresby's diary:

Her rapid passage out, and her admirable performance at sea, had gained for her such a popular reputation, that all the saloon berths were in overwhelming demand, numbers of applicants being disappointed, and the accommodation for the second and third classes quite full. The large number of third-class passengers leaving the colony, I felt disposed to regret. But others, and those anxious for the gaining of labouring men to the colony, took a different view of the case. This returning body, chiefly of the working classes, many of whom carried along with them the fruits of their toils in the goldfields in considerable amounts of treasure, it was considered would be the means of stimulating a far larger number to attempt the same adventure, and thus to yield a large balance, in the way of population, to the rich and promising regions of Australia.

He then went on to describe the eye-watering amount of gold that was being entrusted to Captain Boyce for safe delivery to the authorities in Liverpool:

Amongst the matters of interest on arriving on board was a small steamer lying under the port-quarter, and shipping through a large receiving port, communicating with the lower saloon and the treasure depository, a large amount of treasure in boxes of gold. In this and the preceding day nearly 200,000 ounces of gold had been put on board and safely deposited in a strong, iron compartment below the lower saloon, and secured by a massive trap-door of iron and a Bramah's lock, in boxes generally containing 1,000 ounces. The total weight of treasure taken on board was estimated at nearly ten tons of gold, which with costly jewellery and other precious things might probably reach to the value of nearly a million sterling.

The shipping of such valuable produce has not always been accomplished with safety. In one instance, a daring and successful robbery was carried into effect of a large quantity of gold just put on board a ship bound for England, which was the means of instituting a variety of protective measures which since then have proved safe and effective.

The arrangements for the shipping of treasure are simple, but satisfactory. Some party appointed by the agents or managers for the ship attends at the Bank during the weighing of the gold, and its being deposited and secured in small square boxes of strong hardwood — each box being marked with the weight, the sign of the shipper, etc. Each shipment is conveyed, under police escort, from the Bank to a small steamer lying at the quay at Melbourne (on board which no person is allowed except the crew of the vessel and the authorised parties), and from thence is steamed down the river Yarra alongside of the ship destined to receive it. A custom's officer attends the shipment and notes the packages and quantity for the security of the colonial revenue in respect of a duty of 2s. 6d. per ounce, a charge which though small on a value of £4 per ounce, yields a large annual amount, amounting in the case of the gold in the *Royal Charter* only, to about £25,000. As the labels on the boxes are respectively read off and put down, they are handed below into the treasure room and there packed for the voyage. The Captain, who becomes the responsible party keeping the key of the safe, gives a receipt for the whole.

The 'Royal Charter' began her return voyage on Sunday, the 25th of May, 1856, with around 326 passengers that included William and Georgina Scoresby, as well as a Roman Catholic Archbishop and a popular singer called Catherine Hayes,

This time, there was to be no turning back despite a succession of incidents that could have caused severe damage or worse to Captain Boyce's fine clipper. On the 7th of June, only two weeks out from Melbourne and in a position well to the south of the southern tip of New Zealand, some of the ironwork on the mainmast failed, with the result that one of topsail-yards suddenly dropped from its usual position, showering the deck with pieces of shattered metal. Luckily, it was raining at the time, so that all the passengers were below decks and no-one was injured, but replacing the broken fittings and raising the spare five-ton yard into position proved to be a difficult task, especially as there was rain, sleet and a heavy swell. Mainly due to waves estimated at 28 feet (8 metres) high, the first attempt was a failure, so work had to be delayed until the following day when the massive timber was eventually fixed in place despite a heart-stopping moment when a rope broke. As an experienced shipmaster, Captain Boyce had already fitted extra ropes to stop the yard from falling too far, as it would have penetrated the deck and possibly the hull, had the heavy timber fallen vertically from its position. The failure of the mast-fittings had reduced the speed of the clipper, while icebergs and strong easterly winds slowed her down even more as she battled her way towards Cape Horn at the southern tip of South America. Meanwhile, an ominous problem was developing with the rivets that held the ship together, as one of these fasteners had failed, leaving a hole in the foremost compartment of the ship. Water was pouring through this hole and filling the bilges, the water-level of which could only be held at a reasonable level by keeping one of the boilers fired to provide steam for a 'donkey-engine' that powered the bilge-pump. Further alarm was caused when it was realised that the iron plates at the bow were 'working' (moving relative to one another), with the possibility that the rivets could shear off to displace a whole sheet of iron. As Scoresby wrote in his journal:

.... it was impossible to calculate what the effect of the entire displacement of a plate or plates in the bow might be, or where the mischief might end.

It doesn't bear thinking about - can you imagine a huge hole in the bow of an iron-built ship that was attempting to run the gauntlet of Cape Horn? Something had to be done to ease the pressure on the bow, so the 'Royal Charter' was re-trimmed by transferring 45 tons of copper ore from a compartment near the bow to one near the stern, a task that may have saved the ship from being totally lost without trace.

The 22nd of June was the shortest day of the year in the Southern Hemisphere, and with only around six hours of daylight and one of the passengers having to be buried at sea, this must have been quite a depressing part of the voyage. Scoresby had injured his knee and could not stand or walk without support, and the 'Royal Charter' was now entering an area of icebergs, with six of these huge obstructions being encountered on the following day. Further delays were caused by a failure of yet another mast-fitting, when half-a-ton of metal crashed to the deck, but by the 27th of June, the clipper turned northwards up through the Atlantic Ocean to meet what were described as 'baffling headwinds'.

Finally, on Wednesday the 13th of August, 1856, after a passage that lasted 79 days, the 'Royal Charter' returned to the River Mersey, laden with treasure quoted by the English newspapers as being 181,000 ounces of gold and 10,000 sovereigns. That was a total of over six metric tonnes of the precious metal to top up the depleted war-chest of the British Government.

The Second Voyage - October 1856 to April 1857

THE MAGNIFICENT STEAM CLIPPER

"ROYAL CHARTER"

2,719 Tons Register and 200 Horse Power, with Fire-proof and Water-tight Compartments.

F. BOYCE, COMMANDER,

IS APPOINTED TO LEAVE THE MERSEY FOR

MELBOURNE, PORT PHILLIP,

ON THURSDAY, 2nd OCTOBER.

THIS noble Steam Clipper, built expressly for the Company, one of the finest models yet constructed, combines all the advantages of a Steamer with those of a Clipper Sailing Ship, and offers the only opportunity yet presented to the Public of certainty in the time required for the voyage. She has just made the extraordinary passage of 59 days to Melbourne – a performance never before accomplished. On this voyage she ran one day 358 knots, during which she attained the astonishing speed of 18 nautical miles in the hour. Her daily average for the whole distance to Melbourne was 223 ¾ knots, or 10½ miles per hour. Her accommodations for all classes of Passengers are unrivalled.

FARES TO MELBOURNE.

AFTER SALOON ... 60, 65 & 75 Guineas.

SECOND CLASS ... 25 and 30 Guineas.

THIRD CLASS ...... 16,18, & 20 Guineas.

Including Stewards' Fees, the attendance of an experienced Surgeon, and all Provisions of the best quality, except Wines, Spirits, and Malt Liquors, which will be supplied at very modest prices on board.

Arriving back in Liverpool in mid-August, 1856, it was apparent that the 'Royal Charter' needed urgent modification before attempting a second circumnavigation of the world, so additional stringers or keelsons were riveted into her hull, running along her length. This was done in the graving-dock at Liverpool, adding several tons of iron to her hull and affecting the magnetic properties of the vessel.

With the modifications completed and the ship 'swung' once again to re-calibrate the deviation-cards, the second outward-bound voyage of the 'Royal Charter' was far more comfortable and successful than the first trip, taking only 66 days from Liverpool to Melbourne, although this was still outside the advertised time of 60 days. The embarrassing delay at Plymouth on her first voyage seems to have been forgotten or simply swept under the carpet, and great play was made of her performance during this trip. Only now could comparisons be made as to the advantages and disadvantages of an iron vessel that had the extra ability to make progress in just a light wind, or even in no wind at all. Having corrected most of the problems found on their first trip, her captain and crew should have known how to handle their sleek and beautiful clipper-ship.

Fatal Accident on Board the *Royal Charter*. An inquest was held on Thursday upon the body of John Gunning, who died in the Northern Hospital the same morning from injuries received on board the Australian mail steamer *Royal Charter* on Wednesday evening. The deceased and about 23 other men were heaving the anchor up at about six o'clock, when the chain got foul, and orders were given to walk back the capstan. The pawls were lifted, and the men moved backwards about three times, when they were overpowered and the capstan flew round with the bars in, owing to the compressors at the hawse-hole not being put in.

Scoresby had previously remarked about a problem with the capstan, but his advice seems to have been ignored, and the vessel did manage to leave Liverpool on schedule for a non-stop voyage that lasted 66 days. The weather was favourable throughout the trip, with the Australian newspapers reporting that *'through the efficiency of the commander and his officers, together with the admirable appointments of the vessel, the interval between her sailing and arrival at the port of destination has passed as comfortably to all on board as if they had been on a pleasure excursion'.*

Having arrived safely in Australia, debates started as to whether the combination of sail and steam had significant advantages over a vessel propelled either by sail or steam alone. There was much money to be made or lost, depending on who was right and who was wrong.

AUXILIARY STEAM NAVIGATION.

The particulars furnished of the second voyage of the *Royal Charter* furnish some instructive information with regard to the best method of carrying on the communication between the mother country and Australia - a matter of constant interest to every colonist, and which, after all the experiments that have been tried during the past few years, is still very far from being settled. The earliest attempts to reach Australia by steam failed because it was attempted to apply to a long voyage principles which had succeeded in short voyages. A very little experience showed that the time consumed in stopping to coal* neutralized the speed to be derived from steam. The clipper ships outsailed the steamers, and threw them into disrepute. But the clippers themselves, though signalised by one or two extraordinary instances of success, were on the whole unsatisfactory from their extreme irregularity, and the aid of steam was once more invoked in conjunction with sailing power. But the relative position of the two propelling forces was reversed. In the first instance, sails were used as subsidiary to steam, now steam is employed as subsidiary to sails. The *Royal Charter* was built expressly to endeavour to combine the maximum advantage of the two forces. She has now made two voyages out and one home, none of which can be considered perfectly successful, but none of which have been failures. The early detention on the first voyage was redeemed by a subsequent successful run, but had the bad weather which compelled her to put back to Plymouth been encountered further out at sea, when such a return was impossible, it would have destroyed altogether the prestige of the trip. During the run from Plymouth only 200 tons were used, but the advantage gained was very

clearly perceptible on comparing the log with that of the *Kent,* which relied only on sailing power. On the passage home this advantage was less perceptible. The *Royal Charter* only outsailed the *Kent* by two days, so that there was all the waste of fuel, all the loss of cargo by the room occupied by the machinery, and all the extra cost of an engineering staff on board - to gain two days. This certainly cannot be considered a satisfactory result. The steam power was evidently deficient on the homeward run. There was more demand for its services than the limited amount of fuel on board enabled it to render. The auxiliary power was not auxiliary enough, and did not fully meet the exigency of unfavourable winds. On the second trip out, no less than 218 tons of coal were consumed in order to reach *The Line***, or more than was used during the whole previous voyage, and the use of the screw was called for every day but three. From the equator to the Port Phillip Heads, the voyage was little different from that of a sailing vessel, steam being only used on four days, with a consumption merely of twenty-eight tons of coal. It is clear that if bad weather had been encountered off the Cape, the voyage would have been very much prolonged, as the steam power was rendered nearly unavailable from the almost complete exhaustion of the fuel. But it is not generally probable that bad weather will be met with on more than a part of the voyage. There are, occasionally, instances where the mariner is plagued with calms or foul winds nearly all the voyage, and in such unusual cases a screw-steamer would fare but little better than a sailing vessel. But, on the average, favourable weather may be anticipated for two-thirds of the way, and it is only necessary, therefore, to provide steam power for the unfavourable part. At

* to coal = to refuel

** *The Line* = the equator

the same time, it is clear that, if the *Royal Charter* had possessed more powerful engines, so as to drive more rapidly through the bad weather encountered to the north of the equator, the voyage might have been performed in less than sixty days. Captain Boyce seems to favour this view, and proposes to double the engine power. This, however, is a considerable departure from the principle on which the vessel was planned, and is almost a return to the original style. What will be the best proportion of power and tonnage is a question which can only be thoroughly decided by further experiment, but at present the evidence would seem to incline to the fact that in the *Royal Charter* the power has been diminished too much. If more power were applied it would not necessarily involve more steaming. On the contrary, less might suffice, as while it lasted it would prove more effective. In a calm a small engine will propel the vessel at a moderate speed, but against a strong head wind, it is altogether useless. A larger engine would drive the vessel more quickly through the calms, and be of use also in foul weather. In many cases the total expenditure of fuel would not be much, if at all, greater with a powerful engine than with one of less capability, and the result of the voyage would be more satisfactory. It is not at all improbable, on the contrary it may be reasonably anticipated, that such improvements may be invented as will greatly diminish the consumption of fuel, in which case, it will be possible to increase the engine power without occupying any greater space in the vessel's hold than a small engine with its fuel occupies at present; and then greater certainty will be introduced into the voyage. The *Istamboul,* a vessel belonging to the new company, entitled the Australian Auxiliary Clipper Company, is classed as being of 1,500 tons and only 100 horsepower. Experience will show how far so small a proportion of power answers, but the presumption is that it will not be a sufficient improvement on an ordinary sailing vessel to compensate for the extra expense. The *Golden Age* showed what could be done by a vessel of great steaming power, and the best voyage to Australia on record, as made by a screw-steamer, is still that of the A.R.M.S.N Company's steamer *Victoria,* which was a powerful vessel, and which made the passage from Gravesend to Port Adelaide in 59 days, stopping two days at St. Vincent to coal. The *Oneida,* which will be shortly due, is a vessel of 530 horse-power, and being under command of a captain versed in Australian voyages, will offer a fair test of what a first-class steamer can perform, and help to throw additional light on the extent to which the auxiliary power of the screw is valuable.

The Courier (Hobart, Tasmania)
Wednesday, December 31, 1856

Preparing for the return trip, the 'Royal Charter' had problems obtaining a full complement of seamen, but she eventually cleared Port Phillip on the 18th of January, 1857, carrying 233 passengers, 1,600 bales of wool, 122,086 ounces of gold, 13,400 sovereigns, 120 tons of tin ore and 230 tons of tallow, along with some other assorted cargo. Of special interest was an individual gold nugget that weighed an impressive 323 ounces. The ship was described as being in 'splendid sailing-trim', but made a disappointingly slow passage home, arriving at Liverpool on the 12th of April, 1857, after twelve weeks at sea.

This was Captain Boyce's second and final trip in charge of the 'Royal Charter', and he handed over command to Captain Thomas Taylor, a mariner who had gained previous experience of the clipper when he travelled to Australia as a passenger on her maiden voyage.

The Captains of the 'Royal Charter'

The 'Royal Charter' only had two captains during her short career, with Captain Boyce commanding her on the first two trips around the world, and Captain Taylor in charge for the remaining four circumnavigations.

Captain Francis Boyce

Francis Boyce had a great deal of experience on the Australia run, being recorded as the captain of the 'Earl of Durham' as early as December 1841. This ship of 462 tons register sailed from London to Sydney, and had:

> .... very superior accommodations for cabin, intermediate and steerage passengers, and will carry an experienced surgeon.
>
> The Times. Friday, December 17, 1841

Some years later, in March 1849, he was in command of the 660-ton 'Pakenham' when it arrived in Port Adelaide from Liverpool. At least 262 people were aboard on this voyage, and the ship was advertised as carrying the 'surgeon-superintendent' Edward Kearney, a man who recorded seven births and four deaths during the passage. Compared to other ships of the time this death rate was low. Captain Boyce also commanded the 'Pakenham' on a further voyage in 1850, taking over four months for the return home from Adelaide, during which time he had one passenger put in irons and declared *'a lunatic'*.

By 1852, he was in command of the 'Eagle', one of Gibbs, Bright & Company's ships on the Liverpool to Australia route at a time when many ship's crews were deserting at Melbourne for the more lucrative earnings of the goldfields, but Captain Boyce appears to have recruited some seamen who had made their fortunes at the diggings in Australia, and were prepared to work their passages home to England.

> Ship *Eagle*. -- This splendid ship will convey one of the most valuable cargoes that ever left any part of the world for the port of London. In addition to her gold, she has a cargo of copper ore, wool, and tallow, the value of which altogether, may be fairly estimated at £700,000 sterling! The crew is composed of a splendid lot of men, the majority of whom have successfully visited Mount Alexander and Bendigo, and hold bills of lading for gold on their own account. One man alone holds for 17 lbs. of gold. Several of the passengers are also shippers of gold by the vessel; and Captain Boyce, in addition to an effective stand of arms belonging to the *Eagle*, has obtained from the *Falcon*, belonging to the same owners, her guns, small arms, and ammunition; We heartily pray that the worthy skipper may bring the good ship safe to her destined port.
>
> The Courier. Wednesday, September 1, 1852

There was a great deal of competition on the route between Britain to and from Australia, and he appears to have had great confidence in his own capability and that of his crew and ship, as this challenge appeared in the Australian newspaper.

> Captain Boyce of the fine clipper ship *Eagle,* 1,000 tons, challenges any other vessel to run the passage home for 1,000 guineas. She was to sail 1st July.
>
> The Courier. Friday, July 1, 1853

A guinea was 21 shillings, or £1.05 in decimal currency, so we are talking of a bet of perhaps £50,000 at today's prices. Not surprisingly, there was no great rush from other captains to rise to the challenge, but he did have one reply:

Race-horses of the Deep

To the Editor of the Argus – Sir,

I am rather surprised at not having seen any answer as yet in any of your numbers to the challenge which Captain Boyce of the *Eagle* advertises. I had hoped that the captain of one of the fine ships going home at least would come forward and back his vessel in a race; but as none of them have done so, I am prepared to lay my vessel on for London or Liverpool, and accept Captain Boyce's challenge for £1,000, or more if he likes, provided I can get a sufficient freight to warrant my so doing.

William Gerard, Commander of the American ship *Panama*.

The Courier (Hobart, Tasmania), Monday, July 11, 1853

The Australian newspapers appear to make no further mention of this race, so it seems as if no one actually took up the challenge.

A Quick Passage. - Messrs. Gibbs, Bright, and Co., the owners of the *Eagle*, are about to present Captain Boyce, the commander, with a handsome silver salver, appropriately inscribed, in commemoration of his bringing the vessel from Melbourne to London in the shortest time the voyage has yet been accomplished, namely 76 days.

Liverpool Courier. August 2, 1853

Under Boyce's command, the 'Eagle' carried large quantities of gold and other valuable cargoes back to Britain. His last voyage aboard her was in late 1854, after which he took command of the company's latest vessel, the 'Royal Charter'. After two further voyages to Australia, he relinquished command of that vessel to Captain Taylor and does not seem to have sailed that route again, having probably retired from the sea completely.

Captain Thomas Taylor

Captain Taylor was also an 'old hand' on the Australian route when he took over the 'Royal Charter' from Francis Boyce in 1857, having commanded ships for Gibbs, Bright and Co. for the previous fourteen years. He was described as

.... always temperate in his habits, because he was a smart man. He had a first-class certificate, and was perfectly competent.

In 1849, he was master of the 'Petrel', and later commanded the 'Falcon', another emigrant ship which returned to Britain laden with gold and other highly-profitable cargoes. He was aboard the 'Royal Charter' on her maiden voyage, and aided William Scoresby in 'swinging' the ship in Hobson's Bay to check the deviation of the ship's compasses against the known bearing of several landmarks as '*Captain Boyce's hands being almost wholly occupied in the multifarious work needful to be got through as soon as possible.'* Along with the quartermaster, Captain Taylor recorded the readings on the compass which was positioned on the mast-head. He had gone to Australia for Gibbs, Bright and Co. to fit out an old teak-built East India ship, the 'William Money', in which he returned to Liverpool, carrying a cargo of gold.

The *William Money*, which has arrived from Melbourne, dragged her anchor in the river, and touched the pier head, but was towed off by the steam tug *Blazer*, without apparent injury.

The Times. Monday, March 16, 1857

Frank Fowler, who sailed as a passenger on the fourth Liverpool-bound voyage of the 'Royal Charter', commented on Captain Taylor's appearance:

Brave and rugged as a lion was the captain. His defiant front, his curt, honest conversation, his implacable will, which, like a wave, bore down all before it; his natural humour and intense love of jollity; his large solicitude for his passengers and crew; his all but feminine love for his ship, and his fervent belief that no other craft was fit to touch the waters with her — all these points grow upon me as I write, and cause me to blur the paper as I lash them to the name of Thomas Taylor. I do not believe that man was drunk on the evening of the calamity. This, however, I know, that to those who were not in constant communication with him, Captain Taylor always appeared drunk. He had a ruddy face, a quick, abrupt manner, and a husky utterance, which, to the superficial observer, naturally proclaimed him intoxicated. I never saw Captain Taylor the worse for liquor during our passage home. On the other hand, I heard him pronounced drunk by second and third class passengers nightly.

Fowler also referred to the pressures put upon the captain by the shipowners, in the quest for a rapid passage around the world:

Let me, before proceeding further, explain what I mean. It is a practice with more than one large shipping firm, like that to which the *Charter* belonged, to give very heavy rewards to those captains who are enabled to make 'the voyage' — that is, the passage out and home — within a specially limited time; let us say five months. Captain Taylor, of the *Royal Charter*, told me himself that his owners had promised him five hundred pounds whenever he made the journey from Liverpool to Melbourne and back in one hundred and fifty days. The consequence of this arrangement was that speed rather than safety became the characteristic of Captain Taylor's command. It would be cruel to make this statement if I were not prepared to prove it; but when I add that the *Charter* never made a voyage without an accident of some kind or other occurring — that when I came from Melbourne in her, her gear was so defective that a yard-arm fell, killing one man and wounding others, the very day we left Hobson's Bay, and that throughout the passage her rudder was so faulty that we had to slacken sail whenever the ship attained a speed of twelve knots, — the veracity (or taste) of my assertion cannot be questioned. Everything was sacrificed to speed: a quick passage seemed to be the sole aim of the captain — was, in fact, the sole aim, as, to conclude these prefatory remarks, one little circumstance will show. When I came home in the ship, she happened, from a stress of foul winds, to make an extraordinarily long run. Well, a month before we arrived in port, we were placed on short allowance of food. Rapidity was so relied on that only sixty or seventy days' provisions (instead of, as the Shipping Act provides, one hundred and twenty) had been put on board when we left Melbourne! But, she was a noble vessel; and the captain was a noble sailor. If he was a little reckless, the 'Liverpool System' is rather to blame than he. He had risen, I believe, from before the mast, and was a man of a certain rough amiability, of seafaring energy, and dogged determination. A slight anecdote fits in here as an illustration. Once he was commanding a ship which had sprung a leak, and a number of the sailors, for some reason or other, refused to work. Captain Taylor ordered all the refractory men in irons, and then, fitting up a windmill, pumped out the vessel without any manual assistance whatever.

Thomas Taylor seems to have had a generous personality, as his name heads a list of contributors to a collection for James Potts, a passenger on the 'Royal Charter' in 1859 who had been disabled in an accident at the gold diggings.

The Third Outbound Voyage - May to July, 1857

This was Captain Taylor's first voyage in command of the 'Royal Charter', although he had previously travelled to Melbourne as one of her passengers, and had taken the opportunity to acquaint himself with the ship's officers, her crew, and the peculiarities of a ship powered by both sail and steam. The Rev. Charles Baker was a passenger who kept a diary during the voyage, extracts of which are given here by courtesy of Liverpool Maritime Museum.

13 May, 1857. (Camberwell) This morning I rose early, and seeking an opportunity, proposed to Caroline Bankart, I gave her the letter on the stairs. We settled the business in the Drawing Room -- Miss Edith came in and disturbed us (the rogue!), and so I sent for Mr. and Mrs. Bankart, and the whole affair was agreeably settled in the few minutes. And in an hour from my proposal, I had taken leave to all at Camberwell. Reached home at 7. Mr. Greenbank brought my will, and I signed it. I had to leave in haste to catch the 8-45 express to Liverpool.

16 May, 1857. Came aboard *Royal Charter* at 1 a.m. After supper I retired to my cabin -- No. 9 & 10. 8-30 had breakfast and walked on deck with Mr. Ross, a very agreeable gentleman. Went below and looked over arrangements - found 3rd class divided into streets and squares named after Melbourne. The following advertisement I copied "Found in *Victoria Square*, a small knife with spring back. The owner may have the same by giving a description of the above-named article. Apply to G.H., No 29, Elizabeth Street, Swanston Street, Royal Charter".

22 May, 1857. At teatime, Mrs. Barnett made her first appearance at the table and took her position with her husband at the Captain's end of the table. This was a little too much, as all at that end of the table were disarranged and without so much as a "by your leave." Opposition at once arose and we decided not to allow it. We have a most agreeable set of passengers at our end of the table, and do not wish to be separated.

23 May, 1857. About 9 o'clock a beautiful strong breeze sprang up and all sail was spread. And for the first time we had the screw lifted. This is an awkward operation on account of the capstan being placed forward instead of aft. This is the first day we have had a fair wind. Weather rather squally, but the sea looked beautiful in the sun. It is the finest day we have had yet. Captain Taylor came to breakfast and dinner for the first time, he is very attentive to his duties. The dispute with Mr. and Mrs. Barnett settled by the Captain at dinner, and we retain our old places. An extra half hour granted to the saloon passengers for the future, beginning today - and so lights will be put out at 11 p.m. instead of 10-30.

23 May, 1857. Had some conversation with 'Middy' who were made to scrape the mast. They do not seem very comfortable in their berth.

30 May, 1857. We had an addition to this day to the number of our passengers, owing to the birth of a little girl. " Mother and bairn speeding well." After luncheon, had my wig cropped by the Quartermaster, and almost my ears too. Then washed my hair in a drop of water.

2 June, 1857. The Captain has only been twice to bed since leaving Liverpool. Mr. Dickson informs me that we have six "stowaways" on board.

8 June, 1857. "Neptune Day" We crossed the line this morning at 8 a.m. At 10, Neptune and his crew came on board and made procession around the ship. The procession etc. was very well got up. Neptune was first rate. About nine persons were shaved and ducked, and nearly all the passengers were soaked with the hose. There was a fight between two of the sailors this afternoon, but soon quelled.

13 June, 1857. After tea I went to see Mr. Foster, the midshipman, who I heard was very nearly

killed last evening from the falling of some ropes on his head from aloft. Providentially the rope struck the spar first, or it might have been serious. As it was, his head was cut, and face much disfigured, and he was insensible.

15 June, 1857. Mr. Dickson is slightly "hic" with Miss Yeatman -- she will make him an excellent wife if he gets her.

16 June, 1857. A month today since we sailed from Liverpool, and the time seems to have passed very rapidly. There was one of the most beautiful sunsets that I have ever seen this evening, and we all came up to watch it.

17 June, 1857. A most miserable day, the worst we have had.

18 June, 1857. A storm commenced at 7 a.m. and continued all day without intermission. It was impossible to walk the decks and everyone was rolled everywhere, and it was most amusing to see them. The maintopmast staysail was torn to ribbands at 10 a.m. and we lost the Martingale shortly after. Very few ladies made their appearance today; even the strongest being upset.

19 June, 1857. The gale continued all night, and I was several times nearly pitched out of bed. Have shifted to lower berth in consequence.

21 June, 1857. It has been bitterly cold all day and no such thing as a fire. What a contrast between this Sunday and last. Then, it was beautifully warm, an English June.

22 June, 1857. Bitterly cold all day, and towards night much worse, and the sea washed over the poop and smashed one of the boats. It took four men to steer. The rain poured down in torrents, wet beds were the fashion, and no sleep.

24 June, 1857. My upper bed is soaked through, and it is well for me that I have a lower berth to take refuge in.

25 June, 1857. The *Royal Charter* is a famous roller and it makes us all find our sea legs. A great many of the passengers kept on deck all this night fearing the ship would capsize - as she leaned over very greatly and carried a heavy press of canvas. I slept soundly and knew nothing about it having so arranged myself as not to be pitched out.

26 June, 1857. We have made a splendid run during the last 24 hours -- and only 5 miles short of the best one ever made by the ship. 347 miles!

29 June, 1857. A woman in the 3rd Class gave birth to twins this morning.

1 July, 1857. Scarce anyone slept last night. I had five blankets and yet was hardly warm. I missed my bath this morning in consequence of the sea washing into the saloon. The 2nd class passengers had two feet of water in their berths. One of them, a Mr. Bartlett came to the Captain during the night and told him to take in all the sail or he would report him on the arrival of the ship. Of course the Captain laughed at him. Several of the second-class passengers again remained all night on deck, fearing the ship would be lost. This has been a beautiful day, but colder still - quite a contrast to this day in England. Distance 345 miles, but by the log we have run 400 miles and more, the difference being in consequence of bad steering. I have had conversations with every officer and many of the crew at various times, and all agree that a sailor's life is worse than a dog's. The provisions on board the ship are now very bad. Mouldy biscuit, some bread and no potatoes, tough meat, etc. The saloon is, moreover, miserably cold and cheerless, and no place to sit in.

3 July, 1857. Mr. Bellwood made a beast of himself by getting drunk. This is the second instance of a saloon passenger being drunk in the presence of all the 2nd and 3rd class passengers. It is well the Captain forbids spirits to the other passengers. Bellwood has had his grog stopped for the future.

4 July, 1857. Distance 298 miles Total distance run this week 1,816 miles. Tufty (Kayminsky) has been celebrating American Independence this morning and made himself beastly drunk. In his drunken fit he smashed his cabin furniture, etc., and was put in irons - with his legs tied and then left to cool himself in the bath. At the present moment (having been released), he is shouting "Yankee doodle" and will soon be in irons again. Distance 298 miles. Total distance this week 1,816 miles. Kayminsky was removed to the hospital 'til 12 p.m. and then allowed to return to the saloon.

Leg-irons recovered from the wreck.

7 July, 1857. Distance 265 miles. Fine though squally weather but owing to bad steering have not made such a stride as we might. We are beginning to get accustomed to the cold now although scarcely more bearable than before. Bent a new foretopsail today.

11 July, 1857. Distance run 222 miles Total distance this week 2,002 miles. The 3rd Cabin passengers had stinking tripe for dinner. In the evening they came aft and gave "three cheers for stinking tripe."

12 July, 1857. At 5 p.m. I heard a great noise on the maindeck and found a number of drunken fellows fighting. The Officers separated them once but they fell in again - so I went among them and separated couples, and sent them away to their berths. There must have been twenty or thirty drunk. I had afterwards to remain in the 3rd Cabin for some time to keep them quiet and in their berths, and separated three or four fighting groups. It is a shame that so much drink has been allowed to be sold.

13 July, 1857. The wind gradually sank this morning and at last we had a dead calm, and at 8 a.m. we lowered the screw and furled all sail. It is six weeks since all were furled before. All the passengers are becoming quite crusty and try to set each other by the loss. There are repeated quarrels, and it is difficult to act so as to steer clear of quarrels and be on good terms with all parties.

14 July, 1857. At two p.m., held the last Committee meeting to arrange the programme for final concert in *Victoria Square*. Warm words arose in consequence of my declining to hold the last concert in saloon, although backed by the opinion of Captain Taylor, who did not wish dirty coats to rub against the paint which had just been cleaned. At tea at 7.00, and then I went down and I was loudly cheered. Commenced with three cheers for the sailors who were present. At eight the sailors present went on watch. I then prepared seats of honour close to me for the next comers with their officers. All were lustily cheered on entering. Parry, one of the crew sang four songs. Mr. Stephens also sang "Scotland Yet." We kept up the singing to 11 p.m. and until the candles were burning in the sockets. Before singing "God Save the Queen," Mr. Lawton made a speech and then presented me with an address signed by 156 of the adults of the 3rd Cabin. I thanked them and then led "God Save the Queen." The utmost decorum prevailed, as usual, all through the proceedings. We cheered the Captain, officers and crew, also the Engineer. We have been quarrelling again in the saloon, and Simmons seems to defy and set all by the ears.

17 July, 1857. I proposed an address to the Officers of the ship, as also did Mr. Ross, but petty spite prevented the proposal being carried out.

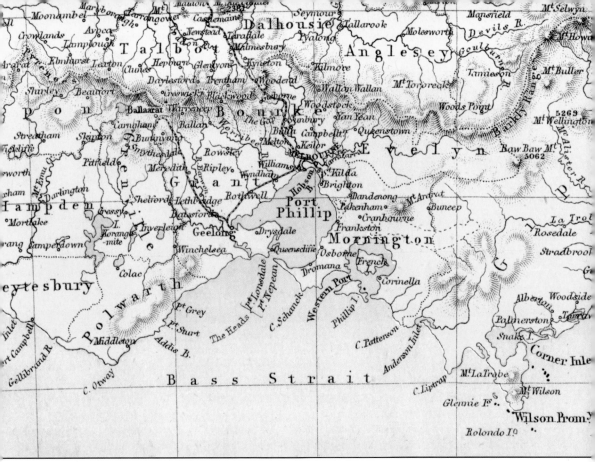

A map of Victoria, showing Cape Otway, The Heads, Port Phillip, Hobson's Bay and Melbourne. Note the area north-east of Melbourne that is named 'Anglesey'.

18 July, 1857. At 10, I went to *Victoria Square* [*one of the third-class areas*] to take leave of the passengers and shook hands with each after saying a few words to all. The sunset this evening was most beautiful. I never saw its equal in my life. The air is warm and balmy, although midwinter, and the atmosphere quite exhilarating. Total distance from Liverpool to Melbourne 14,041 miles.

19 July, 1857. At 6 a.m. fired gun and rocket for Pilot. At seven, the sun rose in most splendid style. At 7-45, the pilot came alongside, and we passed the head about 8-30. At luncheon the address was presented to Captain Taylor and we drank his and various other healths at the same time. We dined at two, and no sooner was dinner over than we found ourselves in Hobson's Bay. Almost immediately the mail boat (a wee little steamer) came alongside for the mails. And a number of these boats with friends of the passengers. We fired salutes and blew away part of the bulwarks. At 4-15 the anchor was dropped. Mr. Ross and I determined to go ashore in the mail boat, and we quit the *Royal Charter* at 4:30 p.m. A good many passengers went with us. We landed at the pier, and at once took a car into Melbourne. The first sight on landing is anything but cheering -- dead and dying trees, bare fields half covered with water, lean looking cattle and oxen. Sunday is a bad day to land, and we were both disgusted with the place. We went to Menzies - but there was only one bed to be had.

The *Royal Charter's* mails were delivered to London early on the morning of the 17th of October, about sixty-three days fifteen hours from their embarkation at Melbourne. Once before this famous feat was approached, namely, by the clipper-ship *Lightning*, which landed the mails in Liverpool in sixty-three days twenty hours, and in London in sixty-four days and ten hours. But the peculiarly favourable circumstances under which that passage was made, the *Lightning*, and her subsequent performances, only indicate that the passages of the latter vessel and the *Royal Charter* will not bear comparison. During the first four days, from August 14 to 18 inclusive, the *Royal Charter* proceeded under steam, meeting with nothing but light, baffling winds, and she progressed but slowly. She proceeded under canvas from the Auckland Islands towards Cape Horn, which she rounded on the 3rd September, being then under 20 days out from Melbourne. This part of the passage brought out the tremendous sailing powers of the *Royal Charter*, for on several days she sailed 306, 307, 320, 335, 340, and even as many as 370 miles in the 24 hours, a performance never before equalled, much less surpassed. She reached the equator in 21 days from Cape Horn, viz., Sept, 24th. During this period there were nothing but light winds from the N. to N.E. The vessel, however, made excellent progress, although retarded at every point; running from the equator to the Western Islands the prevailing winds were N.N.E., and so light and variable as to cause her use of the screw all the time. From the Western Islands to Cape Clear she had light winds and thick foggy weather, which also precluded anything like good speed. When we take all the passage into account, it cannot be denied that the foregoing facts plainly show that wherever the *Royal Charter* had the slightest chance of favourable winds, she dashed along more like a railway engine than a vast ocean steamer fighting against and bidding defiance to the fury and persistence of an angry and maddened sea, and the fierceness of opposing gales. On occasions such as these, the performances of the *Royal Charter* are not only remarkable, but such as no other vessel in the trade has yet approached.

Another instance of the extraordinary powers of the ship is the fact that the Black Ball clipper *Commodore Perry*, which sailed from Liverpool for Melbourne on the 8th of May, eight days before the *Royal Charter* took her departure, had not reached Melbourne when the *Royal Charter* left, although her detention was 26 days in Hobson's Bay. Another vessel of the same size, the *Euroclydon* - which it is said was detained in port two days to race with the *Royal Charter* - started from the Mersey about the same time as the *Royal Charter* (May 16th), yet with all her sailing abilities, she had not arrived at Melbourne when the *Royal Charter* left. This is certainly reversing the statement that the ships of this line can and do "eclipse steam to Melbourne in sixty days." I mention all these facts in justice to the *Royal Charter*; for we are commanded to render " honour to whom honour is due." No doubt much of the success of the passage to which we have been referring is owing to the skill and perseverance of the captain and his officers. We know, from what many of the passengers have told us, that nothing could exceed the skill of the captain. He was not daunted at a heavy gale or a terrific squall; he knew the strong qualities of his noble ship. She could weather storms, and he was determined to carry her through every difficulty and danger until he landed safe back in Liverpool in the space of five months, adding a detention of 26 days at Melbourne. Truly these are wonderful times, and induce the contemplatious minds to ask the question - What next?

The Courier. March 24, 1858

The Fourth Outbound Voyage - January to March, 1858

Fire on board a vessel was one of the most serious challenges facing a captain and crew. There were no smoke detectors on-board other than the ever-vigilant noses of the crew and passengers; fire-fighting equipment was very basic; and there would only be enough space in the ship's boats for a very limited number of survivors should the fire rage out of control and consume the whole vessel.

The 'Ocean Monarch', on fire off Abergele, North Wales.

The burning of the emigrant-ship 'Ocean Monarch' was still fresh in the minds of anyone associated with the port of Liverpool, as this wooden emigrant-ship had left that port for Boston, U.S.A. on the 24th of August, 1848, laden with hundreds of men, women and children. Only a few hours out from the River Mersey, fire was discovered on board, and she burned to the waterline before sinking around seven miles off Abergele, North Wales, with the loss of her cargo and over 170 lives.

The fire on board the 'Ocean Monarch' was reportedly started by a careless accident, but the article reproduced below suggests that fires on board ships could be started by persons shipping goods that were known to produce spontaneous combustion. If several packages of these goods had been placed aboard at different times, there was a good chance that the ship would be consumed by fire and disappear without trace. Terrorism? – No. This was simply a case of greed and wanton disregard for human life, as the dangerous goods would be insured for a far higher value than their actual worth. Huge amounts of money could be made or lost in the shipping industry, but this was a deadly business with a poor safety record that didn't improve until Samuel Plimsoll brought in his Parliamentary reforms in the 1870s.

FIRE ON BOARD THE ROYAL CHARTER
The following statement of a fire on board this fine vessel (which had arrived at Melbourne from Liverpool after a fine passage of 65 days) has been handed to us. On Sunday afternoon, the 24th January, latitude 19 degrees 35 minutes north, longitude 24 degrees 41 minutes west, some of the second-class passengers thought they perceived a smell as of something burning, and mentioned the matter to one of the stewards, but so slight was it that it was believed to arise from the oil-cloth on the table becoming warm from something hot being placed upon it; so this passed off without further notice. However, on the following morning, about 4 a.m., an alarm of fire was raised. The Captain and officers were very promptly at their several posts. The pumps fore and aft were quickly got ready for action. On the after hatch being opened, the dense smoke which poured forth left no doubt as to the reality of the alarm. Some difficulty was experienced at first in discovering the seat of the fire, the hold being full of cargo. The decks were cut away in several places, and the fire at last reached, which was finally extinguished about 8 a.m., to the thankfulness of all on board. Some of the passengers gave what

assistance they were able, care being taken not to crowd the officers and crew in the execution of their duty. Mr. Stephens, the first officer, entered the hold at the outset, but was shortly taken out again, in a state of insensibility. Being removed to the poop, and exposed to the open air and the usual remedies, he was enabled ere long to return to the scene of action. The fire was aft, and in the direction of the magazine. The powder, consisting of one barrel, was thrown overboard, and the rockets, blue lights, and a few charges of loose powder, sent onto the forecastle.

Various at first were the opinions conjectured as to the cause of the fire, but, on removal of the damaged goods, suspicion seemed to point very forcibly to a quantity of partially consumed waterproof coats, which might have fired spontaneously. At 10 a.m., a meeting of the passengers was called in the saloon, and a vote of thanks passed to Captain Taylor for his cool and gallant conduct under so trying an ordeal. Captain Taylor thanked the passengers for the compliment, and assured them that every care should be taken to have the cargo carefully removed and re-stowed, to ascertain whether there were any more cases of a similar description of goods to those in which the fire was supposed to originate. He was aware that there were other cases of the same mark and brand shipped as merchandise only, but as to the nature of their contents it was impossible to say. These remarks from Captain Taylor were in reply to enquiries made to him on the subject.

About 5 p.m. of the same day, another case of the goods referred to was discovered in a highly combustible state. To look at the case, no marks of burning were perceptible, but the heat felt, when touched, left no doubt as to the fire within, as it proved on opening. It is in the power of Captain Taylor to satisfy the curious and enquiring on the subject, as he has retained a small reserve of these goods on hand. The passengers met again in the evening, to seek the opinion of Captain Taylor, or to suggest to him the desirableness of putting in at Cape de Verd, as the ship was then very near, to have the cargo overhauled, or taken out and re-stowed, as danger was apprehended in proceeding further out to sea under the circumstances. Captain Taylor assured the gentlemen then present that they need be under no apprehension or alarm; that, whilst he was decided to keep the ship on her course, every precaution should be taken to guard against any recurrence of a similar disaster, for he himself and his officers would be constantly on the alert in looking amongst the cargo, which they had already done carefully and at different times, and found all cool and in good order.

A few days after this, another case was discovered in the main hold. The smell of the burning oil-cloth led to its discovery. On the removal of sundry goods, it was got at, and so hot was it that it was impossible to handle it with the hands. So as not to alarm the passengers, the case was very adroitly got out and thrown overboard; and I believe but few of the passengers are aware of the circumstance up to the present moment.

These are the simple facts of the whole affair, and the only drawback to the otherwise pleasant passage.

Now, here is a valuable ship and cargo, with nearly 500 souls, that has been jeopardised by a few cases of goods, shipped as merchandise only, or without any notice of care or attention from the dangerous nature of their contents. What protection have persons who are constantly crossing these seas, or indeed the shipowner or underwriter, if goods liable to spontaneous combustion are shipped in this careless manner? Perhaps this case may be a clue to some of the missing ships that are lost annually, and of which no tidings are ever heard.

Daily Southern Cross.
April 16, 1858

94

The Fourth Homebound Voyage - April to July, 1858

Apart from her initial out-bound voyage, the 'Royal Charter' had established a well-founded reputation for a reliable and fast passage in either direction, and she left Australia on the 11th of April, 1858. Unfortunately, this voyage from Melbourne to Liverpool didn't start very well at all.

> It appears that on the morning of the ship leaving Melbourne, a sailor named John Smith was crushed to death in consequence of the upper maintopsail carrying away while the yard was being lowered. The tie broke the engine-room hatch, smashing the glass roof, and falling upon the engines, which, without further damage, were stopped.

This was just the beginning of what was to become a horrendous trip for her passengers. By the beginning of July, the 'Royal Charter' had passed the expected date of her arrival at Liverpool, creating much anxiety for her owners, the relatives of the passengers on board, and those officials of Her Majesty's Treasury who were expecting a huge injection of cash into the government coffers at a time of conflict with China. By the 13th of July, she was long overdue after spending ninety-two days at sea with a valuable cargo of 93,732 ounces of gold and 30,400 sovereigns to a total value of £405,328, or perhaps £50,000,000 to £60,000,000 at today's valuation. That was a thought-provoking amount of money for those on dry land in England, but what of the passengers who had paid for their berths expecting the voyage to be a repeat of her previous passage home, accomplished in 62 days? They were now a whole month behind schedule, and more importantly, they were running short of provisions as reported by the author Frank Fowler, whose comments have been given on page 87.

Having advertised 'Under 60 days' and consistently delivering a journey-time of only a few days over that boast, everyone in England was expecting a repeat of the previous voyage, but three months was far too long a period of time for the journey, and fears were being raised to her possible fate. Had she foundered whilst rounding Cape Horn? Had she hit an iceberg? Had fire broken out and consumed the ship? Even her insurers had given up hope of ever seeing the 'Royal Charter' again, and had already paid out ten guineas (£10 10 shillings) on every £100 of the vessel's insurance cover. Underwriters do not usually pay out without some justification, so that act must have had a devastating effect on those friends and relatives waiting at Liverpool to welcome home their loved-ones.

The following newspaper article certainly brought welcome news to those anxious people on dry-land, as it announced that the passengers and crew of the 'Royal Charter' really had come back from the dead.

> Arrival of the *Royal Charter*. We are gratified to report the safe arrival of the screw steam-ship *Royal Charter* (respecting whose safety some fears were entertained, owing to her lengthened passage) at Queenstown, yesterday afternoon, and reported "all well." After coaling, she would leave for Liverpool, and will likely arrive this (Friday) morning. The *Royal Charter* sailed from Melbourne on the 11th of April and is consequently 94 days at sea. She had on board about 400 passengers (a list of those occupying cabin berths we subjoin), a full cargo of wool, copper and miscellaneous goods, 93,732 ounces 14 dwts, of gold, and 30,000 sovereigns, of an aggregate value of £400,000. The anxiety regarding her non-arrival was so great that ten guineas per cent was paid as insurance, and a disinclination to operate even at that figure. She was compelled to put into Queenstown, short of coal.

Ninety-four days wasn't an excessive period of time for a sailing vessel such as the 'Eagle', another Gibbs, Bright & Co. vessel which took 106 days for the same voyage after leaving Melbourne just over a month after the 'Royal Charter'. However, the 'Eagle' was purely a sailing-ship, whereas the 'Royal Charter' was an auxiliary-steamer that was expected to make some progress even if becalmed or faced with a headwind. Another ship, the 'Shooting Star', left Melbourne fourteen days after the 'Royal Charter' with 42,000 ounces of gold and 50,000 sovereigns, yet she arrived in the River Mersey two hours before her rival. So why was the 'Royal Charter' delayed so much?

Voyage of the *Royal Charter*. The Liverpool and Australian Company's steamer *Royal Charter*, Captain Taylor, encountered very unfavourable weather on her passage homewards, having to steam against a head-wind. She was 94 days out, and for 30 days the passengers were on short allowances of provisions, their stock having run out. Small supplies were obtained from several ships that were met with, but for which they would have been reduced to dire straits. The stock of coals, too, was nearly exhausted, and two days before the vessel's arrival here [*Queenstown*], the captain was glad to avail himself of a favourable wind and run into the harbour. On the voyage, a coal-laden ship was met with, on which the mate of the *Royal Charter* was sent on board to obtain a supply. This, however, was refused unless the steamer hoisted a flag of distress, which, of course, would not be done. The object of this demand was to obtain salvage.

That last sentence shows just how cut-throat the shipping industry was. The collier's captain would not sell the urgently-needed coal to the 'Royal Charter' unless Captain Taylor signalled that he was in distress, but that would almost certainly lead to a salvage claim by the collier, possibly with damages totalling thousands of pounds being awarded against Gibbs, Bright & Co., and the ruination of Captain Taylor's reputation.

Having arrived safely at Liverpool, there was the matter of a compensation claim by the passengers who were not only many weeks overdue, but hadn't been fully provided with food throughout the voyage. Several of them were so disgruntled with the voyage that they left the 'Royal Charter' at Queenstown to complete their journey via the mailboat to Holyhead.

NORTHERN AND SOUTHERN HOSPITALS. The committee of the third-cabin passengers of the screw-steamer *Royal Charter* have handed us the sum of £3 2s. 6d., being the balance of subscriptions collected, as they state "for the purpose of recovering compensation from Messrs. Gibbs, Bright, and Co., the owners of the vessel, for the injuries received and the suffering they endured consequent on their being placed on half-allowance of provisions and water during the last three weeks of the voyage." This sum, we shall with their concurrence, present to the Northern and Southern Hospitals.

Liverpool Mercury. July 22, 1858

The matter seems to have been settled amicably, as there are no further reports of legal action in the newspapers.

The Fifth Outbound Voyage - October to December, 1858

The fifth outbound voyage seems to have been rather uneventful, with very little reported by the newspapers. The 'Royal Charter' left the Mersey on the morning of the 23rd of October, 1858, averaging 200 miles a day for the first week and arriving at Hobson's Bay at the end of December after a passage that lasted sixty-five days.

The following is an abstract of the log kept on board this vessel on her voyage from Liverpool to Melbourne:- Left Liverpool 23rd October, at 10.30. a.m. Steamed down the river with a S.E. wind, which prevailed until the 25th, when it changed to S.S.E. with strong breezes. The distance run from the time of leaving to 1st November was 1,430 miles, or an average of 200 miles a day, and the quantity of coals consumed was 57 tons 14 cwt. From 1st November to the 15th, fresh and steady breezes were experienced from the S. and S.S.E., the vessel steering at the time a south and south-westerly course; and during a portion of this time, no steam was employed. A succession of steady breezes, varying from W to N.W. and W.S.W. prevailed from that time until the 8th December, when the greatest distance run in one day was arrived at, viz., 325 miles. From that time to the arrival of the vessel in Hobson's Bay, nothing of interest occurred, but light and steady breezes from the W. and N.W., and occasionally from the E.S.E. During the whole passage of sixty-five days, the *Royal Charter* only steamed during thirty-nine days.

The Courier. Saturday, January 1, 1859

Perhaps the only item of note was the purser's lack of patience and appreciation of musical talent.

A Non-musical Purser. Brenan v. Lewis. The plaintiff in this case, John Brenan, of School-lane, Church Street, Liverpool, sued the defendant, Mr. Lewis, steward and purser of the ship *Royal Charter*, for £2 5s., under the following circumstances: It appears that the plaintiff was the master of a band engaged by the owners of the *Royal Charter* to play for the amusement of the passengers during her last voyage to Melbourne. Amongst other property belonging to the plaintiff on board was a patent quadrille drum, of which instrument one of the ship's boys grew so mightily fond during the latter part of the voyage that he "did nothing else but beat it up and down the deck from morning till night," much to the annoyance of Mr. Lewis, who admitted that he was not fond of music, and certainly not of drum solos without accompaniments. Perhaps in celebration of the vessel's safe arrival, immediately she reached Melbourne the young artiste performed a fantasia in close proximity to Mr. Lewis's stateroom, and its protracted length and the surpassing brilliancy with which it was executed so excited the ire of the purser that he rushed out somewhat abruptly, and terminated the performance by kicking in the head of the drum and throwing it overboard. The plaintiff, as the proprietor of the instrument, now brought his action to recover its alleged value. His Honour gave judgement for £1 15s.

Liverpool Mercury. Saturday, April 30, 1859

The Fifth Return Voyage - January to April, 1859

Her return home was equally uneventful, being reasonably on time and without any apparent drama, although taking five days longer than the boasted sixty days. Leaving Port Phillip on the 21st of January, she rounded Cape Horn a month later, and crossed the equator on the 14th of March. She averaged 300 miles per day for part of the voyage, with the best day bringing her 396 miles closer to Liverpool, where she could unload her 149 passengers and 27,000 ounces of Australian gold.

The Sixth Out-bound Voyage - May to July, 1859

Sadly, not the 2,159-ounce 'Welcome Nugget', as this one is only around 5 mm in width, and weighs just a few grams.

Despite the reports of the diminishing returns of the goldfields, there had been some really spectacular finds to keep the emigrant-trade alive. The 'Blanche Barkly' nugget of 1,743 ounces was discovered at Kingower, Victoria on the 27th of August, 1857, and the 'Welcome Nugget', weighing 2,159 ounces, was dug out of the ground at Ballarat, Victoria, on the 15th of June, 1858.

By May, 1859, Gibbs, Bright & Co. had settled into a routine whereby their two auxiliary steamships were running in conjunction with the Black Ball Line to offer regular departures for Melbourne, still under the banner of 'Sixty Days to Australia'. A strong advertising campaign in the newspapers even used the name of the British monarch to promote their shipping-line.

STEAM TO AUSTRALIA UNDER 60 DAYS.
PASSAGE MONEY, £14 AND UPWARDS,
GREAT BRITAIN and ROYAL CHARTER
Appointed to Sail Punctually from LIVERPOOL on the 5th and 15th of every month.
The above, in addition to being the only line with Steamers out of Liverpool is composed of the largest, finest, and fastest Merchant Ships in the world.

The above celebrated Steam and Sailing Clippers forming the only lines honoured by a visit from Her Majesty the Queen, and so well known for their rapid passages, punctuality in sailing and splendid accommodation, unsurpassed by any ships in the world, will continue to sail regularly between Liverpool and Melbourne, affording to Passengers and Shipowners, the most unrivalled advantages. The Commanders are men of experience, and noted for their kindness and attention to passengers. The Cabin accommodation is very superior, the Saloons being elegantly furnished with every requisite to insure comfort to passengers, and are supplied with Beds, Bedding, etc.

Judging by the previous record of the 'Royal Charter', the phrase 'rapid and punctual' may not have been strictly accurate, and Her Majesty would certainly not have been amused had she known that some unsavoury characters were escaping justice on one of these ships.

Alleged embezzlement at Manchester – Information was received on Saturday, at the detective-office, that James Hampson, the collector of a Manchester firm, had absconded. The amount of his defalcations, as far as they have been discovered, is £160; but it is expected that that sum will be considerably increased before the examination of his accounts has been completed. About a week since, another person employed by the same firm, left under similar circumstances. On that occasion Hampson assisted the detectives in their attempt to secure his fellow-clerk; but the latter succeeded in sailing from Liverpool for Australia in the *Royal Charter*. A reward has been offered for Hampson's apprehension.

The thief must have had a fast and pleasant journey, as the 'Royal Charter' arrived at Melbourne on the 22nd of July, 1859, after only 59 days at sea.

Was there a sixty-day target?

Much publicity was given to the boast 'Liverpool to Australia in under 60 days', a time-scale that was incomprehensible to the emigrants of only a few years earlier when vessels such as the 'Chowringhee' took 121 days for the same voyage in 1852. But was 60 days a realistic claim, or was there a certain amount of advertising 'spin' that would bring passengers flocking to Gibbs, Bright & Co. rather than to the other Liverpool-based companies? Did the option of auxiliary steam-propulsion make all the difference? It is certainly true that the first voyage of the 'Royal Charter' took less than 60 days from England to Australia, but that journey-time was from Plymouth to Melbourne, and didn't include the eight days from Liverpool to Plymouth or the twenty-one days spent unloading ballast and repairing the ship at Plymouth. What if a modern-day airline advertised Manchester to Sydney in 22 hours, but didn't warn passengers of a three-week stopover at Heathrow airport?

The actual voyage-times of the 'Royal Charter' appear to be as follows, although different newspapers do give differing dates of departures or arrivals, and some use the date of her arrival at Queenstown rather than at Liverpool.

Liverpool	Melbourne	Elapsed time.
Jan 18, 1856	April 16, 1856	8 + 21 + 59 = 88 days.
Oct 2, 1856	Dec 8, 1856	66 days.
May 16, 1857	July 18, 1857	63 days.
Jan 8, 1858	Mar 17, 1858	68 days.
Oct 24, 1858	Dec 27, 1858	**64 days.**
May 22, 1859	July 22, 1859	59 days.

The return trips were no more consistent than the outbound ones, with Gibbs, Bright & Co. claiming 63 days for the run to Liverpool in 1858, when it actually took around 90 days. They obviously had a good advertising agent in those days, with no trading-standards 'watchdogs' to contradict their claims!

Melbourne	Liverpool	Elapsed time.
May 25, 1856	Aug 12, 1856	79 days.
Jan 18, 1857	April 12, 1857	85 days.
Aug 13, 1857	Oct 17, 1857	63 days.
April 11, 1858	July 16, 1858	90 days, but adverts claimed **only 63.**
Jan 29, 1859	April 6, 1859	63 days.
Aug 26, 1859	Wrecked Oct 26, 1859	58 days (to Queenstown).

Even if there had been a 60-day target for the outbound or the homewards bound voyage, the 'Royal Charter' rarely achieved this time. The journey was far too dependant on the prevailing winds and the state of the sea, so it would have been unrealistic for Captain Taylor to have had a strict timetable to meet.

However, according to Frank Fowler, he did have an incentive for a rapid circumnavigation of the world as he would have been paid a £500 bonus had he made the round trip in one hundred and fifty days. This could only have been achieved by a brief stay at Melbourne, and does not appear to have been met either.

HER MAJESTY ENTERING BANGOR, NORTH WALES.

The display made by the Bangorians as a mark of loyalty was, we are informed by the Manchester Guardian correspondent, excellent, not comparatively only, but positively. There was a unity in the decorations which was more satisfactory in its result than had been some of the displays in larger towns where there are fine buildings and broad, long streets. Here, the route of the Royal cortege was, almost throughout, narrow and circuitous, and many of the dwellings along it are of the humblest description. But there was scarcely one, from the poorest cottage to the public buildings or larger shops and hotels, that was not festooned with laurel, holly, or fir, or that had not its front almost embowered by branches of those trees, rich in their finely contrasting shades of green. Bouquets and rosettes, natural sometimes, but often artificial, relieved this part of the display from any suspicion of monotony; and a profusion of flags and banners, national, emblematical, enigmatical, and indescribable, flaunted in the breeze, and served capitally to set off the foliage below. Nor were triumphal arches wanting - arches not to be classed under any of the orders of architecture, but which, not pretending to be solid structures of stone or marble, looked like what they were - impromptu affairs - almost every one of them being a success in its way, and a decided addition to the general effectiveness of the scene. They were generally light frames, thickly covered with evergreens; floral designs, loyal inscriptions, or Chinese lanterns, being added according to the taste of the promoters. The high ground that slopes to the road between the station and the town of Bangor - represented in our engraving - was well filled - a great number of children, chiefly of the local schools, with their flags and emblematical banners, were standing on benches cut out of the side of the cliff; and an immense crowd of country people had gathered here to catch a look at their Sovereign.

Illustrated London News.
October 29, 1859.

CHAPTER SIX

The World in 1859

The world of 1859 was one of great excitement, prosperity, progress and success, mixed with more than a fair helping of disillusionment, poverty and despair. Thankfully, the Treaty of Paris in March 1856 had ended the horrendous waste of life and resources during the Crimean War when the allied forces of Britain, France and the Ottoman Empire fought bitter battles with the Russian army at Sebastopol, Alma, Balaclava and Inkerman, but Europe was soon in the throes of yet another dispute as Austria and Italy were at war, and Britain was forming a Volunteer Rifle Corps as there was a perceived threat of invasion from France. Meanwhile, across the Atlantic, Charles Blondin, the acrobat, crossed the Niagara Falls on a tightrope, and John Brown was hanged in Virginia, U.S.A., after attempting to incite a slaves' revolt at a time when the United States of America was sliding towards a ferocious civil war that was soon to decimate her population.

Running alongside this violent and destructive world, rapid progress was being made in the fields of science, exploration and engineering. Charles Darwin published his controversial book 'On the Origin of Species by Means of Natural Selection' in November, 1859, to be met with a mixture of acclaim and disbelief from the general public, scientific men and theologians. Meanwhile, the boundaries of the known world were expanding rapidly, as brave men such as John McDouall Stuart explored the Australian interior, Captain Leopold McClintock searched the Arctic wastes of Canada in the hope of finding some trace of Sir John Franklin and his ships 'Erebus' and 'Terror', and David Livingstone pushed his way along the Zambezi river in East Africa. Work began on the Suez Canal during this year to create an engineering marvel that would cut many miles off the journey from Europe to India, Australia and New Zealand. This shorter route would remove many of the disadvantages of the steamships, bringing the era of the auxiliary steamship to an end once the waterway was opened to connect the Mediterranean Sea to the Red Sea.

And at home in Britain:

- An average of 379 men women and children emigrated each day.
- According to statistics published in 'The Times', British exports for the year totalled £155,692,975 and imports were £179,182,355. Australia took eleven million pound's worth of British goods, up from four million pound's worth in 1852.
- The chimes of 'Big Ben' were heard in London for the first time.
- The price of gold was £3 17s 10d or U.S. $20.67 per ounce.
- Beef was 6d (2½p) per pound and lobsters were 1 shilling (5p) per pound. Turkeys and geese were 5 shillings (25p) each.
- A five-bedroom house could be bought in the English city of Chester for £350.
- Isambard Kingdom Brunel, the great engineer and creator of the 'Great Britain' and 'Great Eastern', died in September, leaving a legacy that still exists today.
- Another famous engineer, Robert Stephenson, died in October. His Britannia Bridge still conveys road and rail traffic over the Menai Strait onto Anglesey, North Wales.
- Queen Victoria visited North Wales in October 1859, the 22nd year of her reign.

But for the average person in the street, this was a hard, cruel world, and a browse through the British newspapers of that time soon reveals pages full of murder, rape, robbery, embezzlement and other heinous crimes that were met by a strict judicial system that usually handed out long terms of imprisonment, given with 'hard labour', or even the ultimate punishment of the hangman's noose. Horrendous railway-accidents, boiler-explosions, shipwrecks, suicides, infanticide, poisonings, shootings and muggings were a regular occurrence, as shown in this typical page of the Chester Chronicle of October 29, 1859 under the heading of *'Accidents and Offences'.*

- Fatal Accident on the Northern Railway. The train came up to the person, and the buffer of the engine struck him and knocked him down on the hard gravel of the line. .... He leaves a widow and large family.

- Fire and Loss of Life. ..... which has been attended with fatal consequences. It appears that all of a sudden, loud and piercing screams were heard proceeding from the ground floor of the premises. ... The remains were removed to await a coroner's inquest.

- The Railway Accident near Sheffield. .... that the collision occurred in consequence of the facing points at the junction of a siding being opened instead of closed. .... The jury returned a verdict of 'Manslaughter' against the points-man.

- Fearful Gun Accident. .... he seized the gun near the muzzle, and a struggle for possession of it ensued between the two lads. They were near a hedge, and a twig from which chanced to catch the hammer ... The poor lad survived the accident near half an hour.

- Atrocious Outrages. A small stone bottle, filled with powder, hob-nails and fragments of glass, and having a lighted fuse attached, was thrown into one of his bedrooms at three o'clock on Wednesday morning.

- Melancholy Death of a Derbyshire Gentleman. ... who has died from cold and exhaustion in making the ascent of Snowdon. [*Snowdon is the highest mountain in Wales.*]

- Colliery Explosion near Newcastle. Four Persons Killed. .... an explosion of firedamp occurred at Washington colliery, by which three men and a boy lost their lives.

- Serious Accident to Colonel Wetherall. .... his horse slipped, fell, and rolled over ....

- The Wednesbury Murder. .... clearly showed that the death of the woman Owen resulted from a congestion of the brain. .... the prisoner is well-known as a cock-fighter and a dogfighter, and it is said that his temper had been aroused by loss in these brutal sports on the day on which he deprived his wife of her life.

- Another Murderous Outrage .... and that she had sustained other severe injuries. She is not expected to recover.

- Loss of the barque 'Beatrice'. Sufferings of the crew. .... when upwards of 800 miles from land, the vessel sprang a leak, and the whole of the crew pumped for three days without effect. .... the vessel, during a storm, capsized, and a boy named William Smith was washed overboard and drowned ....

- Great Fire in London. .... fortunately, this person was enabled to get out the whole of his horses just as the flames were attacking his stables. The total loss ....

- The Murder of a West Hartlepool Captain .... a Portuguese seaman was indicted for the wilful murder of .... Several other witnesses having been examined, the jury returned a verdict of 'Guilty'. He was then sentenced to death.

And much more ....

October 1859. The 'Great Eastern' comes to Holyhead

To the relief of the shareholders of the 'Great Ship Company', the owners of the 'Great Eastern', their investment was finally afloat by the end of January, 1858. A vast amount of money had been expended, and there was still an immense list of problems to be overcome, not a surprising situation considering the complexity of her machinery and the sheer size of a hull that far exceeded any ship yet known to mankind. At last she was capable of moving under her own power, but decisions had to be made regarding her future. Which seaports could accommodate such a leviathan? What was the best use of such a ship - as a passenger-ship or as a troopship? There were even letters published in the newspapers suggesting that the best use for her was to be a cable-layer, slowly plodding the oceans of the world leaving a thin strand of copper wires encapsulated in a coating of gutta-percha that would establish instant communication between countries and continents around the world. As history was to prove, this idea was to become the most useful and profitable task for her, but in 1859 her owners had come to the decision that she was to be an opulent passenger-liner carrying people across the Atlantic in style, comfort and safety. Could Holyhead Harbour in North Wales be her port of departure from the west coast of Britain? An immense breakwater was then under construction to create a 'Harbour of Refuge' by enclosing a vast area of water that was sheltered from most wind directions except the north-east. These 'Harbours of Refuge' were designed to provide a safe-haven for shipping rather than to provide facilities for loading and unloading vessels. The railway network connected Holyhead to the main centres of population in Britain, and to the coalfields of North-east Wales and South Lancashire that would supply the essential fuel. October 1859 was to provide the opportunity for Holyhead to prove its worth to the 'Great Eastern'. Instead, it nearly became the final resting place of Brunel's great dream.

HOLYHEAD PIER.—VISITORS TO THE GREAT SHIP

The 'Great Eastern' became a huge tourist attraction in Holyhead Harbour.

THE 'GREAT EASTERN' AT HOLYHEAD

The big ship, after her trial-trip (a full account of which, by our Special Correspondent, was given in last Saturday's number of this Journal), dropped anchor within the breakwater at Holyhead on the afternoon of Monday week. Another correspondent thus describes the arrival of the *Great Eastern* at Holyhead :— "Again our ship's head is to the north-east, and the light wind that plays upon our port beam seems but to thrum the harp-strings of Ireland and Anglesea in celebration of our career. When the bugle sounds for dinner — exactly forty-eight hours since it did so as our engines made their first strokes at Portland — the ship is entering the noble harbour of Holyhead. As the viands [*food*] and the wines move along in merry succession, the gun announces the completion of our voyage; and the anchor, with an imperceptible plunge, brings us to a stand. When we return to deck, the spectacle is brilliant in the extreme. Men-of-war and merchantmen, steam-tugs and packets, yachts, smacks, and every description of craft that swims, are dressed in gay colours and resounding with cheering voices. The Rock shines in the western sun, and along its highest margin are visible a crowd of spectators. The Welsh mountains loom grandly in the background on the one side, and a broad path of sunshine stretches along St. George's Channel on the other. Mr. Bold, our managing director, who is also in authority over a steam-tug company at Liverpool, has ordered one of those more useful than beautiful vessels to meet us here. The *Rover* has been trying in vain to keep up with us, but now she is alongside, and in half an hour takes us ashore. The gutturals of the boatmen and porters on the pier leave no doubt that we are in Wales; but there is as little doubt that they are glad, with right hearty Welsh cordiality, to see us here; and here we fancy we could make ourselves happy enough for a few days, while a mob of visitors are in possession of our big ship."

The *Great Eastern* was saluted on her arrival by *H.M.S. Hastings*, Captain Mends, C.B., and by the *Dapper* gun-boat, Lieutenant Eaton, both of which vessels were at anchor inside the harbour awaiting the visit of the Queen. It was a somewhat remarkable coincidence that as the *Great Eastern* entered Holyhead, the *Princess Victoria*, a first class steamer commanded by Captain John Harrison, brother of the commander of the *Great Eastern*, was observed beating up Channel on her outward voyage from Liverpool. Great excitement prevails throughout the principality in reference to the ship.

The Flintshire Observer says:—

"The arrival of this noble ship at the port has occasioned a lively sensation, not only along our own coast but throughout the country generally. On Wednesday last, no less than fifteen excursion trains arrived at Holyhead from various parts of the country, and the arrangements for their ingress and egress was so complete that no accident or delay whatever occurred. The *Great Eastern* rides majestically at anchor within a stone's throw of the pier, and is immediately got alongside of by one of the small steamers plying between her and the pier. There is neither difficulty nor danger in getting on board of her. Securely fastened to her side is a sailing-vessel, from the deck of which a small wooden platform leads into the big ship through one of her portholes, and thus easy and safe access is secured. From her lower decks, special staircases are provided to gain her upper ones, and every facility is afforded to visitors to inspect every part of the monster vessel."

The *Great Eastern* was honoured by the presence of the Prince Consort on Monday, as recorded in another column; and on Tuesday, Prince Napoleon paid a visit to the great ship. Attended by a numerous party, he came on board at eight in the morning, and, having critically examined every part of the ship, breakfasted with Captain Harrison.

His Highness remained on board from eight to half-past eleven a.m., and when he left shook hands with Mr. Campbell and Captain Harrison, at the same time expressing to them the pleasure he had received, and offering his best wishes for the success of the undertaking. On Tuesday the largest number of visitors since the arrival of the *Great Eastern* at Holyhead went on board.

The uncomfortable-looking fishing village of Holyhead (says a correspondent) is full to repletion, and woe-betide the unlucky voyager who comes down by the night train in the expectation of getting a bed. Paltry little dens and roadside alehouses command a price for dingy accommodation which would make our best London houses stare. The daily number of visitors is greater now than ever it was at Portland, and all the chief seaports of the United Kingdom where the *Great Eastern* could stay, and very many also where she could not, are clamorous in their solicitations and invitations to get her round.

In a highly-complimentary article in the Debats on the *Great Eastern* and its illustrious designer, the writer endeavours to convey an idea of the vastness of her structure to his Parisian readers by telling them that her length is rather more than half that of the Tuileries, "from the Pavilion Marsan at one end to the clock-tower in the centre;" that the widest street in Paris, the Boulevard de Sebastopol itself, "would be too narrow to receive her by seven metres; that her depth from deck to keel "is equal to the highest houses in Paris;" and that the circumference of her wheels "is about that of Franconi's Circus." "One of the most competent officers of our own navy," he says, "after having studied her carefully, came to the conclusion that it would be possible to embark on board of her 15,000 troops, or about as many as it is intended to send to China."

Illustrated London News.
October 22, 1859

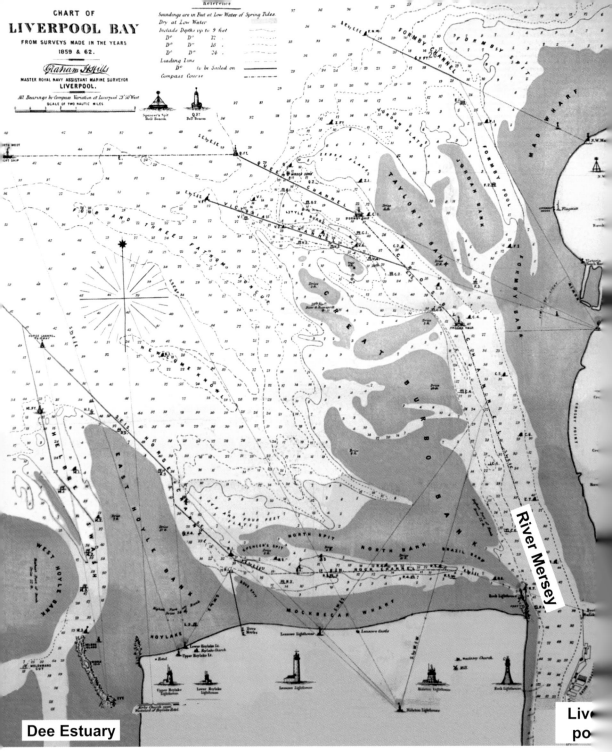

This chart shows the complex maze of sandbanks and channels at the approaches to the mouth of the River Mersey and the docks at Liverpool. Pilots needed to have up-to-date information on the latest conditions so that a vessel could be safely navigated into or out of Liverpool. Hundreds of ships have come to grief here.

PILOT SERVICE OF THE UNITED KINGDOM: LIVERPOOL PILOT CRAFT.

The Liverpool Pilot-boats

As illustrated by the old chart opposite, the approaches to the River Mersey and the Port of Liverpool were very hazardous, as the narrow shipping-lanes meandered between vast sandbanks that dried out at low-tide. That is still the case today, although submerged walls have been installed to improve the situation by directing most of the tidal-flow through the Queen's Channel. This part of north-west England has a tidal range of over 10 metres as measured at the Alfred Dock in Liverpool, with swift currents that can reach over 5 knots in the narrowest part of the River Mersey.

After sailing the oceans of the world, and perhaps having been away from home for several months, a wise captain needed to pick up a pilot before reaching the approaches to Liverpool. This wasn't too much of a problem during normal daylight hours, but poor visibility or night-time required the burning of a blue light to attract the attention of a pilot-boat that was hopefully cruising somewhere off North Wales. A homeward-bound ship could be using outdated charts, and these essential aids to navigation were not to be relied upon unless they gave the latest information.

In normal circumstances, an inward-bound vessel would pick up a pilot off the coast of Anglesey, and use that navigator's local knowledge to guide the ship safely into Liverpool, avoiding the fate of hundreds of others that have come to grief here. The shipping-channels frequently altered as the sandbanks moved, and it was the duty of the Mersey Docks and Harbour Board to constantly monitor the safest route through the danger area, and to place navigation buoys to mark a deep-water passage. The Harbour Board also maintained a series of shore-based lighthouses and marker-beacons that a pilot could use to hopefully establish his position at sea.

THE LIVERPOOL PILOT-BOATS

THE Pilot-boats of Liverpool are among, if not, the finest in the world, and equal to many a first-class yacht. Some thirty or more years ago, they were little better than large-sized fishing-boats, but have wonderfully improved since then. They are twelve in number, and range in length from fifty to seventy foot, more or less, and in tonnage from fifty to upwards of a hundred tons; and carry from fifteen to twenty hands each, including masters (there are two, first and second), journeymen, and apprentices. There are two cruising-grounds, the Hoylake and Westward Stations; the former fifteen to twenty and the latter above sixty miles from Liverpool. From Point Lynas to Holyhead — some few miles — constitutes the Western Station. There are always six boats in dock, and an equal number at sea — two on the Hoylake and the remaining four on the Westward Station.

The mode in which they go to work is this:— A boat leaves the dock with her crew on board (or, as she proceeds to sea, takes them from outward-bound ships), and arrives on the Hoylake Station second in turn. When the boat before her has finished, she then becomes first in turn, and boards all her hands. The vessels that they board on this station consist of coasting vessels, steamers, etc., and sometimes foreign vessels which have passed the Western boats in the night-time. She then proceeds to Liverpool for her hands, and departs the same or next tide for the Western Station; unless, as is generally the case, her hands come down to her on the station in another boat or a tug. She then makes the best of her way west, and arrives on the station fourth in turn; when the other three boats finish, she then becomes first in turn. She then boards all hands but two (unlicensed apprentices, which work the boat, excepted), which she puts on board of the boat taking her place. She then proceeds to Liverpool, in charge of the master and apprentices (the master never going on board a vessel except in case of urgent necessity), and remains in dock till the boat comes up that sends her out.

Originally they were all cutters, but within the last five years they have got six schooners; so that there are an equal number of schooners and cutters. The first schooner, *No. 6,* was launched 9th June, 1852. A good westerly wind gives them plenty to do, whereas a prevalence of easterly winds keeps the ships knocking about in the Channel; and consequently their cruise is prolonged. The wisdom of having so many boats on the station at once will easily be understood — in case of a crowd of vessels coming up there is always a boat ready to take the other's place. The boats in dock are also kept in readiness to go to sea. There is also great wisdom in having two masters; for, while one is at sea with the boat, the other attends to the business of that boat on shore. The committee is composed of half a dozen (or more) of the principal shipowners in the port; there are also a superintendent and a treasurer attached; and it is altogether as well-conducted and as well-regulated as any like establishment in the world.

The boats are on their several stations in all weathers, blow high or blow low; and the pilot's life is an arduous one, and extremely dangerous at times. One of the many dangers to which they are subject is boarding vessels in a heavy sea with the punt. When there is a very heavy sea on, one in which a punt could not live, they board the ship with the big boat, which is done in this manner: — The pilot-boat approaches the ship on the lee side within a yard or two, or as near as she dare; a line is then passed from the deck of the ship through a block on the lower yardarm, and made fast to the pilot's body, who, watching the opportunity, either jumps or is swung on board.

Illustrated London News.
October 3, 1857

Hoisting a pilot onto another vessel during heavy weather.

On the night of the 25th of October, 1859, two pilot-boats were cruising off the coast of Anglesey. Number 11 pilot-boat 'Mersey' was a 55' 7" (17 metres), 47-ton cutter, and Number 4 pilot-boat 'Auspicious' was 60' 5" (18.5 metres) long and of 49.5 tons The night was extremely dark and dismal, and as one pilot was later to testify - *'About eleven p.m., the gale was more violent than before; it was dreadful; the men in the pilot-boat could not hear each other speak at a distance of eight feet on the deck - they could not see the length of the boat before them in consequence of the sea-drift.'*
Can you imagine the scene? Yet they were expected to rendezvous with any vessel that needed a pilot, and then transfer that person over to the other vessel by either launching a small punt or by using a hoist. All in the pitch-darkness, during a raging hurricane!

Connection to the 'Royal Charter'

• Two pilot-boats were cruising off Anglesey on the night of the 25th - 26th of October, 1859, and both senior pilots gave evidence at the subsequent inquiry into the loss of the 'Royal Charter'.

• Although blue lights were seen by one of the pilot-boats, it proved impossible for them to make contact with the ship that had displayed them. That vessel may or may not have been the 'Royal Charter'.

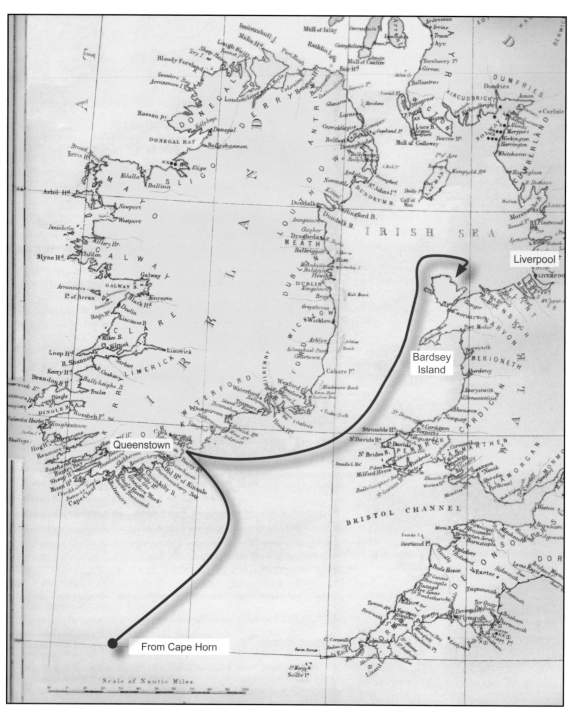

Almost home - The last leg of the route taken by the 'Royal Charter'.

CHAPTER SEVEN

The Final Return, August to October, 1859

TO ENGLAND IN 60 DAYS.

THE BLACK BALL & EAGLE LINE OF PACKETS.

For LIVERPOOL Direct on Wednesday 24th August, The Liverpool and Australian Navigation Company's magnificent armed steam-clipper ROYAL CHARTER 2,500 tons register, Thomas Taylor, Esq., Commander, having arrived after an unprecedented short passage of 59 days from Liverpool to Hobson's Bay, will be despatched on her return voyage on the above date.

The rapidity and regularity with which the Royal Charter performs her passages has rendered her famous, and placed her at the head of the numerous clippers trading to these colonies. The Royal Charter has accomplished the quickest passages on record between Liverpool and Hobson's Bay direct, her six passages occupied 59, 64, 62, 63, 64 and 59 days respectively; and she has made the run from Hobson's Bay to Liverpool in 62 & 63 days.

The accommodation for passengers on board this splendid vessel is beyond comparison.

The saloon is a magnificent apartment of 100 feet long, and fitted up in a most luxurious style. It is separated from the sleeping-rooms by corridors on each side. The staterooms are unusually large, and fitted with every regard to the comfort of passengers, and furnished with every requisite, including bedding, linen etc.

The Ladies' Boudoir is elegantly furnished with lounges, easy-chairs, piano, baths etc. There is also a complete library on board for the use of saloon passengers.

Second-class passengers will find the accommodation on board this vessel superior to first cabins of most ships in this trade, the cabin being furnished with every requisite, exclusive of bedding, etc. Stewards are appointed to wait on this class, the meals being placed on the tables at the appointed hours ready cooked. The ship provides crockery, glass and tableware.

The third-class accommodation is extremely spacious, and well-ventilated by side-ports. The sleeping-berths are all enclosed, and will be found on inspection all that can be desired. The dietary scale is most liberal.

An experienced surgeon will accompany the ship. A stewardess is provided for the comfort of lady passengers.

A cow will be carried for use of saloon passengers.

RATES OF PASSAGE MONEY
Saloon ... ... Per arrangement
Second Cabin ... ... £35.
Third Cabin ... ... £18 and £20.

Who could resist such an appealing advert as this one? Only sixty-two or sixty-three days from Melbourne to Liverpool! That was a fantastic record, but there was no mention of the 94-day passage of the previous year. Those who did answer the advert were a real cross-section of society, with a mixture of those who had become rich from a successful period in the gold-diggings, those who had become disillusioned at their lack of success in the colony, and those heading for England for their own personal reasons. English, Welsh, Scots, Irish, German, Protestant, Catholic, Jew, rich-man, poor-man, successful, failed, respectable, dishonest, jewellers, doctors, diggers, blacksmiths, drapers -- they all gladly booked a berth on the famous clipper in the expectation of being safely in Liverpool before the end of October. However, most of them were soon to die together on the east coast of Anglesey, at the end of a rapid and most pleasant voyage.

Laden with her cargo of human beings, animal hides, wool, a vast amount of gold and 45 tons of copper the 'Royal Charter' steamed out of Port Phillip on the 26th of August, 1859, and headed south into the Southern Ocean. The journey to Queenstown was fast and largely uneventful, except for one near-miss when:

.... on rounding Cape Horn, in the dead of night, they narrowly escaped a shoal of immense icebergs, which took them off their guard, for at first they were supposed to be clouds.

Thankfully, they were safe for the time being as they headed north through the South Atlantic and across the equator to pause briefly at Queenstown on the southern coast of Ireland.

The brief pause off Ireland provided an ideal opportunity for Captain Taylor to report his imminent arrival at Liverpool by sending a message to Gibbs, Bright & Co. by telegraph, and for passengers to post letters home announcing that they would soon be back in England. With no time to waste, the 'Royal Charter' unloaded some of the mail-bags, while seventeen passengers took the fortunate decision to leave the ship here. One of them was a Mr. Lynch, who afterwards made a list of those steerage passengers that he had become acquainted with on the voyage.

Mr. Holland, wife and three children; had been in India, and was in the volunteer corps. Two brothers named Hogarth, from Scotland; one was married, and had a little boy about eight years old. Mr. and Mrs. Lyons, from London, had two sons, one about ten and the other about twelve. Mr. Lyons was a watchmaker. Mrs. Atkey, somewhere near London, had a girl about sixteen. Mr. and Mrs. Kennedy, from Bruff, county Limerick, and three children. Mrs. Willis and two children, one a little boy about nine, and a girl eleven years, English. Mr. Faulkner and little girl, about six years old. Mr. Barrett, belonged to the medical profession, and was employed to take care of Mr. Henry, a lunatic, English. A young man, native of Dublin, about twenty-six, named Kelly, dark foxy hair, worked at Prahran, near Melbourne, brickmaking. A musician, named Harris, an Irishman, but was going to see his brother in London, or some of his friends, age about twenty-eight, foxy whiskers and hair, low size, but stout and smart looking. Mr. Wickett, another musician, about thirty, dark complexion and dark hair. George Taylor, age about forty-five, was going to Belfast, and went out to Melbourne as doctor in the *Ben Nevis*, and was only just recovering from colonial fever; was but a few months in Australia. Henry Laughton, from some part of Lincolnshire, was going home to his wife and children, and was seven years in the colony; he had a son ten years old, who wrote him a letter to come home, and it was signed John Hudson Laughton. William J. Green, London; had been some time in South Australia. Edward Allen, London, red hair, and about thirty years old; was a digger. A fine-looking young man named Bishop, about twenty-five years old, from London. Two brothers named Roe, English. Peter and John Morton, Cornwall, England. Bakewell, a draper, about twenty; tall, and light hair. I think he was from London. A most respectable man, named Wade; tall and slight make, with dark hair, and was some time at the Ovens Diggings; English, age about forty. A respectable man named Thompson; went out in the *Royal Charter*, obtained a situation in Melbourne, and was coming home for the purpose of bringing out his family. Mr. Thompson, aged about fifty: a stout-looking man, an engineer; had left his wife and family in Hobart Town, Tasmania. James Wyatt, a fine stout-looking young man, age about twenty-eight, dark complexion and dark hair, about six feet high; a native of England, and had been at sea before. An Irishman, named Cavanagh, low sized, but very stout; light hair, and age about thirty. I think he was from the county Limerick, but am not certain; had been in America, and had been sailoring for some time, and worked in a steamer that sailed between Melbourne and Launceston, Tasmania. An Englishman named Cowley, age about thirty-five. A stout-looking man named Grice, aged about forty-five. An old man and his son, from about Nenagh; I think their name was Faba. Charles Conway, from some part of England, age about twenty-eight, and was a working jeweller; was of low size and slight make, with light hair. William Ford, age about twenty-five, dark complexion and dark hair, of low size and slight make, and was a smart intelligent fellow; I think he was from London, or some part of England, and was working at the Ovens Diggings for some time. A young man named Purdy, a blacksmith, native of England; of low size, age about twenty-five, dark complexion. Joseph Moss, London, a Jew, age about forty-five; was in Australia before, and sailed in the *Kent*. Mr. Davis, a Jew, low size, dark hair, age about forty-three. Mr. Rea was going to London, and had been some time in New

Zealand, spoke French and English, age about forty, with thin features. A low size, thin-faced man, named Jones, age about forty, very much pock-marked. An old man, over fifty, low size, stout make, worked in a foundry in Castlemaine, was going home for his family. I wrote a direction on two cards for him, one was Dowles and the other Abergavenny; these were to put on his boxes or luggage. I think he worked for Mr. Varian, Castlemaine, and was an Englishman. John Tyreel, age about twenty-three, dark hair; was a native of some part of England. An Englishman named Jacob. George Sieter, a German, age thirty. Francis Weber, German, age twenty-six. A young man named Fowler, a German, age twenty-one. A young man named Hughes. Mr. James P. O'Dowd, of Dublin, who had made several voyages in the ill-fated vessel.

Leaving Queenstown in the afternoon of Monday the 24th of October, the 'Royal Charter' headed in a north-easterly direction towards the welcoming beam of the lighthouse at Bardsey Island at the western tip of North Wales, where she was approached the following morning by the steam-tug 'United Kingdom' which transferred eleven riggers to the clipper, as they needed a passage home to Liverpool. The ship's next landmark was the magnificent lighthouse of South Stack, which was reached at around 4.00 p.m. on the 25th, after which time the masts and superstructure of the 'Great Eastern' could be vaguely made out in the distance as that 'monster ship' lay in Holyhead Harbour. Captain Taylor then continued northwards from Holyhead, keeping the 'Royal Charter' to the west and north of a cluster of islands called The Skerries, thereby avoiding an inshore passage which could have cut several miles off his journey. This shorter route is fraught with danger, and has proved to be the last resting place of many steamships and sailing vessels. The dangerous reefs of the East Platters, Coal Rock, Archdeacon Rock, Ethel Rock, Victoria Bank and Harry Furlong Rocks, combined with the small islands of the West Mouse, the Middle Mouse and the East Mouse, are littered with wreckage from wooden sailing vessels such as the 'Alert' and the 'Frankfield', iron barques such as the 'Earl of Chatham' and the 'Gilbert Thompson', along with the steamers 'Gulf of St. Vincent', 'Minerva', 'Fawn', 'Lord Athlumney', 'Edith Owen' and 'Dakota'. Even the expertise and local knowledge of a Liverpool Pilot was no safeguard from disaster along this northern coast of Anglesey, as evident from the loss of the almost new steamer 'Olinda', which ran onto the Harry Furlong Rocks five years earlier when under the direction of a local pilot. The Board of Trade investigation into that mishap concluded with the following indictment --

Having carefully examined the evidence, I have no hesitation in saying that the loss of the *Olinda* was occasioned by the imprudent conduct of the pilot in attempting a narrow and dangerous passage .... I do think the conduct of Mr. Callister [*the pilot*] most culpable.

So, Captain Taylor was acting very wisely in keeping well to the west and north of the Skerries, especially as darkness was about to fall on a night of a new moon, when there would be no moonlight whatsoever. Despite signalling for a pilot, he had failed to contact a pilot-boat, and the last thing he wanted was to endanger the 'Royal Charter', his passengers, the crew and the ship's golden cargo in the last few hours of his round-the-world journey. However, he had earlier assured his passengers that *'he expected to be on the lee side of Mrs. Taylor'*, so perhaps he did have a good reason to be hurrying home rather than heading for shelter or spending more time in the remote chance of finding a pilot. Rounding the Skerries, and with the guiding light at Point Lynas showing the western approach to Liverpool Bay, the passengers and crew were becoming excited at the prospect of meeting relatives and loved-ones on their arrival at Liverpool within the next few hours.

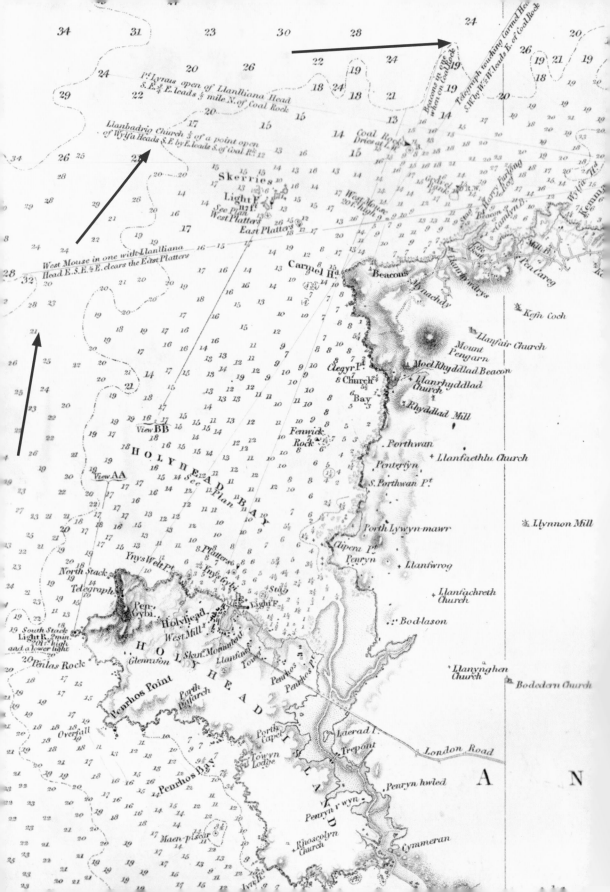

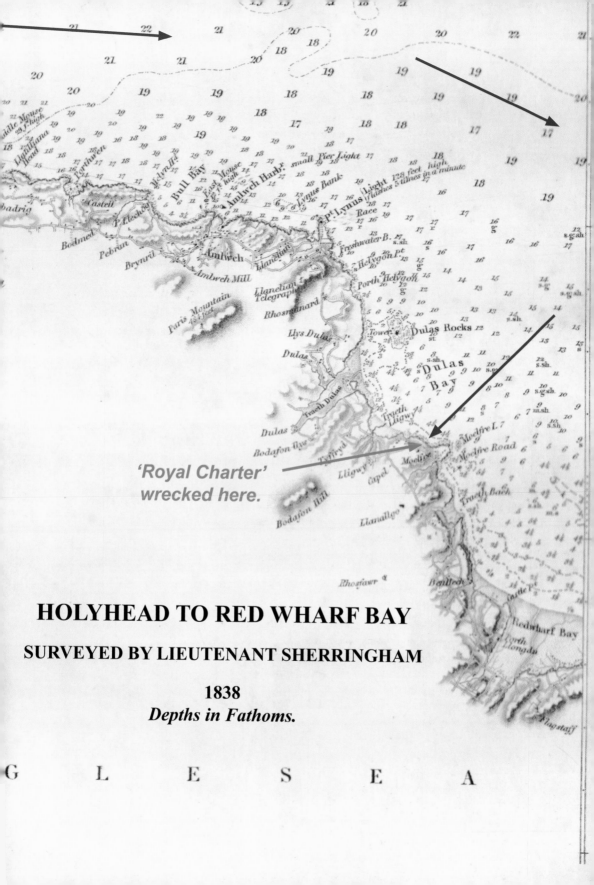

'Royal Charter'
wrecked here.

HOLYHEAD TO RED WHARF BAY

SURVEYED BY LIEUTENANT SHERRINGHAM

1838
Depths in Fathoms.

G   L   E   S   E   A

Image courtesy of The State Library of Queensland (image 164894).

> **"Beaumaris 26th Oct. Received E.T. at 5.55.**
>
> **The *ROYAL CHARTER*, from Melbourne to Liverpool, a total wreck at Moelfra."**

This simple statement, sent by the Electric Telegraph (E.T.) and published in Lloyd's List of Thursday the 27th of October, 1859, was one of the first public announcements of the loss of the 'Royal Charter'. What a shock it must have been to all those who had received news of her safe arrival at Queenstown, especially as some of the passengers and crew had posted letters in Ireland, and these dispatches had been safely delivered to their loved ones waiting in anticipation of a joyful reunion.

Royal Charter, off Queenstown.
Oct. 24, 1859.

Dear father, mother, and sister,
I am writing this from Cork, but we will not be in Liverpool for twenty-four hours, and then I shall write you again. I shall have to remain in Liverpool one day to procure some things, and start next morning, so I shall get into Maryport at night. Isabella, you must make a good apple cake, and should you have any strangers in the house, you must contrive to let father, mother, yourself and me have tea in a place by ourselves. Don't tell anyone I am coming, not even a relation, till I have seen you all. And Isabella, you must come down to meet the night train, and stand in front of the ladies' waiting-room. In order that you may know me, for I am much changed in my appearance since I left, I will call the word 'Brown'. Jonathan and John were quite well when I left, and I hope I will find you all as well as this leaves.

Yours, etc.,
Joseph Robinson.

The Carnarvon and Denbigh Herald

AND NORTH AND SOUTH WALES ADVERTISER

Saturday, October 29, 1859

Loss of the *Royal Charter*.

This splendid clipper steamer, reported to be off Queenstown on Monday, after a passage of only 58 days, now lies in fragments along the north shore of Anglesey, while its treasure and about 400 of its living freight lie beneath the treacherous water.

The vessel sailed from Melbourne on the 26th of August, with nearly 460 passengers, a gold freight of 79,000 ozs., besides wool and hides. After the telegram had been received that the *Royal Charter* was in the Channel*, many of the passengers' friends assembled in Liverpool on Wednesday morning to welcome them back to England, but at that period most of them had passed from time into eternity.

On Thursday morning, she passed Holyhead, taking from a tugboat, which was cruising off the land, eleven men - Liverpool riggers - who had assisted in taking an American ship into Newport. She continued her way down channel, every now and then making signals for a pilot, which were unnoticed. After reaching nearly as far as the Orme's Head, they had attempted to put her about, but failed, the storm at this time raging frightfully. Having drifted as far as Moelfra, in 20 fathoms water, at about 11 o'clock at night, they cast anchor, still keeping the machinery going. The vessel rode well to her anchors till between 2 and 3 in the morning, when her port cable parted. It is supposed that if the captain had at this time acceded to the request of cutting away the masts, she would have been right. Shortly after, her second cable parted, and she went against the rocks head on, and canted to the westward. The masts were now cut away and every means used to signal to the shore – firing of cannon, blue lights, large torches of tow** and tar etc., but without effect.

These efforts failing to attract the country people, one of the crew – a Maltese - swam to the shore with a log-line, and succeeded in getting a hawser fastened around some of the rocks. At this time the vessel was broadside on, beating heavily, and from this time all discipline was at an end, and crew and passengers saved themselves the best way they could. In less than an hour she parted at the main hatches, and shortly after parted in the fore-hatch – leaving all on board to struggle in the boiling waves. The mate was killed at the second parting, one of the boats falling on him. Just before she parted, the captain was seen on the poop, giving orders to clear away the boats, and after the parting he was seen in the after part of the vessel, jammed in by pieces of the wreck. The second mate was killed on the beach, the boat in which he got there capsizing upon him. Little of the struggling of the sufferers was witnessed, the angry waters engulphing them almost instantaneously.

The next tide, a few of the bodies were washed on shore, and when we left the scene of the wreck on Thursday evening, about 45 bodies had been recovered. Thirty four lay in Llanallgo Church. Six in the church of Penrhos Lligwy – the other five were brought up above high water to wait the morning light to place them with the others.

Amongst them was an Irishwoman aged 82; a Jewess, 65; a single woman, 30; a person supposed to be a Mrs. Rose, lately married, daughter of a Mr. Pratt, of London; Miss Russell, daughter of Mr. William Russell, saved, but who lost his wife and two other daughters; an infant boy, son of a Mr. Smith, who with his wife were also drowned; Mr. Henry, a lunatic, supposed

* Channel = St. George's Channel (Irish Sea) ** tow = the coarse part of flax or hemp.

The site of the wreck in an easterly gale (Force 8). It was Force 12 in 1859.

to be highly connected in London; a sailor, whose left arm was tattooed from above the elbow to the back of his hand with various devices, *SAR*, the picture of a sailor holding the English flag, etc. etc. On his left leg was tattooed *J. ROBERTS*, and on the inner ankle a man's face; the sailmaker; and a Mr. Glover, who was going to London to have an operation performed on one of his eyes. £56 were found on him.

Among the sufferers were the following from this neighbourhood – Thomas Jones and Wm. Davies, of this town, sailors; Griffith Jones, carpenter, of Nevin; John, son of Mr. Thomas Rees, of Pistill, Nevin, passenger; William Hughes, of Amlwch; Henry Williams, Cemaes; John Jones, Holyhead; Isaac Griffiths, Moelfra, sailors. The latter was within half-a-mile of his father's house; and Anthony Belt, a native of Newcastle-on-Tyne, shipped as one of the crew at Melbourne.

The following is a list of persons saved, which we obtained by courtesy of John Williams, Esq., of Beaumaris, on the spot:-
SALOON PASSENGERS – W. H. Morse, Esq., Thos. Gundry Esq., Henry C. Taylor, Esq.

SECOND AND THIRD PASSENGERS – Colin McPhiel, John Judge, William John Ferris, James McCappin, William Russell, --- Bradbury, Samuel Grenfell, Carl Bertel, N. Hagen, John Loone, S. Edward Gapper, William Bowden.

THE RIGGERS TAKEN ON BOARD – SAVED – James White, --- Pritchard, Patrick Divine, Thomas Cunningham, William Barton.

DROWNED – Henry Aspinall, Thomas Cochrane, William Thomas, Thomas Neil, Richard Jones, Peter Topham.

THE CREW SAVED – Wm. Foster, carpenter, Geo. Suaicar, boatswain's mate, Owen Williams, quarter-master, David Strongman, ditto, Thomas McCormick, saloon steward, Thomas Ellis, store-keeper, John Stannard, stewards, John O'Brien, Edward Wilson, Thos. Griffiths, Thomas Timms, William M'Arthur, Henry Evans, John Richards, George M'Given, Joseph Rogers, and William Draper, seamen, Wm. Hughes, apprentice.

FROM AN EYE WITNESS.

Beaumaris, Wednesday evening.

I have just returned from the wreck of the *Royal Charter*, off Moelfra, about nine miles from this place. She has completely broken up; iron plates, rivets, beams, - and the shattered remains of the ill-fated ship strew the rocks all round. In the midst of these are innumerable remnants of garments of persons of both sexes, torn and jagged to pieces. When I left at dusk, the only parts of the ship standing were a small portion of the stern, with the wheel and apparatus for lifting the screw, and a fore compartment. From the statements of the survivors, it appears that the ship struck at three o'clock this morning, and broke up at seven. Before striking, she parted her cables, one after another, and tried to steam off the coast, but she rapidly drifted on shore, the winds at the time blowing a hurricane. She was firing guns and rockets, and burning blue lights for hours before she struck. One of the survivors describes the effects as "lighting up the channel." She had no pilot on board. From what I could learn, the loss of life must amount to upwards of 300 including all the officers and all the women and children, not one of whom were saved. In fact, from what I could ascertain by going among and conversing with the survivors, I don't think that more than 20 or 30 persons are saved. Several bodies, including those of two women and two children, were washed ashore before I left. The greater part were found just round the point at the entrance of Red Wharf Bay. The majority of them were greatly mutilated. One very touching incident occurred. In the midst of fragments of massive ironwork, and the shivered remains of a mighty ship, was found, perfect and unbroken on the rocks, a small photograph - the portraits of a lady and gentleman, both young and evidently of superior position. The collector of customs at this port, who, today, is the principal person in authority of the wreck, carries this photograph in his hand and compares it with the lineaments [*facial features*] of the dead washed up, but as yet without having succeeded in establishing the identity of either of the originals. In the distress and confusion that prevailed today, I could not collect any accurate statement of the names of the survivors; and, as a mistake in this particular would be productive of very painful results, I refrain from anticipating the official return.

The survivors are, however, alas! very, very few. On Monday, the passengers entered into a subscription for a testimonial to Captain Taylor, who, in acknowledging this token of their esteem, assured them they would be in Liverpool in twenty-four hours.

It is to be hoped that a competent staff of either coast guard or military will be immediately dispatched to the scene of the disaster, to protect as much as possible so valuable a cargo, which, so far as the passengers' gold is concerned, is very much scattered about. I saw men picking sovereigns out of the holes of the rocks, almost as they would shellfish. They were, however, as well organised by the collector of customs, who is also receiver of droits, as was possible under the circumstances.

All described the sea as being terrific at the time: indeed, yesterday, when the gale had abated, the scene was a very fearful one, and great caution was required in approaching the ledge of the rocks. I have written these few lines under the impression that they may perhaps contain the first information conveyed to the Liverpool public by an eyewitness; if not, do not publish them. The gentleman who bears this, and who accompanied me to the wreck, calls at Messrs. Gibbs, Bright & Co. with the view of affording them any information he can.

Yours etc,

J. H. Gregory

P.S. - I have neither time nor spirits, after what I have just witnessed, to make a copy of this, I fear in some parts, almost illegible letter.

'fragments of massive ironwork, and the shivered remains of a mighty ship'.

LATEST PARTICULARS

Mr. Wagstaff, a visitor to the scene of the wreck, has reached Liverpool, and states that the vessel drifted into Dulas Bay, where two anchors were let go, the screw, however, being kept in motion, to mitigate the strain upon the cables.

The bodies which have so far been discovered are for the most part dreadfully mutilated. The rocks were strewn with money and valuables belonging to passengers. A bag containing one hundred sovereigns was picked up, and large quantities of loose sovereigns also found. The boatswain's mate (saved), brought away £400* with him. Mr. Smith, the collector of customs, was indefatigable in preserving order and preventing plunder after the wreck. It is confidently expected that the bullion will be recovered. A detachment of men from the *Hastings* frigate (lying in the Mersey) has been sent to assist the local authorities. As the *Royal Charter* had the latest dates, her passenger list was not fully known, nor can it be known until the arrival of the next overland mail. When the vessel first struck, Captain Taylor went down into the saloon, and told the passengers to keep up their spirits, and that there would be little danger if they kept calm and obeyed the instructions of the officers. A clergyman, the Rev. Mr. Hodge, was most assiduous in giving religious comfort and offering up prayers. The repeated strokes of the vessel, however, upon the rocks told too plainly the story of the destruction, and soon the passengers became fearfully alarmed and excited. When she parted, large numbers of the passengers were crushed to death beneath a falling funnel and other portions of the machinery. Mr. Stephens, the chief officer, was killed by the falling of the rigging. When last seen alive, and he was the last man seen on board, Captain Taylor was clinging to a spar. He cried "There is hope yet", when, according to one report, the boat fell from the davits upon his head, and he perished.

* Suaicar, the boatswain's mate, later denied this under oath.

Glass and a rowlock from the wreck.

The vast majority of the information given in this and other descriptions of the wreck of the 'Royal Charter' is second-hand, usually being a newspaper reporter's version of what was said in court or by a survivor, or it was a visitor's description of the scene written days, weeks, or even months after the event. There are only a few descriptions of the catastrophe given by those who were there at the time, but the following letter was written by Samuel Edward Gapper, a second-class passenger who had been earning a living in Australia by operating agricultural machinery. He was fortunate to survive the disaster thanks to the heroism of the men of Moelfre who rushed to the scene and plucked him and others from certain death in the raging surf, but he lost his personal savings of around £50 in the process. He later gave evidence at the inquest and the inquiry, and wrote this eyewitness account of his lucky escape and the horrors that he saw on that fateful dawn of the 26th of October, 1859.

Moelfra, Anglesea,
November 27, 1859.

My Dear Friends,
I hope and trust you will have received my two former letters ere this, in which I informed you of my shipwreck on the above coast. It was a fearful scene, one I shall never, never forget. Picture to yourselves four hundred and fifty individuals in a space of 336 feet long by 41 broad, on the deck of a ship, encumbered by the cordage of fallen masts, all the spare yards (of which there was an abundance) broken, and tattered sails. The houses on deck all in pieces, bulwarks smashing, decks breaking up, with the waves breaking from eight to ten feet over all, and within 50 yards of shore, inhospitable in appearance, being a craggy limestone — sharp points jutting out here and there through the tremendous surf. Picture this, if you can, to your imagination, and you have before you what I had before me in reality on that dreadful morning. After an hour of this, the ship parted amidships, the death warrant of hundreds; then came the dreadful work, but no wild shouts, no desponding, noisy cry, but a deep, terrible, stunning groan of "All is lost!" "All hope is gone!" It was now about half flood tide, the waves increasing in height every moment. When the ship parted, I went on the poop deck. The first thing I saw was a number of ladies struggling in the water on the poop — I rescued one. Some of them went overboard, others, as the water ran off, came round again. Then two or three tremendous waves came thundering over us, smothering everything, and drove me and the female that was in my arms away to leeward. Again I was able to get up and return to where I was standing before, in the companionway from the saloon to the poop. Many now came on the poop; males, females,

and parents with children in their arms. Now came a fearful scene. The quarter boats were still fastened in their places, the keel on the rail of the poop; and many were trying to lower the leeward boat into the water, and I also had hold of the davit line. On looking round between the seas, I saw that the boat to windward was adrift, and hung by the davits; thinking the next wave might tear it all adrift as the ship righted, I again ran and stood inside the companionway. At that moment, a wave appeared to come over the deck, dashed the boat against the saloon skylight, and capsized over to leeward, killing and crushing all who were in its way. The boat, in passing across the deck, smashed everything that it struck, and I escaped by a few inches only. The next wave drove this, and the leeward boat, with all who stood there, into the sea, and I never saw them more. I now saw our Captain on the weather side of the deck, struggling with the water; he had hold of the davit line which the boat carried across with it, but he could not get on his feet, being a very heavy man, and having on an overcoat and leggings. It was reported by some one that he was drunk, but I saw Captain Taylor many times that awful night, walking the deck with the telescope under his arm, and occasionally looking at a light called Point Lynas, steady, sober, and doing, to the best of my judgment, his duty as a seaman. After struggling about a quarter of an hour, he was washed to the leeward, being driven off the poop into some of the wreck that lay alongside, and there drowned. I, about this time, took off my coat and trousers, and threw them and all I had away, except my knife; I also took off from the lady I had rescued, all her clothes except her chemise, corset, boots and stockings, as I now saw we must soon leave the ship, or we should be engulphed with the wreck as I could feel the vessel working beneath my feet. At this time, I saw between the waves that all in the saloon was being smashed to atoms, but I could hear no noise save the crashing masses of water and the howling of the cold north-east wind. Some of the saloon passengers came on the poop, but were dashed into eternity in a few moments. I saw one young lady, a Miss Jane Fowler, standing to leeward of the stump of the mizzen mast, for I should think five minutes. After a tremendous wave had passed, I turned to look for her, but she was gone. The ship now appeared to be breaking up amidships, the forecastle and poop still holding together, but I saw I must be going, and seeing a studding-sail boom laying end on from the wreck to the rocks, the thought flashed across my mind, that I should perhaps be able to get, hand over hand, to the end of it, and from that to the shore. I must try the chance. No sooner thought, than I tried to do it. I took the lady in my arms, got her over the ship, stood by her side holding on by the leeward davit rope while a tremendous wave passed over us; I then fell into the water, held open my arms, and shouted to her to drop. At that moment a wave, if possible larger than any before, tore me from her, and dashed me away among the debris of the wrecks. I now thought of myself, as I could not reach the ship again; the first trial convinced me of the imminent danger I was in. I never felt afraid until now, but it even now, was not fear, it was a sense of drowning, as I could not get my head to the surface to breathe. At last I got my nose above water, breathed, then down, down again; at the surface, I caught sight of a piece of the wreck passing me, grasped it, the next moment it was torn from me, but it brought me clear of the ship into the surf. This was not half so bad, as I had time to get breath between the waves, and I think the fourth took me on the rocks. From this time I can remember but little. It was a struggle for life. I was much bruised, but thank God I am able to get about again, my arm is the only thing that troubles me; you may well suppose I did not spare it in that awful struggle for life. When I was well up on the rock, one of the fishermen in the neighbourhood jumped down and picked me up, and the boatswain's mate assisted him in carrying me to his house.

S. E. Gapper.

The Carnarvon and Denbigh Herald

AND NORTH AND SOUTH WALES ADVERTISER

Saturday, November 5, 1859

Further Details of this Dreadful Catastrophe George Suaicar, the boatswain's mate, says:- "On Monday we left Queenstown in the afternoon, after putting some passengers on board the pilot-boat *Petrel*, who desired to be landed. We proceeded on with calm weather and water smooth. We made Ballycotton Light at half past seven, p.m., and Youghal Light, on the Irish coast, at half past eight. Reached the Menay Light at nine, made the Nook Light in half-an-hour, and sighted Tusker at about half-past eleven. On Tuesday morning, saw Bardsey, at which time the wind began to freshen. Off Bardsey, the steam-tug, *United Kingdom* came alongside, and handed on board some newspapers, asking if we would give a free passage to the eleven riggers, as we were going to Liverpool and the tug was not going until she got a tow. The riggers were taken on board. The wind increasing, we took in the square sails; and at ten a.m., the wind increasing, we took in all the fore and aft sails. In the afternoon, made Holyhead at half-past one, and at half-past four were right ahead of Holyhead harbour. Could see the steamship *Great Eastern*. At a quarter to eight on Tuesday evening, were abreast of the Skerries, distant about a mile and a half. At this time the wind had increased to a heavy gale, and the ship was making little or no progress through the water. She was driving up with the strength of the tide, and nearing the shore; the steam had no effect, but we did all we could to keep the ship off. The main topsail was lowered, but she still drifted. Clewed up the main topsail, and the hands were sent up to furl it. The wind had now increased considerably, almost blew the sail from the yard, and it became entangled on the starboard side. It was difficult to get the sail stowed. At this time, Mr. Bean, the third officer, with several seamen and myself, were trying to make the sail fast, but could not succeed in accomplishing it. Shortly afterwards, orders were given to cock-bill the port anchor, and let go. This was done, giving her seventy-five fathoms of chain. The vessel was steaming the whole time. Finding she was dragging, we paid out all the port chain. The vessel was still steaming. We let go the starboard anchor. Still finding her dragging, and the wind had now increased to a perfect hurricane. We then went to get the stream-anchor up, and while doing so, the starboard chain parted. I then felt the ship canting over to port, and fancied the wind had changed. Orders were then given to cut away the mainmast, which was done, and in a few minutes afterwards she struck on a bank. The captain gave orders to the engineer to give her as much steam as he could, to harden her on the bank. It was then about three-quarters ebb tide.

The place where she struck was at the west of Moelfre, eastward of Point Lynas. Heard the captain give orders to starboard the helm, to keep her on the shore, so that the sea would not have so much power on her broadside. When she became hardened on, the chief officer gave me and the boatswain orders to cut the main and maintop mast stays, as they were lying across the boat, so that the boat could be cleared in case of need. We did so. The chief boatswain and myself were afterwards sitting on a spar, on the deck-house, the sea at the time making a complete breach over the ship. I then went forward to look out and ascertain whether we were on sand or rock, when I discovered the land about thirty yards away. I went back and told the chief officer that it was land; and he said 'we will loose the foretopmast staysail, and, when the tide makes up, run her up'. I said it would be as well to give her the foresail. It was then getting daylight.

I volunteered to go ashore with a line to get a hawser ashore, immediately after which I felt the ship striking heavier than ever, supposing it was in consequence of the tide making. The sea still making over her with even greater violence than ever.

The captain was at this time on deck, standing by the steam telegraph. I told the chief officer again I was willing to go ashore with a line, and do everything in my power to save life. Asked him if he would allow me a few minutes to put my lifebelt on, and he said of course he would. I afterwards told the boatswain I was going to try and get a line on shore, and he said it was useless, the sea was running too high. Afterwards had a small line slung around my body, and wished someone to volunteer to attend to it while I swam ashore. After some hesitation, a man volunteered. Just as I was being lowered into the water, someone called out that there was a line onshore from forward. Upon hearing that, I did not go. A hawser was got onshore and made fast to a rock, and with this myself and some of the other seamen saved our lives. The hawser was made fast by several of the inhabitants onshore, who came to render assistance. After the ship struck, all the passengers were directed to go aft until the hawser could be properly got out, so that as many as possible might be saved. Shortly after this the vessel parted amidships; and a large number of passengers, standing on the deck where she parted, were swept into the sea and drowned. The boats were smashed to pieces by the fury of the gale, and the others could not be lowered, so that none of them could be made available. The passengers saved were driven onshore by the force of the waves. Sixteen of the crew got ashore by the hawser. An endeavour was made to get a second hawser ashore to rescue the female passengers, but this could not be accomplished. Not a single female passenger was saved. In three hours after the vessel struck, she began to go to pieces. Saw about seventy passengers on the port bow, all anxiously awaiting some means of getting them on shore, but a heavy sea which struck the starboard bow, stove it in. The ship gave a lurch, and the people were all driven into the sea and drowned. Some of the passengers saved were thrown upon the rocks, and picked up by the crew and others who came to render assistance."

AFTER THE CABLES PARTED
The scene after the cables parted was described as follows:- "On entering the saloon, Mr. Allen, the head steward of the second cabin, came and told the passengers that they had better not go on deck, as it might cause confusion. The order was implicitly obeyed. Time passed anxiously and wearily; the storm still raged. Suddenly the vessel struck, not violently, not even with sufficient force to throw the passengers off their seats. Water then came pouring down into the cabin. A voice shouted for the second-class passengers to go into the lower saloon, as the mainmast was going to be cut away. The passengers nearest to the entrance doors attempted to open them (they were hinged in the ceiling), and finding some difficulty they were immediately smashed. Still there was no hurrying or crushing; all silently took their seats. On deck, sailors and officers, stripped to the waist, laboured to cut away the mainmast. The vessel rolled and thumped so heavily, that in delivering their blows the men were many times thrown on to the deck, but the motion of the vessel assisted the work; the waves, too, lent their aid and soon the mast tottered, then fell with a crash overboard. Immediately afterwards the raging sea threw the vessel higher up upon the rocks. The foremast was then cut away, and almost at the same time the mizzen-mast broke off at the mizzen-mast head. Boats were lowered, but the moment they touched the waves, they were carried away with irresistible force against the rocks, and their inmates were either crushed or drowned in the sea. No boat could live in such a storm. There appeared scarcely any

need of boats, so close upon the shore was the vessel. Having struck, the vessel slewed round port side to the rocks. When in the lower saloon, about this time, an apprentice boy, Charley, entered, telling the passengers from the captain that they were to keep up their hearts; all was well; they were only on a sandbank. The passengers still remained quietly in the cabin. Mr. Cowie, the second mate, accompanied by the purser and two men, came down; they were stripped, having on only their shirt and trousers. They passed through the saloon to the powder magazine; as they went bidding the passengers keep up their hearts, they were not far from the shore. The water entered the saloon at the same time, and the waves striking more heavily, the vessel thumped harder. Those in the lower saloon then passed into the upper one. There they found assembled some of the first and third class passengers. No words were spoken, hope and fear struggled for the mastery in their countenances - by this alone, was it seen that life and death were in the balance. The stillness of the assembly was broken once - a young lady, about twenty, Miss Murray, who was on board with her father, mother, and brother, fainted, and was immediately carried to her cabin, from whence she never emerged.

Daylight now began to dawn. They had been tossing on the sea and labouring on the rocks all night. Shortly after daylight, a third-class passenger came down; he had on only his trousers, and had been in the bows of the vessel for several hours. He said that the forepart of the vessel and the bows touched the land; everyone could wade ashore. All hopes of saving the vessel having disappeared, and the boats having been rendered unserviceable, the captain ordered a hawser to be got ready. A Maltese seaman, named Joseph Rogers, volunteered to swim ashore with it. The line was made fast to his body, and the noble fellow gallantly dropped overboard and breasted the waves with the resolution of a British sailor. For a time he was lost to sight, as

wave after wave dashed over the vessel and broke upon the rocks; then the line tightened, and the man was seen clambering up the rocks. The villagers crowded round, the hawser was hauled ashore and made fast to a rock, a boatswain's chair was slung on to the rope, and a number of sailors ordered ashore to work it. Every order was obeyed without confusion. Amongst others landed were two brave fellows – George Suaicar, Malta, boatswain's mate, and Wm. Foster, Liverpool, carpenter. Word was passed down to the saloon that the ladies were to come on deck. There was a movement immediately towards the staircase. At the same time the ship's timbers began to creak; then there were two heavy thumps experienced, and the ship broke in two across the main hatch. A great number of passengers were standing amidships, and when the vessel parted they disappeared for ever. At the same time, a boat abaft the fore-rigging fell. The chief officer, Mr. Stephens, and the chief engineer, Mr. Rogers, were standing under it, and both were killed. A second line was attempted to be carried on the shore, but failed. Mr. Russell, his wife, and two children, on gaining the deck, found that they were on the stern part of the vessel, separated from the fore part by a yawning chasm, into which every moment human beings were dropping or being driven by the waves. It was a moment of the intensest anguish. As each clung to the rail, at the top of the stairs, a hurried farewell was spoken; then they awaited death calmly. Mr. Russell had several times essayed to get a rope. So close were they to the shore, he imagined he might fasten the rope around his family, cast the rope ashore and save them. In vain were his efforts. They were still clinging to each other, when a huge wave came and separated them. When the wave had passed, Mr. Russell's eldest girl was missing; a box had been washed on her leg. Mr. Russell moved the box and liberated her. Again for a few minutes they were united. Another wave came - they lost

Dive-boats over the 'Royal Charter". Note how the wreck lies very close to the shore.

hold of the rail; Mrs. Russell, and the twin girls were washed against the side of the vessel, Mr. Russell overboard. As the water returned, Mr. Russell sprang at a piece of iron, which hung from the side, seized it, then caught a rope; in another moment he was on deck. His youngest daughter was nearest to him; he attempted to lay hold of her, had his hands just on her, when another wave came, broke over the ship, poured down with irresistible force, and washed him overboard again. For a time he was struggling in the waves convulsively; he clutched at something which he felt against his body; it was only a piece of canvas; another moment he felt seaweed under his feet. A wave came, he was almost insensible, yet he saw a man standing before him. Was it a dream, or a reality? He stretched out his hand, he grasped another hand; yet another wave came, and, hand unloosed, he was borne back again; a mightier wave broke, and his hand was again grasped - it held him - he was saved. In a moment or two he recovered his senses, he was lying on a rock; he turned his eyes seaward, there was no living creature on the stern of the vessel. He then became insensible again and was born by the villagers to the hospitable cottage of Mr. and Mrs. Lewis, in the neighbourhood. There were one or two scenes just before Mr. Russell was finally washed off the wreck which imprinted themselves on his memory; words uttered which no time can ever obliterate; they were the last glimpses caught of fellow-voyagers; the dying expressions of old companions.

Mr. Henderson, a merchant, of Melbourne, on his way to London, was holding onto the binnacle with a gentleman named Watson, one of the firm of Watson, Passmore and Co., of Melbourne, and he exclaimed "Oh Watson, all is gone!" A Jewess, named Markes, was jammed in near a place where the vegetables were kept, and her husband, in vainly endeavouring to release her, tore all her clothes to rags. They had two children on board, and came from Ballarat.

A gentleman, named Welsh, while in the lower saloon, tied two black canvas bags of gold around his neck: he was lost. Several other passengers fastened money about their persons: all were lost. Mr. Taylor, one of the saved, had £35 in his pockets when he jumped into the sea; on reaching shore he had £10 remaining. Mr. Gapper, another saved, lost about £50 out of his pockets while he was being carried ashore by the waves. A gentleman, named Bradbury, who was on his way to Manchester, dislocated his right ankle on board, and in endeavouring to free himself, he broke his leg; he afterwards lowered himself overboard into the sea, exchanged one piece of wood for another, shared it with a gentleman called Lewis, who was not hurt at all, was dashed against the rocks several times, was saved, and his companion was lost. When the vessel broke, an awful shriek – the death-cry of hundreds - was heard above the violence of the storm. On shore, the villagers and the sailors who had escaped unhurt, linked hands, and the bravest stepped into the surf to catch hold of those whom the waves bore towards them on their crests before they were drawn back into the sea. Foremost in one link was George Suaicar, and he was instrumental in laying hold of nine out of those rescued, until exhausted he fell senseless on the rock, and was borne away. William Foster was another who joined in forming the link. The vessel struck finally about seven, and broke about nine o'clock. On board were the officers of three vessels coming from Australia, and they, with the captain and officers of the ill-fated *Royal Charter,* were all lost."

PASSENGER'S NARRATIVE

Mr. James Russell, a passenger, belonging to Scotland, who had been seven years in Australia, and acquired considerable wealth, was below in his berth when the vessel struck. He had with him his wife and two young children, one aged ten and the other two and a half years. He was aroused by hearing a commotion on deck, and a fellow passenger, Mr. Smith, saying, "Oh, Mr. Russell, we are gone; we are drifting on shore." On getting to the deck, his worst fears were confirmed, as it appeared evident that little, if any, hope of rescue existed. The sea was breaking over the ship with terrific fury, and the persons on board were running frantically about the deck, in a state of despair. Having brought his family from below, he held them together as they stood on deck, the waves surging over them at every moment. In a minute or two, a surging sea carried away his wife and two children, and he never saw them more. He himself was then washed off the decks towards the shore, but a succeeding wave brought him back again. Another sea then struck him, and he was driven forward on the beach, and, as he himself described it, was saved by the miraculous hand of Providence. Mr. Russell had a considerable sum of money on board, the product of his enterprise and skill in Australia, and is now, comparatively speaking, penniless.

Mr. Wagstaff, of Liverpool, who visited the wreck on Thursday, says:- "I saw them bringing up another body, and of all the frightful sights I ever witnessed I never saw anything like this. Both legs were broken about a foot above the ankle; and his feet, which only hung by the skin, had been bent backwards, and tied to keep together. The bones were visible, his head was twisted round, and his bowels protruded. Another body we noticed with half a head off. One ear was hanging down, and the brains had been washed out. We went to the beach, and the first object we observed was the body of a female, apparently fourteen or fifteen years of age, but a friend said he noticed a ring on her finger. She had on a black jacket and a petticoat. Her face was very much cut with being knocked about among the rocks. While we were standing there, another body was brought up, which was identified to be that of the sail-maker – a fine, powerful fellow, who presented no marks of injury. There were some four or five bodies further on, but we did not go near them; in fact, our feelings were so harrowed by what we had seen that we could go no further, and came away."

Edward Wilson, a seaman, says:- "The scene on board was indescribable; nothing but confusion on deck, fore and aft. Passengers - saloon, cabin, and steerage all mixed together - fathers and mothers clasping their children in their arms, wives clinging to their husbands, shrieking, and crying, 'Save me, save me, don't leave me,' etc. Captain Taylor, who was perfectly calm and collected, did all that he could to allay their fears. The captain then sent word to the ladies to come forward and they should be put ashore on the hawser, but as soon as they came on deck they were washed overboard. Shortly after the hawser was got on shore, the ship began to go to pieces; she broke up aft, and a large portion of the deck fell on about 100 passengers, who were crowded together, completely crushing and mangling them. None of this group were seen again. After he got onshore, he sat down upon the rocks, watching the progress of the wreck, for it was impossible to render those upon the ship any assistance, and he described the sight as dreadful to look upon - mangled bodies floating about; men, women, and children standing upon the deck shrieking for assistance, while others were on their knees praying, others being dashed through the cabin doors by the waves and washed overboard. He states that when the ship went down there was a large number of passengers huddled together on deck, and the shrieks of the poor creatures as they met their death were utterly appalling.

The following is the narrative of the escape of James Dean from the wreck of this unfortunate vessel. He says he was in bed in a berth with four other passengers when the ship struck, and he was aroused by one of his fellow-passengers exclaiming "I think we're lost". He dressed himself, and after a few minutes prayer, ascended on deck, where he had not been more than a very brief period when the vessel parted in the centre "like the snapping of a tobacco stump." The people on board stood petrified, as it were, seemingly unable to make the slightest struggle for their lives, whilst their terror was increased by the awful scene presented, as unfortunate creatures fell and were crushed to atoms in the chasm separating the two parts of the ship. He never for a moment lost his presence of mind. He saw that most of those in the water struggled towards the large pieces of the wreck, and he saw also that most of those who trusted to these heavy portions of the vessel were crushed to death, and the bodies dreadfully mutilated against the rocks; mangled corpses, arms, legs, and even heads being discernible on the crest of many retreating waves. Though totally unable to swim, he jumped overboard, and just seized a box he saw floating near him. Almost at the very moment he grasped this, a head was thrust under his arm, and a second claimant appeared. Dean said it would not support both of them; so as soon as possible, he left the box for another piece of wood, and with this he was thrown upon the shore. He left his support and tried to gain a position of security, but ere he could do so, a wave overpowered him and carried him back to sea, where he became entangled in the floating remnants of the vessel, and it was with the greatest difficulty that he extricated himself. When he had succeeded in this, he was again thrown onshore. Whilst momentarily expecting the arrival of another wave, a rope was thrown to him, and by it he was finally drawn out of danger without experiencing any injuries or bruises, other than of very trifling description. He soon recovered strength, and was able to leave for Wigan on Friday morning. He was bringing home a cheque for a considerable sum of money, and before his voyage he had taken the precaution to enclose this in a waterproof belt which he kept around his waist. This cheque was therefore saved, and his only losses were his clothes and a small sum of money which was with them.

Timescales

From these and other narratives, we can get a rough idea of the logical sequence of events, although it must be borne in mind that the survivors recollections do not always agree with each other. It is also possible that some of the pocket-watches may not have been accurately set.

All times are approximate.

- Monday, October 24th. 1.00 - 4.00 p.m. The 'Royal Charter' called at Queenstown, in southern Ireland.
- Tuesday morning, October 25. She took on eleven riggers off Bardsey Island. The wind began to increase at 10.00 a.m.
- Tuesday, 1.30 p.m. She approached Holyhead, and passed that port at 4.00 p.m. There was a south-easterly wind.
- Tuesday, 6.00 to 8.00 p.m. With the floodtide to her advantage, she passed north-west of the Skerries in a north-easterly gale.
- Tuesday, 9.00 p.m. As the wind increased, Point Lynas was within sight.
- Tuesday, 10.00 p.m. to 10.45 p.m. - Attempts were made to stay the ship (i.e. to go about onto the other tack) but these failed.
- Tuesday, 10.15 p.m. High water. From now on, she was battling against the tidal-flow as this increased to full-ebb.
- Tuesday, c. 11.00 p.m. The port anchor was let go, then the starboard one. However, Mr. Morse said that this wasn't done until midnight.
- Wednesday, October 26. 01.30 - 02.00 a.m. The port anchor-cable parted, shortly followed by the starboard one. However, one report says that the starboard anchor-chain held until 02.30.
- Wednesday, 02.00 - 02.30 a.m. Less than an hour after the chains failed, the keel grounded on a sandy seabed while the tide was still falling. Some reports say this did not happen until around 03.00 to 3.30 a.m.
- Wednesday, 02.30 - 03.00 a.m. The mainmast was cut away, and in going over the side, it took the mizzen-top overboard as well.
- Wednesday, 03.45 am. The ship's crew began to cut away the foremast.
- Wednesday, c. 04.45. Low-water.
- Wednesday, 05.30 - 6.00 a.m. The rapidly-rising tide began to push her onto the rocks, putting an immense strain on the rivets holding the hull together.
- Wednesday, 06.00 - 6.30 a.m. With the oncoming of daylight, Joseph Rogers volunteered to take a line ashore. As the night turned from black to grey, the wreck was noticed by the local villagers, who immediately rushed to the scene.
- Wednesday, 07.00 As dawn broke over the wreck, Rogers succeeded in getting a line ashore so that he and the local helpers could establish a strong hawser between the ship's bow and the rocks.
- A boatswain's chair was set up to take passengers and crew ashore.
- Wednesday, 7.15 - 7.30 The ship broke up, trapping many passengers below and throwing others into the sea. Many of the passengers' pocket-watches stopped at around this time.

Tides and the underwater-terrain

Liverpool Mercury	HIGH-WATER	AT LIVERPOOL	
Tuesday, October 25.	MORNING	EVENING	HEIGHT
	Hour Minutes	Hour Minutes	Feet. Inches.
This Day	... 10. 41.	.... 11. 02	...... 17. 11.
Tomorrow	... 11. 23.	.... 11. 43	...... 18. 2.

Around the coast of Anglesey, both high- and low-water occur earlier than at Liverpool, so high-water at Moelfre on Tuesday the 25th was around 10.30 p.m., after which time the 'Royal Charter' would have been steaming eastwards directly into the fierce ebb-tide off the north coast of Anglesey. There were spring-tides on the 25th and 26th, perhaps the highest tides of the year. As Captain Taylor passed the guiding beacon at Point Lynas, he would have encountered the ferocious hurricane from the north-east, and by 2.00 a.m., the tidal-flow would have been at its peak, trying to carry his ship away to the west-north-west. In the early hours of Wednesday, October 26th, these two elements, wind and tide, were now attacking the 'Royal Charter' from points of the compass that were at least ninety degrees apart, putting a tremendous strain on the anchor-cables. It's no wonder that they snapped under the extreme load.

According to the evidence later given in court by the quartermaster, David Strongman, the port anchor-chain snapped at around one-thirty to two o'clock in the morning, followed shortly afterwards by the starboard one, and the ship first hit what they thought was a sandbank at around three to three-thirty in the morning. Low-water occurs at a little over six hours after high-water, so the tide would have been at its lowest point at a little past four a.m., although the ferocity of the onshore-wind may have altered these times somewhat.

Broadly speaking, the chains snapped on the full ebb-tide, and she first hit the sand at perhaps an hour before low-water. The seabed where she came ashore consists of gently-sloping sand to within about thirty metres of the high-water mark, but this then changes abruptly to steep-sided limestone cliffs. Needing at least seven metres to float in normal conditions, the clipper would have first come into contact with the seabed at the trough of a wave while still several hundred metres from the coast, and in the darkness it is no wonder that the captain said that they were embedded in the sand and would all be able to walk onshore within ten minutes.

Unfortunately, they would have been some distance from the actual coast as it was now approaching low-water on a spring-tide, and in the total darkness none of the ship's officers could have appreciated that they were in no position to walk or even swim ashore, and that the rising tide would soon pick up the 'Royal Charter' and fling her onto the rocky coast where, in the words of someone calling himself 'An Observer':

A large portion of those on board were engulphed or crushed to death, but previous to this, a great many had been washed away as the sea swept over the vessel or killed by the falling of masts, or lost in attempting to swim on shore. Directly the vessel divided, her destruction was very rapid, and in less than an hour, the *debris* thickly covered the shore in perfect splinters, there not being a piece of timber of any size (excepting masts) amongst the whole.

Mr. Smith, the local Receiver of Wreck, was to say at the inquiry under oath:

Saw the watches of several persons who had been washed ashore. They had all stopped somewhere between twenty minutes past seven and eight o'clock.

And still the tide was rising, the hurricane was blowing, and people were dying in their attempts to reach the safety of the rocks, only a few yards away.

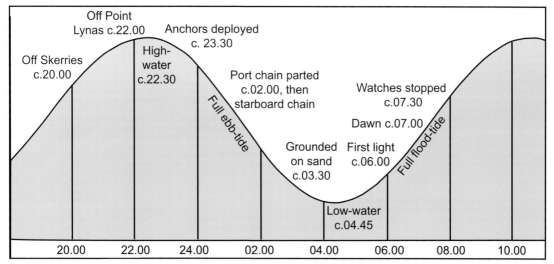

Off Skerries c.20.00

Off Point Lynas c.22.00

High-water c.22.30

Anchors deployed c. 23.30

Full ebb-tide

Port chain parted c.02.00, then starboard chain

Grounded on sand c.03.30

First light c.06.00

Low-water c.04.45

Watches stopped c.07.30

Dawn c.07.00

Full flood-tide

20.00 22.00 24.00 02.00 04.00 06.00 08.00 10.00

The above diagram shows the probable variation in the depth of water (tidal-range) at Moelfre on the 25th & 26th of October. Low water was at around 04.45 a.m., a little after the time that the 'Royal Charter' first came ashore. The tidal-range at Moelfre exceeds 7 metres (23 feet).

'We were in hopes it was ebb tide; but it was nearly low water when we struck. As the tide rose, the waves increased and smothered the ship fore and aft.' - Samuel Gapper

FLAT SAND

NORTH

SUBMERGED ROCKS, CLIFFS AND GULLIES

APPROXIMATE HIGH-WATER LINE

An electronic scan of the wreck-site showing the underwater terrain. Imagine an aerial photograph with the sea totally dried out. Below water, the flat sandy seabed changes abruptly to a rocky shore-line. The scan shows about 100 metres of the coastline.

131

The beautiful lighthouse at South Stack, near Holyhead.

Inquest at Holyhead. On Friday, the 18th instant, an inquest was held before W. Jones Esq., the county coroner, on the body of John Jones, who had been killed while in the execution of his duty on South Stack Island, as light-keeper, during the fearful hurricane of the 25th ult. The deceased lingered from the time of the accident until within few days previous to the inquest.

Henry Bowen, principal light-keeper at South Stack Island said deceased was his assistant, and he had known him for the last seven years. On the morning of Wednesday the 26th, after the storm, went to see if all was right. Saw deceased in a posture half sitting, and half lying, alone. His face was covered in blood. Found his cap within a few yards of the bridge, and the spot was covered with blood. There was no blood where he lay. There were several loose stones where the cap was found. Did not know of stones falling down before. Saw no people at the top of the rocks. When witness first saw deceased, he was calling out dolefully, waving his hand and groaning. Witness went for help and returned back with Wm. Parry. It was a severe storm and raining – the spray washing over. The storm must have brought the stones down.

Dr. Jones attended the deceased the same morning. He had a compound fracture of the skull. There was no hopes of him when first seen by the doctor.

Anne Rogers, the deceased's servant was examined, and her evidence corroborated that of Mr. Bowen as to how and where the deceased was found – between the pillars of the bridge on the shore side of the island.

The jury returned a verdict that deceased was accidentally killed by a stone falling upon him from the rocks on the shore side of the bridge, and added the following recommendation:-

The jury upon the inquest on the body of John Jones, light keeper, at South Stack Island, finding that the deceased was accidentally killed by a stone falling upon his head from the rocks on the shore side of the bridge leading to the island – strongly recommend that some immediate steps be taken to remove the loose stones lying on the steep cliff immediately over the entrance to the island to prevent the recurrence of such a lamentable accident.

(signed) John Jones, Foreman
18th Nov., 1859
Caernarfon & Denbigh Herald
November 26, 1859

CHAPTER EIGHT

Other Damage

South Devon Railway, near Teignmouth.

The effects of the storm at Minehead.

The prelude to the storm was first noticed by the Channel Fleet of the Royal Navy while exercising near the Eddystone Rocks off Plymouth at around three o'clock on Tuesday the 25th of October. Nearby, on the south coast of England, the South Devon Railway was washed away by the sea at four different places, with coping stones weighing a ton *'tossed about like corks'.* Further east, at Portland, severe damage was caused to the breakwater under construction for the Harbour of Refuge, and houses at Hastings were flooded to a depth of around one metre. People at Eastbourne found bathing-machines in the middle of town, having been blown there from the beach, while three lives were lost when the master of the schooner 'Pilot' misread the lights at the approach to Dover Harbour and accidentally ran ashore.

The ferocious weather then caused even more damage as it swept northwards into Somerset where *'broken boats and the masts of wrecked vessels strewed the shore'.* Continuing into the Principality of Wales, a house was blown down at Cardiff, eight bodies were washed ashore nearby, and the mast-heads of a small vessel were seen protruding from the sea near Cardigan Island. Further north, the hurricane struck Anglesey, killing John Jones, the assistant keeper at South Stack Lighthouse near Holyhead. It then overwhelmed the partially-built breakwater of the nearby Harbour of Refuge, and very nearly destroyed the 'Great Eastern' anchored there. The brig 'Agnes' was wrecked near Point Lynas at the north-east tip of Anglesey, with the loss of two lives, and the underwater telegraph cable along the North Wales coast failed between Anglesey and the Great Orme. Sweeping onwards, the tempest washed away part of the Chester to Holyhead railway at Penmaenmawr, severely damaged the pier at Llandudno, and then headed for Liverpool, where it caused the clipper 'White Star' to go adrift in the Mersey. The 'White Star' then ran foul of the 'Gladiator', and had to be rescued by the guard-ship HMS 'Hastings'. Steaming from Belfast to Liverpool, the 'Gladiator' had been badly battered by the storm and arrived at Liverpool a frightful state, with her holds full of dead cattle and pigs. Even as far away as the east coast of England, forty-five vessels were blown ashore at Hartlepool alone, with five of these being described as *'total wrecks'.* Then, only a few hours after the 'Royal Charter' was wrecked, the wind decreased rapidly so that by noon it was described as a *'brisk breeze'.*

133

Llandudno. A correspondent writes –
"After breakfast, I got on my 'dreadnought'*
and prepared to face the weather, to witness
the effect of the gale during the 'last quarter
flow' and the 'first quarter ebb', which I
expected would cause great damage around
the bay, especially to the pier. I had not
to wait long before it began to show its
powers. At half past nine o'clock, the storm
raged with great violence, with a very
heavy sea running direct into the Bay from
the N.N.E. At a quarter to ten o'clock, part
of the Railway, with a large portion of the
roadway of the New Pier erected this year,
was carried away by a heavy wave; and
shortly after this, about ten o'clock, one
grand wave completely swept over the pier
from one end to another, and which for a
second or two was completely concealed
from view, and at the same moment struck
the timbers with such violence as to cause a
report like distant thunder, and to shake the
earth under my feet, at a distance of nearly
a quarter of a mile. In another moment,
piles, thirty feet long, sprang with great
violence into the air, and the sea had made
a complete breach through about one third
of the pier. At about high tide, another wave
swept over the inshore portion, and carried
away about one third more, with equal, if
not greater force. The oldest man here says
that he never witnessed a more severe gale
in this quarter. I have just returned from
viewing the effects of the gale, now that
the sea is out, which is dismal indeed. The
whole of the beach is covered with wrecks,
and the Esplanade with hundreds of tons of
shingle and large pieces of rock, which will
cost some hundreds of pounds to repair.
There is a vessel at this moment laying
at anchor, about four miles from shore,
without masts or rigging, with two men and
a boy on board, and we have no lifeboat or
any craft fit to go out to them."

Caernarfon & Denbigh Herald.
October 29th, 1859

POINT LYNAS

The brig *Agnes*, of Amlwch, Owen Evans,
master, bound from Liverpool to Barrow in
ballast, was caught in the gale of Tuesday
se'nnight about ten miles from her port
of destination, unshipped her rudder and
was obliged to run before the wind, and
came on shore on the rocks at Point Lynas.
The captain's brother and another of the
crew, William Parry, were drowned. The
remainder of the crew, four in number,
succeeded in getting on shore. An inquest
was held on the bodies washed ashore, by
W. Jones Esq., the coroner, and a verdict in
accordance with the above facts returned.
On Wednesday, a schooner was seen on
the sands near Red Wharf. The crew were
in the rigging. When the tide receded, the
crew effected a landing. She still remains
on the sands with her masts standing. She
was laden with iron ore, and nearly new.

RED WHARF BAY

On Tuesday last, a brigantine was seen
approaching the scene of the late wreck of
the *Royal Charter*. Great excitement was
created among the people on shore, as she
approached the rocks, the sea rolling in
frightfully. The lifeboat was launched. The
people ran along the highlands towards
Dulas. She was seen to embed herself in
the sands, and the crew left her – leaving,
as it is said, one hand on board. The water
became smooth, and the crew returned.
She proved to be the *Maria,* of Barrow,
with iron ore for Swansea. She had fouled
a vessel in the Channel, got disabled, and
afterwards struck upon a rock. When the
water smoothed and the crew returned, she
floated and was brought into Dulas Bay,
where she now lies.

Caernarfon & Denbigh Herald
November 5th, 1859

* dreadnought - a heavy, woollen coat.

The Carnarvon and Denbigh Herald

AND NORTH AND SOUTH WALES ADVERTISER

Saturday, November 5, 1859

The *Great Eastern* during the late Gale. 'The Times' special correspondent on board the *Great Eastern*, writing from Holyhead, says:-

"On Tuesday se'nnight the wind allegedly freshened and appearances became threatening. By six o'clock, it was pretty generally seen that it would be a 'dirty' night. The sea and wind kept rising as the glass fell, and before eight it blew a heavy gale from the eastward, with fierce squalls and storms of rain. The night was very wild, and dark as pitch, though tolerably clear too, showing with sufficient distinctness the dull red light on the head of the breakwater, and the lamps on the pier astern, but that was all. Everything seemed to auger very badly, so the fires were carefully attended to by the indefatigable chief engineer, Mr. M'Lennan, and Captain Harrison gave orders to have steam ready in case of being suddenly obliged to slip and stand out into the Channel.

As night wore on, the wind increased and came in fearful gusts, tearing away among the spars and rigging with a hoarse, sustained roar that was awful to listen to, especially when one bore in mind that the glass was still falling, and that what we then saw was only the commencement of the gale. Sea after sea ran tumbling by, only discernible through the darkness by its snow-like foamy crest, or the heavy jerk it gave to the great ship as the chains surged and rumbled in the hawseholes, as though she was going adrift altogether. Vessel after vessel could be seen in the gloom by their bright lights dipping and rolling over the heavy waves, as they bore up for the protection of the breakwater, glad to run for any shelter in so wild a night, and one which was hourly becoming worse and worse. At ten o'clock, the rain set in like a second deluge. Each gust of wind seemed longer and worse than the last, striking down upon the ship, as sailors say, with a blow like a hammer, and testing everything in the way of masts and rigging to the very utmost they could bear. Still, in spite of all, the *Great Eastern* rode steadily and lightly, head to wind, and without perceptible motion, although a fierce sea was rolling in, and we could see by the rapidly-moving lights among the other shipping, far outside the harbour, that they were dipping heavily and making the worst of the bad weather. From eight o'clock, Captain Harrison never left the deck or bridge, but was either sounding the lead overboard to see if she dragged, giving directions about the steam, or watching the chain-cables, as under the strain they rose up out of the water like bars of solid metal.

Everything that could be done under the circumstances was done, and there was nothing for it but to hold on and wish for daylight. This latter Captain Harrison did most devoutly, for the wind almost equalled the force of a hurricane at times, jerking at the masts as if it would snap them off at the deck, and making the *Great Eastern* tremble perceptibly throughout her immense length and breadth, as if some giant hand was shaking her. From this time till between two and three o'clock in the morning, the gale increased in violence till the din was appalling, and the rain and hail, driving with the force of small shot, made it painful to face it. The gusts revelled over the huge expanse of deck till none dared stand before them. Well was it for the great ship that nothing happened at this time, or her chance would have been poor indeed. The air was filled with spray, torn from the jagged waves – the darkness was impenetrable, while the hoarse roar of the wind drowned every other sound save the dull, threatening booming of the waves upon the rocks and breakwater, the sound of which came up on the gale like peals of distant thunder. Words of command would have been useless, and even if heard, neither men nor ship could have struggled long against the gale which was rushing past. Those who heard its deafening roar that night from sea are never likely to forget it. Between one and two o'clock, Captain Harrison went forward and endeavoured to pierce the thick gloom, and see what was going on ahead. On his way along the deck, his waterproof coat was blown to ribands off him, and he was himself at last carried before the gale and thrown down, and tumbled along with such violence as to receive some most severe contusions. Towards two or three o'clock in the morning, the gale seemed at its worst. To the roar and scream through the shrouds, other and more unpleasant sounds were soon added, as the wind blew up the saloon skylights, dropping them down with a bang and a crash of glass that, to those below, was startling in the extreme. Crash after crash, the glass in these skylights went, one after the other; the rain and wind pouring down through the apertures into the saloons, and, above all, into the grand saloon, to decorate which so much that was really needed in the ship has been deferred. It wanted not such aids to let in wind and water, for the upper wooden deck was leaky at every seam, so that on all the sofas, carpets, and tables below was an array of vessels of every size and kind which could contain the ceaseless drippings from above. Yet, in spite of this, the lower decks were sopped and plashy* and seemed under the mattings to be much like walking on an ill-drained marsh. At four o'clock, a wistful look out was kept for the light on the breakwater, for it was evident that if the gale continued much longer, the *Great Eastern* must endeavour to run to sea. Two anchors were down, one of seven tons, with eighty fathoms chain on the starboard bow, and one of 3 ½ tons, with 60 fathoms to port. The cables of both seemed tautened to the very utmost which they could bear, and, though it was quite possible they would hold on through still worse weather, yet, with what was then feared to be bad holding-ground and a rocky lee shore, it would not do to calculate too finely. Therefore was the light on the breakwater kept anxiously in view, as a point to be carefully rounded in case of the worse.

Fortunately, it was easy enough to see this dim, red beacon at intervals; that is to say, when the sea allowed it, for the tremendous rollers came tumbling in, lashing over the timber work on the head of the breakwater, and shielding the light in a cloud of foam and spray. At last, after a most anxious night, the cold dawn broke in doubtful haze, till it was hard to say where the water ended and the clouds began. Above, all was thick and gloomy; below, the water seemed lashed to fury, and the waves came hissing and writhing in, "curling their monstrous heads," and breaking upon the rocks like avalanches of snow. It was, in truth, a very wild and dreary scene.

Over the lighthouse on the inner pier-head, the waves seemed to surge almost unimpeded, while the breakwater itself was so completely hidden that the tremendous jets, spray and foam which cloaked it from end to end more resembled in their distant boom and snowy clouds the constant discharges of heavy artillery than the break of waves, however dangerous. Within the very extremity of the breakwater, where one would have thought the Channel fleet might have ridden through any gale, much damage had been done. High and dry ashore under Holyhead Mountain, lay a fine barque, and around her, in the same predicament, were three smaller vessels. Out in the centre of the harbour the tops of two slender tapering

* plashy - abounding with puddles.

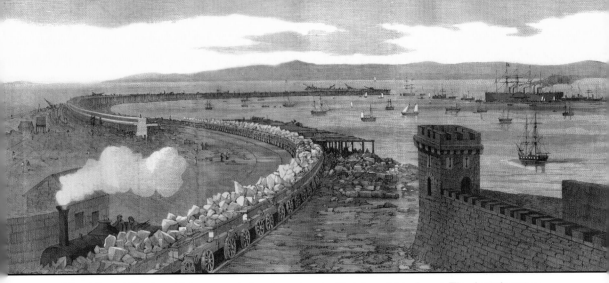

The 'Great Eastern' lying serenely at anchor in Holyhead Harbour. The breakwater was still under construction, using facing-stones that had been quarried at Moelfre.

masts showed where Captain Henry's beautiful schooner yacht, the *Marquita,* had gone down bodily. Immediately behind this last was another and larger vessel, which had apparently only escaped the same fate by driving on the rocks, and which, with a fierce sea breaking over its hull, and its jagged and tattered sails blown out to riband streamers by the wind, looked the very picture of a melancholy wreck. Other vessels there were too, which, though still afloat, seemed very little better off than those that were ashore, and which, dipping bows under to the angry sea, appeared about to illustrate by fresh examples the force of the tempest which now howled and worried around on all sides. It was, indeed, what sailors call a 'wicked' gale. Very little could be distinguished through the drifting snow, half rain, half cloud, which was driving through the air. Only occasionally could the headland to the north be seen, like a heavy fog-bank, with the breakers surging up to 100 feet into the air, as they came thundering in against the iron coast.

At six o'clock, there were symptoms of the storm breaking, and, as usual, the last gusts were the worst, and the situation of the *Great Eastern* was a matter for deep anxiety on the part of Captain Harrison and his officers.

Inside the breakwater, the sea ran high, with waves of a deep yellow hue, while the ocean without resembled hills of muddy, half-thawed snow, reflecting their whitish glare upon the clouds above, as if the very laws of nature had been reversed, and light came from below. Both wind and tide were rising, and as the great billows came dashing in upon the massive framework of timber which marked the end of the breakwater, it became a nice calculation which would yield first, the timbers or the gale. Wave after wave swept in upon the mass of stone and wood, and seemed to explode in a cloud of smoke-like spray. Yet still the red light in the lighthouse held on, and shone out cheerily above the desolate and angry scene around. Sorely was it tried, minute after minute, and well must the framework have been put together to hold aloof so long the destruction which all could see was inevitable. At last, soon after six o'clock, a monstrous wave came in upon the horizon. Nearer and nearer it rolled, a white crest towering high above the green wall of water as it reared up its monstrous bulk and seemed to gather might for one great rush upon the prey. In another second, the foam towered a hundred feet

137

over the head of the breakwater, and the red light was seen no more, while the wave, broken, but not disabled came tearing on, hurling aloft, as if in triumph, a black mass of timbers, which seemed like rocks among the seething waters. This was introducing, so to speak, the thin end of the wedge, for the work of demolition, once commenced, went rapidly forward, and the massive timbers began to disappear by a hundred feet and more at a time, melting away into the angry sea like a mere fretwork of sugar candy. The cranes and machinery at the top dropped off into the water one by one, as if the sea possessed the properties of a universal solvent; for when once the waters covered them, obstacles were seen no more. Some lengths of framework, however, held out long and gallantly, resisting every effort to overthrow them, till the tide was at its height, and at last they too disappeared, some in splinters and chips like firewood, as the beams were rent to pieces, some in great angular masses, as if an island of timber had come to sea. The whole harbour was covered with such rafts, till their black masses showed up like reefs of rock in all directions. Still the storm swept on as wild as ever, and where the breakwater makes that most injudicious inward curve and forms a concave surface for the sea to act on, the waves broke high and fiercely, each here damaging the cranes upon the high scaffolding, and threatening a clean breach into the harbour. Matters now began to look very bad, and such tremendous evidences of danger on the part of the wind and sea were by no means overlooked by those on board the *Great Eastern*.

In fact, it was with most considerable anxiety that Captain Harrison saw the turn affairs were taking, for the wind was now dead from the north-east, and the whole sweep of the Channel was pouring into the harbour. Some profitable bargains might have been made in *Great Eastern* shares, had the shareholders been on board and seen the state of the weather – the lee shore behind, and the timber work of the breakwater (the great and only shield ahead) disappearing by hundreds of yards at a time. Yet still the *Great Eastern* rode out lightly for her bulk, and without a sign of dragging, though the chains apparently could bear nothing more. The whole harbour was now one immense mass of wreck wood, the huge piles tumbling over and over one another, and rearing up 15 and 20 feet from the water, as the waves tossed them to and fro like playthings. The sea had set in too, so violently that it was necessary at once to do something to relieve the ship from the strain upon the cables, and to effect this, the screw was set to work. But here an obstacle intervened of the most serious kind, as the masses of timber-wreck were round the ship, going down upon the screw at every minute, and once or twice so fouling it as to force the engines to a dead stop. To clear these, it was necessary to put the helm hard a-port, though this was only a choice of evils, as the vessel's head played round and threatened soon to foul the anchor chains. The latter accident, in fact, took place at last, and the heaviest anchor and longest scope of cable on the starboard bow appeared to be doing nothing to retain the vessel, while the small anchor appeared to be doing too much, and its cable flipped up out of the water with every surge in a startling and ominous manner.

Towards eight or nine o'clock, the wind went round more to the N.E, sending in a beam swell, to which the *Great Eastern* began to roll heavily. As the surge swept in, the position of the vessel hourly became worse, and at last, at ten o'clock, Captain Harrison had no alternative but to try and raise the heaviest anchor, get the vessel's head more under the lee of the breakwater, and then let it go again.

This was a difficult and most critical task, for every part of the harbour was now so completely covered with drifting beams that the screw could only be used with

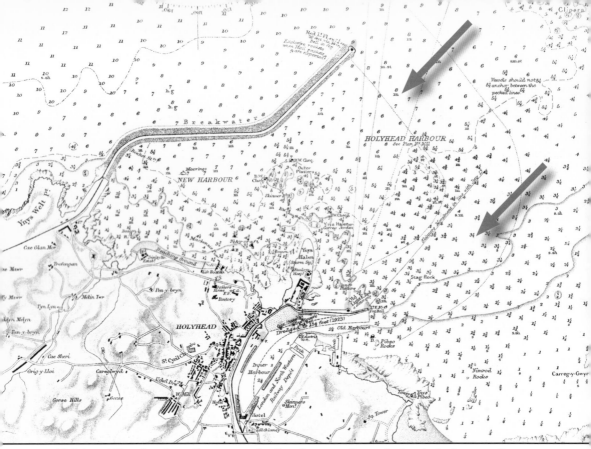

Holyhead Breakwater offers no protection from north-easterly winds (arrowed).

the utmost caution. The paddles, unless in case of a most dangerous emergency, could not be used at all, as the timbers would, of course, knock the floats to pieces. Gradually, therefore, the *Great Eastern* was brought up to her starboard anchor, though with the utmost difficulty. Before the screw could well get play, it was fouled and had to stop. Directly this occurred, the steam from the screw boilers was let into the paddle engines, which in turn went ahead till the propeller was free and able to work again. At last, after some time, the anchor was under the bow, the slack chain hove in, and the huge mass of iron got up to the bow ready for letting go again in a better berth. But the wind now allowed no choice of situations. The vessel had partly swung off into a beam sea, which was then sweeping over and past the breakwater with awful force, and the *Great Eastern* began

to roll quickly and heavily. In spite of the relief afforded by the screw, the cable of the remaining anchor kept tautening more and more, until, at about half-past ten, it sprang up like a cord out of the water, and in another moment the *Great Eastern* was adrift, rolling and tumbling like a drunken ship towards shore. So quiet and orderly was everything when this most alarming incident took place, that very few knew what had really happened, though all could pretty well guess by the heavy lurches of the vessel that something had indeed gone wrong. Captain Harrison and Mr. Kett were forward, and in an instant all was ready for letting go a second heavy anchor, while word was passed to go ahead with the screw, for the great ship, lurching from side to side, was making rapidly for shore. The second anchor was let go and the screw moved ahead, but the vessel had now great way on her, and she could not be easily stopped on what seemed her road to destruction. Just as the screw began to tell, an immense mass of wreck wood fouled it, and brought the machinery to a dead stand. Not a second could be lost in waiting till it cleared, so the steam was at once turned into the paddle engines, which were driven round at a good speed, though the floats got hurt among the mass of wreck, and the great iron-work of the wheels was bent in many places. To avoid this and the serious damage it might occasion, the screw was set to work again the instant it was freed, but it was seldom able to revolve more than a few moments without becoming jammed again, when the paddles were again resorted to. But for the *Great Eastern*'s double engines, very little could have been done. The anchor which was let go, 'bit' at once, and as much scope was given to the cable as dare be let out when the vessel had driven back so far and the lee shore loomed so close astern. Still, for a time, the position continued dangerous in the extreme, as, in spite of both wind and steam, the great ship lay open to the sea, rolling dangerously for such a place, and making way as if nothing would hold her. At last, she brought up, though she seemed to make desperate efforts to break from the grip of her new holdfast – tugging and rolling to her chain as though she would pull up a mountain. Fortunately, both chains and anchors held fast, as they did before in heavy weather at Portland when two screw colliers, each with 800 tons of coal on board, two brigs, two dummies, and a large galliot, all hung onto the *Great Eastern*, riding at the same single chain and anchor. After one or two more ineffectual efforts to break away, her head at last swung round, and she rode lightly to the gale as before. In this last struggle, some of the links of the chain cable were actually dragged out one-third longer, and one which passed under the sharp bows of the vessel was bent nearly double. The cable on the port bow was then hove in, when it was found

that the shank of the anchor, after bending considerably, had been torn in half about a foot below the crown, showing good anchor and holding ground both.

From this time (about twelve o'clock) the glass began to rise fast, and the worst of the gale was over, though it still came down occasionally in wild and heavy gusts, rendering every precaution necessary in the way of full steam power, for with such a ship and such a sea, none knew what next might happen. Soon after one o'clock, two schooners came upon the coast; one with good way on her stood right down upon what remained of the breakwater, unaware of the fact that much of it had been swept away, and that the head which they ran for was far inside a dangerous reef of breakwater debris, on which even the *Great Eastern* herself would be beaten to pieces in an hour. Fortunately, both vessels saw their danger when almost on the breakers, and one weathered safely round the awful shoal. The second, in trying to recover herself, lost way and drove too much inshore, and for the next two hours had to struggle with the gale, poised between life and death, and hundreds looking on at the unequal contest with breathless interest, but unable to aid in any way.

Happily for the little ship, and all on board, she fought a successful, though arduous battle. One minute she seemed carrying on well, and hope beat high as with her little rags of sail she faced the storm and, all hid with foam, broke doggedly through the great antagonists which rose around on all sides. Another minute, and, reeling over under the effects of a tremendous wave, she fell off before the wind and again drove rapidly towards the dismantled breakwater, over which the sea was now roaring in a succession of cataracts. Twice did she seem overpowered amid those fearful breakers, and yet again emerged, her little black hull rising sharp and clear above the line of foam. Her utter destruction appeared almost impossible to avert, and Captain Harrison had ordered twelve hands to be ready for lowering away in one of Gladstone's boats, in order that no effort might be spared to save those on board, when the little vessel made another effort and, aided by a momentary lull, stood further out to sea, weathered the dreadful reef, and reached the harbour. From this time out the gale continued to decrease in violence, so that in afternoon the *Great Eastern* again screwed ahead, and dropped a second anchor more under the lee of the breakwater, and rode secure. Then, and then only, was Captain Harrison enabled to leave the deck, and take that rest which he so much needed after his labour and long anxiety."

A few days later, just as life was beginning to return to normal, the country was hit by a second storm which, although not as fierce and destructive as the first, was still capable of creating mayhem and death. At least forty-two people lost their lives on November 1st, with the worst casualties occurring along the South Coast of England and in the Bristol Channel. John James, a shipwright's apprentice, aged nineteen and the son of poor parents, lost his life attempting to save another crew-member when the 'Elizabeth' sank near Milford. Once this second storm had subsided, the fearsome power of the wind was shown for a third time only a few days later, when scores of elm-trees were flattened near Bristol, *'as if by a giant hand'*.

Back in Holyhead, the 'Great Eastern' still lay within the New Harbour, but it was evident that the partially-built breakwater had offered little protection from the north-easterly hurricane. The monster vessel had survived only by the skill of her captain, the strength of her anchor-chains, the immense power of her engines, and with a certain amount of good fortune, but the future was looking rather bleak for her financiers, and as 'The Times' reporter had remarked:

some profitable bargains might have been made in *Great Eastern* shares had the shareholders been on board and seen the state of the weather.

By this time, the vessel's first commercial voyage was long overdue. She had been stuck on the slipway for several months, suffered an enormous explosion on her maiden voyage, and the financial state of the 'Great Ship Company' was dire. Holyhead had proved to be unsuitable as her port of departure due to the lack of protection from the wind, so she was taken to Southampton Water on the south coast of England where she could be moored in a far safer location.

The arrival of the *Great Eastern* at Southampton caused immense excitement, and the water is crowded with boats conveying visitors on board and around the huge vessel. The excursion trains of the South-Western Railway are running at low rates of fare, and large numbers of persons are availing themselves of the opportunity of visiting the ship after its third and most successful trip.

Illustrated London News. November 13, 1859.

It might have been the Great Eastern's most successful trip so far, but it began with a problem in raising the anchors, with one of Trotman's best *'breaking in half about a foot or so below the stock'*.

Then, despite having saved his ship from destruction at Holyhead, Captain Harrison was drowned at Southampton in an accident the following January, so it was Captain John Vine Hall who was in command when the 'Great Eastern' began her first transatlantic voyage on the 16th of June, 1860.

Llanallgo Church, where some of the bodies were placed to await identification.

The Devoted Services of the Reverends S.R and H.R. Hughes.

Every one who has from time to time pursued the distressing particulars connected with the wreck of the *Royal Charter* must have admired the humane and Christian services rendered to the shipwrecked passengers and their friends by the Reverend S.R. Hughes, incumbent of Llanallgo, and his brother, the Reverend H.R Hughes, parish minister of the adjoining village of Penrhos Lligwy. The pious cares and the laborious charity of these reverend gentlemen are thus detailed in the letter of a correspondent of *The Times*:-

"They are the resident pastors of the two parishes in the island of Anglesey, on the united borders of which the *Royal Charter* struck and went to pieces. Their stipends are moderate, as their duties are hard – not exceeding £130 per annum. Yet it was to these gentlemen's unaided means and unassisted personal exertions that the burial of 230 bodies out of 500 lost in the ill-fated ship was necessarily committed; and not the burial only. The ignorant and superstitious peasantry absolutely refused to touch the dead bodies as they were thrown up from the sea; it fell, therefore, to these two clergymen to take off the clothes from the dead with their own hands, and in many instances to perform the last offices to the remains. It became their duty to preserve all marks, clothes or property by which each body could be identified; and, lastly, to comfort, console, satisfy, and give hospitable shelter not only to those who had escaped the engulphing sea, but to the relatives and friends of the deceased, who, as soon as the fatal tidings had spread far and near upon the wings of the telegraph, came hastening from all parts of the kingdom to learn tidings of the lost and loved."

Caernarfon & Denbigh Herald. December 31, 1859

Perhaps it isn't surprising that the local people were reluctant to touch the corpses, as at least one person was arrested and charged with theft whilst under instruction from the Reverend S.R. Hughes to recover any clothing that could help to identify the bodies.

CHAPTER NINE

The Aftermath of the Wreck and the Inquest on the Bodies

Hundreds of lives had been lost and dozens of bodies were being washed up on the Anglesey coast and beyond, so inquests had to be held to try to determine the identity of the deceased and the cause or causes of their deaths. That was the purpose of a British inquest, whereas a Court of Inquiry (see Page 185) had a different objective, that of establishing the cause of the wreck, and if there had been any negligence by the captain or crew, or if the design, construction or operation of the ship was deficient in any way.

The interior of Llanallgo Church.

In the absence of a suitable mortuary, the recovered bodies needed to be kept somewhere secure and in a suitable location where the relatives and friends of the victims could view them in the hope of identifying the corpses before decomposition rendered this unenviable task totally impossible. Places of worship were deemed to be the most suitable locations, so the churches at Llanallgo, Penrhos Lligwy, Llaneugrad and elsewhere were used as temporary resting places where the sad work could be attempted under the guidance of the Rev. Stephen Roose Hughes, his wife and two sisters-in-law, and his brother, the Rev. Hugh Robert Hughes.

They met the bereaved at the door; they interrogated them; then they went into the valley of the shadow of death, and sought the corpse which some mother, perhaps, had come to reclaim, and they would go out and bring in the sorrowing one blindfold, until she stood where she might see her boy without being stared at by the things once human that surrounded her. A pitch fire burned in the place to disinfect the atmosphere, and when the bodies had been identified, in cases where identification was possible, they were solemnly buried. Stephen Roose Hughes, the most Christian pastor of Llanallgo, laid in their last bed 145 bodies, sometimes having to exhume them for inspection by the friends of the missing. The funeral services were invariably performed, the dead were buried in their clothes, and all the neighbouring people were busy for a while making coffins; and this within a few steps of the clergyman's door, on which the white surplice, ever ready, hung; and thus the victims who perished with the *Royal Charter* will sleep close beside the hearth of the noble-hearted man who, though he could not save their lives, was to them in death as a friend and a minister of the Most High. Nor shall the name of his brother be omitted - Hugh Robert Hughes, of Penrhos Lligwy, who interred 34 bodies in his own churchyard, and vied with Stephen Roose Hughes in the abundance of his Christian charity.

One bizarre aftermath of the wreck concerns the Fenwick family. Mrs. Fenwick was travelling to Liverpool with her four children, her brother-in-law, her sister and their four children, all of whom died at Moelfre. Mr. Fenwick was the coroner at Beechwood, Melbourne, and had stayed behind in Australia. About five days before the wreck, he wrote a letter to a friend in Tasmania telling of a dream in which his wife and children were *'battling with the waves, and calling to him for help'*. This certainly preyed on his mind, with the following result:

Mr. R. W. Fenwick, the Coroner for this district, committed suicide this morning [*November 3, 1859*], at half-past 3 o'clock, while in a state of insanity caused by excessive drinking. The deceased was an inmate of the hospital at the time, and escaped from the custody of those who had charge of him to a neighbour's house where he had been residing. Here, he seized a carving-knife, and cut his throat in so fearful a manner that he died within an hour and a half.

There was no telegraphic communication between England and Australia at that time, so had Mr. Fenwick correctly predicted the terrible disaster so many thousands of miles away, or was he simply depressed at the departure of his loved-ones?

Meanwhile, William Jones, the County Coroner for Anglesey, needed to quickly assemble a suitable jury, a task that wasn't going to be straightforward as the majority of the local inhabitants used Welsh as their native language when the evidence given in court would be given by English-speaking witnesses. This situation could easily have led to a verdict that didn't truly reflect the events of that fateful night, and a suggestion was made to the coroner that the jury should consist partly of '*English gentlemen*'. However, a jury of '*the most respected farmers*' had already been notified to attend court, and to alleviate the language-barrier, Mr. Robert Pritchard, an auctioneer from Bangor, was appointed as a translator. This must have caused considerable delay and confusion at the inquest, as the witnesses all gave their evidence in English which then had to be translated to the twenty-nine members of the Welsh-speaking jury. At least one newspaper reporter was very unimpressed by the court, the jury and the local constabulary, stating:

> This must prove a very tedious process, but it will cause less concern than the behaviour of the jurors. These gentlemen do not appear to appreciate, in the most remote degree, the serious importance of the duty they have been called upon to perform; they have to be watched like schoolboys by a policeman, and indeed this latter functionary seems as much inclined as his wards to steal out of the school-room whenever an opportunity presents itself. We do not always perhaps expect to find Coroners' Juries composed of the most intelligent men of the community; but we cannot help observing that these Welshmen have conducted themselves with a clownish levity which, in the interest of the public, we must stigmatize as utterly disgraceful. The jury was composed of very humble-looking men — small farmers and seafaring persons.

These were totally unjust comments on those members of the jury who had animals to feed or whose boats were lying idle, especially at a time when terrible damage had been caused to walls, fences, roofs, fishing-nets and lobster-pots. Winter had arrived, and the local people had their own priorities to attend to rather than listening to the evidence. Another newspaper had this to say:

> The jury, who were sworn in in Welsh, were not provided with seats, and as they mixed with the spectators, it was difficult to tell who were the "good men and true" who were sworn to investigate one of the most important and painful cases that have ever engaged the attention of a jury. During the day, the Coroner called out to an official not to allow the jurors to leave the room, it being then supposed that about one-half of them had made their exit from the room during the taking of the evidence.

The scene at the inquest must have been one of total confusion, with a mixture of English and Welsh voices, jurors coming and going, newspaper reporters trying to generate a sensational story, and the tears and cries of the distraught relatives and friends all adding to the chaos of the court.

The Carnarvon and Denbigh Herald
AND NORTH AND SOUTH WALES ADVERTISER
Saturday, November 5, 1859

THE "ROYAL CHARTER".
INQUEST ON THE BODIES
(From our own Reporter.)

The inquest on the bodies of the unfortunates lost in this truly melancholy catastrophe was opened at Llanallgo Church on Friday last, before William Jones, Esq., coroner, and two highly respectable juries from the parishes of Llanallgo and Penrhos Lligwy. After viewing the bodies, the inquest was adjourned *pro forma* to

WEDNESDAY,

when it was resumed at the National School-room, Llanallgo. From the numberless rumours circulated with regard to this frightful catastrophe, considerable interest was manifested by the large attendance of persons at the inquest. Mr. Bright, from the firm of Bright and Co., and other owners of the vessel were present, and took part in the proceedings by examining the witnesses. There were also present several gentlemen representing the London and local press. The coroner held an inquest at noon on the same day at the parish church of Penrhos Lligwy, on two bodies which have not been identified.

In opening the court, the Coroner addressed the jury as follows:- "Gentlemen of the jury, it has become my painful duty to call you together for the purpose of enquiring into the cause of one of the most distressing occurrences that ever took place in this country - distressing from the number of valuable lives lost, and its other lamentable results. I hope you will enter on your duties calmly and impartially, dismissing from your mind all reports that you have heard or that have been circulated through the press, as it will be your duty to arrive at your verdict solely on the evidence which will be produced at this court. I will afford every facility to the owners, Messrs. Bright and Co., and to the representatives of those unfortunate persons who perished. I trust that in adopting this course I shall best perform my duty towards you and the public. I should have been happy to have attended to a suggestion which was made to me by putting some English gentleman on the jury, had that suggestion been made before the present jury had been empanelled. They are, however, the most respected farmers in the two parishes, and from their intelligence, I have every reason to expect a satisfactory result. It has, however, been suggested and urged upon me to call in the assistance of an interpreter as the evidence would necessarily be given in the English language. Concurring with the propriety of the application, I am happy to inform them that I have secured the services of Mr. Robert Pritchard, of Bangor, who is perfectly conversant with both languages, and he has had considerable experience as an interpreter. With these observations, I will now propose to examine the witnesses."

The first witness called was Mr. W.H. Morse – He deposed. "I was a saloon passenger on board the *Royal Charter,* the vessel wrecked in this neighbourhood on the morning of Wednesday, the 26th ult. She sailed from Melbourne on the 26th of August last. The captain's name was Thomas Taylor. She was bound to Liverpool. There were 61 saloon passengers when she sailed, and about 300 second and third-class passengers. She did not touch at any place on her passage. It is said she was 3,500 tons burden. She had two 80-horsepower engines. She had a good supply of coal, and a full complement of crew – 110 in number, including officers. She showed no deficiency or difficulty up to the night of Tuesday, the day previous to the wreck. We first saw land on Monday, 24th at day-break. It was the Irish coast. We put about fourteen passengers on shore on board the pilot-boat. We passed Holyhead about four or half-past four o'clock on Tuesday evening, 25th. We did not land any passengers at Holyhead. The wind was blowing fresh ahead. Cannot say from what point. Nothing wrong occurred until she was wrecked. We passed two lighthouses, and the storm continued to increase into a hurricane. She was drifting when the anchors were let go. We were, I think, within sight of Point Lynas. We had passed it. Can't say how long we had passed it when the anchors were let go. I had no conversation with the captain. I saw him during the progress of the storm. I did not hear any person remonstrate with the captain or desire him to turn back. I saw him giving orders on deck up to five o'clock on Tuesday evening. I was not much on deck myself after that time. At the time the anchors were let go, there was nothing the matter with the machinery as far as I know. The anchors were let go about twelve o'clock. She parted the first cable about two o'clock in the morning. She parted the other cable in about an hour. Before we came to Point Lynas, the captain made signals – blue lights and rockets – which were continued until day-break on Wednesday morning. She struck about three o'clock. I was not on deck, but I understood she went head on. It was a slight shock at first. I went on deck once after that. She divided about seven o'clock, or half past. It must have been about four hours after she struck before she went to pieces. A hawser was taken on shore shortly before she broke up. I did not see it. I escaped by swimming. All I know about the hawser is from hearsay. I had no conversation with the captain after she struck, but he came down to the cabin to speak to the ladies. I believe I saw him once in the cabin after the vessel struck. I heard him tell the ladies there was no danger, and

that they would soon be able to walk on to the shore. He was then perfectly sober. I did not see him or any of the officers at any time during the voyage the worse for drink. Everything went on comfortably until the storm came on. He knew what part of the coast we were on. I heard Captain Withers, one of the passengers, say we were on a sandy coast. I had no conversation with the captain after half-past three."

In reply to Mr. Bright:- "There was a testimonial given by the passengers to Captain Taylor. It was joined in by all the saloon passengers excepting two. There was a slight difference between the 2nd and 3rd class passengers and Captain Taylor. It was, I believe, because he refused to allow of their dancing on the poop. When the anchors were let go, I heard him speak cheeringly to the passengers. He was calm and collected when speaking to the ladies. During the evening, after she anchored, he went down to the cabin two or three times, always calm and collected. I cannot say that the Captain saw the Point Lynas Light. He came down to cheer the ladies, and once to order coffee, of which I partook. I do not recollect seeing Captain Taylor drink anything that evening. He was not at dinner in the Saloon that evening. I heard Captain Taylor tell the passengers in the Saloon that he had been forward, and that there was no strain on the cables."

In reply to the Coroner - "Cannot say how far the vessel was from the land when the anchors were let go. There were sixteen fathoms of water."

In reply to Mr. John William Mellor, of Oldham - "The testimonial was presented to the Captain on the evening of Saturday or Monday before the wreck. I cannot say which. After leaving Cork we took some riggers on board from a steam-tug. Cannot say how many. We had not such rough weather on any part of the voyage as we had on Tuesday, the 25th. We encountered a storm off the River Plate* which was not

* River Plate in South America.

146

as bad as on Tuesday. The weather was not so bad when the anchors were let go as it was afterwards. The storm off the River Plate might have been as bad as the storm was on Tuesday before the anchors were let go. I do not know when the riggers were shipped. I was below at the time. I came up and saw a vessel leave the side of the ship. I do not know how long we lay off Queenstown – I believe about two hours. I had no way of judging. I was on deck while she lay off Queenstown. I was on deck once after dark before the vessel struck. Cannot say what time. I did not expect any accident, and therefore took no notice. I did not know what part of the coast we were on; nor do I now, excepting that it was near Point Lynas. I did not see the captain the last time I was on deck. I did not speak to Captain Taylor after half-past three o'clock in the afternoon. I was on the deck several times after, but I do not recollect seeing him more than three times after. He was below – in the saloon, I have no doubt of this. I saw him in the saloon before the ship struck. He was speaking to the ladies. He was in the saloon at the time the vessel parted anchor. I heard a messenger tell him so. I know nothing of the management of a ship. No person spoke to the captain in my hearing about going into Holyhead or into any other place. It was when the first anchor parted that the captain was in the saloon. He had only shortly come there. He did not dine with us that day – because, I think, he had been up two or three previous nights, and had gone to rest."

Mr. Mellor remarked that if everything had gone well before, why did the captain remain up the two or three previous nights?

In reply to Mr. Bright – "The captain might have been on deck after I saw him, without my taking notice of him. When he heard the cable had parted, he instantly went on deck."

At the close of Mr. Morse's evidence, Mr. Bright said that the real tonnage of the vessel was 2,719 tons, and that the engines were of 200 horse-power.

Mr. Henry Carew Taylor, a saloon passenger, deposed - "I am no relation whatever of the captain of the *Royal Charter.*"

Mr. Taylor not being in the room the whole time Mr. Morse was examined, the coroner read over the evidence to Mr. Taylor.

Mr. Taylor said "That was right as far as I know. Mr. Morse knows more that I do. The passengers who landed at Cork were sent in a boat to the pilot-boat. When we were taking our dessert on Tuesday about half past four, one of the stewards came down and said, 'Mr. Taylor, would you like to go on deck and see the *Great Eastern?*' That's how I know when we were passing Holyhead. The wind was against us, and it was very rough. I do not recollect seeing Captain Taylor the whole of the day on deck or until after I jumped overboard. I saw him in the saloon after the vessel struck. It was before light broke. He came into the saloon, spoke very cheeringly, and said we should be on shore safe in ten minutes. Captain Withers was with him, and spoke similarly. The captain said we were embedded in the sand, and in ten minutes they would all be able to walk onshore. I was deputed by the ladies to make enquiry as to the state we were in, when I met Captain Withers coming in before Captain Taylor, and from their appearance and from what they said, I was convinced we should be all safe. I was so convinced at 11 o'clock that all was right that I went to bed, and, until I heard Captain Withers speaking to a lady "Come directly - no time to be lost," and that he would take her child, I was not aware of any danger. When I went to bed I heard some one say 'She rides nobly,' and I said 'I'll go to bed.' When I heard Captain Withers, he said 'Come directly, there's no time to be lost.' I heard it was half past two. I jumped out of bed, opened my cabin door, looked up and down the saloon, saw no-one. It was to Mrs. Woodruffe that Captain Withers spoke. I knew it was, though I did not see her. I then heard the ship strike and give two or three heavy jerks, and I knew then the cause of Captain Withers calling the lady. The vessel was evidently beating heavily. I put on my trousers, coat, slippers, and great coat, and went into the saloon, and saw several ladies and gentlemen, who were in a state of great consternation, crying and praying, and Mr. Hodge, clergyman, prayed extemporaneously. I went to seek my nurse and child at the other end of the saloon. I found the lobby of the saloon perfectly full of men and women, of first and second-class passengers, so crammed, but I could not go through to look for the nurse and child. The thumping went on more violently, and quicker than at first. I at last found my child. The thumping at first was at intervals of a minute and a half, but went on, continuing more and more, until I jumped overboard. I was perfectly wet through for hours before I left the ship. I was told it was half-past seven. I went on deck and was knocked down several times with Captain Taylor, by the waves. He was tied to a log of wood, and lay on the deck. I said, 'Oh, Captain Taylor, what a fearful scene this is.' He did not reply. Another wave came in. I took off my greatcoat and jumped overboard. I, first of all, laid hold of a log of wood, on which was a man. I saw a yard, and got upon that – when I came to shore, after one or two failures, I was laid hold of by a man, Robert Lewis, and two others, and drawn on shore by my fingers. I was taken to Mr. Lewis' house. He put me in his own bed, and afterwards furnished me with his own clothes, and treated me with every kindness. My clothes were torn to rags, and held on only by a belt around my waist. My child and nurse were drowned. The vessel appeared to me to have been thumping for hours before she went to pieces. She beat so severely that it was unsafe to go across the cabin. I saw Captain Taylor with Captain Withers after

the vessel struck. He lashed himself. He was as sober as any man could be. Indeed, I never saw him in the slightest degree intoxicated, or anything approaching it. He always appeared the reverse. If I thought Captain Taylor drunk, I would not have gone to bed, but would have gone and looked after some valuables that I had on board; but I was perfectly satisfied with his conduct. I lost all excepting ten sovereigns and my gold watch. It was blowing hard all Tuesday. I did not remonstrate with Captain Taylor, nor did I hear any other person say anything to Captain Taylor about going into some harbour."

In reply to Mr. Bright – "I saw Captain Taylor struck down by a wave, and then I saw him lying on the deck. He was tied to a log, and had been struck down several times before, and did not get up as soon as I did. When I got up and saw the state of the ship, I jumped overboard."

In reply to Mr. Mellor – "I saw Captain Taylor struck down two or three times. When off Holyhead, I went on deck to see the *Great Eastern*. We were going very slowly all that day. I remarked it to several gentlemen on the poop deck and thought we should never get to Liverpool at the speed she was going. We were off Holyhead nearly all day, but it was seen by several before me there was a great fog over it. I did not see Captain Taylor on deck on Tuesday, and I am not aware that I saw him in the saloon, except when he came down to cheer us up and said we should all be saved. It was about half-past two on Wednesday that Captain Withers woke me. It was after this I saw Captain Taylor. I did not dine at the table Captain Taylor did, and he might have been there without my noticing him. When I went to bed at eleven, the port anchor was out, and I heard some one say she was riding nobly. I went up on deck a little after dark, about tea-time, to see a rocket sent off. I saw two let off. It was for the purpose of signalling the pilots. And I saw a man get into the boat on the poop with a light, which he shook backwards and forwards. I never heard a gun fired. I did not see the masts cut away. I, with others, was ordered down to the lower saloon when they were doing so. I know not whether the tide was ebbing or flowing. Cannot say the vessel could be got out to sea before the port anchor was let out. I know nothing more about it than my little daughter did. I heard Captain Withers and Captain Adams say that the ship would not wear. I never heard Captain Taylor say so, nor did I hear it said in Captain Taylor's presence. I had heard Captain Withers say it two or three times on our passage home, when we were talking of nautical matters. When Captains Withers and Taylor said all was safe, the ladies remained in the cabin, and became pacified, and Mrs. Fenwick gave clean stockings and shoes to put on her children to go on shore. I felt both ways. I did not know what to think - whether it was right or wrong, but when I saw the ship divide, I knew it was all wrong."

Mr. Thomas Gundry, a saloon passenger deposed - "I have heard nearly all that the previous witnesses deposed to. I agree with them up to the time we were off Queenstown. She arrived there about half-past 12 at noon, on Monday. I believe thirteen passengers went on shore there. We reached Holyhead between four and five on Tuesday. It was blowing rather fresh, the weather was thick, but I did not consider it foggy. The storm increased. Between six and seven the Captain gave the first signals for a pilot. A gun was fired about nine o'clock. It was when the anchors were let go that we first thought there was danger. It was about eleven o'clock. I saw the Captain about ten o'clock on deck. I had no conversation with him. I never heard anybody remonstrate with him to turn into any harbour, nor did I myself. He was at that time quite competent, as far as sobriety was concerned. He gave orders to the men. I never saw him in the least the worse for drink. I cannot account for her being where she was, excepting by her drifting before the severe storm. I am not aware that she became unmanageable before the anchors were let go. I believe the screw engines were all in perfect order. The first anchor was let down about eleven o'clock. Cannot say how far we were from shore, but I recollect just before seeing the light at Point Lynas looking over the stern. I think she parted from her first anchor about two o'clock, and I think the other parted immediately after. She struck on the rocks about three o'clock. While at anchor, I believe the steam was up, and the engines at work. She began to break up a little after seven. I heard immediately she struck orders given to turn off the steam, fearing the boilers would burst.

The Captain was on deck until half past one from ten the previous night, when he went to the saloon to order coffee. He said she was riding very easily. Don't recollect him saying there was no danger. He was called up, and came down again about four o'clock. He then did all he could to calm the ladies, and said it would be all right when it dawned. She broke in two about seven, and I then jumped overboard. I did not see him after four o'clock until I was in the act of jumping overboard."

In reply to Mr. Bright – "I believe Captain Taylor did everything that could be done to save the vessel. I heard the remark made that if the masts had been cut away before she parted with her anchors, she might have rode. Cannot say who made the remark, nor did I hear it was said to Captain Taylor. I am convinced that Captain Taylor was quite sober, and fully competent to manage the ship."

In reply to Mr. Mellor - "I don't think anything more could be done to save the lives of passengers than was done. We were waiting for daylight. The hawser was sent ashore very nearly about seven. If it had been daylight, nearly all the lives would have been saved. It was pitch dark. The hawser might have been taken ashore earlier. Operations might have begun earlier. I am not aware it was light enough at six to send the hawser on shore. I should say it was seven when the hawser was completed. I knew of no means of sending the rope on shore from the vessel except by a man taking it. I believe it was Joseph Rogers, a Portuguese, who took the rope on shore. I believe the screw was working at the time the vessel struck. The screw was powerless to keep against the sea. There was almost a dead calm when at Queenstown, and the vessel was under steam alone, or with only very little sails, after entering the Channel. We had no sails off Holyhead. I remember when she was off the River Plate, she encountered rather a violent storm there. The storm on Tuesday night was as violent before the anchors were dropped as when she was off the River Plate. I believe the vessel was then hove to. She had more sails on when off the Plate that she had on Tuesday night. I cannot give an opinion what effect there would be if the sails were up. The wind was either E. or E.N.E. we had very little if any change of wind that day. I am not aware there was any change of wind after eleven. I have heard some remark before that she would not tack. Cannot say who made it. It was in conversation. I heard it said to Captain Taylor."

In reply to Mr. Bright - "There was no occasion to tack the vessel on the voyage home. I cannot say from any failure that it was so. I am not aware that there was any change of wind on Tuesday of any note. When passing the Skerries the wind blew about East. Cannot say how the ship was then steering."

It being now five o'clock and a great portion that the parties interested in the investigation having to go long distances to rest, the inquest was adjourned to ten o'clock on Thursday.

THURSDAY

The Coroner entered upon his duties this morning, at about half-past ten, by taking view of four bodies which he had not before seen. This concluded, he took his seat in the schoolroom, as on the previous day.

The double jury, Llanallgo and Penrhos Lligwy, having been called over (twenty-nine in number).

Mr. Samuel Edward Gapper was sworn. He said "I was second-class passenger on board the *Royal Charter*. I worked thrashing-machines in Australia. I was not present the whole time the witnesses were examined yesterday. The *Royal Charter* was off Queenstown at half-past one on Monday. Eleven or thirteen passengers went on shore there. The vessel was off Holyhead, I think about half-past four on Tuesday evening. The weather was hazy, blowing fresh. Do not know from what quarter. Before reaching Holyhead, the tugboat *United Kingdom* came alongside, and put some men on board - cannot say how many. I do not recollect seeing the captain on deck on Monday. I saw him several times on deck on Tuesday. After passing Holyhead it came on to blow very hard. The wind was on the port bow. The first signal given for a pilot that I saw was about eight o'clock at night. The signals were rockets, blue lights, and sometimes a gun was fired. The anchors were let go about eleven o'clock, after passing Point Lynas. I never heard, at this or any other time, any person ask the captain to turn back to some harbour. I think it was about half-past three on Wednesday morning when she first struck. She parted with her anchors about two o'clock. It was too dark to see the length of the vessel. She first struck on the sands. It was about six o'clock when she struck on the rocks, and she was about three-quarters of an hour on the rocks before she parted. As soon as it was light enough to see, a rope was sent ashore, and a hawser afterwards. During the three-quarters of an hour she was on the rocks, I saw the captain on deck several times. I saw the captain many times during the night. I saw him on the quarter-deck in the intervals of firing the signals. Signals were given up at the time of letting go the anchors. I saw him frequently on deck before the anchors were let down. Did not hear him speak. He walked to and fro, looking at Point Lynas lights over the quarter. He appeared to me perfectly sober. I had no conversation with him after she struck. I heard him speak to the ladies in the saloon about half-past four in the morning. He said 'Ladies, we are on shore, and I hope it is a sandy beach. I hope to God we shall all go on shore when it becomes light.' I did not see him in the saloon afterwards."

In reply to Mr. Bright – "When off Holyhead, we were near enough to see the great ship very dimly. Between Holyhead and Point Lynas the wind increased very much, and still more after passing Point Lynas until we anchored. The wind was blowing tremendously, and much stronger after letting go the anchors. There was a change in the wind. It shifted about ten o'clock, for we examined the chart with Captain Adams, who was returning home, after he had been run down by the *Red Jacket* off Buenos Ayres. He said 'It is impossible to get her off, and I should not be surprised if we should be on shore before morning.' The vessel was lying then to the eastward of Point Lynas. I never saw Captain Taylor the worse for liquor on board."

In reply to Mr. Pitcher – "I heard a desire expressed in the cabin that the captain should go near Holyhead for the purpose of seeing the *Great Eastern*. The wind was blowing N.E. on the port bow when off Point Lynas. I did not hear any order to keep the ship out to sea. Captain Taylor was not present when the wish to approach Holyhead was made. I know the message was taken to him. Cannot say by whom. The message returned was, we might sight the *Great Eastern*, but he could not go out of his course."

In reply to Mr. Mellor - "I know the times I have mentioned by the change of watch more than by anything else. The first signals I know of were given at eight o'clock. I cannot say this was the first signal. We examined the chart with Captain Adams three or four times before ten o'clock, and afterwards. Point Lynas bore at 10 o'clock on the starboard quarter. Cannot say what chart we examined. I never studied charts. (A similar chart produced, on which the witness pointed out the spot.) Capt. Adams said at ten o'clock the ship was in her course. I cannot say that it was at ten o'clock when he said that he should not be surprised if we should be on shore before morning, but he did say so. I am not confident as to the time. It was after the anchors were let go - he said so, and that we might have to swim for it. When off Holyhead we saw the *Great Eastern* very dimly. It was on account of distance and thickness of weather. I cannot say it was very hazy. The wind was not shifting off Holyhead; but from six in the evening until we anchored, it was continually shifting. It was not dark off Holyhead. It was after the anchors parted that the masts were cut; cannot say how soon after it was before she first struck that the mainmast was cut. Capt. Adams was called up to consult with Captain Taylor and Captain Withers on the best means of saving the ship. He was called by Mr. Coombe, the fourth officer. It was before the mainmast was cut, after she parted with her anchors. There were two guns on board, both were used for signals. The weather gun was full of salt-water when they last went to fire it. It was not safe to fire the lee gun. She ceased to use the screw when she was hard and fast on the sand. She was half-an-hour alongside the rocks before she struck. She lay on the sands from half-past five to six. They were close to the rocks. There was no rocket with rope sent on shore. I never saw a mortar on board. Several parties put their lifebelts on; but there was no preparation made by the ship's crew to send a rope on shore until it was light. Cannot say that any light was shown on the ship from half-past five. I do not think I was on deck after that time. There was a light previous to half-past five over the telegraph. It was a globe light. I noticed it because I had not seen it there before. Rockets and blue lights were let off at intervals during the whole night. Cannot say that any were let off after the ship parted from her anchors. Do not know the result of the conference between Captains Taylor, Adams and Withers. Saw Captain Adams afterwards. Had no conversation with him afterwards. It was before the interview that I had heard Captain Adams say he should not be surprised if we were on shore before the morning."

Mr. Mellor here stated that after this he should confine his questions to the course the vessel took, unless he was requested by some other parties to put different questions.

Mr. George Suaicar sworn – "I reside in Liverpool. I am a mariner. I was the boatswain's mate on board the *Royal Charter*. She left Melbourne on the 26th of August. She was bound to Liverpool, and did not call anywhere on her passage. We stayed off Queenstown about three hours. Do not know for what purpose. There were some passengers landed by a pilot-boat. She afterwards proceeded towards Holyhead. We were within four or five miles of Holyhead. There was no time lost in passing Holyhead. We took on board eleven riggers when off Bardsey Island; no time was lost in doing that. The steam tug *United Kingdom* came alongside to put them in. When off Holyhead, the weather was hazy, wind S.E., blowing fresh. The storm increased. At dusk, the Admiralty regulated lights were put out. It was then near five o'clock on Tuesday evening, the 25th October. The wind increased, turning to the eastward. We passed Point Lynas light in a stronger gale than when off Holyhead. She was still going ahead, the tide driving her up. Rockets and blue lights and one gun were fired at a quarter past eight. It was continued all night, and when our danger was apparent, we then burnt signals of distress – torch lights and firing guns. We passed Point Lynas about half-past nine, the gale was then stronger than at Holyhead. When we let go anchors, Point Lynas light was out of sight, the weather being thick. The anchors were let go about eleven. They parted – first, about two or a little after. The second, at near three o'clock. She grounded in about fifteen to twenty minutes after. It was, I believe, on a sandy bottom. We could not see the shore, it was too dark. In about two hours, when the tide made, she struck on the rocks. She was on the rocks an hour and a half before she parted. During that time, it was impossible to send a rope on shore – it was too dark. It was at dawn of day that the rope was sent ashore. I can't say the time. It was sent, I believe, by a man jumping overboard. At the same time, I endeavoured to take a line on shore from amidships. I failed, and I was hauled on board. The only person who attempted besides, was Joseph Rogers; he was the man who succeeded. We were then enabled to get a hawser on shore. There was only time to get on shore sixteen before she parted. It took a little more than an hour to do this. The villagers made fast the hawser on the rocks. She had parted at her main hatch before half the sixteen went on shore. Everything that could be done to save life was done. Captain Taylor was on deck nearly the whole night. I was sent to different parts of the ship, and did not see him all the time. I had myself received orders from him. During this time he was perfectly sober. No person asked him to turn back during that night in my hearing. I first apprehended danger when she parted her cables. I have been to sea twenty-two years. I can give no opinion as to the possibility of taking her out to sea. Every effort was made to put her about before letting go the anchors. I heard orders given by Captain Taylor to stay the ship to clear the land. Those orders were obeyed. We first tried her under steam, by backing the after yards, and putting out a spanker. She came up so far to the wind that the strength of the wind blew her off again. We made a second attempt. We brailed in the after yards in the same way, squared in the head yards. She came up to the wind, but the strength of the wind paid her off again. We then tried her by the lower main top-sail. The ship under a heavy gale of wind can never stay."

In reply to Mr. Bright - "We were steering in passing Holyhead E.N.E. I am not aware of the course from Holyhead to Liverpool. We first made signals off Point Lynas. This was for a pilot. When we passed Point Lynas, the wind turned to E. It went to the N.E. and N.N.E. It was from the latter point the wind blew strongest. The lead was cast before coming to Point Lynas. We continued casting the lead all night until we came close under the rocks. The anchors were let go in sixteen fathoms. The captain was on the forecastle deck when the first anchor was let go. I saw that it was let go. When on the rocks, two torch lights were shown. We tried to fire the gun, which was too wet to go off. When we first attempted to stay, I was sent down by the captain to the first engineer to put as much steam on as it was possible. The sailors were sent on shore to assist in drawing the passengers ashore. An attempt was made to take a second hawser on shore when the ship parted. The reason why we took the riggers on board was that the master of the tug begged for a free passage for them as he was not going to Liverpool. It was after we lost sight of Lynas Light and we parted with the port anchor that we made signs of distress. I am perfectly sure that Captain Taylor was sober."

In reply to Mr. Mellor – "I have seen the chart. When I said I have not seen it, I meant I did not see the course, as I am not an Englishman. I may explain myself. I am a Maltese. I merely looked at it in the hands of Mr. Bright and Captain Martin to see how it varied. I cannot say for what I looked at it. I cannot say how long I looked at it. I had a conversation with Captain Martin and Mr. Bright about it. I cannot say when I said the first time the course we were steering off Holyhead. I do not remember saying it at all before I stated it here. I may have done so, but I do not think I have. Nobody showed me the course on the map from Holyhead to Point Lynas. Nobody has showed me on the map the ship's course from Point Lynas to Liverpool. We tried to stay the ship three times and failed before we anchored. Twice with after yards squared, and once with lower main-topsail, steam going all the time. Steam was never off. I cannot say exactly how we steered from Holyhead to Point Lynas, I think E.N.E. Never was on this coast before. The vessel was on the port tack when we passed Point Lynas – she was as close to the wind as she could lie. Cannot say how the ship lay from Point Lynas, as I did not look at the compass. Cannot form an opinion whether a ship could get out of Moelfra Bay N.N.E. When we tried to stay, the wind was N.E. If she had not missed stays, we should have been able to clear Point Lynas. (The witness afterwards said she could not have.) Cannot say how often I have sailed from Liverpool past Holyhead. From 10 to 15 times, and about the same number of times back. I do not know where the ship was when she missed stays. All I know was she was in 16 fathoms of water. I have been in the *Royal Charter* for the voyage out and home. I had nothing to do with the steering of the ship; there were four men engaged for that purpose. I have seen her stay often; never saw her miss stays before – and I have been in several ships which have missed stays in hard weather when they had not good way upon them. There was not sufficient room to wear the ship after she missed stays. I did not hear any one apply to the captain to cut the masts away. I am not aware that I said so to any person. I never told any person that I had been thrice to the captain to ask permission to cut the masts away, and he refused. I never told you (Mr. Mellor) in the presence of Mr. Russell and Mr. Welch - you have mistaken the person. I do not remember even saying to you that if the master had cut the masts away the vessel would be saved. I never told anybody since the wreck that the captain was drunk the night of the wreck. I did not tell you in the presence of Mr. Russell and Mr. Welch that the captain was drunk the night of the wreck."

In reply to Mr. Bright - "After parting with the anchors, I was running along the bridge. I saw the captain near the steam telegraph, and then met Mr. Stephens, the chief-officer, with a line in his hand. He said 'Suaicar, I am quite willing to take this line ashore, but I cannot swim.' He said 'Can you swim?' I said 'Yes'. 'Will you swim ashore with this line?' I said, 'Yes, sir, anything I can do to save life.' He said 'Come forward.' I asked him for a few moments to put a life-belt on. After putting a life-belt on, I went forward with the chief-officer, and saw three of the villagers on the rocks. We called to them to come down as close as they could, and we would heave the line to them. They did so. We hove eight or nine times and failed. The line was washed out of our hands, and we very nearly with it. I asked after the second anchor parted of the second officer, who was standing by me, if anything was to be done to the rigging. The captain said 'No, not yet, my boy.' I did not escape with £400, and whoever says so tells a falsehood."

Mr. Mellor called Mr. Thomas Welch, who swore "I was present on Thursday with you and Mr. Russell at Moelfra. I heard the last witness Suaicar say that Captain Taylor was drunk on the night of the wreck. I believe he repeated it. I heard him also say that he applied to the captain three times to cut the masts away. I am sure it was the witness Suaicar."

In reply to Mr. S. Martin - "I believe I asked witness if the captain was sober or drunk. I cannot give the precise words of his answer. I thought him sober at the time. It was on Thursday night, the day after the wreck. I think he knew perfectly what he was saying. It took place at the cottage in which he lodged, between half past seven and eight o'clock. I knew Foster, the carpenter. He was present, and made the same statement."

Mr. J.W. Mellor, of Oldham, solicitor was then sworn. "I had a brother and cousin on board the *Royal Charter,* both of whom are lost. I came here on Thursday last to make enquiries about the wreck, and to see if I could find their bodies, and in the course of my inquiries I met Mr. James Russell, one of the survivors. I went with him and the last witness to the house where Suaicar and Foster the carpenter lodged; whilst there Mr. Welch enquired from Suaicar what was the condition of the captain and he said he was drunk on the night of the wreck. He also said that several persons applied to the captain to cut away the masts, and that he himself had asked him three times to do so and he refused. I put the question to him again, and got similar answers. I did not take his answers down in writing. The answers were given in the presence of the carpenter, William Foster, but I do not remember what he said. I was vexed at the loss of my brother and cousin. I called at the office of Messrs. Gibbs, Bright and Co., in Liverpool. I believe it was on the following day. I told a gentleman in their office that there was a rumour at Moelfra that the captain was drunk. He said it was a great lie, and asked who had dared to tell such a lie. I told him I declined to give any name then, but would do so at the inquest. The time Suaicar made the statement to me, he appeared perfectly sober. The person I saw at Messrs. Bright and Co.'s office was giving answers respecting the wreck."

The steep shoreline where the 'Royal Charter' struck in the dead of night. This photograph was taken just before high-water.

In reply to Mr. Martin - "When I made enquires I did so from many persons, and I was told by one of the passengers that the captain was drunk. It was Mr. James Russell who told me. I asked other passengers. I asked Mr. Gardner and he said that he never saw him drunk. I was guarded in my enquiries then. I enquired the condition of the ship and the officers. I spoke to another passenger. I believe it was Mr. Gapper and he said that the captain was sober. I have since ascertained, on pushing my enquiries with Mr. Russell, that he had no personal knowledge of the captain being drunk that night; that he spoke from information. To my mind the evidence given is conclusive that the captain was perfectly sober."

Mr. William Foster sworn – "I was carpenter on board the *Royal Charter*. Nothing occurred wrong to the ship from the time she sailed until we reached Queenstown, nor up to Point Lynas. The wind was right and ahead of us, but do not know from what quarter. When off Point Lynas, it blew a good stiff breeze. We were obliged to give signals for pilots off Point Lynas; it was between eight and nine o'clock on Tuesday the 25th of October. Cannot say where the wind blew from on passing Point Lynas. We were from three to four miles outside Point Lynas. An attempt was made to take the vessel out to sea by bracing the after-yards. I afterwards saw them try to put her about by bracing the fore-yards - and I lent them a hand to set the lower maintopsail. They failed to put her about. The port anchor was let out about eleven o'clock. She dragged it with, I think, ninety fathoms of chain. We were obliged to let go the other anchor. She still dragged – and was kept steaming all the time. I saw the captain on board giving directions. While these things were going on, she parted her bow chain between three and four o'clock on Wednesday morning – and soon after, the second chain. We then cut away the mainmast and she grounded between four and five o'clock*, and in about an hour got on the rocks."

The room at this time becoming dark, the Coroner adjourned the Court until ten o'clock on Friday morning.

* These times are different to those given by other witnesses.

This photograph shows the total destruction of the 'Royal Charter'.

Loss of the *Royal Charter*.

The *Royal Charter* was built at the Sandycroft works, within five miles of this city, on the banks of the Dee. She was deemed a model of naval architecture, and in the voyages she has made to Australia has fully justified the high expectations which the builders formed of her. Her latest trip, out and home, was pre-eminently successful, until her sad loss in the gale of Tuesday night, on the rock-bound coast of Anglesea. The high reputation of this vessel has assured her a large and valuable freight, and the full complement of passengers, many of the latter having with them the savings of a laborious residence in the Southern hemisphere. Her loss has thrown a general gloom over the commercial interests in Liverpool, and the fearful loss of life has plunged many families into deep grief. The event conveys a fearful lesson to all. Here one of the finest vessels afloat, successfully combated and triumphed over the perils of a long and hazardous voyage - her passengers and crew were full of high hopes on reaching the shores of their native land - all had the most joyful anticipation at meeting relations, friends, and the dearest connections; and suddenly, by one of the most awful dispensations of Providence, the gallant ship was wrecked, the wealth with which she was laden plunged in the remorseless sea, and her living cargo grasped by the grim arms of death in its most terrible form. May this severe lesson have its moral with the living. May we recollect, that in the most apparently secure and prosperous moments, we are liable to the most dread visitation; and that it is our own Maker's will that disposes of us, for his own purpose. The decrees of Divine Providence are inscrutable, and our duty is to bow to them with resignation.

Chester Chronicle.
October 29, 1859

THE "ROYAL CHARTER".
THURSDAY, NOVEMBER 10

To-day being calm, the divers began operations about eleven o'clock, but, although they were indefatigable until five – low water – nothing of any moment was brought to light, a few of the ship's articles of domestic use being the sum total.

Letters of inquiry continue to be received in large numbers by the rector, who is really unable to reply to all; but from our own personal observation, the friends of missing passengers may be assured that instant notices will be sent to them of all who may be identified, or may have anything about them by which relations or friends could distinguish them, as the bodies are all examined personally by the rector, and any trinket or article found upon them is reserved for their friends.

The shore ground is still guarded by the coast guard and police. The underwriters are represented by Captains Fell and Lodge, the Board of Trade by Mr. Smith, the Collector of Customs at Beaumaris, and the owners by Captain Martin. The latter gentleman has engaged boats to be out from light to dark every day, sweeping the whole bay for the bodies, and every care being taken of them, as they are discovered, removed to the several churches near the coast, from the idle gaze of the inhabitants. Mr. James Russell and Mr. Gapper, two of the survivors, are detained on the spot in order to identify as many as possible. Up to this time, 72 bodies have been found, of which eight are in the church of Penrhos Lligwy, five are in Llanddona, two in Llanbedrgoch, and three at Pentraeth.

The following is a list of the bodies identified:-

John Smith, infant, four years old – parents not yet cast up. Miss Russell, daughter of Mr. James Russell, one of the saved. Mrs. Lyon, of Melbourne. Miss Jane Fowler. Rich. Reed, Plymouth. Jacob Roberts, fireman. James Walton, second steward, --- Milliken,

A head-stone at Pentraeth to six unidentified bodies washed ashore nearby.

3rd-class passenger. William Smeaton, apprentice. John Watkins. James Eddowes. Henry Aspinall, rigger. J. Grave, £56 found on his person. Rich. Fernibough, sailmaker. --- Wilson, boilermaker and first engineer. William Barratt, five years old. John Rees, Pistill, Nevin. Michael Henry Davies, a Jew. --- Lambert, seaman. --- Russell, seaman. William Bishop, seaman. Mrs. Fenwick. Master Pitcher. Master Hogarth. A female with stockings, one marked Lewis, the other Robinson. Mrs. Hogarth, clothes marked G. Pringle, £5 on her person. Miss Anne Fawlen. A body washed onshore at Amlwch was too decomposed for recognition. Also a body at Cemaes and one at Llanrhyddlad. Today there was picked up, on Redwharf Sands, a piece of shirt marked C.G. Baker 12, a child's linen drawers, marked Ida Fowler 5, a shirt marked J. Murray 3.

Caernarfon & Denbigh Herald.
November 12, 1859

The Carnarvon and Denbigh Herald
AND NORTH AND SOUTH WALES ADVERTISER
Saturday, November 12, 1859

Conclusion of the Evidence and Verdict. The following is from our second edition of last week:-

FRIDAY

The court opened at ten o'clock this morning.

Mr. William Foster's evidence continued:- "The vessel remained thumping against the rocks from half-an-hour to an hour, when she broke right across the main hatch. Previous to this, a rope had been sent ashore. A man of the name of Joseph Rogers jumped overboard and swam ashore with a rope. A hawser was afterwards sent ashore. There were some people standing upon the cliffs, and they assisted to fasten the hawser on the rock. This hawser had been sent ashore and secured about an hour, or an hour and a half, before the vessel broke across the main hatch. I think about sixteen persons went ashore by that hawser - they were the crew of the vessel. There was some female who hesitated to go ashore by the hawser, and there was half-an-hour's delay in everything. The female refused to go, and I then went along the hawser and was thus saved. About three of the crew came onshore in the same way after me. The chief part of the passengers and crew were at this time on the poop, and some below in the saloon. There were others on the forecastle head. A heavy sea came across the starboard bow and broke the vessel across the forecastle, and swept from sixty to seventy persons who were on the forecastle into the sea. I saw the captain frequently that night, and he was perfectly sober. I have been four or five voyages to sea. Considering the gale that occurred that night and Wednesday morning, the captain could not have done more than he did to prevent the vessel running upon the rocks."

In reply to Mr. Bright:- "I paid no attention and cannot say whether the wind changed after passing Point Lynas, but it blew stronger and stronger. We took soundings the whole night, both with the hand line and deep sea line. It was my duty to sound the water, and to examine the pumps, and the vessel made no water after thumping upon the sands. It was in about one hour after she did so, and when she slewed round it was then I first observed her making water. After parting from her anchors, signals of distress were made. We fired guns, rockets, and blue lights; and torches made of oakum dipped in turpentine. The anchors were dropped in sixteen fathoms of water. I assisted to cut away the masts. We first cut away all the lee rigging, then cleared away all the running gear, and what would hold the masts and prevent them going down. We then cut away the weather rigging. The sixteen of the crew sent on shore first were for the purpose of getting another hawser on shore, and an attempt was made to get a second hawser on shore, but failed, from what cause I cannot say, as I was on the rocks. It was just then that she broke across the main hatch. When the vessel was upon the rocks, there were signals shown on board, and Mr. Cowie, the second officer, was showing a blue light."

In reply to Mr. Mellor - "I could see Point Lynas Light after letting go the anchor. I cannot say how it bore. Cannot say how soon I lost sight of the light after the anchor was down. I think we were three or four miles off Point Lynas Light when the anchors were let go. Cannot say how far from the place we anchored to the place she first struck. I heard some part of Suaicar's evidence yesterday. I heard Suaicar say that he was going to take a line on shore. It was thick weather when we passed Point Lynas; but I am sure I could see the light when we anchored. Suaicar and I did not sleep in the same house that night."

In reply to Mr. Bright – "I never heard Suaicar say the captain was drunk."

In reply to the Coroner – "I have no recollection of seeing Mr. Mellor and Welch at our lodgings on Thursday week. It is impossible; hundreds have called there. I never heard Suaicar say that he had asked permission of the captain to cut the masts away, and that the captain had refused. I never made such a statement myself, either to Mr. Mellor or Mr. Welch."

Mr. J.B. Marsh, Reporter of Chester – "I conversed with Suaicar at his lodgings about half past eight to nine o'clock on Thursday week. Foster, the carpenter, was present. After taking down Suaicar's and Foster's narratives in writing, I asked Suaicar if he had anything more to tell me. He said 'Some man on the beach had been saying that the captain was drunk; but he was as sober as I am now. I should like to meet the man who had said the captain was drunk.' He afterwards added – 'I was running about nearly all the night carrying messages between the captain and crew, and I can swear that the captain was not drunk.'"

The coroner suggested that some nautical evidence should be produced. Mr. Bright acquiesced. The Coroner suggested that as Captain Fell was on the beach and had no distinct interest, he should like to hear his evidence. Mr. Bright suggested that his honour should send a subpoena for him, which was done.

Mr. James Russell, a second-class passenger, was then called and sworn – "I had my wife and two children on board with me. The *Royal Charter* sailed from Melbourne on the 26th of August, bound for Liverpool. Nothing to mention occurred from the time we sailed until we reached Point Lynas. There were some passengers landed off Queenstown. She might have been detained from two to three hours, as near as I can judge. We were off Queenstown about one o'clock, and left about four o'clock on Monday afternoon. The vessel reached off Holyhead as the sun was sinking, and we could just see the *Great Eastern's* outline. Could not say how near the land we were. The wind was blowing fresh, and had been blowing fresh all day, but rather more so at that period. I was not on deck off Point Lynas. The last time I was on deck we were passing a light off Holyhead. The first thing I knew of afterwards was about two o'clock on Wednesday morning. I was coming out of my cabin, and I heard Mr. W. Watson say something to Mr. Smith at the cabin opposite mine. Mr. Smith said to me 'Oh, we are drifting.' I went back into my cabin and finished dressing my children. This was about two o'clock. In about an hour or three quarters of an hour, the vessel struck. Cannot say when she got on the rocks, for I could not perceive any difference to the bumping. I was below in the lower saloon and second cabin until about half an hour of dawn. When she parted, I was in the saloon passage, and saw it. I was then making my way to the deck, and I then went to the poop. I saw a rope from the fore-part of the vessel to the shore. I believe some of the crew had got on shore then. My wife and children were with me on the poop. I told them to hold on by the rail, and I fastened them, and I went for a rope. I tried one rope and then another, but I could only get one end loose. My intention was to fasten my wife and children to the rope, the edge of the vessel being close to shore, and to throw it ashore. I could not get it. I returned to my wife, and said 'We are all gone.' I did not see any of the vessel break, but every wave was breaking her piece by piece, and I was washed overboard and the waves washed me ashore. How, I cannot tell. It was then blowing a strong wind;

stronger than at any other time. I did not see the Captain the whole of that night. I did say the captain was drunk, but when I said it, I told the enquiring parties (Mr. Mellor and others) who told me. I was told by the boatswain's mate, and I was also told by Walter Hughes, and a person of the name of Bradbury. The two latter are now lying in the village, unable to move from injuries sustained. The boatswain's mate expressed it the evening after the wreck in the presence of Mr. Welsh and Mr. Mellor. I believe the boatswain's mate was sober. He appeared to be so. I did not see any signals. I believe there were signals, for I saw Mr. Cowie, the second officer, more than once go into the magazine for powder. I never saw Captain Taylor, at any time during the voyage, intoxicated."

Thomas Griffiths, one of the crew, sent for by Mr. Mellor, from Amlwch, presented himself for examination. On being sworn, he said – "I was one of the crew of the *Royal Charter.* She left Melbourne on the 26th of August. There was not much wrong until the vessel had passed Point Lynas. Off Holyhead – the morning – Tuesday – was fine. The wind blew fresh about six in the afternoon. The vessel was then near Skerries, outside. We put out signals for a pilot off Cemaes. We did not get one. We continued signals until passing Point Lynas. I do not understand navigation. The vessel was, from my own knowledge of the coast, in her proper course. She was on the track to meet a pilot if there were one out. I saw the captain giving directions all that night and morning to the crew. The first anchor was let go about eleven on Tuesday night. I cannot say how far we were off Point Lynas Light before we let go the anchors. I was up aloft when the second anchor let go. She did not hold to her anchors, but drifted and struck about half-past three in the morning, and got on the rocks about six – at the breaking of day. She parted at the main hatch, and soon after became a total wreck. Before the anchors were let go, the captain tried to stay the vessel. He tried two or three times, and failed to get her round. She was too light, and the wind blew too hard to allow her to go round. I mean by being too light that she was not low enough in the water. She was stiff enough when she left Melbourne, but she was lightened by the quantity of coals burnt. I do not think she had sufficient coals to steam all the way across. She did not steam all the way; but I cannot say how many days she did not steam. She was more than a week not steaming. This was my first voyage with the *Royal Charter.* I never saw her stay, nor attempt it, until she came here. I have nothing more to say. I know of nothing against the captain."

Mr. William Parry of Manchester wished to ask a question – He stated he had a friend on board who went by the name of Henry Williams, but whose real name was Charles Parry, and a second-class passenger called Mary Ridley. He heard of the wreck on the day of the occurrence.

Witness replied – "The vessel, I believe, was sufficiently off the land when the anchors were let go to clear Point Lynas, and go back to Holyhead, if she had stayed."

In reply to Mr. Bright – "The vessel drew 21 feet aft and between 19 and 20 feet before. We were 39 days from Melbourne to the Line. Cannot say how many days we steamed during that time. She steamed during that time four or five days. It was said she had 700 tons of coal on board when she left. The bunkers were full. There was coal in the lower hold. It was full. I cannot say how much. The orlop deck was full. I don't know how the wind was when we dropped anchor. I believe it was N.E."

Captain William Martin, of Liverpool, Marine Superintendent – "I am employed by Messrs. Gibbs, Bright and Co., in that capacity. The *Royal Charter* belonged to the Liverpool and Australian Steam Navigation Company, and in this country she was under my charge. Her registered tonnage was 2,719 tons, and of 200 horsepower nominal – capable of driving her with the screw, eight knots an hour, or nine and a half miles an hour. She has made, under sail, 18 knots an hour. I was out with her on her first trial trip. We came down with her as far as five miles to the eastward of Point Lynas. We had on board, at the time, a number of scientific gentlemen to prove the capabilities of the ship. Our first trial was under steam, and it was fully proved that, in a calm, she could make 8¼ knots an hour. Our next trial was under canvas, a fresh breeze blowing, say topgallant breeze. There was a great deal of ambition on board as to who should put the ship in stays* first. The captain (Mr. Boyce) gave up his right to Mr. Parry, the pilot. The helm was put down and the ship stayed to the whole satisfaction of all on board. So thoroughly satisfied were we all that we did not think it necessary to try again. We steamed out all day trying every experiment with the ship, and sailors and engineers agreed that the vessel was complete. Her draught of water at the time was 18ft 4in aft, and 18ft forward. That was my only trial with the ship. The *Royal Charter* was examined every voyage, and she had on board the certificate of the Board of Trade. The *Royal Charter* was fully equipped in every possible way, and I may just add, at this particular time, as the looking after her and fitting out all rested with me, I have always been extremely careful that everything that would make the ship seaworthy, and add to the comfort of the passengers who travelled in her, should be done; and have never in one instance failed to comply with the regulations of the Board of Trade. Gibbs, Bright and Co. have always given me instructions not to allow anything to go wrong. Her compasses were fully adjusted before sailing, and everything else completed that could add to the safety of the ship. I was nineteen years at sea, five years as commander, and

have frequently sailed in screw boats. I have been to Australia. I know the course of vessels from Liverpool to Melbourne, and from Melbourne back. I recollect the night of Tuesday, the 25th of October. It was very stormy. I have attended to the evidence of the several witnesses examined here carefully. I have a chart before me, and looking at it, I think I can form an opinion where the vessel was when the anchors were let go. All nautical men that understand the course, will agree, that when a vessel, after leaving the South Stack and Skerries, has steered her proper course, the next object will be to get her safe past Point Lynas. The *Royal Charter* reached that point safely, and all the witnesses I have examined proved clearly that the ship was three to four miles to the north of Point Lynas. I'll show the position at three miles - and I have no doubt that at that point there were thirty fathoms of water. Here we have Captain Taylor looking for a pilot. He then comes up to the regular pilot ground eastward. There are three pilot stations: the first outside the Northwest Lightship; the second is the Ormeshead station; and the third is Point Lynas, or Westernmost station. If a captain fails in getting a pilot at Point Lynas, his next safe course is to steer for the Ormeshead station; and it is on that course we can trace him five miles to the eastward of Point Lynas. The next thing we hear is that he is encountering a very heavy breeze from N.E. to N. according to the evidence, he having tried to stay the ship. Failing in that, we find him leaving go his anchors in sixteen fathoms water. Sixteen fathoms water is rather more than four miles from shore; and I have no doubt of his having been driven previously at least five miles to leeward. The position of the ship was wrecked in goes to prove that the wind must have been somewhere N.N.E., and there can be no doubt, from the manner in which the ship broke up, that the hurricane was very severe. It was

* in stays - to change to the other tack.

impossible for the captain to stay that vessel before he let go of the anchors, nor any other vessel under the circumstances of the wind in such a hurricane. It would have been certain destruction to wear her. I knew Captain Taylor 17 years, and have commanded vessels for this company about 16 years. I have always known him to be a temperate man, and he was selected for the command of the *Royal Charter* from being a very smart man, fully competent in everything to command such a vessel. He had a first-class certificate."

In reply to Mr. James Russell - "The *Royal Charter* was never altered after being launched. The *Royal Charter's* draught was certified by the Board of Trade to be 21 feet. She would be more manageable at 18 feet forward and 19 feet aft than at 21 feet. I should rather go out in her thus. From the position of the wreck, and the quarter from which the wind blew, it is my opinion she must have been nearly five miles to the eastward of Point Lynas when her anchors were let go."

Captain Alfred Fell, of London, agent for the London Underwriters, deposed - "I have been twenty years at sea, being in command in the East Indian and Australian trades, and seventeen years as an agent to the Underwriters in London. I was not present at any part of the investigation until this evening. The position shown upon the map, is the position in which the vessel was supposed to be when her anchors were let go. It was at the last of the flood - wind at N.E. I would say it was impossible to stay that vessel. I have heard the evidence given by Captain Martin, and I agree with him that Captain Taylor did all that could be done under the circumstances to save the ship. I should have done everything that Captain Taylor did."

This ended the evidence.

The coroner here said, addressing the jury:- "As I told you at the commencement of this enquiry, I now repeat that you must leave out of your consideration all that you may have heard previously, and try to recall to your recollection the evidence which had been adduced. If you wish me to do it, I will read over to you the whole of the evidence given, but in order to make everything plain, I got Mr. Pritchard, of Bangor, a gentleman who is perfectly conversant with both languages, in order to translate to you the evidence as it proceeded, so that the matter should be sifted to the uttermost. I thank you for your great patience during this melancholy enquiry – a circumstance which never before had its parallel in this country, where so many lives were lost in so short a space of time, or where so many families had to mourn the loss of wives, husbands, and children. Our object in this enquiry has been to find out whether this has occurred from any mismanagement on the part of the captain, or was caused by any fault in the construction of the vessel. The first question, therefore, for your consideration is, was Captain Taylor in fault in bringing the vessel to the spot where she was wrecked. We have the evidence of Mr. Morse, Mr. Gundry, and Mr. Taylor, saloon passengers, and of Mr. Gapper and others, distinctly proving to my mind, that Captain Taylor was perfectly sober during the whole time, and I think you will also be satisfied that such was the case. An attempt was made, and I wish the gentleman was present now, to prove that he was not sober; but the evidence, I think, clears him completely from such a charge, and in justice to the unfortunate captain's memory, I must say I believe he was sober, and did all that could be done, under the circumstances in which he was placed, to save the vessel and the lives of the passengers under his charge. He (the Coroner) had no wish, however, to warn the opinions of the jury. If they differed from him, they would say so from their verdict.

They should first consider whether the delay at Queenstown was unnecessary, and if so, whether it affected the position of the vessel when the storm caught her. It was evident she could not have got into Liverpool before the gale, and it had been proved that it was impossible for Captain Taylor to get the vessel out. Such is the evidence of Captains Martin and Fell; but I regret that none of the ship's officers survived to give us true evidence of the exact position of the vessel. The next question is, was every means used, after the vessel had become a wreck, to save the lives of the passengers. He (the Coroner), thought that such was the case, but it was for the jury, by their verdict, to say whether the circumstances occurred from any negligence of Captain Taylor." His honour then read the dictum of a judge to show that if the accident had occurred from want of judgement only, there was no criminality.

The room was then cleared. In about ten minutes, Mr. Pritchard, the interpreter, was called in to write out the collective verdict of the jury. On the admission of the public, the following was read.

"Having carefully attended to the evidence, we are unanimously of opinion that James Walton and others were unfortunately lost in the *Royal Charter* by pure accident: that the captain was perfectly sober, and that his conduct proves that he had done all in his power to save the ship and the lives of the passengers."

When the jury had delivered their verdict, Mr. A.H. Smith, collector of customs at Beaumaris, read the following communication, which he said had that moment reached him:-

Custom-house, London.
Nov. 3, 1859
To the Collector of Customs at Beaumaris,
Sir, The Board of Trade having directed an inquiry into the loss of the *Royal Charter*, I beg to acquaint you that I propose leaving London for Beaumaris by tomorrow evening's train, and have to request you will in the meantime notify to the witnesses now under examination before the coroner that such inquiry is about to be held, and their attendance will be required. You will also be so good as to inform Messrs. Gibbs, Bright and Co. of Liverpool, that this inquiry has been directed.
                         J. O'Dowd, solicitor,
              Merchant Shipping Department

The management of Gibbs, Bright & Co. must have given a huge sigh of relief at the verdict of the jury, as there was the certainty that legal action would have been taken against them if there was any hint that their principal employee on the 'Royal Charter' was unfit to be in charge of such an important vessel. Thankfully, witnesses had testified under oath that Captain Taylor was perfectly sober on that fatal night, and the jury had decided that all those lives had been lost by accident, and not by negligence on the part of the ship's master.

Certainly, there had been many cases in the past where seamen had drunk alcohol to ease the pain when faced with certain death, but the following report appeared in one newspaper supporting the idea that the ship's officers fully understood the potential danger of drunkenness at a time like this:-

It is stated that one of the crew of the *Royal Charter*, at the time she struck, rushed to the store-room and broke all the bottles containing spirits, fearing that his fellow-seamen might intoxicate themselves.

It is highly unlikely that a seaman would have carried out this task on his own initiative, and it is probable that he was acting under the direct orders of Captain Taylor or one of the ship's officers, who needed every crew-man to be fully capable of carrying out his duty without question or delay.

The paddle-steamer 'Rothsay Castle', wrecked in 1831.

Perhaps still at the back of people's minds was the memory of the great loss of life in August 1831, only a few miles from Moelfre, when the 'Rothsay Castle' ran onto the Dutchman's Bank, a vast sandbank near Puffin Island, while en route from Liverpool to Beaumaris, Anglesey. Despite having recently been fitted with a new boiler, this wooden paddle-steamer was so old and leaky that she rapidly broke up, with only sixteen passengers, four of the crew and one musician being saved.

Shortly after, the captain seemed more on the alert, and betrayed signs of alarm and great irritation. He swore at the men for not trimming the vessel by means of a box running on wheels and containing heavy chains, which was on the mid-deck, and which they ought to have moved from side to side as occasion required. He was several times asked, "What shall we do to be saved?" and on one occasion he answered, "If you are afraid, go to prayers." I put a question relative to our situation to the steward, who replied, " How can you be afraid when you see us all so merry?" The crew were either sea-sick or drunk; they staggered along the deck, and became very talkative. The captain stood in the midships, swearing at the men; I am convinced, indeed, that they were all drunk except the man at the wheel. The male passengers were in great anxiety; the women were wailing and crying; the children were overpowered by sickness, and lay chiefly in a helpless state on the deck. The steam, which had recently been applied, again became short, and the captain ordered "All hands to the pump." Some cried out to hoist the sail, others said "No". It was not hoisted, and the vessel lay without either steam or sail until she struck on a sand-bank.

From 'The Wreck of the Rothsay Castle', published in 1833

The Passengers and Crew

Who was actually aboard the 'Royal Charter', and how many of the passengers and crew lost their lives? That was an easy question to ask, but finding the answer in 1859 proved difficult, and the true extent of the loss of life is probably still unknown even today. We have the list provided by Mr. Lynch (see page 112), but quite simply, the most accurate passenger-list was carried on board the ship and was not recovered. Other sources may or may not be correct, as some people were travelling under assumed names, perhaps fleeing from justice or their creditors.

> A person named William Gardiner, a commission agent, residing in Melbourne, made an unostentatious exit from the colony by the *Royal Charter*, taking with him property worth £4,000. He shipped in the name of Garden. He has since been declared an insolvent.

Caernarfon & Denbigh Herald. November 26, 1859

Was this the Mr. Gardiner who was listed as a saloon passenger? If so, he appears to have left the ship at Queenstown, leaving his wife on board the doomed clipper.

In his 'All the Year Round', Charles Dickens says 446 persons were killed; the 'Amhurst and Back Creek Advertiser' in Australia says 449 lives were lost; but 459, 460, and 470 deaths are quoted by other sources; the 'Liverpool Albion' newspaper says 480; and Sir James Elphinstone in his Parliamentary report on anchors and cables says that a total of 497 men, women and children died in the tragedy. This latter estimate is probably more accurate than the others, as it was written several years after the disaster, although the death-toll would have been even higher had the 'Royal Charter' not paused at Queenstown.

> Amongst the eleven persons who effected their escape from the *Royal Charter* by going ashore at Queenstown in the pilot-boat was a lady, who would have gone on with the vessel for Liverpool, but she apprehended her near approach to confinement rendered it unsafe for her to run the risk. She proceeded to her destination in the County Tipperary, and was yesterday safely delivered of a son, "who with the mother are doing well." Thus were two human beings providentially saved from a dreadful death in Moelfra Bay.

Liverpool Mercury. Thursday, November 3, 1859

By this time, it was a lack of coffins that was causing concern, as more bodies came ashore in need of identification and a decent burial.

> Sir,
>
> Having been to visit the scene of the wreck of the ill-fated *Royal Charter*, I venture, through the medium of your columns, to suggest to the owners of the ship the humanity and propriety of sending down from Liverpool a number of coffins to bury the unfortunate bodies washed on shore, as the difficulty of procuring them is very great and the charges exorbitant. One gentleman on Sunday last was too glad to get a wretched thing nailed together and called a coffin for £5, and in some cases they cannot be procured at all. I would also suggest there being for the next ten days or a fortnight a person remaining on the spot to photograph any body that may not be claimed up to the time of its being necessary to bury it, as many of those unfortunate creatures may remain unclaimed, their friends not perhaps expecting them on this vessel. This arrangement would prevent much confusion and disinterring of bodies hereafter. Lastly, it strikes me there should be a proper person who understands such matters there to take charge of deeds and papers which are continually being washed on shore – of course, saturated, but still which could be preserved or restored if in the hands of persons who understand such matters with the aid of chemicals. Nothing can exceed the

kindness of Mr. Smith, the collector of wreck and Customs House officer, who is untiring in his exertions to give every assistance in his power to the numerous inquires after relatives and friends. Should you think those suggestions worth inserting and that they would be the means of relieving one anxious heart, my object will be fully attained.

I remain your obedient servant,

SYMPATHIZER

The Times. Friday, Nov 4, 1859

This immense loss of life so close to the Anglesey shore spurred many minds into action, in the hope of preventing such a tragedy from occurring again. Surely anything that would float could have saved lives in the circumstances, as the 'Royal Charter' didn't carry dedicated lifeboats with enough space for all passengers and crew, just four pinnaces that were commonly used for ferrying stores and passengers ashore in relatively calm conditions.

A Mr. Richie already had a patented life-saving device, while a Mr. Williams had a similar idea that could be used to save human life in an emergency.

LOSS OF THE ROYAL CHARTER.

Why do not SEAMEN and PASSENGERS avail themselves of RICHIE'S PATENT CORK BEDS, which would be invaluable as Life Buoys in case of shipwreck?

E. Marsden, 16, Union Street., Liverpool.

SOLE AGENTS

Preservation of Life From Shipwreck.

Gentlemen, it appears very extraordinary to me that in Liverpool and other large seaport towns where emigration is carried on to a great extent, something has not been devised by which, in case of shipwreck or foundering at sea, human life might be spared. My object in writing to you is to point out a remedy, unquestionably a feasible one, and easily obtained at a comparatively low price when human life upon the ocean is considered; and I am more surprised that Government has not taken the matter up by passing an act to force upon all the masters and owners of emigrant ships the necessity of supplying their vessels with efficient life-buoys. The present system adopted, as far as I can learn, is that all the first and second-class passengers are provided with bed and bedding, the bed or mattress being filled with feathers, hair or flocks, in place of which I would suggest the necessity of having the beds and pillows made of the best and most improved macintosh material. Each bed and pillow a perfect life-buoy, the former sufficient to sustain and keep afloat six persons; in case of foundering at sea, fifty of these life-buoy belts would keep 300 souls from sinking. They could also, when inflated, be lashed fast to the side of the ship's boats, which would prevent any possibility of the boats sinking or upsetting; this, of course, refers to the time when there is no alternative left but to abandon the ship. If you think it is advisable or worth the trial, the experiment can easily be made at the plunge baths in Cornwallis Street or St. George's Pier-head. You will then have practical proof as to the utility and value of the same in saving life. I am satisfied they would be cheaper for the merchant, lighter for the vessel, and a good preventative of those offensive and obnoxious vermin bugs so common to ships trading to warmer climates.

Yours etc.,
J.J. Williams,
King Street, Chester.
24th Nov., 1859

Liverpool Mercury. Thursday, December 1, 1859

The North Wales Chronicle

AND ADVERTISER FOR THE PRINCIPALITY

BANGOR, SATURDAY, NOVEMBER 12, 1859

List of the Passengers of the *Royal Charter.* SALOON -- Hugh Bethune, Mr. and Mrs. Bruce, infant, and servant, Mr. W. Beamer, jun., Mr. and Mrs. Davis, two daughters and two sons, Mr., Mrs., and two Miss Fowlers and servant, Mrs. Fenwick and four children, Mrs. Foster, Mr. J. and Mrs. Grove, Mr. and Mrs. Gardiner (Mr. Gardiner landed at Cork.), Mr. Gundry (saved), Mr. F. T. Hutton, Rev. Charles Hodge, Dr Hatch, Mr. J. S. Henry, Mr. and Mrs. Jenkins and five sons, Mr. Walter Lafargue, Mr. J. B., Mrs., Miss and Master Murray, Mr. J. M'Evoy, (landed at Cork), Mr. Mellor, Mr. Molineux, W. H. Morse (saved), Mr. R. F. Macgeorge, Mrs. Nahmer and child (landed at Cork), Mr. W. H. and Mrs. Pitcher, two children, and servant, Mr. Rufford, Mrs. Tweedale, Mr. Henry C. Taylor, child and servant (Mr. Taylor saved), Mr. Welsh, Captain Withers, Mrs. Woodruff and child, Mr. G. Watson.

SECOND CLASS -- Mr. Allen and two children (landed at Cork), Captain Adams, Mr. Barrat and child (son), Charles Callis, Mr. and Mrs. Dodd, or Todd, and two children, Miss F. Davies, Mr. Eddowes, Bird, Edgar Gates, S. E. Gapper (saved), Mrs. Glover, John Griffiths, Wm. Houlden, Mr. Henderson, John Loone (saved), — Lethlaine, L. E. Mention (saved), John Maule, Mr. M'Nab, T. Macreadie, — Nicholas, Mrs. Norman and two children, Mr. Portway, Mr. Parry, Edmund Pearce, Mrs. R. Rose, Mr. and Mrs. Russell and two children (Mr. Russell saved), Mr. and Mrs. Smith and three children, Solomon Samuel, Mr. Sanson, Julius Stirks, (landed at Cork), Miss Elizabeth Ward, Miss Mary Ellen Wrigley, Edward Watson, John Wilkes, Mr. Watson.

THIRD CLASS AND STEERAGE -- John Bradbury (saved), Mr. Lyons and family (wife and three children), two sons, J. Triesteman and family (two children), Henry Burns and child (? landed at Cork), Nathaniel Nathan, Alice Newton, Jos. Churton, John and Catherine Duggan (landed at Cork), John Judge (saved), Maurice Boyle, James Dean (saved), Wright Lockwood, Jos. Moss, Mr. Faulkner and child, Robert Jeffrey, P. De La Landa, David Thompson, Mrs. Kennedy and family (two children), Thomas Willis, T. Wickett and party, C. Jackeman, Messrs. Jones and Rice, C. Kisterman, Messrs. Culins, Sturt, and Lyon, Charles Conway, Bates and Rosely, James Johnston, James Pardy, Joseph Spyaglio, George Chesney, Thomas Byrne, John Grice, Matthew Scott, Houghton and Thompson, T. Wood, Thompson and Milliken, Noah Lyons, William Green, Robert Tuck, Joseph Gibson, John Wotherspoon, John Lynch (landed at Cork), Charles Anderson, P. Thompson, E. Fowler, H. Ivey, L. Porrit, Michael Kavanagh, Antonio Albergetti, Duffin and Rolls, Morrelli and Cavagna, John and P. Martin, George Leito, Henry Lawton, Mr. Kirkbride and two sons, Mr. Kennedy and family (wife and three children), William Banks, David Thomas, C. R. Ross, W. J. Ferris (saved), J. M'Cappin (saved), T. Taylor, Robert Hogarth, Henry Enghams, William and John Row, Messers. Trippit and Lowe, William Makepiece, Thomas Fawcett, William Bowden (saved), James King, Denis Collins (? landed at Cork), William and T. Murray, John Buchanan, Coll. M'Phiel (saved), Jos. Robinson, A. Pottinger, George Taylor, Samuel Grenfell (saved), E. Allen, John Anderson, L. Dalton, Wm. Storey, W. Crowley (landed at Cork), Mrs. Ross and family (two children, one an infant), D. Travers, F. Wyatt, James Sullivan (landed at Cork), James Turner, Mr. Carling, or Conlin, and family (three children), B. Bladier, Mr. Padditte, Wm. Bishop, Mrs. Willis and family (two children), John Gillespie, Thos. Kelley, Mr. Mitchell and wife, R. Oliver and party, P. Hogarth and family (one child), Wm. Ford, C. Shanahan (landed at Cork), David Bell, Wm. Wilson, Geo. Smith, Michael Frawley, Messrs. Derose and Kenny, John Famby or Formby, R. Longstaff, Frank Webber, Geo. Watson, Mr. Holland and family (wife and three children), Isaac Stephenson, Mrs. Atkey and child, T. Newton, Agett Richards, Jas. Stanard (saved), Edmiston and Ellis, Mr. Terril, Jessie Thornden, Baptiste Phillipine, Wm. Fleming, Jno. Scott, John Muhlmann or Nuhlmann, Chas. Parkinson, John Parkinson or Ranson, Jas. Pamplin, Miss Davidson, Henry Sims, John Marrion, Samuel Mosely Wade, Nicholaide Page, Mrs. M'Leod and family (two children), William Tany, John Inglis, Rd. Davies, Joseph Potts, Frank Hoyland, E. Willray, Miss Susanna Morton or Merton, John Mason, T. Bakewell, Jas. Black, and Beratti Vingenga.

From the Belfast newsletter.

Mr. M'Cappin and Mr. Ferris, our townsmen, who were so miraculously saved from the wreck of the *Royal Charter,* have visited our office within the last few days, and have given us some particulars in reference to their most extraordinary escape and the appalling scenes they witnessed on that dreadful morning on the Welsh coast. They have been urged to deliver in public some description of the catastrophe from the moment the vessel struck until the time they left the wreck on their way to Belfast; and for many such an account would possess a very melancholy interest. Among the property which Mr. M'Cappin had on board was a box containing several valuable rings made from gold nuggets, brooches, and other articles of jewellery, and a valuable silver Orange medal, bearing on one side the image of King William. The box went down with the vessel, and after a desperate struggle with the raging elements, its owner succeeded in reaching the land with his life. The next day, having got himself temporarily clothed in such stray articles as were cast up by the tide, he went along the beach searching for some of his lost property, when he found, partly embedded in the sand, a small nugget, which he at once recognized as one of the most unique in his collection, and probably the most beautiful for its size on board the *Royal Charter*. In appearance it appears an exact resemblance to a small opal, the quartz being, as it were, set in the gold, in the same manner as a stone in an ordinary opal. Further on, one of the Coastguard asked if anyone had lost a medal. Mr. M'Cappin replied that he had, and having given a description of it, it was produced, and found to be the same as he had packed up with the nuggets and other articles in his box. How these articles, small and heavy, torn from the box, were carried on the waves, and left where they were uncovered by the receding tide, when strong and vigorous men, battling for life, were swallowed by the billows, must remain one of the many wonders in connection with this deplorable occurrence.

THE "ROYAL CHARTER"
LIVERPOOL, Tuesday. A subscription list has been started here for the relief of the sufferers by the loss of the *Royal Charter*. Upwards of £1,000 has already been contributed.

Note that this passenger-list is incomplete and inaccurate. Further details are available on our website.

The Carnarvon and Denbigh Herald

AND NORTH AND SOUTH WALES ADVERTISER

Saturday, November 26, 1859

The *Royal Charter* and her late officers. The following interesting letter is from Mr. W. Gilmour, of Aylesbury, for two years surgeon-superintendent of the *Royal Charter*:-

"Having been surgeon of the unfortunate vessel during four voyages from Liverpool to Australia and back, I feel myself called upon to give a few reminiscences of the ill-fated ship and her late officers, who are now no more.

First of the ship. At sea with a good breeze on her quarter, which was her best sailing point, she was the best sailer I ever saw; we used to pass everything we came up with. I have known her to sail 18 knots an hour, and yet go steady through the water; but in a very rough weather, with a headwind, she laboured very much, and shipped a good deal of water, which made her a very uncomfortable ship for passengers, more especially the third-class. I have very often seen the water knee-deep between decks, and in sloppy wet weather, the main deck always leaked, supposed to be from the working and straining of the ship. Indeed, I have seen the boards of the deck working up and downwards, like the keys of a piano, and the seams a mass of froth. This, I have frequently pointed out to the captain and chief officer. I have also seen and felt her vibrate from bow to stern, like a fishing rod, and often, when great press of sail was on her, have heard the rivets rattling in her sides, but I must say, never saw her leaking in any part only once, and that was a small one in her bows. These things I have more particularly noticed during the last two voyages before this unfortunate one, as I am thankful to God that I was not in her the last one. During those two voyages, but more especially the last one, I lost much of the confidence I had in her, and determined to leave her as soon as I could get a chance of settling down on land; in fact, such was my anxiety to get out of her that I had a presentiment which haunted me continually, that sooner or later, she would be lost. This I have often told Mr. Stephens, chief officer, Mr. Rogers, chief engineer, and Mr. Lewis, Purser. I never had the same confidence in her that I had in the *Great Britain*, of which ship I was surgeon at the time she was engaged in Her Majesty's transport service during the Crimean War, which was a period of 18 months, and all that time I never saw her decks wet by a wave, but the *Charter's* deck, I have many, very many times; indeed, I once very nearly lost my life from a huge wave, containing many tons of water, which nearly washed me overboard one night, as I was going to the surgery. I have to thank the boatswain of that voyage, whose name was Albert, for saving my life. He jumped right into the water, and seized me as I was being washed into the lee scuppers. The same wave stove in one of the boats.

Almost every one of the late unfortunate officers was most intimately known to me, as we were more than a 'band of brothers' than anything else; but, poor fellows, they are gone, and they deserved a better fate. To begin with Captain Taylor. A better commander and seaman never had charge of a ship; he was a strict disciplinarian with his officers and crew -- almost too much so; he was very fond of carrying all the sail he could possibly have spread out; he too had every advantage of the wind; but it was thought by some that he sometimes carried too much sail, which strained the ship more or less; but of this, from my own knowledge of nautical affairs, I cannot give an opinion, but I can safely say that when at sea, I never on any occasion felt the least nervous or uneasy at the quantity of canvas he had on her -- I mean, as long as we had plenty of sea room; but I felt rather nervous that voyage before last, I think it was, that I was in her coming up Channel. We were steaming, and there were a great many vessels passing us, and one ran right across our bow, so close that I could have almost stepped on board of her, but this was no fault of Captain Taylor. What I used to say of him was that he was a "rough diamond", as almost every one is who has risen from the ranks of the forecastle. He never had been a gold-laced kid-gloved middy, with more money than brains, but had got up to what he was by his own perseverance and proficiency. He has left a widow and, I think, he told me, nine children.

The chief officer was W. B. Stephens. A more gentlemanly, better educated, cool-tempered chief officer, there did not exist. He was one who always had a pleasant word for everybody, and who did everything in his power to make all on board happy and comfortable. He was the life of the deck during his watch aloft, as very many of the passengers who sailed in her will remember. He had been twice shipwrecked before, and was in the steamship *Cleopatra* as chief officer all the time she was employed in the transport service during the Crimean War. Poor fellow! If he had been spared, he would have been an ornament to the mercantile marine service; but it was willed otherwise. Many, very many hours have I spent in his company, and I can safely say a better young man I never knew. He was a good Christian, a good seaman, a fond and tender husband, an honourable and true son of the ocean. He has left a widow and two children, who are residing in Bootle. He was a native of Scotland.

The second officer, Andrew Cowrie, was also a very promising young man, a good seaman, well educated, and fearless of danger. He was once shipwrecked on the coast of South Australia. He came home with Captain Taylor in the old *William Munny*, which showed that he was fearless of danger in trusting himself in such a craft. He was also a Scotsman, and married; his wife resided at Govan, near Glasgow.

The third officer, Mr. Bean, I did not know much of. He was of a more reserved and quiet disposition, but always pleasant and agreeable to the passengers; and he always did his duty on all occasions as a true British seamen. I cannot say if he was married or not.

The fourth officer, John Croome, had been a cadet, or middy, on board, ever since she first started from Liverpool. He was appointed as fourth officer, the voyage previous to the last. At the time of the appointment, he had not served out his time, but he was a very clever and gentlemanly young man, a good scholar, and clever draughtsman, which talent he inherited from his father, who is a mechanical draughtsman to the firm of Penn & Son, and Co, the celebrated marine engine boilermakers of London. He was a mere youth in years, but was a man possessed of sterling nautical qualities.

The purser, John Lewis, commenced his sea life on board the steamship *Great Western*. In her, he made several trips across the Atlantic. He afterwards entered on board the *City of Pittsburgh* steamer, belonging to an American company. She was burnt to the water's edge, and he lost his all, and suffered much privation, both bodily and mentally. He afterwards entered on board the steamship *Great Britain*, and in her was promoted to the post of chief steward, which he filled without complaint all the time he was with her, more especially while she was in the transport service, when he came more especially under my notice. On her being paid off by the Government, he was transferred to the *Royal Charter* as purser, which situation he has well and truly filled to the satisfaction of all – owners, passengers, and crew. He was allowed to be the best Purser that ever sailed on the sea; he well knew how to make the most of everything on board. He was most gentlemanly in his manner; he was very engaging and pleasant in his conversation, and many, very many passengers will remember the pleasant hours spent in his cabin after the business of the day was over. He belongs to Bristol, and has left a widow and two children.

I come now to a person whose talents and education were of a different kind - poor John Rogers, the chief engineer. He was the second engineer in the *Great Britain* in the transport service, and for some time previously, I believe. He had made altogether six trips to Australia, and this unfortunate one was the seventh. On the *Royal Charter* being ready for sea, he was promoted as chief in her, which situation he has filled ever since. He was a good, practical engineer, and one who was complete master of every part of his trade. He was very fond of his violin, and, when not steaming, many a pleasant hour have I spent in listening to the beautiful Scottish airs he used to play. But his little engines were his chief delight. He used to call them his children, and often, in the midst of our amusement, he would say, "Come and see how my children look." He was a Scotchman, born in Edinburgh, but for many years, his family had been residing in Liverpool. He has left a widow and six children to mourn their loss.

The second engineer's name I cannot recollect, but his Christian name was 'Frank'.

The third engineer was named Hosken, son of Captain Hosken, who was in command of the *Great Britain* when she was wrecked in Drundrum bay. He played very well on the cornopean*, and when the ship was lying in Port Phillip bay, used to enliven the tedium with the strains of his music. He was a very gentlemanly young man, and attentive to his duty.

The fourth, boilermaker, whose name was Wilson, I did not know much of, only that he was a Scotsman, and could "spin a good yarn."

The principal store-keeper, Robert Clucas will long be remembered by the many passengers and others who were acquainted with him. He always gave satisfaction to every person, and when the toils of the day were over, the many invitations he had to the passengers' concerts, parties etc, told how he was beloved. He could sing a good song and tell a good story. He belonged to the Isle of Man, and had a brother living in Liverpool.

The barkeeper was Edward Lewis, brother to the purser; he had been at sea many years; I think he told me that he had been shipwrecked on the coast of South America. His situation was a difficult one to fill, more especially on board a passenger vessel, and to give satisfaction to all was a most difficult task; but yet he managed to please everyone, and to carry out the regulations to the best of his ability. He was also married, and had a son in Australia and a wife and several children in Bristol.

And now for the one solitary middy on board, whose name was Frederick Foster, an orphan. He was fonder of his bunk than the deck, and many an hour he spent at the masthead as punishment, and many a bucket of cold water he had about him to wake him up. He was also very fond of "foxing" or feigning ill when he came under my notice. He never would have made a sailor, but now all his troubles are over.

The chief steward, Mr. Emery, I did not know much of. He was of a reserved disposition, but always paid particular attention to his duties, as the excellent table that used to be spread in the *Charter* could testify. He belonged to Liverpool, and was married.

The chief steward of the second-class saloon was Mr. Allen. He had been first

* A musical horn

steward to the officers' mess-room. On being promoted to the saloon, the officers presented him with a purse, in remembrance of his kindness and attention to them. He was afterwards promoted to the situation of chief of the second-class, which situation he ably filled during several voyages. He was one of the smartest stewards that ever were on board a ship, and the many presents he received fully testify as to how he did his duty. He has left a widow and family, who reside on the Cheshire side of the Mersey.

The stewardess was Miss Wearing, whose father has been in Mr. Bright's employ very many years. She was a very good, modest young woman. She had made two trips in the ship, and was universally liked by all the lady passengers in the saloon; but her services and attention were very often given to the second-class as well, and often have I seen her in the very bows of the ship visiting some poor third-class passenger who was sick - indeed, even to the common sailors when any of them were ill. Well do I remember her attention and kindness to one poor fellow, a sailor, who one night fell from the main yard on to the deck and had one of his arms taken off. She tried to take him the nicest part of her meals, and nursed him like a sister, till he was able to go about again.

The above are what may be called the permanent staff of officers. Though not so engaged, yet they one and all had such a love for the *Charter* that they used to remain disengaged the time she was in dock, and when about to sail, engage again. But there were some minor characters that I cannot pass over without mentioning here. There was Mr. Oatwick, the pantry steward; the two bedroom stewards, Thomas Cormack (who is one of the few saved), and Hugh Kane, who was also the captain's steward; he was a very smart young man, a native of Westport, Ireland.

And so now for Joe Rogers, the Maltese who swam ashore with the rope to which the hawser was attached that was the means of saving several lives. He was a hero indeed to overcome the death-dealing waves. This feat will be ever remembered by every true British seamen, but many a time have I seen him go out on a yard-arm when it was blowing "great guns", when no other sailor would venture. He has often told me that he never knew what fear was, and bless God that such a brave fellow has been spared to perform more deeds of daring.

I will now close with a few words on a character whom every passenger by the *Charter* will remember - I allude to "Piping Judd". He was one of the sweepers between decks, but his avocations were multifarious, as you would often find him scrubbing on deck. A few minutes afterwards might be heard the lively strains of his tin whistle when hoisting up coal, etc; and in the evenings many a dance has been performed to its music, and many a concert on board has he been a performer at, when he would play some of the most delightful pieces from celebrated operas. He played all by ear, not knowing a note of music, but now his piping is over, and he and his pipe lie in the same watery grave.

I remain etc

W. Gilmour"

Dr. Gilmour had left the ship after spending two years on her, apparently after having had a foreboding idea that she would be wrecked. He was called as a witness at the Board of Trade inquiry, where he repeated his thoughts under oath. The Chester Chronicle reported him stating:

I had a presentiment that she would be ultimately lost, and I left on that account. I told Mr. Stevens, and Rogers, and Lewis, that I expected the ship would be lost. I never told anybody now alive.

From his observations as Surgeon on board the 'Royal Charter', Dr. Gilmour's letter gives us an interesting view of the ship and her crew, but these were his own personal opinions that were not going to be left unchallenged. There would be serious consequences if he was correct that:

- the boards of the deck worked up and down like the keys of a piano.
- he had heard the rivets rattling in her sides.

These statements implied that the ship was unseaworthy, inadequately maintained, and dangerous, a public challenge that could have great implications for her owners, Gibbs, Bright and Company. Captain Taylor was dead, but Captain Boyce and James Hosken immediately replied to Doctor Gilmour's comments as shown below. Hosken corrected Gilmour's errors regarding those still serving on the ship, but is he corroborating Gilmour's assessment of the seaworthiness of the 'Royal Charter'?

"Sir - my attention has been drawn to Dr. Gilmour's letter, and, having been in command of the *Royal Charter* the two first voyages, I can speak with greater authority as to her seaworthiness than any ship's surgeon could possibly do.

When Dr. Gilmour joined the *Royal Charter* her hull and decks were as tight as any ship afloat, and no water entered her 'tween decks except through carelessness in washing decks or during heavy weather when some of the side windows or companion doors were left open, which is the case in all other ships.

The rattling of the rivets, etc. must be pure imagination on Dr Gilmour's part, for if they were loose, the ship must have made water. I am not aware that she made any during the voyages he was surgeon on board, and he himself says 'I never knew of her leaking in any part; only once, and that was a small hole in her bows.'

In conclusion, Dr. Gilmour says of the officers that, though not so engaged, yet one and all had such a love for the *Charter* that they used to remain disengaged the time she was in dock, and when about to sail, engaged again - a statement which in itself is the best contradiction to his remarks.

I remain, Sir, your obedient servant,

Francis Boyce
[*Former captain of the "Royal Charter"*]

"Sir - in your impression of today, you published a letter from Mr. W. Gilmour, in which that gentleman has made a few mistakes, consequent on his leaving the *Royal Charter* almost immediately on her last arrival at Liverpool, and not knowing the changes afterward made in her staff, which may lead many of the friends of those whom he mentions into error. Mr. Croome, father of the fourth officer, is a consulting engineer of good standing. The name of the second engineer was Frank Rockliffe, of whom you might speak, as of Mr. Rogers, the chief, as being a sterling, good-hearted fellow, and devoted to his professional duties. The stewardess and captain's steward, who were intimated as being on board, were married soon after the arrival of the ship on her previous voyage, and did not go out again in her. And with regard to myself, whom Mr. Gilmour supposes to have gone out in her on her last voyage, I and he were the only officers who left her that voyage.

Trusting that you will insert these few lines to correct the unintentional errors in Mr. Gilmour's letter, which in every other respect, I feel most happy to corroborate.

I remain, Sir, yours respectfully,
James Hosken,
Late third engineer of the *Royal Charter*
Stapleton,
Bristol,
Nov. 19.

The Carnarvon and Denbigh Herald

AND NORTH AND SOUTH WALES ADVERTISER

Saturday, November 26, 1859

THE "ROYAL CHARTER".

During the past week, 25 bodies have been washed ashore. Eighteen of them were deposited in Llanallgo Church, four at Penrhos Lligwy, and three at Amlwch. Of those at Llanallgo Church, five were identified -- Mr. Isaacher Marks, a Jew; John Hodson, of Preston, a sailor; James Davies, of Woodside; John Lewis, purser of the ship; and Miss Florence Davis; and at Penrhos Church, one male body; had stockings on which were marked "W.B.". The linen of another body was marked "Edmund Smith". The body of Captain Withers was brought ashore at Bull Bay, on Thursday week afternoon. The body had all the clothes on, except the coat. On his person were found a gold watch and chain, two gold seals, £36 in gold, and a silver snuff box with the inscription -- "Presented by the passengers of the ship *Gloucester* to Captain Withers, November 7, 1838". His watch had stopped at half-past seven.

On Wednesday week, two bodies, a male and female, were brought ashore. The male was a powerfully-built man, above 50 years of age, face disfigured. He had on a macintosh, monkey jacket, waistcoat, red shirt, flannel vest, fustian trousers, flannel drawers, woollen socks, and Wellington boots. Round the shoulders was a leather belt containing a leather purse, with six sovereigns and a half, a bag containing two or three ounces of nuggets and gold dust. In the trousers pocket, a portemonnaie containing four half sovereigns, four half-crowns, and four shillings; also two small keys, and in the jacket a memorandum book, supposed to be in German, with the name "A. Weyrawy" and "Hanrich Brandes" written four times; also a small illustrated book, printed in Old English, supposed to be in the German language, Roman Catholic Prayer Book, and a sheet of paper containing a log, commencing 15th September. The female was respectably dressed, wearing patent elastic boots, stockings and dress of black corded silk, and patent stays, all of the best quality. Nothing was found about her person that could lead to identification; face and lower extremities much disfigured, supposed to be a married lady, about 30 years of age and of middle stature.

The divers have been at work, and much of the upper portion of the wreck has been transferred into the lumpers; several ingots of gold, to the value of £3,000 or £4,000, have been recovered, and it is expected that when the upper portion of the wreck has been removed the bulk of the golden freight will be saved.

The number of bodies recovered, is stated to be 85, and the quantity of gold £5,700. Mr. Arthur Rich, of Moelfra, in a letter dated November 19, says - " Messrs. Gibbs Bright and Company, having considerably ordered that one of the divers should be sent down to examine part of the coast pointed out by the Rev. Mr. Hughes, their instructions have been carried out this morning, though, I regret to say, without success, the great depth of water and nature of the bottom rendering the search fruitless and the operations dangerous; but strange to say, soon afterwards, a body rose from the very spot, which, from its appearance, still bears out the opinion expressed. It was evidently that of a gentleman, 6 feet 1 inch or 6 feet 2 inches, light hair, red moustache and whiskers, and perfectly recognizable, but no mark on linen. Another body of a sailor was found this morning, but not identified. Two other bodies were yesterday taken to Llanddyfnan Church – one, socks marked "J.T.", and the other that of a tall man, but not recognizable."

An inquest was held at Drogheda on the body of a man which was found off Holyhead on Wednesday evening week by a coasting vessel. It was proved to be the remains of Mr. John Emery, the chief steward of the ill-fated *Royal Charter*, by Edward Wilson, who had been a seaman on board the *Royal Charter*, and was one of those who escaped by the rope; he is now a seaman on board the *Agnes*, of Preston, and happened to hear of the body being brought into town. The witness also stated that the deceased was a married man, and that he had seen his wife and family in Liverpool, where they resided. He did not know of the captain having neglected his duty. He was blameless. He remained on deck 'til the vessel went to pieces. No blame should be attached to anyone on board, for no human power could save the vessel. The Coroner believed they could arrive at no other verdict than that the deceased came to his death by the wreck of the *Royal Charter*, on the night that ill-fated vessel was lost. The jury found their verdict accordingly.

'They had all stopped somewhere between twenty minutes past seven and eight o'clock' - Receiver of Wreck.

Bodies were now being washed ashore everywhere along the coastline of Anglesey and other parts of North Wales, the Isle of Man, and even the east coast of Ireland --- wherever the vagaries of wind and tide decided to take them, but these rapidly-decomposing human remains needed to be quickly identified wherever possible, and another inquest had to be held before they could be buried according to his or her religious beliefs.

In the meantime, Gibbs, Bright and Co. had caused more than a little consternation with a £100 donation that was made public in a letter that they sent to the Caernarfon & Denbigh Herald, and was published on the 12th of November, 1859.

The Rev. Stephen Hughes,
Moelfre

Dear Sir,

Enclosed you will find £100, one half of which we must beg you will distribute among the poor at Moelfre. The other half we beg you will accept yourself, as we feel sure that in the late deplorable accident to the *Royal Charter*, you have, through your kindness of heart, been put to some expense. Begging to return you our sincere thanks for the attention and unwearied exertions you have made in providing for the distress of the surviving relatives of those lost.

We are, dear Sir,

Yours very truly,

Gibbs, Bright, & Co.

As we will see, Joseph Rogers was the publicly acclaimed hero of the day, and quickly received much press-coverage and financial reward. Yes, he was an exceedingly brave person who certainly risked his life to get the line and hawser ashore, but the option of doing nothing would probably have resulted in his own death. Was there to be no recognition of the bravery exhibited by the local people who rushed to the windswept shore in the early hours of the 26th of October? After all, they were risking their own lives and the financial future of their families at a time when there was urgent work to be done repairing the damage caused by the hurricane. They had rescued Joseph Rogers from the surf, hauled on the thin line that he carried, and secured a sturdy hawser to the rocks so that a boatswain's chair could be rigged up to save some of the passengers and crew. Nothing had been done to reward them a month after the wreck, when this letter appeared in the Caernarfon & Denbigh Herald of the 26th of November, 1859.

THE RESCUERS OF THE WRECKED AT MOELFRE

SIR, - we beg to request you to lay these observations before the public, relative to the rescue of lives at Moelfre, through the medium of the 'Herald.' In the first place, we beg to state that we have been assembling together on two previous occasions, to examine and identify those who were diligently employed on the rocks and in the water, at the risk of their own lives in rescuing those who came along the hawser; and most of us were in very dangerous positions. There were five or six of us hand-in-hand in the water; and were in danger of being swept off by the furious billows. The courage and gallantry of Joseph Rogers are worthy of attention; but had it not been for the assistance we rendered him, he would have been among the drowned, according to his own statement. The rope had got entangled about his body, and he was on the eve of being carried off. When information of the catastrophe reached us, we volunteered to go down to save as many lives as we could.

We wish to state that we have received no remuneration up to this date for what your paper may call gallantry. In confirmation of what we had previously stated, we request you to insert the two following statements, copied from the autographs of two of the passengers, and which are subjoined to our list.

"I, John Bradbury, do hereby state that I could not have been saved had it not been for the assistance I received from a portion of the above-named men, who lifted me out of the sea at the danger of their own lives. I also believe that these men were the means of saving all that were saved: for I think there were not any that reached the shore, (unless by the rope) but required to be lifted out of the water, and carried to some house in the neighbourhood"

"I, Samuel Edward Gapper, hereby affirm that had it not been for the assistance rendered on my reaching the shore, I should have been lost."

The following is a list of those who were actually engaged on the rocks and in the water on the occasion:-

Thomas Roberts*, Cogyn; Owen Roberts, Tynypwll; Owen Roberts, jun., ditto; David Williams, Llain Swch; Mesech Williams, Cogyn; Robert Lewis, y Big; Thomas Hughes, Ty Newydd; John Hughes, Tinfyny; William Owen, y Big; Richard Hughes, Ty Newydd; Evan Williams, Post office; John Parry, Pen Llain; John Owens, Llainfargriad; Thomas Parry, Bryn Goleu; John Lewis, Moelfre; Joseph Williams, ditto; Thomas Owen, Tai Bricks; William Williams, Tyn Graig; Richard Mathew, Moelfre; Israel Mathew, ditto; William Pritchard, ditto; Owen Hughes, Tyn-y-Gongl; Richard Evans, Moelfre; David Owen, Glan Traeth; John Lewis, jun., Moelfre; William Owen, Moryn; Lewis Francis, Moelfre, and John Francis, ditto. We would feel thankful for the insertion of this list.

We remain, sir, yours respectfully,
The Above Named.

* The North Wales Chronicle gives this person's name as Thomas Hughes.

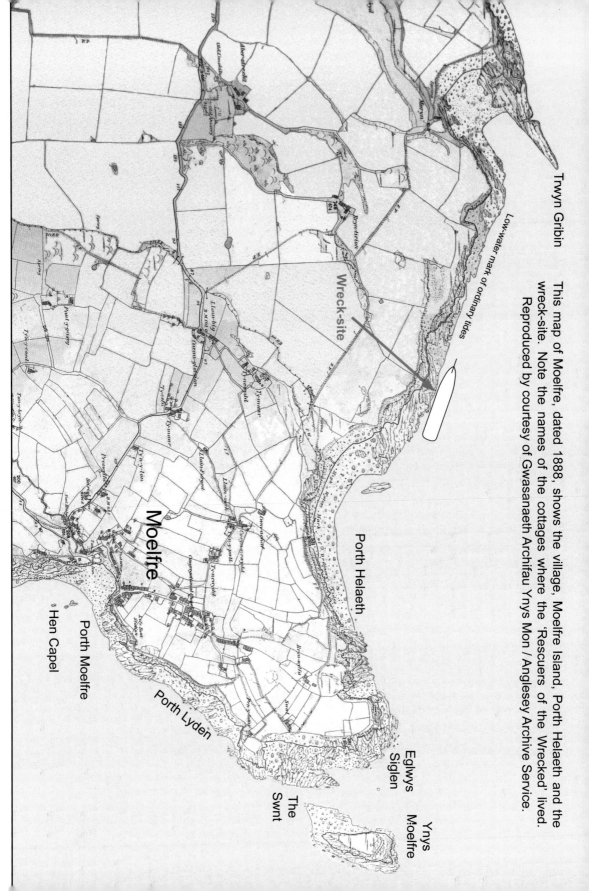

Trwyn Gribin

This map of Moelfre, dated 1888, shows the village, Moelfre Island, Porth Helaeth and the wreck-site. Note the names of the cottages where the 'Rescuers of the Wrecked' lived. Reproduced by courtesy of Gwasanaeth Archifau Ynys Mon / Anglesey Archive Service.

Low-water mark of ordinary tides

Wreck-site

Moelfre

Porth Helaeth

Porth Moelfre

'Hen Capel

Porth Lyden

Eglwys Siglen

The Swnt

Ynys Moelfre

This was followed up in the Caernarfon & Denbigh Herald by ---

Moelfre, Llanallgo, 26th Novr., 1859

Messrs. Gibbs, Bright, and Co.,

Gentlemen, - The general report about here is that you have remitted the sum of £100 to the Rev. Mr. Hughes, Rectory; and that it was to be applied in the following manner:- £50 for himself, and the rest to be distributed among us who were diligently employed on the morning of the catastrophe, in rendering assistance to the survivors:-

In the first place, we should feel thankful for the following explanation, viz. what is meant by the poor of Moelfre? Whether it includes the owners and captains of vessels, or the landlords of the neighbourhood, or the poor people, or whether it means those men who rendered assistance on the above occasion? We should feel extremely thankful if you will favour us with this explanation. We enclose the piece of paper, which contains our marks, and which contains a correct list of those men who were actively engaged on the occasion. An early reply would greatly oblige.

We remain, gentlemen, your humble and obedient servants,

The Above Named

The "Moelfre List,"

Care of Mr. Evan Williams,

Postmaster,

Moelfre,

Anglesey.

To which Gibbs, Bright & Co. replied --

Liverpool, 29th November, 1859

The "Moelfre List"

Care of Mr. Evan Williams, Postmaster, Moelfre, Anglesey.

In reply to the communication which has now reached us, we beg to say that we cannot pay attention to any claims so made; but if any of the men whose names are given can prove to the satisfaction of Mr. Smith, of Beaumaris, and the Rev. Mr. Hughes, of Llanallgo, that they were the parties who exerted themselves so gallantly and effectually, at the risk of their lives, to save the crew and passengers of the *Royal Charter*, we shall be glad to do what we can to remunerate them in some measure for their assistance.

As regards the money given to the Rev. Mr. Hughes, we are quite satisfied to leave it in his hands to employ in the manner he considers best, and meet in accordance with our wishes, nor can we countenance the interference of any one else in its distribution.

We are, your obedient servants,

Gibbs, Bright & Co.

So, the final arbiter was to be the Reverend Stephen Roose Hughes, who certainly had many other things on his mind apart from adjudicating as to who deserved a financial reward from Gibbs, Bright & Co., but he quickly moved to distribute some of the money to the 'Rescuers of the Wrecked' and other true heroes of the disaster, as reported in the local newspaper of December 3rd.

With reference to a letter which appeared in the 'Herald' of last week, from 28 persons who assisted in saving the crew and passengers from the wreck, we have it on the best authority that each of them received 10s. [*50 pence*] from the Rev. Mr. Hughes, as did eight others whom Mr. Hughes found had been equally active, and smaller sums to a boat of persons who made themselves useful later in the day.

We have great pleasure in giving a Portrait of Joseph Rogers, seaman, of the *Royal Charter*. This brave fellow, it will be recollected, swam ashore with a rope, to which the hawser was attached that was the means of saving some lives, and which, but for the sudden break-up of the vessel, might have been instrumental in saving hundreds more. The particulars which can be gathered of Joseph Rogers' life are but meagre, as he is of a very retiring disposition, shrinking with an air of bewilderment from the praises bestowed upon him, as though quite unconscious of having done anything out of the common. All we know of his antecedents is that he was born at Malta, in the year 1830; that for ten years he sailed from Malta to ports in the Red Sea; and that subsequently he made five voyages in the *Royal Charter*, having joined her in the second trip. Mr. W. Gilmour, for two years surgeon-superintendent of the *Royal Charter*, in an interesting letter giving particulars of the officers and others on board that vessel, writes of him as follows: — "And now for Joe Rogers, the Maltese, who swam ashore with the rope to which the hawser was attached that was the means of saving several lives. He was a hero, indeed, to overcome the 'death-dealing waves'. This feat will be ever remembered by every true British seaman. Many times have I seen him go out on the yard-arm when it was blowing 'great guns', and when no other sailor would venture. He often told me that he never knew what fear was; and I bless God that such a brave fellow has been spared to perform more deeds of daring."

Joseph Rogers gave the following evidence, on Thursday week, before the commission appointed by the Board of Trade to inquire into the circumstances connected with the loss of the *Royal Charter*:- 'I was an able seaman on board the *Royal Charter*. Between four and five o'clock on the afternoon of the day of the wreck, it was my watch. Boatswain Smith called me to go down below to stow the small sails. The sails unbent were the mizzen maintopgallant staysails. I came on deck again at eight o'clock. I was sitting aft the engine-room when I was called to reef the maintop-mast staysail, about nine o'clock. It was hauled down again in about ten minutes afterwards. About half-past ten o'clock the watch was called to put the ship about. I went aft to haul in the spanker-sheet on the port side. After the main-topsail was set, they clewed it up again. They went up aloft to furl the sails, and the wind was so strong that the roving-poles were broken. I was nearly pitched off the yard. I came down, and said, 'I could not furl the sail,' and Mr. Stephens told me to go back again, and make it fast to the yard-arm. Shortly after this the port anchor was let go, and after that the starboard anchor was let go. When both the chains parted, we cut away the masts, and she went ashore. Captain Taylor gave me an order to clear away the port lifeboat. The mizzen stay, being cut away, came down by the run, and fell upon the lifeboat. When the ship struck upon the rocks, I was on the forecastle, and I asked the boatswain's mate what he was going to do, and he said, 'You go ashore, and I will

go too.' I went inside the forecastle, and found a chap with a line, and he said, 'Are you going ashore?' I said 'Yes.' I went on the top-gallant forecastle, and made the rope fast round my waist. Mr. Stephens asked me what I was going to do, and wanted to give me a life-buoy, and I said 'No,' and I lowered myself down by a flying jib-boom. I was washed back three times to the ship, but at last succeeded in getting ashore, where I saw some people, and they said, 'Give us the line,' and they took me away. I wanted to stop to pull the hawser ashore, but they would not let me."

The committee of the National Life-boat Institution, to mark their sense of Rogers' gallant conduct, determined to present him with a valuable gold medal, the sum of £5, and a suitable vote of thanks embossed on vellum. The presentation was made at Liverpool on Wednesday week through Mr. S. R. Graves, chairman of the Local Marine Board, in the dining-hall of the Sailors' Home. Mr. Graves was attended by the other members of the Local Marine Board, Mr. H. Bright (of Gibbs, Bright, and Co.), Captain Gray, of the screw-steamer *Great Britain,* the officials of the Sailors' Home, and a number of the boarders in that establishment. Rogers was attended by Suaicar, Bryan, and Foster, three of the seamen who also escaped from the wreck of the ill-fated vessel. In making the presentation Mr. Graves dwelt eloquently upon the gallant conduct of Rogers; who, in a brief reply, said that he should be glad to perform the same duty again under similar circumstances. Mr. Graves afterwards presented Rogers with £2, subscribed by the employees of the Sailors' Home. The proceedings terminated with three hearty cheers for Rogers and his companions. Rogers, at the invitation of the committee of the Sailors' Home, then sat down to dinner with the boarders and officers of the establishment.

Illustrated London News.
November 26th, 1859

Joseph Rogers was awarded £5 and a gold medal by the committee of the National Lifeboat Institution, but the Board of Trade report for 1859 also lists a reward of £10 and a silver medal from the Mercantile Marine Fund. Several newspapers had initially reported that Rogers was a Portuguese sailor, so a testimonial was arranged in that country and presented to him, despite it becoming known that he was a Maltese-born sailor.

The Nationality of Joseph Rogers.

We have been shown a copy of some correspondence which has taken place between Messrs. Charles Brounlie and Co. of Liverpool, and a Portuguese firm in Lisbon, named Torlades, respecting the nationality of Rogers, the seaman who swam ashore from the wreck of the *Royal Charter,* with a rope, which was the means of saving several lives. It appears that some benevolent people in Lisbon having credited the first reports concerning the nationality of Rogers, to the effect that he was a Portuguese, set on foot a subscription in his behalf, in order to testify their admiration of his gallant conduct as a "fellow countryman."

Before handing over the amount, Messrs. Torlades wrote to Messrs. Brounlie, of Liverpool, inquiring whether Rogers was really deserving of such a tribute; also, if the English Government had rewarded him, and to which province he belonged to. In their reply, Messrs. Brounlie corrected the error regarding Roger's nationality, informing their correspondents that he turns out to be a Maltese, in corroboration of which they enclosed an extract from one of the local journals, giving an account of a presentation made to him on behalf of the English Government. The same gentlemen subsequently state that they have ascertained from Rogers himself that he is a Maltese, born in Malta of English parentage; and they very properly add, that the amount subscribed in Lisbon could not be better applied than in being handed over to him, as he was quite worthy of it, irrespective of any special nationality.

In a subsequent communication, Messrs. Torlades enclose a draft for the amount of subscriptions, which appear to have reached the sum of £19 14s. 5d. sterling, and they request Messrs. Brounlie and Co. to hand over the same to Rogers. They state that the subscribers evinced no desire to withdraw their subscriptions when they heard that Rogers was not a Portuguese, thus proving that real humanity is above the influence of difference in nationality. We understand that Rogers is at present at sea, having gone on a voyage to Australia in the *Great Britain.*

Caernarfon & Denbigh Herald.
February 11, 1860

The story of Joe Rodger's bravery had spread far and wide, and he continued to be employed by Gibbs, Bright & Co. Further rewards were heaped on him when he next arrived in Melbourne.

The *Royal Charter*. Jose Rodgeurs, the Maltese sailor who behaved so nobly on the occasion of the wreck of the *Royal Charter*, has arrived in Melbourne in the *Great Britain,* and has been warmly welcomed. A purse was to have been presented to him at Cremorne, but owing to a misunderstanding between the Mayor of Melbourne and Mr. Coppin, the presentation did not take place. A purse containing forty sovereigns was given to him on the boards of *The Royal*, by the manager of that theatre.

Caernarfon & Denbigh Herald.
April 14, 1860

'The Volunteer', a painting by Henry Nelson O'Neil. Many believe this to be a depiction of Joseph Rogers and Captain Taylor, but an article by the Society of Fine Arts states that the painting was started before the 'Royal Charter' was wrecked.

Even George Suaicar wasn't totally forgotten by the British public, as he had shown similar bravery but was beaten to that desperate swim ashore by his fellow Maltese countryman, and so didn't receive quite the same adulation and financial reward as Joseph Rogers. However, his daring conduct was recognised by the residents of a small village in Northern England, and he was awarded a medal bearing the words:

Presented to George Suaicar, for his daring conduct in saving six lives from the wreck of the *Royal Charter*, on the 26th October 1859.

In the first excitement relative to the wreck of the *Royal Charter*, the principle interest connected with the survivors culminating upon Rogers, the boatswain, who swam ashore with the rope by which so many persons' lives were saved, and, as is well known, he was presented not only with several testimonials, but also with a handsome sum of money. Rogers, however, was not the only seaman on board that unfortunate vessel who behaved with great bravery, and assisted in saving the lives of some of the surviving passengers. George Suaicar, boatswain's mate, was the first person who tried to swim ashore with the rope; and although he did not succeed, and nearly lost his life, he was subsequently of great assistance in rescuing passengers from the unfortunate vessel. These facts having been noticed by some of the inhabitants of Stanhope, a village near Durham. They subscribed among themselves and purchased a medal bearing a suitable inscription; and this medal, at their request, was on Tuesday presented to Suaicar at the Liverpool Sailors' Home, in presence of all the boarders in that establishment.

Caernarfon & Denbigh Herald.
Saturday, March 24, 1860

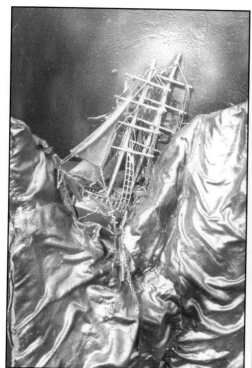

These are maquettes (scale models) of bronzes created to commemorate the 150th anniversary of the disaster. The actual bronzes are on display at Moelfre.

At long last, the bravery and heroism of the men of Moelfre was recognised in 2009, the 150th anniversary of the final, fatal voyage of the 'Royal Charter', with the creation of two bronze plaques by Sam Holland, scale models of which are shown above. Often referred to as 'The Twenty-eight Men of Moelfre' or 'The Rescuers of the Wrecked', these allude to those persons who added their names to the letter written to the local newspaper, but there were other brave fellows who received a reward from the Reverend Stephen Roose Hughes. Ten shillings (50 pence) might seem rather paltry in comparison with the forty sovereigns given to Joseph Rogers, although ten shillings would probably have the purchasing-power of at least £50 at today's values.

At the same time, a reward was also given to eight men involved in the rescue of the crew of the 'Esther Anne', and it is possible that these are the eight men previously referred to as being rewarded by Stephen Roose Hughes.

Benllech, Anglesey ---Through the kind application of the Rev. W. Williams, Rector of Llanddyfnan who superintended the operations, those eight men who co-operated in the rescue of the captain and crew, of the schooner *Esther Anne*, Ulventon, stranded on this coast, have been rewarded for their gallant effort. The Rev. W. W. Williams received a £12 cheque from the Shipwrecked Mariners Society, to be equally divided among them. The names of the heroes are the following:— John Price, Mindon; Wm. Thomas, Red Wharf; John Owen, Tyddyn-volyn; Thomas Williams, Tyddyn (Sergeant); Edward Williams, Erw; Hugh Hughes, Groes; and Hugh Jones, Penybont. The Rev. W. Williams took a prominent part in relieving the sufferers.

North Wales Chronicle.
Saturday, November 12, 1859

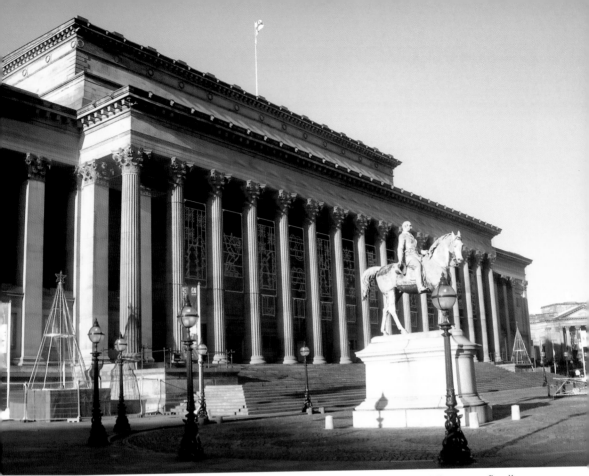

St. George's Hall, Liverpool. Work began in 1842, and the building was finally completed in 1855 to incorporate a concert hall and the court-rooms.

A Government Inquiry was held in the Crown Court of St. George's Hall, Liverpool, in the November and December of 1859, with the purpose of establishing the reason or reasons for the wrecking of the 'Royal Charter'. This was the normal procedure after the loss of a major vessel, as valuable lessons could be learned from a tragic event such as this.

- Was there an inherent fault in the design, the materials or the construction of the Royal Charter?
- Why did the anchor-cables fail?
- Was the captain drunk? This question was to be raised yet again, despite the verdict of the coroner's inquest at Llanallgo.
- Did the crew obey their orders?
- At what stage did Captain Taylor order the masts to be cut down, and what were his reasons for delaying that task?
- Why did all of the women and children perish?
- Did the Liverpool Pilots do their duty to the best of their ability?

CHAPTER TEN

The Court of Inquiry

𝕿𝖍𝖊 𝕮𝖆𝖗𝖓𝖆𝖗𝖛𝖔𝖓 𝖆𝖓𝖉 𝕯𝖊𝖓𝖇𝖎𝖌𝖍 𝕳𝖊𝖗𝖆𝖑𝖉
AND NORTH AND SOUTH WALES ADVERTISER
Saturday, November 19, 1859

THE "ROYAL CHARTER".

Board of Trade Inquiry.

The inquiry commenced at Liverpool on Tuesday morning, in the Crown Court, St George's Hall, and was conducted by Captain Harris, R.N. and Mr. Mansfield, stipendiary magistrate of Liverpool. Mr. O'Dowd appeared for the Board of Trade, instructed by Mr. Tyndall of Liverpool; and Mr. Aspinall (barrister) for Messrs. Gibbs, Bright, and Co., the owners, instructed by Messrs. Lowndes, Robinson, and Co.

Mr. O'Dowd, in opening the case, said that within his own experience, and he ventured to say within the memory of man, no event had occurred so distressing in its character, and so lamentable for the extent of its sacrifices and losses as that which they were about to investigate. By the official register, the *Royal Charter* appeared to be the property of Gibbs, Bright, and Co., who represented the Liverpool and Australian Navigation Company; her official number was 1,355, and her registered tonnage, 2,164 78 100. She was built at Sandycroft, Flintshire, in 1855, under the superintendence of Mr. Wm. Patterson, of Bristol. Having quoted from the register and also from Dr. Scoresby's Journal as to the size, construction, steam power, etc., of the ship, Mr. O'Dowd said that the space within the body of the ship was divided transversely by bulkheads, and comprised altogether seven watertight compartments. The *Royal Charter* was commanded by Captain Taylor, a gentleman of the highest respectability in his profession; the crew consisted of 112 persons; and the cargo consigned to Messrs. Gibbs, Bright, and Co., consisted of wool, sheepskins, and a large quantity of gold. But the vessel had a more precious cargo still – three hundred and seventy five passengers, or thereabouts, though of the precise number it was impossible to speak with accuracy, as the whole of the ship's papers were lost. The vessel left Melbourne on the 26th of August, and arrived at Kinsale Head, on the 24th October. After landing 13 of her passengers at Queenstown, she proceeded on her voyage, and came abreast of Holyhead, where she took in 11 riggers from the United Company's steam tug. At this time the wind blew fresh from the E.N.E. At 7.45 that day she passed the Skerries, and the wind becoming more northerly, increased to a gale. About eight o'clock, signals of distress were made, and rockets and blue lights exhibited. This, indeed, had been done during the whole evening, and continued almost to the time of the wreck. Point Lynas was made about 10 o'clock, and the evidence as to the distance at which it was passed varied very much, some witnesses giving it as three, others four or five, and one witness 15 miles. The gale had increased to a hurricane, and at ten o'clock, Captain Taylor gave orders to loose the main-topsail, and set on the ship, the only canvas being the main-topsail and spanker; but notwithstanding this, she drifted rapidly under the pressure of the storm. These means having failed to prevent the drifting of the ship, the sheet anchor was let go, and immediately afterwards the starboard anchor. Every effort had been made to take soundings during the whole evening, and almost to the time of the occurrence of the wreck. At the time the anchors were let go, she had 100 fathoms of chain at the port anchor, and 70 at the starboard, with a sufficient number of hands standing by to give her plenty of cable. About half-past one, the port chain parted, and before the order could be given to bring up the two stream-anchors the ship drifted rapidly and struck upon the sand. The utmost confusion ensued, during which Captain Taylor did all he could to encourage and assure the passengers, ordered them below, and gave directions to have the boats hung in tackle. As a further precaution, he ordered the masts to be cut down. The quartermaster in his evidence described the captain as being unceasing in his exertions, and stated that he was repeatedly knocked down while giving his orders. A man named Joe Rogers heroically went ashore with a hawser after the vessel had struck on the rocks, and by this means a few lives were saved, while a few other persons were saved by being washed ashore. With these exceptions, all on board perished. The vessel broke across the main hatchway, and went to pieces. Mr. Smith, of Beaumaris, who would be examined, would, from his observations of the subsequent position of the wreck, give the court excellent information on this subject. There were two most important considerations suggested by this inquiry; first, that this shivering to atoms of an iron vessel seemed not only to indicate a deficiency of strength, but positive weakness; and, secondly, as regarding the captain, though it was with the greatest reluctance, that he (Mr. O'Dowd) would throw the slightest imputation upon his memory, or ask the court to review his conduct censoriously, yet the interests of the public demanded that Captain Taylor's proceedings should be as rigidly and thoroughly investigated as though, instinct with life and professional pride, he were that day in court, seeking to protect that commission which authorised him to pursue his profession. Upon these points, he (Mr. O'Dowd) should not obtrude any opinions of his own, convinced that the court would do the strictest justice in the matter. He then proceeded to call evidence.

David Strongman was the first witness called. He deposed that he was quartermaster on board the *Royal Charter* for about two years. She sailed from Melbourne on the 26th August last. The voyage was good up to the time of the arrival off the Irish coast; it occupied 58 days up to the landing of some passengers at Queenstown. Thirteen passengers were landed there on board the pilot-boat *Petrel*. The passage up the Channel as far as Holyhead was very fine. They reached Holyhead about half-past four o'clock p.m. That was on Tuesday, the 25th October. The wind was then from the S E. When witness came on deck at four o'clock it was very thick. The vessel did not go close to Holyhead; she kept about five miles off. In the early part of the day, before they got to Bardsey, they took on board some riggers. That was about noon. It was witness's watch below before they reached Holyhead, and he came on deck at four o'clock, and he stayed on deck till six o'clock, at the wheel. He then went below to his supper, and was on deck several times after, but was not himself doing duty. Saw Point Lynas Light about twenty minutes or a quarter to seven, then went below and remained there till eight o'clock. The light appeared six or seven miles off, and was broad on the starboard bow. Witness, however, did not know the exact position of the vessel at this time. At eight o'clock, witness relieved John Hudson on the watch. The wind had freshened after leaving Holyhead, and was at this time blowing very hard from the north east. Witness did not see Capt. Taylor on deck at night, but he saw him there at a quarter to nine. The captain ordered the helmsman to starboard, in order to bring her head to the wind. The man at the wheel said the helm was hard a-starboard. This was after nine o'clock. At a quarter to ten witness was ordered by the captain to heave the lead, and he did so from the starboard bridge. The first soundings were eighteen fathoms. The spanker was then the only sail on. The screw was going, and the vessel was steering E.S.E. He hove the lead a second time, about ten minutes afterwards, and got sixteen fathoms. The vessel was then drifting so fast that the line got under her bottom, though he threw it as far as possible to leeward. Captain Taylor, after the first cast of the lead, ordered the lower maintop sail to be loosed, and after the second cast gave orders to prepare to let go the anchors. About half-past ten, or a quarter to eleven, an unsuccessful attempt was made to stay the vessel. Captain Taylor then ordered the chief officer to try to wear her, but witness did not know whether this was done, being engaged with the lead. The third time witness hove the lead, he got fifteen and a half fathoms, the wind still increasing. The captain ordered the chief officer to let go the port anchor, which was done, and about a quarter of an hour afterwards, he ordered him to let go the starboard anchor. She dragged the port anchor a little, but it appeared to bring her head somewhat to the wind. Before the second anchor was let go, the captain told witness to get the deep-sea lead up in order to try whether the vessel was drifting. When the starboard anchor was let go, the vessel ceased to drag. This was about half-past eleven, and he was relieved about twenty minutes to twelve. The vessel brought up some-what when the starboard anchor was let go. Witness then went to the wheel, and remained there until ten minutes to twelve. The helm was still hard a-starboard when he went. When relieved, he went forward to the port bridge, took hold of the line, and found that the vessel was not dragging. At this time, rockets and torches and blue lights were burning, and guns firing, and had been since eight o'clock. After being about twenty minutes in the forecastle, witness again went to the bridge, and found

that the vessel held fast still. About half past one or two, she parted her port chain with a very heavy pitch, there being a great sea on. Captain Taylor then gave the orders to get up the stream-anchor out of the after hold. The stream-anchor was brought up on deck, but was not bent*. The starboard chain broke, and the vessel's head turned right around and she went ashore. It took nearly an hour to get the stream-anchor out of the hold. She struck about three o'clock, or half past. Some hands began then to clear the boats, and in about a quarter of an hour after the vessel struck, the mainmast was cut away. It fell over on the port side, the lee rigging being cut away afterwards. Witness thought the wreck was clear of the screw. It ceased to work a few minutes after the striking, and before the mast was cut away. The cutting away of the mast eased her a little. She was broadside on to the sea when she struck, and everything on the starboard side was carried away. The captain was the only person on the poop then, and he was knocked down several times. Witness helped him up. After the vessel struck, but before she broke up on the rocks, witness took the lead and sounded inside. There were 3½ fathoms aft, and 2 forward. Witness never went aft again, but remained in the forecastle until he thought it was time to be moving. Orders had been given to get out the boats before she struck, but witness did not think that the men were 'told off' for the boats' crews. The lifeboats were ready for swinging, but were not swung out over the ship's side. A great many of the crew were in the forecastle, and also large numbers of the third-class passengers, but not on deck. About five o'clock witness was able to make out the loom of the land. Wilson, Joseph Rogers, and himself determined then to make an effort to get on shore. Rogers went out on the jib-boom, taking a hawser with him, and having dropped into the water, succeeded, after being washed about for some time, in making it fast. A boatswain's chair was then

* bent - attached to the chain.

fastened to the hawser, and by this means several persons, including the witness, escaped. There was great scrambling for the chance of going in the chair, as the ship was fast breaking up. He himself was on board when she began to break up; before he left, he saw the poop go down altogether. The vessel parted at the main hatchway, and then lengthways, fore and aft. Only about three quarters of an hour had elapsed from their commencing to get the hawser on shore until she broke up. Witness saw no lifeboats pulled out from shore. It was getting daylight when the vessel struck, and broad daylight when he landed. He never saw such a hurricane before, although he had been in a typhoon. In reply to Captain Harris, witness stated that it was quite calm when they passed Tuskar light.

Mr. Morse, a passenger, and a magistrate of New South Wales, was then examined. His evidence was extremely favourable to the character of the captain as a seaman. Mr. A.C. Taylor, another passenger, made a statement to the effect that Captain Withers often said during the voyage that the *Royal Charter* would neither wear nor tear, and that her masts were wrongly placed. After this evidence the inquiry was adjourned to one o'clock on

WEDNESDAY

The first witness examined was Owen Williams - The witness deposed that he was the late quartermaster of the *Royal Charter*. His watch on Tuesday morning, October 25, was from eight to half past twelve. Was at the wheel from ten to half past twelve. After half past twelve he went below. Came on deck again at four o'clock. Remained there until six. Was engaged in various duties on deck during these two hours. Took the wheel at eight o'clock. East by south was the course given to him. The vessel had only the fore and aft sails at that time. The maintopmast, staysail and spankers were the only sails he saw. Remained at the wheel until twenty-five minutes before twelve.

The lower maintop sail was set before that time. The yards were braced the other way, and squared in order to stay the ship, but she would not stay. The helm was put hard a-starboard. The port anchor was thrown out about eleven o'clock. Some time after, the starboard anchor was let go. Witness was at the helm after that time, and does not know what the hands on the main deck were doing. Kept steering the same course, the helm hard a-starboard. When the anchors were let go, she came up east half north, and fell off south-east again. After the two anchors were let go, the vessel became very steady. She did not appear to be drifting. The screw was kept going all the time. She continued in that state until the parting of her anchor. The lower maintopsail was furled after the anchors were let go, and the spanker was brailed up. Has heard that the main topmast staysail was reefed during the second dog-watch, and set again. About a quarter past two, the port cable gave way. About twenty minutes past three, the ship struck upon the sands. The engines were going all the time. About five o'clock, she struck upon the rock. Witness was at that time in the forecastle. She did not stand more than three quarters of an hour after her first striking on the rock. She then went to pieces. Witness saved himself by getting ashore in the boatswain's chair on the hawser. Saw Captain Taylor on deck several times. The last time he saw him was about four o'clock in the morning. Captain Taylor was then on the poop.

To Mr. Aspinall – Saw Mr. Stephens, the first mate, forward while the hawser was being got ashore. Does not know whether it was he who first called for volunteers to take the hawser ashore; he was giving orders there about it. As soon as the hawser was got ashore and hauled taut, Mr. Stephens ordered witness to go aft and get the lady passengers forward. Mr. Stephens said the lady passengers should be first sent ashore. Witness went aft for the purpose, but before he could get to the passengers, the vessel broke up. Witness was in the forepart when she broke up. The port side of the vessel was up, and she had a list to windward. Witness came forward again, and told Mr. Stephens the vessel had broken. Mr. Stephens had charge of the hawser at the time. He then left the hawser and went aft, and witness never saw him again. Mr. Stephens appeared most anxious to save the ladies. Had he wished to go ashore himself, Mr. Stephens could have done so. The third officer, Mr. Bean, was there too, and he acted in a similar manner. There was a woman on the forecastle, a third-class passenger, and Mr. Bean was very anxious she should go ashore, but she was afraid. She was the only woman in that part. There were some minutes lost in endeavouring to persuade her to go. Neither Mr. Stephens nor Mr. Bean made any efforts to save their own lives.

To Captain Harris – Heard from the fourth officer that the vessel had 300 tons of coal on board when she entered the Channel; she had 700 tons when leaving Melbourne. She did not steam at all until after passing the Horn. The weather was very calm off Queenstown. There was very fine weather when passing the Tuskar, and only a ripple on the water. Witness was at the wheel when they passed the Tuskar. There was no wind to speak of until about five o'clock that afternoon. Witness was below when they were passing Holyhead, and when he came on deck again, they had passed the Skerries. There was very little wind then. It began to blow pretty fresh about half-past nine o'clock. At eight o'clock, witness was at the wheel, and the vessel was steering east by south. She was carrying a slack helm. Cannot tell the reason. She was not in the habit of carrying a slack helm. There was not much sea then, and there was not much wind. Although the wind was freshening, she carried a topgallant sail at eight o'clock. It was near ten o'clock when she made Point Lynas. She was going six knots between Holyhead and the Skerries the last times they hove the log. When crossing from Queenstown to Holyhead, all the square-sails were set, the main skysail yard was aloft, and the sail on it. The hawser which was got on shore was their best hawser. It was a 10-inch manila. Joseph Rogers carried a rope on shore, and the hawser was made fast by this means on shore. The people on shore appeared to give every assistance as far as he could see. Did not see lifeboat or lifeboat's crew.

William Foster, examined by Mr. O'Dowd - was carpenter on board the *Royal Charter*. On the 24th of October, she was off Kinsale Head and reached Holyhead about half past four; the wind was ahead when the vessel was passing Holyhead. About 10 o'clock that night, witness was on the main deck, and the wind was blowing pretty stiff. Shortly after that, the ship was drifting strongly towards the shore, and the port anchor was let go in about 16 fathoms water to check it. At first there were from 40 to 50 fathoms paid out, and it was afterwards increased to 90 to 100. Witness was in the forecastle when the chain was being put out. There were hands enough at the compressor to pay it out as quickly as was required. The vessel held for a little, but then it began to drift, and the starboard anchor was let go to hold her. The vessel was steaming all this time. She was still drifting after both anchors had been let go, although the steam was kept going. Does not think she held for any considerable time after the second anchor was let go, but she did not drift to leeward as rapidly as before. The port anchor parted about two o'clock. More chain was then given to the starboard anchor. Witness assisted in paying it out. About 80 or 90 fathoms were paid out. Some hands went aft to get up the stream-anchors. They were got up on the deck, but before they could be let go the starboard chain parted. The stream-anchors then could not be of the least service. Mr. Stephens the chief officer, told witness to cut away the mainmast. This was about 20 minutes or half an hour after the starboard chain had parted.

The mast was stout and very heavily rigged. It was about three feet eight inches or three feet ten inches, witness thinks, in diameter. Does not think she had struck upon sand at this time. The foremast was about the same diameter as the mainmast. The diameter of the mizzen mast was about 32 inches. In obedience to Mr. Stephens' orders, witness cut away the mainmast. This had some effect in stopping the drift of the ship; cannot say whether it stopped the working of the screw. It might have been between two and three o'clock when the vessel struck on the sand. Witness cut away the foremast shortly after. Mr. Stephens gave the orders to do so. Cannot say whether it would have been prudent to have cut away the masts earlier. Saw Captain Taylor on the forecastle-head when both anchors were down. Witness was on the forecastle-head when the vessel broke up. The tide had slewed her broadside on to the rocks, and she was beating very heavily, the sea making a clear breach over her. She was beating there about half an hour or three quarters before she broke across the main hatch. The forepart of the after-body of the vessel went down, and the stern hove up. This was witness's first voyage as carpenter in the *Royal Charter*. She had seven watertight compartments. She appeared to have struck on sand forward in the first instance. She then slewed broadside on to the rocks. Was employed before this last voyage in executing some repairs of the vessel. It was in May last. There were about thirty or forty other men employed for the same purpose. They were employed for about three weeks. Messrs. Brown and Martin had the charge of the repairs. They are shipwrights. They do not build iron ships. The repairs consisted of caulking the passenger decks, and a great part of the upper deck and several other little jobs. Does not think there was anything done other beyond the ordinary repairs of a vessel after a long voyage. Such large ships usually require as many as 30 or 40 men to do these repairs.

Cannot say whether her iron plates or rivets underwent any repair.

To Mr. Aspinall – The vessel made no water until after she got onto the rocks. Witness sounded the pumps himself. She began to make water after striking the rocks. Nothing could stand the beating she got there. She was a very strong ship. Witness would have been glad to go out in her again if she had had the luck to get home safe, and if they would have taken him. Off Point Lynas, signals were made for a pilot, and these signals were continued the whole night throughout. Torches made of oakum dipped into turpentine were burnt as well as blue lights. Was present when Mr. Bean endeavoured to get the only woman who was forward to go ashore on the hawser; she would not go. It was after she refused to go that witness went. An effort was made to get a second hawser out amidships, but witness does not know why it did not succeed. The end of the line from the shore was lost, or something of the kind happened.

To Captain Harris – They had the wind well aft in running from Melbourne to Cape Horn. Did not observe that the vessel strained or that her decks worked. She was perfectly tight during the voyage. Witness sounded the wells every morning and evening, and never found any water of any consequence. There were two barometers on board; one in Mr. Stephen's cabin, and one in the captain's.

Thomas Cormick, second steward, examined by Mr. O'Dowd - "On Tuesday night, I turned in about ten. Got up between one and two, being aroused by the chief steward who said the captain had given orders to have coffee ready for the saloon passengers, which he had prepared. The cutting away of the masts made a little hole in the deck, through which water came into the saloon. Heard the fourth officer say he hoped, with the help of God, they would soon be all on shore. Witness remained in the saloon until about seven. The passengers remained in the saloon, by order of Captain Taylor. They were not obliged to remain there; they might have come up if they chose. When witness went forward at seven, he saw that the ship was in two; the forward part of the ship was higher than the after part; witness then went up the companion, when he was struck by a wave, and washed down to the lee side of the vessel. Saw Captain Taylor on deck, and a lady; both were prostrate on the deck. Witness went to the after-part of the forward boat on the poop. Got hold of a belaying pin. Put a rope around it, and let himself down into the water, and got on some spars which were lying alongside. Had not been there many minutes before the captain was washed overboard. Witness pulled him up on one of the spars, and he said 'There's hope yet'. Another tremendous wave broke over them and washed the captain off the spar. Witness succeeded in getting him up a second time. The forward boat was just then washed from its davits, and witness got into it, pulling the second officer, Mr. Cowie, with him. A second-class passenger also got in – the latter was saved. Mr. Cowie was not saved. The boat went down into the water, and drifted those who were in it onto the rocks. Was picked up by the boatswain's mate and others on shore. The second officer went back with the boat into the water as she split. He was in the after part of the boat, when witness being in the fore part was washed onto the rocks. An ordinary ship-boat could not have lived in the water between the ship and the rocks. It would have been impossible to swim there. The distance was about ten yards. Witness was the last of the surviving crew who saw the passengers in the saloon. The deck of the saloon was not damaged very much. In a few places, water was coming in. Should think when the mizzen fell, the passengers would have been all swept into the sea. Was aboard the *Royal Charter* during three voyages. During the voyage before last, they encountered a severe gale round the Cape of Good Hope."

Mr. Mansfield mentioned that he had received a guinea, enclosed in a letter, from the members of the Sons of Friendship Lodge, No. 631, Order of Druids, as a contribution towards the fund being raised for the survivors of the wreck.

Mr. James Russell was examined by Mr. O'Dowd –

Was a passenger on board the *Royal Charter*. His wife and two children accompanied him. Remembers the vessel being off Holyhead. Was on deck when she passed Holyhead. She appeared to be two or three miles from Holyhead. The wind was ahead, and blowing a little fresh. Saw Captain Taylor very frequently during the voyage. From what he saw of Captain Taylor during the voyage, never knew him in an improper state, or one in which a gentleman ought not to be. Had frequent opportunities of seeing him, as a second-class passenger during the voyage. Witness was saved from the wreck by being washed overboard and flung upon the rocks.

To Captain Harris — Went into his cabin at eight o'clock. Knew that it was blowing fresh, but did not know until two o'clock in the morning that it was blowing to an alarming degree. Heard Captain Johnson (a nautical man) remark in the forenoon of Tuesday that from the appearance of the weather it seemed likely to blow hard. Heard Captain Adams say it would be rough. That was about sunset. About two o'clock witness met Captain Adams, who told him there was great danger. He therefore went on deck; there were some others there, four with whom he was intimately acquainted, and some others. None of those with whom he was acquainted were saved. When witness got on shore, he was very kindly treated by the people at Moelfre.

To Mr. Mansfield — The sea broke clear over the vessel. That part of the sea between the vessel and the shore was somewhat calmer than that outside, the ship appearing to act as a kind of breakwater. Witness thinks if more people had come on deck when he did, many of them might have been saved.

To Mr. Aspinall — All the afternoon the wind seemed to be freshening. Did not much observe the effect until eight o'clock. Mr. Aspinall, at this stage of the inquiry, produced a letter from Mr. Bradbury, one of the passengers by the *Royal Charter,* who is at present lying ill at Moelfre, and who was anxious to contradict a rumour which had appeared in the papers, to the effect that he had stated that Captain Taylor was intoxicated on the day of the wreck. The letter was addressed to Mr. Smith, the local receiver of droits, by whom it was forwarded to Mr. O'Dowd. Mr. Bradbury stated that he had not the least knowledge of ever having made the statement imputed to him, and declared that if he had done so it must have been during a state of unconsciousness such as had frequently occurred to him during his illness; because, had he been conscious, he never could have made a statement so untrue. He declared that never during the voyage had he seen Captain Taylor or any of the ship's officers in any but a perfectly sober condition. Mr. Bradbury also forwarded a surgeon's certificate to explain his inability to attend the inquiry,

Mr. Samuel Edward Gapper examined by Mr. O'Dowd: Was a second-class passenger by the *Royal Charter.* Has heard the evidence given by the other passengers. There was nothing in it he dissented from, excepting some of the evidence as to the state of the wind after the vessel entered the Irish Channel. It was a light breeze. One of the witnesses said it was strong-breeze, and in that opinion witness did not agree.

To Mr. Aspinall - Some of the passengers were very anxious to get near Holyhead to see the *Great Eastern*, but the captain declined going any nearer.

To Captain Harris - Was acquainted with Captain Adams; saw him several times on the evening before the wreck, and during the night. Had several conversations with him about the weather and the ship. After the anchors were let go, Mr. Croome, the fourth officer, came down to the second cabin and told Captain Adams that Captain Taylor wished to speak to him immediately in the saloon. Capt. Adams went immediately. Witness waited until he returned, and then asked him whether there was any danger. Captain Adams said, "Yes, there is." He looked witness in the face, and said, "If it were possible to sing the song of 'The White Squall' it might now be sung with feeling." He added, "I have no doubt we shall have to do this (making a motion as if swimming) before we get ashore." He pointed to witness on a chart the places where they were, and said that from the quarter the wind was blowing from he did not see how they were to get out of it. Earlier in the night, about 10 o'clock, heard Capt. Adams say he had had a consultation with Capt. Taylor and Capt. Withers with respect to the weather. The screw ceased to work for a few moments after the starboard anchor was let go: it did not cease immediately on the vessel striking on the sand: did not come on deck himself until the vessel had parted, as he waited to observe how long the screw would go, thinking there was hope so long as it kept going. Witness lowered himself from the poop into the water, and got upon a topsail yard; before he did so he lowered a lady who was in his company into the water. There was a studding sail boom close to the vessel, and he thought he might get on it and be carried ashore. He was washed off, and was flung on shore. Never saw the lady afterwards. Was much bruised when thrown on shore.

To Mr. Aspinall - Word was passed aft for the ladies and children to go forward, and the door was just opened for the purpose when the vessel parted. This was while the hawser was out to the shore. Witness did not lower himself into the water for an hour and a half after. Heard Mr. Croome say they hoped to

Ladies' dresses were voluminous, heavy, and not designed for swimming!

pass the ladies onshore in one of the boats at daylight, and advise the ladies to put on as much of their clothing as they could; this was after the ship had parted amidships. In witness's opinion, all the officers behaved even better than, under such circumstances, could have been expected. Saw them trying to lower the boats after the ship parted. Many were washed away in doing so.

Joseph Rogers examined by Mr. O'Dowd - Was an able seaman on board the *Royal Charter*. It was his watch on deck at four o'clock on the afternoon of Tuesday; the mizzen and maintop gallant staysails were unbent, the three royals and topgallant studding sail had previously been sent below. Witness was engaged below with sailmaker in stowing the sails; came on deck again at eight; was sitting aft, near the engine room, when about nine o'clock he was called to reef the maintopmast staysail, which had been set about ten minutes and was then hauled down again. About 10 or half past 10, the watch was called to put the ship about. Witness went aft to haul in the spanker sheet on the port side. The main

yard was then rounded in. The maintopsail was set, but clewed up again. It took from two to three hours to furl the sail. The force of the wind was such that the robing poles were broken away. Witness was nearly pitched off the yard. Went down on deck to ask Mr. Stephens, the chief mate, what was to be done, as they could not furl the sail. He said to go back and make it fast to the yard, which they did. Shortly afterwards, the anchors were let go - first the port and then the starboard anchor. Witness went forward himself to lend a hand to bear away the chain. Witness described the snapping of the cables, the cutting away of the masts, and the other events immediately before the wreck. Witness went to help in clearing away the lifeboat, by Captain Taylor's orders. The vessel had four lifeboats. He went to clear away the front lifeboat. The mizzen-stay had been carried away and fell on the lifeboat. When the vessel struck on the rock, witness was inside the forecastle. The boatswain's mate was there. Witness asked what they were going to do. He said he would try to go ashore; and witness said he would do so too. Went into the forecastle and found a chap with a line. Witness made the line fast round his waist, and went on the topgallant forecastle. Mr. Stephens was there, and offered him a life-buoy. Witness said he did not want it; he was a Maltese, and could swim ashore. Went out on the flying jib-boom, caught hold of the guy, which had been carried away, and lowered himself into the water. He was three times washed back to the ship, but at last succeeded in getting to the shore, where he saw some people, to whom he called to bear a hand. He got upon the rocks, and gave the men on shore the end of the line. Witness wanted to stop, but they said he must not stop there, but must go away and get dried, and he was then taken away to a house.

To Captain Harris - Has been 10 years at sea. Joined the *Royal Charter* on her second trip. Does not know whether she had storm staysails or storm staysail stays on board. Never saw storm staysails set during the last voyage.

Mr. Bateson (solicitor) said the owners would be able to prove by evidence that the vessel had storm staysails and stays on board.

Examination continued - The sea between the ship and the rocks was very heavy. Partly swam and partly was washed ashore.

Rowland Hughes examined – Is master of the lifeboat at Moelfre. It is a self righting boat, the crew 16 in number, being a double crew, but six men and the steersman only go in her at a time. On the night of the wreck witness was at Red Wharf; the lifeboat was not there. Is the owner of a small smack, and had her at Red Wharf. Did not see any lights or signals of distress. Was out until half past 12, and did not see anything of the kind. Did not hear from the people at Moelfre that they had seen any; even if he had, he could not have given any help; no lifeboat in the world could have given any assistance to a vessel that night. Got up at six o'clock next morning; about half past six saw a schooner onshore at Red Wharf sands. Could not relieve her, the sea was too high, and the wind was blowing too hard. It would not have been possible to get out a boat at that hour to relieve a vessel in distress.

To Mr. Aspinall - Had lived a long time on that coast, and never saw such a storm in his life before. Between 10 and 11 o'clock that night, the wind chapped round to the N.E. and it then began to blow a complete hurricane. Up to that time the wind was east by south. The sea up on the beach was such as he had never seen in his life before. Conversed with an old man, 81 years of age, living at Moelfre, who told him he never saw such a storm in his life.

To Captain Harris - The launching of the lifeboat was left to his own discretion, as captain of the boat. Thomas Owen was the other master of the boat, and it was his duty that night to be with her.

George Suaicar, boatswain's mate, deposed that he made an effort to take a line ashore from amidships, at the same time that Rogers went from the fore part, but when he was lowering himself into the water, Captain Withers and some others pulled him back, and said if he went in, he must be lost, owing to the suction under the ship. Meanwhile, Rogers had succeeded in getting his line ashore. An effort had been previously made to throw a line ashore, but the sea carried the line away.

Mr. O'Dowd said this witness concluded that portion of the evidence with regard to the circumstances of the wreck, and he had to apply for an adjournment to allow him to get up other evidence he proposed to offer. The issues he meant to raise were, whether the *Royal Charter* was built with the usual strength of iron ships destined for such a voyage; and secondly, whether that strength was sufficient for the purpose.

After some conversation, it was agreed that an adjournment should take place to one o'clock on Wednesday next.

The Carnarvon and Denbigh Herald

AND NORTH AND SOUTH WALES ADVERTISER

Saturday, November 26, 1859

The Wreck of the *Royal Charter.*

RESUMPTION OF THE INQUIRY

The inquiry was resumed before Mr. Mansfield and Captain Harris, in the Crown Court, St. George's Hall, at one o'clock on Wednesday. Mr. O'Dowd attended on behalf of the Board of Trade, and Mr. T.B. Aspinall appeared for the owners of the vessel.

Mr. Smith, the Receiver of Wreck at Moelfre, was placed in the witness-box, and produced a deposition sworn to before him by Mr. Bradbury, third-class passenger in the *Royal Charter,* who is himself unable to attend the inquiry, being under surgical care. The deposition contained a number of answers given by Mr. Bradbury to questions drawn up by Captain Harris. Mr. Bradbury stated that the barometer was noted every four hours, and during changeable weather still more frequently. The captain's log was written up to Saturday the 22nd October. On Tuesday the 25th, at twelve midnight, the barometer was last noted; believes that between 28 and 29 were the figures then noted. There was no remark made to him by the captain or by any other person on the 25th October about the state of the barometer; nor was any remark made about it in his hearing. Did not himself take the height of the barometer on the 25th. Believes there were three barometers on board – one in the captain's room, one in the chief officer's (Mr. Stephens) room; and he did not know precisely where the other one was.

Mr. Smith produced a meteorological record of observations of the state of the weather kept by the keeper of Point Lynas Lighthouse, from which it appeared that on the morning of Tuesday, the 25th, at 9 a.m., the wind was S.E. and light, clear weather; in the afternoon at three, wind S.E., strong, dull and hazy – sky dull and gloomy all day; 9 pm., S.E., strong breeze; 10 pm., fresh gale, raining, wind E.N.E.; 11 pm., N.E., heavy gale and rainy weather; 12 pm., heavy gale, rainy weather; October 26th, 1 am., wind N.E., heavy gale, with rain; 2 and 3 am., heavy gale, and rain; 4 am., wind N.N.E., heavy gale and rain until 1 pm., then the wind veered to the north, and moderated.

A record of observations made by Mr. Hartnup, of the Liverpool Observatory, was put in. The storm did not appear to have reached Liverpool in any violence until several hours after the wreck at Moelfra. A singular circumstance was that during the 24th, 25th and 26th, the barometer scarcely varied its height at all.

In answer to Mr. Aspinall, Mr. Smith stated that the *Royal Charter* appeared to him to have been one of the strongest vessels he had ever seen, for it took three boiler-makers three days (working when the tide was out) to loosen one of the plates. Saw the watches of several persons who had been washed ashore. They had all stopped somewhere between twenty minutes past seven and eight o'clock.

Mr. Mellor, of Oldham, solicitor, asked leave to put a question to Mr. Smith, stating that he had himself lost a brother and cousin in the vessel.

Mr. Mansfield thought it would be better, for the sake of regularity, that the question should be put through Mr. O'Dowd.

Mr. Mellor said the question he would ask was, what had been done for the recovery of the bodies?

Mr. O'Dowd said that the question did not appertain to the present inquiry, which merely referred to the loss of the vessel. In justice to Messrs. Gibbs and Bright, it should be said that Mr. Smith had stated already in his evidence that everything which could possibly be expected had been done for that purpose.

Mr. Mellor said he wished to ask what had been done?

Mr. Mansfield ruled that the question could not be put.

John Shepherd, master of No. 4 Liverpool pilot-boat, was examined by Mr, O'Dowd – He deposed that his boat is sloop-built, registered 23 tons; it carries a light at the mast head, and uses a flash-light every quarter of an hour; has a crew of six on board. Remembers Tuesday the 25th of October; was out on that day; was cruising between Middlemouse Rock and Puffin Island the whole of the day and night; the wind, about seven that afternoon, commenced to blow very strong; it increased very much in violence after eight; there was rain and lightning. About eleven p.m., the gale was more violent than before; it was dreadful; the men in the pilot-boat could not hear each other speak at a distance of eight feet on the deck. The wind had got to the N.E. The boat's lights were put out by the wind; they were lighted again, and again put out. Vessels bound for Liverpool seldom came up without taking a pilot, if the weather allowed of their getting one on board. Witness sounded a little before day-light, and had twenty-five fathoms; it was about seven then; they could not see the length of the boat before them in consequence of the seadrift. Got a glimpse of Point Lynas once, but lost it again, and it was eleven o'clock before they got sight of land. They were under close-reefed sails. They lost their storm-jib and stay-sail during the night, and drifted in consequence about eight miles.

To Mr. Aspinall – Has been thirty-nine years a pilot, and twenty-nine years a master pilot. Never knew such a hurricane before – the wind blowing fresh from that point of the compass. On this coast, it is more usual for an easterly wind to back to the south than to the north. He never saw a heavier sea in his

PILOT BOAT

The Pilot Boat Inn, near Llanallgo.

lifetime. There could not be a worse place for breaking vessel up anywhere on the coast than where the *Royal Charter* went ashore, with such a wind.

To Captain Harris – at five p.m. on the evening of the wreck, witness telegraphed to Point Lynas, to know if there were any vessels in distress round the coast, but got no answer. Must have been cruising close in the track of the *Royal Charter* during the night. The place where the *Royal Charter* may be presumed to have anchored is, under ordinary circumstances, tolerably good anchoring ground; but thinks no ground would have held during such a night. Witness's boat was reported as lost that night.

Richard Parry, master of pilot-boat No. 11, examined by Mr. O'Dowd – Was off Point Lynas at seven o'clock in the evening of Tuesday, the 25th of October. Left Holyhead at a quarter before three. The wind was then about E.S.E. About seven p.m. saw what he thought was a blue light, from a vessel off Point Lynas, to the west. It was reported to him about half-past six p.m. that rockets were seen below the Skerries. The vessel from which he saw what he supposed to be blue light might have been seven or eight miles off Point Lynas. About seven p.m. it was blowing hard. They had all their reefs in, having reefed at half-past five; it began to blow east by south, increasing in strength as it backed to the north; lost sight of Point Lynas about eight o'clock, and did not get sight of anything again until about eleven the next day. Agrees with the last witness as to the extraordinary violence of the gale.

To Mr. Aspinall – Easterly gales more usually back to the southward, but of late years they have sometimes, as in this instance, backed to the northward. The place where the *Royal Charter* went ashore is as bad a place for breaking up a ship as could be found – there could not be worse.

To Captain Harris – Even if he had fallen in with the *Royal Charter,* that night, he could not have boarded her in such a storm. The barometer was low all that day; about six p.m., it had fallen to 29; from midnight to four a.m. it had reached 28.70. Did not notice the thermometer. Lost seven or eight miles that night.

Mr. William Patterson, shipbuilder, of Bristol, was examined. He said – "I am a shipbuilder. I am engaged in building both wooden and iron ships. The *Royal Charter* was built in the year 1855. She was contracted for by Messrs. Charles Moore and Co., of Liverpool, with Mr. George Cram, of Chester. Messrs. Gibbs and Bright subsequently purchased her, and I became inspector for them. She had been commenced, and I took her in the state she was in when Messrs. Gibbs and Bright became owners. Nearly all the frames were up, and part of the frames were commenced. I went down to superintend the building. When the frames had been put up, in the year 1854, Messrs. Cram failed in business, and I then became the builder. At that time, the greater portion of the iron was on the premises. I took to her, and prior to that I had brought my own foreman from Bristol to look particularly at the iron and the riveting. As the ship progressed, we were particularly careful to see that the riveting was good. Lloyd's rules at this time were not in existence for iron ships. The keel plates were 1 inch thick. The following plates were $\frac{7}{8}$ in. and $\frac{3}{4}$ in. up to the turn of the bilge in the mid-ship body, and continued to within 30 feet of each end of the ship, the two ends being $\frac{1}{16}$ th less. The plates opposite each tier of beams were $\frac{5}{8}$, extending 250 feet of the length. The keel was 12 in. by 4 in., or something more than 4 in. The rivets, I think, were $1\frac{1}{4}$ in., but I am not quite clear upon that point. The rivets in the sideplates were 1 in. round the turn of the bilge. From the larboard strake up above the turn of the bilge, they were 1 in. diameter. All the plates and butts were double-riveted. The frames were 18 in. from centre to centre; they were 5 in. by $3\frac{3}{4}$ in. thickness. There were two wing keelsons, one at the bilge and the other half-way between the bilge and the middle keelson. The lower tier of beams were 10 inches by $\frac{5}{8}$. The upper edge of the beam had an angle iron riveted on, 3 by 3 by $\frac{1}{2}$ inch. The second tier of beams, 9 inches by $\frac{5}{8}$ angle iron, riveted on to upper edge 3 by $3\frac{1}{2}$ inch. The upper tier of beams were 8 inches by $\frac{9}{16}$ th less. Angle iron the same size as in the former instance. The upper tier had two plates, extending fore and aft. There were shelves on the ends of the beams; angle iron on the top; they were riveted down to the beams with a vertical plate next to the angle iron of the frame, and with an angle iron in the angle of the vertical and horizontal plate. This vertical plate extended fore and aft. All the tiers of beams were so secured. The middle tier had longitudinal plates on top of them, and were secured with plates, riveted to each stringer and upon each beam. On each, strong, teak waterway pieces, 14 or 15 inches square, were batted to the shelf-pieces and the beams. There were six standing bulkheads, five of them watertight, about $\frac{1}{2}$ inch. The bulkheads at the after part of the engine-room had a passage leading into the screw tunnel; there was no door, but an open archway; to meet that, we made the tunnel watertight. There was a watertight bulkhead immediately at the foreside of the stuffing-box; this was further secured by a watertight deck over it; these bulkheads were put into the ship before she was launched, and after she had been designed for a screw-steamer. They were riveted to the angle irons of the floor, round up the side of the ship to the middle deck beam. They were riveted to the middle deck beam, and supported by vertical angle irons about every 2 feet 9 in. The stringers passed through the bulkheads. This applies to the whole of the bulkheads throughout the ship. The whole of the fastenings and everything throughout the ship were made of the best iron. The greater part had been contracted for before I took up the ship, but I examined them, and found them all of very good iron. Some of the rivets were made afterwards, and were of the best iron. Anything which appeared defective, I had put aside. The ship in every way was well secured. She was lengthened before I took to her. She was not lengthened in her midship body, but only at her two extremities; her original keel was never touched; the frame at either end had not been bent into shape before the alteration in her design took place. Every care was taken to have the work done well, and I believe for that purpose the workmen were paid higher wages for riveting than I have ever known given before in such cases. I have seen her in dock after each voyage, with the exception of the last outward voyage, and I never found a loose rivet, and I can say the same of the *Great Britain*. I built the *Great Britain*. I did not observe any signs of wear and tear in the rivet heads. Sometimes, especially with a sugar cargo, I have known the rivet heads loosen from the action of the bilge-water after a very few voyages. At the launch of the *Royal Charter* on the River Dee, she got stuck in the sand. There is very little water in the Dee. She was stopped there for some time until the sand had been dug from under her. The ways were under her all the time. She had no appearance of having strained or injured herself. When the spring tides came, she was towed out by steamer. While being towed down the Dee, she ran ashore at Flint, and broke her keelson. She was subsequently put into dry dock at Liverpool, and the necessary repairs were executed."

Mr. Aspinall said that the Liverpool shipbuilder who executed the repairs (Mr. Vernon) would be produced as a witness.

Examination continued – "The damage done by the accident was such as could have been effectually repaired. (A report of a survey made of the ship after the accident was put in.) I am of opinion, from what I have heard, that the ship striking the rock at Moelfra injured her bottom – almost divided it – and that the effect of the sea striking upon the two ends was enough to break her, as you would break a stick across a knee. I believe that any ship in the same situation and in the same weather would have met with the same result, and I am borne out in this opinion by understanding that even the waterways, large as they were, of teak timber, were knocked to pieces. I believe she was as strong, if not stronger, than any other ship of her day. I think her length was seven times her beam. I am of opinion that, with proper regard to strength, you may safely go as far as eight times the beam."

To Mr. Aspinall - "I was ordered by the owners to spare no expense in making her a good ship. After the repairs of the accident on the Dee had been completed, she was, in his opinion, as good a ship as ever."

To Mr. Mansfield - "Had she been built stronger, and consequently heavier, her fate on the rocks would not have been protracted."

Captain Harris – "If she had been built like one of our floating batteries of 4-inch iron, her own weight would have beaten her to pieces on the rocks."

The court adjourned at half-past five.

The Carnarvon and Denbigh Herald

AND NORTH AND SOUTH WALES ADVERTISER

Saturday, December 3, 1859

Loss of the *Royal Charter.*
Conclusion of the Official Inquiry.

On its being resumed on Thursday morning:-

Mr. Patterson was examined by Mr. O'Dowd. He said – "I believe the *Royal Charter* could have been classed A1 at Lloyd's in 1855 if the owners had desired it. The foreman I brought to look after the rivets was in my employment the greater part of the time. I consider him a very competent judge in matters connected with iron workmanship and riveting. When I took to the ship, the whole of the angle-iron frame, the floor plates, and the beam iron were provided. There was a quantity – not very large – which I rejected as unfit for the purpose. I consider that what I rejected would not stand the sudden bend which was required. That was the only objection. The rivets were 1¼ inch diameter in the keel, I believe. I have not lately seen one of the keel rivets, and I believe it is not possible to procure one. The plate rivets were one inch. I think all the rivets were sufficiently large for such a vessel as the *Royal Charter.* I consider that the beams she had were numerous enough for such a vessel. I have always used boiler plates for sheathing. I believe these were used in the *Royal Charter.*"

To Mr. Aspinall - "I was asked to look at the ship before Messrs. Gibbs and Bright purchased her. I did so; very little of her was put together then as she was only just commenced. Messrs. Penn and Co., of Greenwich, supplied the engines; the price paid for them was very high, £55 10s per horse-power."

James Berry, examined by Mr. Aspinall - He was Mr. Patterson's foreman. The iron used in the bulkheads of the *Royal Charter* was 5/8 th of an inch. He agreed generally with Mr. Patterson's evidence. The iron in the *Royal Charter* stood its work well from beginning to end. In all cases, some portions have to be thrown away for slight defects, such as a sand-flaw or blister. There was not much of the *Royal Charter* iron rejected for such causes.

To Mr. Aspinall - "There never was a large lot of iron for the building of a ship out of which some had not to be rejected."

To Captain Harris - "The iron was of the kind normally applied to the building of iron ships. Was employed in the building of the *Great Britain.* Was employed as foreman of the works in repairing the damage done to the *Royal Charter* when she grounded in Flint. I was in her when she grounded. She was brought to Liverpool, put in dock, and repaired. She broke 33 or 35 flooring angle-irons. She bent her main keel amidships. It was bent 2½ inches in a distance of about twelve feet in the midship part. The midship keelson was broken. The garboard strake was bent a little. The butts of the garboard strake were strained in some places, but not broken. Four or five of the stanchions of the whole beam in the midship body of the ship were bent; some of the rivets were started in the bottom, just where the great pressure came, and nowhere else. Many of the rivets there were shaken; these were replaced. Stronger plates were put in the main keelson, at the sides and top, for the space of about 40 feet. It was a very workmanlike job, and the vessel was properly and effectually repaired. He last saw her at Plymouth, when she put back in 1856; this was after the repairs just described. She put back because of the leakage in her waterways. Witness superintended her repairs. There was nothing the matter with the hull of the vessel, but she leaked her waterways. She was not put in the graving dock. There were carpenters on board who recaulked the waterways, and put in some additional bolts, and she was lightened of about 300 tons of stone ballast." (A certificate of the government surveyor in Plymouth, declaring that the work had been satisfactorily executed, and the vessel made fit for sea, was put in.)

Mr. Aspinall said that Mr. Patterson was of opinion that the vessel originally had five keelsons, not three, and that two were afterwards added, making seven in all.

The witness adhered to his opinion, that three keelsons were the original number.

Mr. O'Dowd said he was informed that when a Board of Trade inspector visited the vessel in 1857, there were only five keelsons there.

Mr. Aspinall said he had now in his hand the original specification between Messrs. Charles Moore and Messrs. Cram, and it specified one main keelson, and two bilge keelsons on either side. It was not likely that the number was afterwards reduced.

Capt. Harris – "Then the probability is that she was built as Mr. Patterson thinks."

Mr. Aspinall – "It would seem so, and that Mr. Berry is right as far as the fact is concerned that two keelsons were added subsequently to the original number."

Mr. John Vernon, shipbuilder, of Liverpool, deposed that he put a fore and aft stringer into the *Royal Charter* in October 1856. It was done in the public graving-dock. Was requested by Messrs. Bright to suggest what kind of stringer would be best fitted for strengthening the ship, and he suggested a fore and aft. This was after her first voyage. No expense was spared by Messrs. Bright. There were some crutches put in the forefoot of the vessel for the purpose of giving her additional strength in that place. She showed some slight symptoms of weakness in the upper works then. Did not attribute this to her heavy masts. Attributed

it rather to her great length. Considered her construction remarkably well adapted for the purpose for which she was intended.

To Mr. Aspinall – The kind of stringer witness introduced was afterwards adopted by several large steamers. Has had many opportunities of judging of the strength of the *Royal Charter*. She was a ship possessed of very great strength, but liable to more strain than other vessels because of her great length and fine ends. The material and riveting were capital. With the stringer in, witness considered her a very strong ship.

Mr. John Jordan, examined by Mr. O'Dowd – Was surveyor to the Liverpool Underwriters' Association. He examined the *Royal Charter* after each of her voyages, for the purpose of furnishing information to the underwriters. As regarding her strength, found her an average specimen of the usual class of large screw-steamers.

Mr. W. Gilmour, who had acted as a surgeon to the ship, differed in opinion from the gentleman previously examined, and stated that he had less confidence in the vessel to such a degree that he resigned the post he held in her. Some letters to the owners were put in, however, in which Mr. Gilmour said he left the ship solely to commence practice in England.

On Friday, on the inquiry being resumed, William Foster, the carpenter, was recalled at the request of Mr. Mansfield, and stated that there were about six inches of water in the vessel after she stuck on the sand. He asked the engineer about her, and the engineer said that she was all right. Did not sound her after she got on the rocks. The cargo was hides and wool, copper ingots, and gold. There were about forty-five tons of copper ingots.

Captain Harris asked if the exact weight of the cargo could be ascertained.

Mr. Tyndall Bright said they had not received any manifest.

Captain Harris - "Then, in fact, you

absolutely do not know what was in the ship."

Mr. Bright - "We do not."

Captain Harris - "She had a light cargo?"

Witness - "Yes; she was drawing 18 feet 5 inches forward, and 20 feet 6 inches aft."

To Mr. Aspinall - Did not hear Cormick's evidence. Does not know up to what time the chief engineer reported. The time he had mentioned was the last time he saw the chief engineer.

Captain William Martin, examined by Mr. Aspinall – "I am marine superintendent of the firm of Messrs. Gibbs, Bright, and Co., and of the Australian Steam Navigation Company. In that capacity I looked after the *Royal Charter* whenever she was in port, and I had constant opportunity of seeing her while being built. I assisted Mr. Patterson, the builder, for some months. I superintended the masting and rigging of her in Liverpool. I can confirm Mr. Patterson as to the quality of the materials and the care taken in building her. Nothing was left undone, nor any expense spared to make her as good a ship as could be built. There was the greatest anxiety on the part of the owners she should be made so, and we all laboured very hard for the purpose. There were three best bower anchors on board, Trotman's patent; 50cwt. 24lbs., 50cwt. 3qrs. 16lbs., 51cwt. 18lbs. were their weights. There were 300 fathoms of 2½ inch bower-cable. The cables were proofed at 72 tons each. They were supplied by Henry Wood and Co., of Liverpool, and proved at Chester. I was not present during the proof. (The certificate of proof was handed in and read.) The weight of the cables was 18 tons 9 cwt. 0 qrs. 16 lbs., and 18 tons 7 cwt. 2 qrs. 11 lbs respectively."

To Captain Harris – "There is no compulsion to have chains up to a certain proof, either Admiralty or corporation. It is usual to take the builder's test. We had Trotman's stream anchor of 15 cwt. 1 qr. 10 lbs., and the full complement of cable. The price of the bower anchors was 45s. per cwt. The spare bower anchor was also 45s.; it weighed 51 cwt. 18 lbs. The stream anchor cost 36s. per cwt. The kedges were also 36s. per cwt. The bower cables were 13s 6d. The stream cable the same. The chains were all stud-linked. The sheet anchor was stowed down the fore hatchway, with the ring uppermost, ready to use. It is not usual in Liverpool to carry the sheet anchor on the gunwhale; there would be some difficulty in getting in and out of dock. She had standing channels about 14 inches broad."

To Mr. Aspinall – "The anchor and chains were full size for a vessel of her class. In caulking her before the last voyage, there may have been as many as thirty men employed for a day or two, in order to get through the work as quickly as possible. We had the berths out, and took the opportunity of caulking between decks. There were no actual repairs going on. From the log-book, I perceive that she wore and stayed admirably. I have been on board her myself, and she stayed very easily in what we would call a top-gallant breeze. She was found to have much greater stability than was expected, looking at her great length and her narrow beam."

To Captain Harris – "She was the largest auxiliary clipper I had seen at that time. Anticipating from her construction that she might possibly be crank, a very large amount of ballast was put in. When she had to put back at Plymouth, she was overloaded with ballast. When lightened, she sailed capitally. The heavy sails all throughout the ship were No. 1 canvas up to the upper top-sails. She would have lain to under her lower maintopsail. We did away with topsails in the *Royal Charter,* because we found from our experience that such large vessels in heavy gales do better under their lower maintopsails. We never had trysails in the *Royal Charter*. I cannot account for the statement of two witnesses that the *Royal Charter,* after rounding the Skerries, went along with her helm hard-a-starboard without coming up, except that I believe the men must have been mistaken. I once went round from Liverpool to the Tuskar in the *Royal Charter* in a heavy gale of wind; we never averaged less than 3½ knots an hour during the whole time the ship was steaming head to wind, or a point or two on the bow. I was surprised to find that with so strong a wind and so little power, she steamed and answered her helm so well. She had a draught of 20 feet 6 inches aft and 19 feet 4 inches forward. No doubt the force of the gale in the instance mentioned by the witnesses must have prevented her from coming round. I remember now that in the case I have been referring to, she did come round; the masts were very nicely proportioned and very nicely balanced; they were not put with reference to gaining space, but to make the ship more efficient. When under sail, she would go along for half an hour on the wind steering herself without the helm at all. The reason she would not steer on the occasion of her first passage between Liverpool and Plymouth, as described by Dr. Scoresby, was because of her being in improper trim, and too much by the head. I have been 19 years at sea, and in all kinds of vessels. I have heard the evidence as to the letting go of the *Royal Charter's* anchor. I have heard that she rode for four hours. I think it is difficult to say whether from experience Captain Taylor ought then to have cut away the mast; the moment you cut away a mast in a screw-steamer, her engines are useless."

Captain Harris - "My own humble opinion is that if the masts had been cut away in the first instance, those lives might have been saved. She rode so gallantly for four hours."

Captain Martin - "It is a very dangerous process to cut away large masts and yards at a time like that. A commander might defeat the very object he had in view. If a large yard were to strike the vessel in a heavy sea the chances are fifty to one that one of her decks might have been knocked in. That would be just as likely as anything."

Captain Harris- "For a slight built ship it might be."

Captain Martin - "I think under the circumstances a shipmaster would think a great deal before he cut away his masts, if he were depending upon his screw."

Mr. Aspinall remarked that all conclusions in this case were drawn from very imperfect evidence, while Captain Taylor, who had consulted with two other nautical men, had the state of the case actually before his eyes.

Captain Harris said he made every allowance for that, and his enquiries were rather directed to obtain opinions, with a view to the guidance of others in future contingencies.

In answer to Mr. Aspinall, Captain Martin stated that the *Royal Charter* cost £34 per ton ready for sea. Captain Martin also described the present position of the vessel, from which it appeared that she came on the rock, right in her middle.

Captain Francis Boyce, examined by Mr. Aspinall - "I was on board the ship one voyage, while Mr. Gilmour was there. There is no truth whatever in the story about the rattling rivets. She made no water or whatever, even in the between decks. I commanded the *Royal Charter* on her first two voyages."

To Captain Harris - "She wore and stayed very well. I have frequently stayed and wore her, both in violent and fine weather, without the aid of the steam power. She wore and stayed as well as any other vessel. I cannot explain why she should not have answered her helm on the night of the wreck. She must have had no way on her. She always answered her helm well, so far as I ever saw. She was splendidly rigged and splendidly sparred."

Mr. R.S. Steel, examined by Mr. Aspinall. "I am an insurance broker, of Liverpool, of the firm of Rathbone, Martin, and Co. The *Royal Charter* was insured at 70 shillings out and home. That was considered a low rate. On this occasion, the reports of the surveyors were not received, not being thought necessary, the insurers had so good an opinion of the ship."

To Captain Harris - "We make no distinction between a wooden and an iron ship. A steamer would be taken lower than a sailing-ship."

Mr. William MacDonald, examined by Mr. O'Dowd - "Is superintendent of the Liverpool corporation testing machine. He tested some plates from the wreck of the *Royal Charter* furnished by Mr. Smith, the receiver of wreck. There were some gentlemen present at the experiments. The object of the machine is to test the tensile power of iron. Repeated the experiments that day. Tried six plates, four the previous day and two that day. The first plate tried was 3 by ⅝ inches. It broke at 41 tons, but it broke at the bolt eye and he therefore did not consider it a fair test. The next was 3 by ¾ inches. It broke at 45 tons 10 cwt. That was a fair break, right between the centre. The next was the same dimensions, and it broke at 42 tons. The next was 3 by $^{13}/_{16}$ inches and it broke at 45 tons. Those of that day were first one of 2 by $^{11}/_{16}$ inches, which broke at 32 tons; the next 2 inches by $^{11}/_{16}$ and $^{1}/_{32}$ inch, and it broke at 28 tons.

Mr. O'Dowd said the average of the five fairly-tested plates was a pressure of 20 tons 15 cwt to the square inch. This quality of iron he understood was higher than good Staffordshire plates. Fairbairn's average of good Staffordshire plates was 1½ tons less. To Mr. O'Dowd – I cannot say whether it necessarily follows that because iron has a great tensile power, it must be fit for building ships."

Mr. William Clay, examined by Mr. O'Dowd. - "Is the superintendent and manager of the Mersey Iron Works, and was present at most of the experiments made by the last witness. Is practically acquainted with the manufacture of iron. Tensility, although a very essential element in the strength of iron for all purposes, is not the only element. Lowmoor iron bends well when heated, but it is not stronger when cold than good iron of other kinds. Is of the opinion that the iron tested by Mr. Macdonald stood an extraordinary strain. Considers it above the quality of iron which is generally used in the building of iron ships. The government, in the construction of the steam rams, contracted for a tension of 22 tons to the square inch, and had great difficulty in having it complied with. Believes that is the only test they required."

Mr. O'Dowd - "That is all the evidence I propose to offer."

Mr. Aspinall said the price of iron was £12 10s. per ton, which was a high price, as iron ranged at the time. Evidence could be given on that point, but probably the court would be satisfied with that statement. Mr. Aspinall then briefly addressed the court on the evidence which had been offered. He maintained that neither the court nor the public could point to anything which had been omitted in the construction of the *Royal Charter*. Everything which energy, skill, profuse expenditure and mercantile enterprise could do had been done to render her one of the finest ships which ever sailed out of the port. Every witness called to speak to that point, the builder, the superintendent, the officer at the Board of Trade, the officers of the insurers, had all borne testimony to the beauty and strength of her construction. It was impossible that after all this mass of evidence, the greatest grumbler amongst the public could hold up his hand and say there was anything to be found fault with. They had seen yesterday an instance to show how certain statements got before the public, and the court and the public had seen how lamentably the assertions of one person had failed, and how utterly his statements with regard to the ship were without foundation. Mr. Aspinall quoted several passages from Dr. Scoresby's work to show the "peculiar and splendid qualities" of the *Royal Charter* in a gale. In one instance, Dr. Scoresby remarked that "her rolling was as smooth as a swing, and it was evident that there was no straining which could affect the general fabric of the ship." He (Mr. Aspinall) expressed a hope that the court would come to a conclusion which would in no way disparage the memory of the brave officers of the vessel, who were no more. There was no extraordinary weather in the early part of the day before the wreck, and nothing which could have warned Captain Taylor against coming in where he did to look for a pilot. Then came that sudden and extraordinary hurricane, unlike, witness after witness told them, anything which had ever been seen on that coast before. Under the pressure of the circumstances which followed, he maintained that Captain Taylor took the course which the circumstances demanded, and he urged that even the most experienced seaman could not now place himself in such a position as to venture on pronouncing a judgement unfavourable to Captain Taylor's conduct. In regard to the question of cutting away the masts, he referred to the instance of the *Prince**, off Balaclava during the Crimean war, and reminded the court that in that instance the master of the vessel had been accused of causing her wreck by cutting away the masts and fouling her screw. Captain Taylor had not merely acted upon his own judgement, but there was evidence that over and over again he resorted to the opinion of those who were most competent to form an opinion of the facts before their eyes, and the course which ought to have been pursued. He consulted not only his own officers, but three nautical captains who were on board. It must be inferred that their views coincided with his, and Mr. Aspinall called upon the court to presume that there must have been some circumstances not now apparent to justify and render necessary a course thus unanimously adopted. That everything had been done up to the last to save life, Mr. Aspinall declared that the evidence had fully proved. No idea appeared to have entered the minds of Captain Taylor or any of his officers, of saving their own lives until they had first rescued the helpless persons committed to their charge. The officers and sailors might easily have saved themselves had they thought fit to abandon the passengers, and especially the women and children. It would be difficult to imagine a picture more creditable to the bravery and the honour of English seaman than that presented, after the courage and gallantry of Rogers had established a connection with the shore, by the officers and seamen who kept guard at the hawser even after the ship had actually parted, in the hope that some of the women and children, or even the one woman who was forward, might first be saved. The conduct of the passengers Mr. Aspinall declared to be in itself worthy of equal praise, so free was it from the slightest instance of selfishness or of any discreditable conduct. In conclusion, Mr. Aspinall declared that the owners and the public felt deeply indebted to the Board of Trade, to Mr. O'Dowd, and to the court for the manner in which they had conducted the inquiry.

At the close of the enquiry, Mr. Mansfield said his colleague and himself entirely concurred in everything which had fallen from the learned counsel with reference to the heroic gallantry shown, not merely by the captain and crew, but also by the passengers of the *Royal Charter* up to the last moment. Everyone appears to have done his duty, even with almost certain death before him, intrepidly and unflinchingly to the last. Perhaps a nobler spectacle was never witnessed, except in the memorable

* See page 209.

case of the wreck of the *Birkenhead** and it was even perhaps more remarkable in the case of ordinary passengers of the middle and humbler ranks of life, whose conduct was such as to make one proud of being their countryman. Notwithstanding what had taken place in that court during the very long inquiry, he understood that some persons still perceived in the most malignant imputations against the late Captain Taylor, with reference to his sobriety. It was well known that the Board of Trade had been most anxious to receive any communications whatsoever which bore on the inquiry. Indeed, the Post-office had been like the Lion's Mouth in Venice, from the number of accusations which had been dropped into it. The Board of Trade invited every person who had any communication to make or suggestions to offer to appear before them. Nothing of the kind has been brought forward. On the contrary, some names had been given as authorities for that most malignant imputation, but the parties, on being referred to, entirely denied it. It seemed therefore so groundless that Mr. O'Dowd, in his opening, declined going into it. The whole story was entirely baseless, and he (Mr. Mansfield) should not even mention it in the report to the Board of Trade. There could be no doubt that Captain Taylor was a gallant and brave seaman, and it could only be from the vilest malignity, or in some other unworthy motive, that an attempt was made to leave the stigma upon his character in that respect.

The following were the remarks of Mr. Aspinall, to which Mr. Mansfield referred:-
"As long as it continued dark, Captain Taylor evidently thought that it was safer to wait for daylight than to make any attempt by boat or otherwise in such a sea to reach an unknown coast. As soon as the light came, the communication was established under the orders of the officers with the shore by means of the heroic conduct of the Maltese, Rogers. But for the unexpected breaking up of the ship, the bravery of that man would probably have saved almost everyone on board. When the hawser was passed from the ship to the shore, there was presented a picture than which it is difficult to conceive anything more illustrative of the nobleness of British seamen. Not a man attempted to get to land except by order of the officers. Messengers were despatched for the women and children; at that moment, the ship broke up. When that was told to the chief officer, Mr. Stephens, he left the hawser and went aft in the direction where the females were, and was doubtless lost in trying to reach them. Even at that frightful moment we have evidence that the fourth officer, Mr. Croome, and the crew spent some twenty minutes in trying to save the only female in the fore-part of the ship. As regards the conduct of the passengers, - up to this time the conduct of the soldiers on board the *Birkenhead* who kept their ranks until the ship went down has been thought the greatest heroism on record, but if it were possible that that should be exceeded at all, it is so now, because here we have a mass of persons not subject to command, or habituated to discipline; men, women, and children behaving in a most admirable manner, and showing an amount of courage and a total absence of selfishness which ought to make every Englishman proud of his countrymen."

* Built in 1845 at Laird's shipyard in Birkenhead, the iron-hulled paddle-steamer 'Birkenhead' was lost off Danger Point, South Africa on February the 26th, 1852, with great loss of life. The steamer was carrying over 600 British Army officers and men, along with a number of wives and children. On a calm, clear night, she hit an uncharted rock, and quickly filled with water despite her supposedly watertight compartments. Military discipline was rigorously maintained while the women and children were given the few available places in the ship's boats so that all the women and children survived, but around 450 soldiers and sailors were drowned.

The hull of the 'Royal Charter" consisted of iron plates held together by rivets.

Although the inquiry raised no criticism of the construction of the ship, William Patterson, the builder of both the 'Great Britain' and the 'Royal Charter', had stated *'Lloyd's rules at this time were not in existence for iron ships',* showing that the introduction of iron into the shipbuilding industry was still a new and revolutionary technique. He also said that *'we were particularly careful to see that the riveting was good',* emphasizing that the ironwork needed to be securely fastened together, and perhaps hinting that there were known problems with faulty rivets in other ships.

James Dean, one of the survivors, stated that the vessel suddenly parted in the centre *'like the snapping of a tobacco stump.'* The construction and maintenance of iron ships was still under development, and solutions to the various problems were being sought and introduced as the difficulties arose. One cause of concern was the fact that sand-laden water sloshing about inside the ship could effectively sand-paper the heads off the rivets that were holding the hull-plates together, as pointed out by Mr. W. Litchfield in the Chester Chronicle only a week after the disaster.

Iron steam vessels have arrived home from foreign stations to a certain extent leaky, and after being paid off and cleared out, have been taken in hand for the necessary repairs. On the insides of a vessel's plates being examined, it has invariably been found that the whole of the rivet heads, wherever the wash of the bilge water reached, had been worn off as cleanly as if cut by a hammer and chisel. This has led to a composition or cement being used over the surface of the plates of sufficient thickness to raise the surface of the plates to an equality with the head of the rivets, and in some cases, bricks have been laid on this cement, thus presenting a smooth surface to the wash of the bilge water and preventing its action on the head of the rivet . . . . Her Majesty's troop ship *Megaera*, now in the steam basin at Portsmouth, and lately returned home from foreign service, is an illustration of what I have stated, and thousands of rivets are now in her bottom which can be knocked out by a common punch from the inside. The plates of the *Royal Charter* may have been protected in a manner that would preserve their fastenings, or they may not have been.

There appears to be no record of the inside of her hull being protected from wear and tear by a layer of cement, so could the stress of six circumnavigations of the world have contributed to fact that the 'Royal Charter' broke up so quickly?

During the same week, 'The Times' newspaper reported:

> It has also been stated, since this subject has been so painfully forced upon the attention of the public, that the heads of the rivets by which the plates are held together in iron ships are apt to get loose, and that this could be prevented by the employment of a very simple process, which is not used in ninety-nine cases out of a hundred.

And only a month later, the same issue was raised at the Australian inquiry into the loss of the 'Admella' (see below* and page 14); so was the problem of weakened rivets occurring throughout the shipping industry on a worldwide basis?

> We also wish to call attention to the circumstance detailed in the evidence, of the *Admella* having broken at the water-tight bulk-heads. We are aware that the attention of engineers and builders of iron ships has been directed to the fact that the rows of rivet holes necessary for securing these bulkheads tend greatly to weaken the hull of a vessel so fitted - and we would strongly advise that, if possible, some means should be devised of providing against this defect; as we think it probable that if the hull of the *Admella* had held together, the majority would have been saved.

What the news-reports seem to be implying is that the rivets holding a ship together were likely to wear away during a long voyage, that there was a known cure to the problem, but in most cases this solution was not being implemented. No doubt there would be a considerable cost and weight of a layer of cement throughout a ship's bilges, and that this modification would have had an effect on the viability and profitability of the shipping company, but could it have saved lives and property by protecting the ship's hull from wear and corrosion? The problem with the rivets of 'H.M.S. Megeara' was successfully treated with a layer of cement, although parts of her hull were later coated with an experimental mixture which actually increased the rate of corrosion of her hull. There was no suggestion that a problem with the rivets had

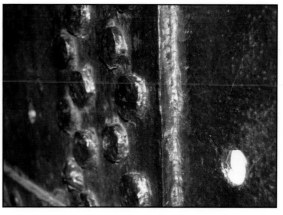

A close-up of rivets from the 'Royal Charter'.

caused the 'Royal Charter' to be cast ashore, but once an iron-built ship had done so, there was a possibility that these weakened rivets could prematurely fail and lead to such a great loss of life as had occurred on the 'Admella' off South Australia and on the 'Royal Charter' at Moelfre.

We will never know if Mr. Gilmour, the former surgeon-superintendent of the 'Royal Charter', was correct when he stated in his letter *'have heard the rivets rattling in her sides'*. Despite being denied by Captain Boyce and Captain Martin, this may have been true, and if so, had anything been done to prevent or cure the problem before the fault could cause lives to be lost?

* Admella - From the names of the cities - ADelaide, MELbourne, & LAunceston.

This photo of the 'af Chapman', a steel sailing-ship currently moored at Stockholm, shows the complex array of masts, spars and rigging.

The inquiry also discussed the possible reasons why the masts were not cut away before the anchor-cables snapped instead of waiting until she was aground, but why would a captain order his crew to cut away the masts on his ship? After all, they were a fundamental part of the propulsion system on a sailing vessel. Without the masts, there was no means of setting sail, and the cost of replacing them was so enormous that Captain Taylor would have had to be certain that this was a totally necessary course of action. To even consider this seems rather strange, but the reason for cutting away the masts was to reduce the strain on the anchor-cables due to the wind resistance of all the timber-work and rigging up aloft. But there was great danger in pursuing this line of action - can you image all those tons of wood, metal and rope crashing down all around you from a great height? Where would you run to? Where could you shelter? Even on dry land, would you stand under a fully-grown tree while it was being cut down? It would have taken a very brave man to stand there while the masts and rigging were chopped through, and this was certainly no place for the women and children, who had been ordered to stay below deck where they were hopefully out of harm's way, and had put on extra clothing in the expectation of being able to walk ashore. There had been a terrible precedent in the loss of life aboard the steamship 'Prince' only five years earlier during the Crimea War, and no doubt this was still fresh in the minds of Captains Taylor, Withers and Adams. The Board of Trade inquiry stated:

> It is very likely that the captain of the *Royal Charter* was deterred from this course [*cutting the masts away*] by the apprehension that the falling rigging and spars might foul her screw, thus repeating the catastrophe undergone by the *Prince* in 1854, off Balaclava.

The newspaper article opposite describes the loss of men, medical supplies, uniforms and munitions at a critical period of the Crimean War. A total of 18 British and 12 French vessels were lost when their anchor-cables snapped, but the Chester Chronicle of December 9th, 1855 had a slightly different story from the Illustrated London News, telling a tale that perhaps reflected badly on those in charge of the 'Prince'.

> The loss of the *Prince* seems to have been partly owing to the negligence of her officers. When she arrived at Balaclava, she let go one of her anchors in 30 fathoms of water. It appears that the cable had never been clinched [*fastened*], and the whole of it ran out. Anchor and cable were lost together. She then let go the other anchor, the cable of which was so inefficiently fastened that she lost this also.

This infers that they let go both anchors without fastening the chains to the ship. Oops!

LOSS OF THE STEAM-SHIP "PRINCE".

The following statement of the loss of this vessel, on the 14th ult, about three cables' length eastward of the entrance to Balaclava Harbour, has just been received:— While lying at anchor in 25 fathoms water, with two anchors down, about half a mile from the shore, the wind blowing a terrific hurricane from the southward and westward, No. 16 Transport fouled us, doing us some damage; and we were obliged to cut away all masts. About 9 a.m., the port cable parted (all hands being on deck at the time): endeavoured to steam ahead; but, on account of some of the wreck being foul of the screw, were unable to do so. About five minutes afterwards the starboard cable parted, and the ship drifted in rapidly towards the rocks.

Captain Goodall, who had been on deck from the commencement of the gale, called all hands aft, and, with Captain Baynton R.N., Transport Agent, pulled off their coats, Captain Goodall, at the same time, saying, "Now, my lads, I've done the best I can for you; every man must try and save himself."

About 9.15 a.m., the ship touched the rocks, and, owing to the great force of wind and severe sea sitting in at that time, in fifteen minutes after, not a vestige of her was to be seen. After thumping about five or six times, the ship broke in halves about amidships, and I jumped out of the mizzen chains on part of the wreck, and, being about ten minutes in the water, was washed ashore. After remaining on the rocks about five hours, with six of the crew of the *Prince*, we were hauled up by parties from the *Medway, Trent, Tonning,* and *Harbinger* (who had been engaged all day with life-buoys and lines, endeavouring to save lives) over an almost perpendicular cliff, of about 250 feet in height. Out of upwards of thirty vessels anchored in this place, only three rode the gale out with masts standing, and I believe about ten were lost entirely.

H. G. F COTGRAVE, Late midshipman,
G.S.S.S. Company's steamer, *Prince.*

Illustrated London News.
December 16, 1854

Connection to the 'Royal Charter'

- The loss of the 'Prince' was cited at the inquiry as an example of what could happen if a sailing vessel's masts were cut down, causing debris or rigging to foul the screw. The 'Prince' was a steamship of similar size and power to the 'Royal Charter', although she had a non-lifting 3-bladed screw rather than the 2-bladed one of the 'Royal Charter' that could be lifted clear of the water.

The Carnarvon and Denbigh Herald

AND NORTH AND SOUTH WALES ADVERTISER

Saturday, December 10, 1859

The Committee of Privy Council for Trade have received the following report from Mr. Mansfield, the Magistrate of Liverpool, and Captain Harris, nautical assessor, who held the late inquiry at Liverpool relative to the wreck of the *Royal Charter* steamship:-

"My Lords, - In accordance with the instructions which I received from the Board of Trade, I have, with the assistance of Captain Harris, nautical assessor, conducted an inquiry into the circumstances attending the loss of the auxiliary steam clipper ship *Royal Charter*. The ship was originally ordered to be built by Messrs. Moore, of this town. The builder was Mr. Cram, of Chester, and the keel was laid at Sandycroft, on the River Dee. Before any considerable progress had been made in her construction, the firm of Messrs. Gibbs, Bright, and Co., who are managers for and now represent the Australian Steam Navigation Company, the registered owners of the *Royal Charter*, took her off the hands of Messrs. Moore. At or about this time, Mr. Cram failed, and the further progress of the shipbuilding was conducted by Gibbs, Bright and Co. on their own account. Some changes were made to fit the vessel for the purpose which was ultimately attained; an addition was made to her length at either end, and the original specification was departed from in other respects. It is not material to dwell upon this part of her history at any great length, as, at the time of her transfer to Gibbs, Bright, and Co., her keel only was laid, and a portion of the frame set up. Nearly all the material had been provided by Mr. Cram, and was on the premises; this, after an examination by the builders employed by Gibbs, Bright, and Co., was used in the construction of the vessel. A portion of this iron, recovered with great difficulty and expense from the wreck, has been produced before and tested by the Liverpool corporation machine. It is decidedly above the average strength of iron plating used for shipbuilding, and the average strength assigned by Mr. Fairbairn for good Staffordshire plate. When the ship was completed, it was necessary to launch her diagonally, owing to the shallowness of the river at Sandycroft. During this operation, she stuck fast on her ways, and great efforts were necessary to get her afloat. It does not, however, appear that she received any injury at this time. In proceeding down the Dee, she took the ground off Flint, and here her keel and the adjoining portions amidships received serious injury, so as to necessitate extensive repairs in the graving dock at Liverpool. There is some discrepancy in the evidence, but it is probable that on this occasion she was strengthened by the addition of two bilge keelsons, having originally been constructed with a keelson and two sister keelsons.

Of her rigging, it is sufficient to say that her masts and spars seem to have been amply sufficient, and, though very large, not out of proportion to the size of the vessel. Her tackle seems to have been generally good, and her heavy sails were of 'No. 1 and No. 2' canvas – the quality of stormsails in ordinary ships. The ground tackle seems likewise to have been free from objection. She carried two bower anchors and a sheet anchor of requisite size, all of Trotman's model. She was provided with 300 fathoms of chain cable with full 2½ inches in diameter, tested by the maker, Mr. Wood, of Chester, to 72 tons. From the performance of this cable immediately previous to the loss of the ship, it is reasonable to suppose that the material and workmanship were good. Her engines, which worked a two-fan screw, were of nominal 200-horsepower, and were able to propel the vessel in dead water at the rate of about eight knots an hour. Upon proceeding upon her first voyage, she was very heavily ballasted, as her builders apprehended she would be crank [*in danger of overturning*], owing to her narrow beam. In the Bay of Biscay, however, she encountered very rough weather, and put back to Plymouth. Here, she was examined by the Emigration Officers and Surveyors, who recommended some trifling repairs to obviate her making water, as it was supposed, through her deck. These, however, had nothing to do with the seaworthiness of the ship.

In accordance with their recommendations, she was lightened of 400 tons of ballast, the result of which was that her sailing properties improved, and she was enabled to stay and wear with facility. I am assured by the witnesses who have subsequently made voyages in her that she was far from being defective in this respect, regard being had to the greater time necessarily requisite to bring a long vessel round. Upon her returning from her first voyage, it was observed by the surveyor of the Liverpool Underwriters' Association that some of the paint had cracked at the joining of the butts outside amidships, and that in these places there were streaks of rust. This, he stated, was invariably the case with long iron vessels on their return from a voyage. It does not, however, appear that wooden ships, encountering heavy weather, are free from an analogous indication of a strain in their butts. Some suspicion, however, seems to have noted upon the minds of the owners; and, with a view to giving her additional longitudinal strengthening, a massive stringer, the greater part of the length of the ship, was introduced on either side between decks. After this, nothing further of any importance as regards the strengthening of the ship seems to have been done.

It may be proper, at this point, to state that, from the evidence, I have arrived at the conclusion that the *Royal Charter* was, at the least, fully equal in strength to the average of ships of her class built at the same date (1855). Whether this be sufficient is a question which in reality does not arise in the present enquiry. Even if it did, I should hesitate to generalise from an isolated instance, on very imperfect evidence, and where so much is left to conjecture. A much wider induction is necessarily applied to the subject by Underwriters in the ordinary course of their business; and to those of the public who may be ignorant of the fact it may be of interest to learn that, *ceteris paribus* [*all things being equal*], there is no difference in the premium paid for insuring wooden or iron vessels of the same class.

Upon her last voyage the *Royal Charter*, after an unusually quick passage from Melbourne, arrived at Queenstown on the 24th October. She proceeded up Channel and passed the Tuskar Light about 4 a.m. on the 25th. About half-past 4 or 5 p.m. she was abreast of Holyhead. Up to that time the weather had been fine, with a light breeze ahead. A change then took place, and it became hazy over the land. The vessel proceeded in her course, rounding the Skerries at 6 or half past 6 p.m. Point Lynas Light was in sight at a quarter to 7 p.m., at a distance of 6 or 7 miles on the starboard bow. At 8 p.m. the wind was from NE to ENE, veering and blowing very hard, and had been increasing in strength from the time the ship passed Holyhead. She was heading at the time about E by S. At a quarter to nine, Captain Taylor gave orders to starboard the helm, to which the Quartermaster at the wheel replied 'The helm is a-starboard already.' At a quarter to nine, orders were given to take a cast of the lead. In a quarter of an hour they first succeeded in getting soundings with the hand-lead in 18 fathoms. The screw propeller was at work, but the ship, notwithstanding, was drifting rapidly to leeward, as denoted by the lead. Shortly after this soundings were again taken in 15 fathoms, and about half-past 10 p.m., an attempt was made to stay the ship. This appears to have failed, for shortly afterwards the port anchor was let go, and 100 fathoms of chain cable payed out. At 11.15 p.m. the starboard anchor was let go with 70 fathoms of chain. The two anchors brought the ship up. At 1.30 a.m. of the 26th the port chain parted outside the hawse-hole. Orders were then given to get up the stream-anchor, which weighed only 15 cwt, and was stowed in the after orlop. The sheet anchor of 50 cwt was stowed in the fore hatchway. It took about an hour to get up the stream-anchor, and when this was done, at about 2.30 a.m., the starboard cable parted. At about 3 or 3.30 a.m., the ship took the ground; her heel seems to have struck first, and her head canted round to the westward, broadside on to the wind and sea. It appears that the screw stopped when the ship struck. The mainmast was then cut away; it fell abeam, and not in the direction of the screw. The foremast was also cut away, but did not fall till the ship washed upon the rocks, about 5 a.m., or two hours after she first struck

About 7.30 to 8 a.m., the vessel parted amidships, and a melancholy loss of life ensued. Such is the narrative afforded by the few survivors of the loss of the *Royal Charter*.

In reviewing the evidence before me, it is my painful duty to notice the apparent want of preparation to encounter stormy weather shown by the *Royal Charter* in her course up Channel. She came up Channel with her skysail masts on end, and yards across. It is true that the weather was fine in the morning, and there might have been no indication of the coming hurricane; but it is certain that in such a dangerous area, and at a time of year when storms may be expected, the staunchest merchant ship would be only prudent in making all snug aloft, and the best-equipped man-of-war would infallibly do so.

I have no evidence before me to show whether the barometers gave any indication of the approaching gale. There were two, if not three, of these instruments on board. If they had been noticed, they would in all probability have suggested caution. At 5 p.m., there were two courses open. The *Royal Charter* was close to Holyhead, and might have run there for refuge, or she might have put her head to the westward, and kept the Irish Channel open. At 6 p.m., the Skerries were rounded, and the wind increased to a gale. At 9 p.m., the wind and sea had increased so much that, though under full steam, the ship refused to answer her helm.

It was then found that the ship was drifting bodily to leeward, and no course remained but to let go the anchors. To the anchors it will have been observed that the ship held for four hours, and it is to be lamented that the resolution was not immediately given to cut away the masts. Had she been so relieved, her only chance of safety, viz – holding on to her anchors – might possibly have been secured. It is evident that, with the top hamper aloft, the steam power was inadequate to keep the ship under command. Had the masts been sacrificed at first, as they were ultimately, the steam power might have availed the ship more effectually.

It is very likely that the captain of the *Royal Charter* was deterred from this course by the apprehension that the falling rigging and spars might foul her screw, thus repeating the catastrophe undergone by the *Prince* in 1854, off Balaclava; but it should be remembered that the *Prince* was supplied with a three-bladed fan, while the *Royal Charter* had a two-bladed one only, which could be hoisted up in a short time and with little labour.

I am well aware that in making these animadversions on the measures taken by the *Royal Charter,* I may encounter some difference of opinion; but, having the advantage of judging from the event, I cannot but help concluding that a fair chance of safety was sacrificed by the course pursued. I may here also advert to what appears to be a dangerous practice – viz. to steam ahead to the anchors in a gale of wind and in a seaway. A gale of wind, as is well known, is not uniform in strength, but there are moments of comparative lull. During these, the steam power not being readily controlled is apt to shoot the ship ahead. After this, when a violent gust occurs, the ship drops astern, bringing up with a sudden and severe jerk on her cables – a kind of strain most likely to make them part. It is not impossible that such may be the true explanation of the parting of the cables of the *Royal Charter*.

All the evidence concurs in showing that the force of the gale was terrific and unexampled on that coast. Nothing conclusive can be arrived at towards solving the question whether a wooden sailing-ship would have held together longer, or so long as the *Royal Charter*. As far as I have had information on the subject, I have no ground to impute blame to the lifeboat people.

The Coastguard were early on the spot, though stationed 10 miles off. The two pilot-boats, according to the regulations of the port, were in their proper cruising ground off Point Lynas. One of them saw a blue light, probably from the *Royal Charter*, and kept a sharp lookout accordingly, but immediately afterwards the darkness was so great and the rain so thick as to make it impossible to see from one end of the pilot-boat to the other. The wind also became so high as to put out her lights repeatedly; and even had she neared the *Royal Charter*, there was such a sea running as to make it impossible to put a pilot on board.

The officers and crew to the last were indifferent to the preservation of their own lives and solely intent on their duty. Taking into account the unexampled fury of the gale, which entirely neutralised the powerful action of the screw propeller so that the ship was no longer under command - a circumstance which Captain Taylor could not have anticipated; and considering also the apprehension he may have entertained, while at anchor, that the masts would foul the screw if they were cut away, and possibly that the action of the screw to ease the cables could not be safely intermitted - I do not think that this is a case in which I could report that the ship was lost by the default of the master."

J.S. MANSFIELD,
Stipendiary Magistrate,
Liverpool,
Nov. 28, 1859

I concur in the above report.
Hy. HARRIS,
Nautical Assessor.

Reference was made at the inquiry to William Fairbairn, the well-known authority on iron ships and bridges. He wasn't called to give evidence, but two years after the disaster, he gave a lecture in which he criticised the construction of the 'Royal Charter'. The following item was reported in the newspapers:

Iron ships were amongst the most valuable discoveries in modern ship-building. He could speak of iron ships experimentally, having been employed as one of the first persons to investigate and report on their practicality. The lecturer [*William Fairbairn*] next illustrated, by diagrams, the maximum degree of strain upon the bow and stern of a steamer, pointing out very lucidly the defective construction of the *Royal Charter*. Having obtained the various sections of the ship, his wonder was, on examination of the same, that the vessel was not lost long before it reached that country [*i.e. Australia*]. The lecturer next showed the action of the waves on the bottom of the vessel, the undulations of each end, and which would act upon the middle of the vessel like the two ends of a beam, thus accounting for the *Royal Charter* having been broken right in two. The plates around the vessel were not strong enough to resist one half of the strain; and many other vessels were equally unseaworthy, being liable to break and go to pieces – a fact which he had demonstrated before Liverpool and London audiences.

The Other Captains

On the fateful night when the 'Royal Charter' was wrecked, Captain Taylor had several passengers aboard who were also qualified shipmasters. None of them survived.

On board were the officers of three vessels coming from Australia, and they, with the captain and officers of the ill-fated *Royal Charter*, were all lost.

Captain James Withers

Travelling first-class from Melbourne, Captain Withers was mentioned several times in the newspaper accounts of the wreck.

Bad Luck! Loss of a Guano Vessel. From information received in Liverpool on Tuesday, it appears that the ship *Virginia* was wrecked at Nantucket Island* on the 16th May [*1859*] last, when on an expedition in search of guano, and is totally lost. Fourteen of the crew remained on the island until the 25th of July, when they were taken off and safely landed at Honolulu on the 14th of August. Captain Withers, the master of the ill-fated vessel, with nine men suffered great privations, having been nineteen days in an open boat, after which they put into the Feejee Islands whence they were conveyed to Sydney, where Captain Withers heard that the *Royal Charter* was at Melbourne about to sail for Liverpool. With the view of reaching England, he took a passage on board that vessel, but was among the ill-fated passengers who perished in Moelfre Bay.

* This Nantucket Island is in mid-Pacific, rather than the one off Boston, U.S.A.

The body of Captain Withers was brought ashore at Bull Bay on Thursday week afternoon. The body had all the clothes on except the coat. On his person were found a gold watch and chain, two gold seals, £36 in gold, and a silver snuff box with the inscription "Presented by the passengers of the ship *Gloucester* to Captain Withers. November 7th, 1838." His watch had stopped at half-past seven.

Captain Adams

Travelling in the second-class accommodation, he was another of the shipmasters to whom Captain Taylor turned to for advice when events turned sour. He had been captain of the 'Elizabeth Walker' which sank after colliding with the 'Red Jacket' in the South Atlantic, while sailing hundreds of miles off the Brazilian coast.

The White Star ship *Red Jacket* arrived at Port Phillip Heads at sundown on Saturday, and reached Hobson's Bay late yesterday evening. Captain Kirby reports the loss of the *Elizabeth Walker* from collision with the *Red Jacket*. The following particular are extracted from the log :— "June 13 [*1859*] at 1 a.m., clear moonlight, ship's course, southeast half south, wind south-east, rate of sailing nine knots per hour, all plain sail set and the port foretopmast studding-sail. The man on the lookout reported a ship on the port bow. Orders were immediately given by Mr. Robertson, officer of the watch, to show the port light. On ascertaining the tack and position of the ship, the officer of the watch gave orders for the helm to be put to port, as the strange vessel was nearly on a parallel on the opposite tack to ourselves. The *Red Jacket* went off from south-east half-south to south south-west. The strange vessel then showed a flaming torchlight. At the same time it was discovered that she had put her helm to starboard, and was keeping off the same as ourselves. The officer of the watch seeing by the two vessels continuing the same course that a collision would be inevitable, ordered the helm of the *Red Jacket* to be put to starboard, with the view of passing under the stern of the strange vessel, and almost simultaneously, the helm on board the strange vessel was put to port, which luffed her across our bows, and a collision took place. Orders were immediately given to throw all aback. To describe the confusion amongst the passengers at the first shock is unnecessary; suffice it to say that the *Red Jacket* had cut into the main-hatch coamings of the other vessel, carrying away her mainmast, mizzen topmast, yards, etc, the *Red Jacket* losing foretopmast stunsail boom, and some of the head gear being carried away. On looking over the bows of our own vessel, I immediately saw the dangerous position of the other one, as she was evidently filling very rapidly with water, and called out to them on board to leave her at once. With much difficulty the crew got on board the *Red Jacket*; and in less than eight minutes from the first shock, the strange vessel went down under the bottom of the *Red Jacket*. At the earliest opportunity, the crew of the strange vessel were mustered. They were all on board, and, with the exception of the man that was at the wheel, they were all uninjured. The ship proved to be the *Elizabeth Walker*, of Glasgow, from Buenos Ayres, with a general cargo. The captain told me he had just time to jump out of bed to save himself, and had not ascertained the particulars of the collision. The chief mate, who had charge of the deck at the time of the accident, stated that, on first observing our ship, he ordered the ship to be kept off, or the helm to be put to starboard, and afterwards ordered the helm to be put to port, which luffed her again across our bows. The ship kept lying to until 11 a.m., when all was completed and sail made, with the intention to proceed on the voyage, and to put the crew on board of the first ship that we found homeward bound."

Rescued by the 'Red Jacket', Captain Adams arrived in Melbourne in July 1859, and had the misfortune to book his passage back to England in the 'Royal Charter'.

Captain Adams said, "Yes, there is." He looked witness in the face, and said, "If it were possible to sing the song of 'The White Squall' it might now be sung with feeling." He added "I have no doubt we shall have to do this (making any motion as if swimming) before we get ashore."

A witness report by Samuel Edward Gapper

Captain Johnson

Very little was reported in the newspapers about Captain Johnson, who was travelling as a steerage or third-class passenger. He does not appear to have been consulted by Captain Taylor, and was mentioned only briefly at the inquest.

Heard Captain Johnson (a nautical man) remark in the forenoon of Tuesday that from the appearance of the weather it seemed likely to blow hard.

Captain James Morris

Several books refer to a Captain Morris being lost aboard the 'Royal Charter'.

Picked up afloat at Moelfre, a body on which was found a pocket-book with name "Captain James Morris, *Achilles* – Messrs. Ferguson, Runkin and Co., Bathurst, Brunswick, North America". Also photographic likeness of female and child.

However, the body was actually that of Mr. Cowie, the Second Officer of the 'Royal Charter'.

The mis-identification of the second officer's body, about whom I was interested, as his poor widow is one of my parishioners, arose from his having in his possession a pocket book with the name of his late brother in-law, 'Captain James Morris', inscribed in it, who, sad to say, was lost only two years ago while in command of the *Tempest*. - Rev. R. G. Weldon.

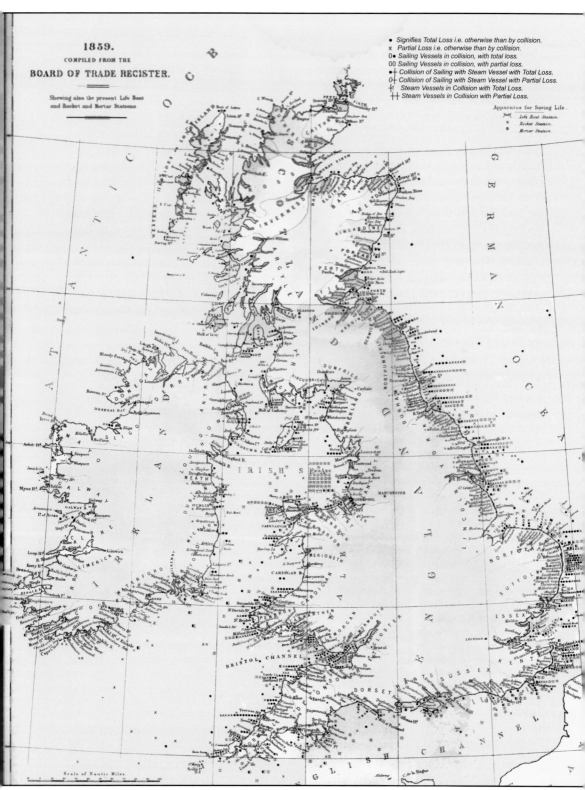

Each black dot or cross represents a shipping accident during 1859.

The Board of Trade Wreck Returns for 1859

Table 1. Wrecks and Casualties for Five Years ;

Months in which Casualties happened.	Number of Wrecks and Casualties in				
	1855.	1856.	1857.	1858.	1859.
January	—	149	281	124	115
February	—	154	64	116	139
March	—	96	166	148	136
April	—	74	76	115	126
May	—	57	33	48	32
June	—	32	34	30	27
July	—	48	33	61	34
August	—	51	75	33	52
September	—	98	66	91	86
October	—	99	135	148	343
November	—	129	94	120	170
December	—	166	86	136	156
TOTAL	1,141	1,153	1,143	1,170	1,416

In the United Kingdom, it was the responsibility of the Board of Trade to ensure that records were kept of shipping casualties, and to prepare a formal report to be published during the following year. Details were collected of the number of lives lost and saved, the rewards given for saving life from wrecks, and the expenses incurred in maintaining lifeboats and other life-saving apparatus. The statistics for 1859 were made public on the 11th of February, 1860, when it became clear (see the adjacent table) just how bad life had been for the seafaring community compared with previous years, and how incredibly terrible the casualty figures were for just two days during the month of October. Up to the 22nd of that month, only one vessel is recorded as being wrecked in a situation that involved loss of life, but for the 25th, there are fourteen casualties listed in which a total of fifty-six seamen died. The entry for the 26th was even worse, with a further fifty-five sloops, schooners, smacks, ships, brigs and barques all being lost in situations where 294 seamen died. And those figures do not include the tragedy of the 'Royal Charter'.

In North Wales, the 25th saw four lives lost on the 34-ton smack 'Beatrice Catherine' and one seaman on the barque 'Villa', both on the north coast of the Llyn Peninsula, while the smack 'Messenger' had three of her crew killed at Penmon, Anglesey. The 26th saw the destruction of the smack 'Claudia', the sloop 'Priscilla' and the schooner 'Eliza' on the Llyn Peninsula. Eleven lives were lost on these three coastal-traders, with two more deaths on the brig 'Agnes' at Point Lynas, Anglesey.

The actual number of ships and lives lost throughout the whole year is simply staggering, as shown on the map opposite, where each symbol represents the total or partial wrecking of a vessel during 1859. The following paragraphs give a brief overview of the detailed statistics contained in the full report.

As compared with 1858, there are 1,416 casualties against 1,170, and 1,645 lives lost against 340. This Increase is chiefly attributable to the violent gales of October 25 and 26; and of October 31, and November 1 and 2. In the former gale there were 133 Total Wrecks and 90 Casualties resulting in serious damage, and 798 lives were lost. This number, however, includes the loss of 446 lives in the *Royal Charter*. In the latter gale there were 27 Total Wrecks, and 27 Casualties resulting in partial damage, and there was a loss of 51 lives. Besides this, 424 lives were lost at once in the *Pomona,* on the 28th of April, and 56 in the *Blervie Castle* on or about the 20th of December.

From Table 9, which shows the force of the wind when each casualty happened, it will be seen that a marked increase has taken place in those which happened during force 11 (or "Storm"), viz., 88 against 57 in 1858, and at force 12 (or "Hurricane"), 87 against 11.

ROBT. ROBERTSON, Captain R.N., Surveyor General.

217

The steamship 'Olinda', wrecked in January 1854 at Cemlyn Bay, North Anglesey.

WRECKS

WILLIAM HUGHES, of Bull Bay, Amlwch, Anglesey, and JOHN OWEN, Captain of the sloop 'Sarah' were, on the 21st of February, 1854, severally convicted of having in their possession and concealing goods, part of the Wreck of the Ship 'OLINDA'; and the said WILLIAM HUGHES was fined TWO POUNDS and Costs, or One Month's imprisonment with hard labour, in the County Gaol; and the said JOHN OWEN was Fined Five Shillings and Costs, or Fourteen Days imprisonment with hard labour; and

Notice is hereby Given

That the Magistrates of the County of Anglesey have determined to visit with the severest punishment any persons who shall be convicted of Robbing Wrecks, or of keeping possession of, retaining, concealing, or removing Wreck Goods. And have ordered that the names of offenders so convicted shall be made as public as possible.

.... a young lady of easy virtue and who had been the greater part of her life an inmate of Mr. Evan's establishment at Ruthin, [*Ruthin Gaol*] was again sent to her old quarters for six weeks, charged with being drunk and disorderly at Ruabon on the Fair Day. A number of other drunk and disorderly cases were disposed of.

Amlwch. Tuesday, Feb 21. Before the Reverend James Williams.
Stealing from the wreck of the *Olinda*. Wm. Hughes, of Bull Bay, Captain John Owen of Amlwch Port, and Ellen Williams were brought by P.C. Ellis, charged with having in their possession a portion of the cargo of the steamer *Olinda*, which was wrecked a short time ago. William Hughes was fined £2 19s. 6d. for stealing 12 singlets, 10 yards of cloth and 24 yards of black silk velvet; Ellen Williams was likewise fined £1 for stealing 80 yards of merino and 6 shawls; and Captain John Owen 17s. 6d. including costs, for having in his possession a Britannia metal pint measure. A week was allowed them each to pay the fine and costs.

North Wales Chronicle. February 25, 1854

CHAPTER ELEVEN

Court Cases

Stealing from a shipwreck was seen as an extremely serious offence, as announced by the poster opposite after the loss of the 'Olinda' on the Harry Furlong Rocks at Cemlyn Bay, North Anglesey in January 1854. By modern day standards, a fine of two pounds sounds very trivial, but it was a serious amount of money for a person to pay out in the mid-1800s. Can you imagine a month spent in the County Gaol at Beaumaris, especially if the punishment was given 'with hard labour'?

However, despite the attendance of the coastguard and the severity of the punishment for anyone convicted of theft, the knowledge that there was so much wealth scattered along the east coast of Anglesey proved an irresistible attraction to many who knew about the disaster, either from the local or national newspapers or had heard about it by word of mouth. Unfortunately, along with the usual cases of theft, there were some genuine mistakes made, as in the situation where the Reverend Stephen Roose Hughes had instructed several of the local people to collect any scattered property and bring it to him in the hope that this would help to identify some of the bodies lying at Llanallgo. Another person was caught with property from the wreck, but he was acquitted because he was totally drunk!

So what constituted theft? By law, anything retrieved from the beach or lifted from the wreck needed to be reported to a government official known as the 'Receiver of Wreck'. For Anglesey, this would have been Mr. Smith of Beaumaris, the local customs official who was staying at Moelfre in order to collect and record anything recovered from the wreck. It was legal to pick up an article on the beach and take it to the Receiver of Wreck, but the situation would quickly deteriorate into a criminal offence unless the article was reported to the authorities.

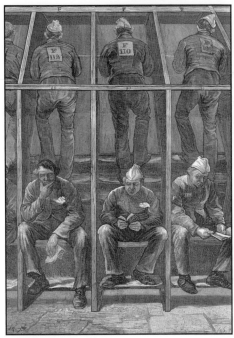

Punishments were severe, including floggings or spending hours on a treadwheel. © llyfrau-magma.co.uk

The authorities soon realised that the wreck, the bodies and the cargo needed to be protected as quickly as possible, so members of the coastguards and the police were sent to Moelfre to be joined by naval detachments from 'H.M.S. Hastings' and 'H.M.S. Sea Mew'.

Security was quickly established around the wreck, but who was watching the watchers? There were coastguards and police allocated to the task of protecting the coastline at Moelfre and any property that had been washed ashore, but rumours were bound to circulate, and these needed to be corrected where they proved to be false.

> There has been some objection on the part of the authorities, as they apprehend that thefts might be committed by some of the persons going out in the boats; but if rumour speaks truly, the watchers themselves require watching. It is unfair to make charges against men having a responsible duty to perform, but one of the police inspectors has told me that he himself caught a coast-guardsman in the act of thieving.

Frank Fowler - "The Wreck of the 'Royal Charter'"

But in the middle of this criticism, letters were written to the local papers praising the work of those guarding the wreck during those cold, wet, winter months of 1859.

> The *Royal Charter* - A report having obtained general circulation that one of the Anglesey Police Force had been sent to prison for robbing property from the *Royal Charter*, we are happy in having it in our power to state that such report is entirely without foundation. On the contrary, they are most indefatigable in their endeavours to discover missing or stolen property; and in *The Times* of Tuesday we read a letter from a gentleman who had relatives on board the *Royal Charter* highly complimentary to Captain Griffith and his force.

North Wales Chronicle. November 12, 1859

Perhaps some of these rumours were actually true, as one person from 'H.M.S. Sea Mew' was to reveal many years later in a letter to the 'Melbourne Argus' of September 29, 1923, where he stated:

> The morning after the wreck, my father, who commanded the *Sea Mew,* received a telegram to say that the *Royal Charter* was wrecked, and to give any assistance possible. We left next morning, and arrived in Moelfre Bay on the north coast of Anglesea on the same day. The sea was like a millpond, and covered with splinters and chips of wood of the ill-fated vessel. The only fair sized piece of wood found was the figurehead, which we picked up and later delivered to Gibbs, Bright, and Co, agents, Liverpool. We also picked up a small piece of wood with a woman's handkerchief attached to it, but not marked. I saw another piece of wood with a large portion of human skin on it. On our arrival at the scene of the wreck, my father went on shore, and the man in the bow of the boat was the only one allowed to land, he holding the boat's painter*. This man picked up a bar of gold weighing 4 lb 7 oz. without being noticed, and foolishly said nothing about it at the time. He had a disagreement with his mess-mates afterwards, and the gold was salvaged and the proceeds divided amongst the whole ship's company. Had the man spoken at the time, much more may have been salvaged. The country people who came to the wreck found quantities of jewellery and gold, which were never given up.

Then amidst all the confusion, the judicial system started moving, with the first court-case taking place at Menai Bridge on the 7th of November, less than a fortnight after the catastrophe. Examples of several prosecutions are given on the following pages.

* painter - the rope attached to the bow.

The Carnarvon and Denbigh Herald

AND NORTH AND SOUTH WALES ADVERTISER

Saturday, November 12, 1859.

Local Petty Sessions – Menai Bridge. November 7th, 1859. Before W. Bulkeley Hughes, and R. Briscoe Owen Esqrs.

William Parry, a lad between 13 and 14 employed as a farm labourer at Castell, Llanwenllwyfo, Anglesey, was brought up in custody, charged by Police Inspector Owen with having feloniously stolen a gold watch, two gold chains, two seals, and a key from the wreck of the *Royal Charter*, on the shore at Moelfra Bay, on Thursday, the 27th of October.

Police Inspector Owen deposed that he was directed to look after the wreck. In consequence of some information which he had received, he proceeded to Castell, Llanwenllwyfo, on Tuesday morning, the 1st of this month. Saw the farmer, Robert Evans, his two servants, and the prisoner, and asked him if he knew anything about a gold watch. He replied 'There are the servants. You had better ask them.' Enquired of the servants if they had been at the wreck? They said they had. One of them said they had brought home some pieces of trousers and such rags. Pressed him to say whether or not he had got a gold watch. He said that he had not. Asked the prisoner, William Parry, and he also denied that he had found one. Witness then said that he would examine their boxes, and asked the other servant, John Thomas, whether he had seen the watch. He said he had. William Parry said it was a yellow, German silver watch, for which he had paid half-a-crown, and that it was at the watchmaker's. Witness felt his pockets. He then said it was in a box. His master was present, and remarked "If you know anything about it you had better tell the truth." John Thomas made the same remark. Prisoner said he would go for it, and witness followed him to the servants' room. There was only one box; it was locked, and belonged to John Thomas. He then gave up the gold watch now produced, and said that he found it in a black rag amongst the stones near the wreck, that several persons had kicked it before he took it up. He said that he did not think it wrong to do so, as he had seen others remove things on the beach. Witness than apprehended him, and the watch has been in his possession since.

The watch produced was a gold horizontal lever, with a strong engine-turned case, a massive guard chain, a chain with two gold seals and a watch key appended. One of the seals bore a lion *gardant*, with the motto 'Courage'. It had no number, nor the master's name.

John Roberts, another youth, deposed – "I live at Pensarn. I overtook the prisoner on Thursday, returning from the wreck. He showed me a watch like the one produced; he said he expected the owner would call for it, and that he did not intend to keep it. He told me that he found it on the shore in a black rag. He also told me that he had picked up some herrings."

John Thomas, servant at the farm, who gave his evidence in a very unsatisfactory manner, during which he was severely rebuked by the bench, deposed – "I went to see the wreck with the prisoner and others on Thursday afternoon. I left him on the road, and did not see him until the following morning, as I did not return that night. Did not know the day nor time of day when I first saw the watch. It was in the bed-room. He said he found it somewhere near the sea shore. On Sunday, he gave me permission to put it in my box, for he had no box of his own."

The prisoner when called upon, with the

usual caution, said that it was not his intention to keep the watch, but that when it was restored to its owner, he expected to be remunerated. He also produced testimonials to his previous character.

Mr. Bulkeley Hughes, after consulting with the other magistrate, addressed the prisoner. 'The evidence against you in this case is quite clear, and the defence you have made cannot justify your conduct. Being so young, we have the power of trying and adjudicating your case at this court. You ought to reflect upon the heinous sin that you have committed by stealing the watch of an unfortunate person under such a distressing calamity. I only hope that you are the only one at Castell who was a party to this transaction. This being your first offence, you will be sent to jail for fourteen days, as an example to other persons in the neighbourhood."

Hugh Roberts was indicted for stealing two bills of exchange, two rings and two watch keys. He pleaded not guilty.

Mr. MacIntyre prosecuted and Mr. M. Lloyd defended.

Mr. MacIntyre, in stating the case, said it was of a peculiar character. On the 26th of October, when the *Royal Charter* was wrecked near Amlwch, the prisoner was working there. Various things were taken by the people. There was a man on the coast, placed there to receive things that were picked up. Prisoner came one morning afterwards on the omnibus from Amlwch to Llanfair station, and after he had been on his journey for some time he showed the bills, but it was fair to state that prisoner was in a state of partial intoxication. As he was showing them, a passenger took one up and it was dated 1859. Prisoner stated he was away three years ago. The rings which were shown on the coach were never found.

John Williams, draper, of Amlwch,

THE AMLWCH AND MENAI BRIDGE OMNIBUS
Will leave AMLWCH every Monday, at a quarter before six, morning, and Thursday evening at 2.30, and return from the BULKELEY ARMS, MENAI BRIDGE, every Wednesday and Saturday on the arrival of the Prince of Wales steamer from Liverpool.
To commence MONDAY 24th inst.
Performed by the Public's most obedient Servant,
HENRY HUMPHREYS.   19th October, 1859

remembered the wreck of the *Royal Charter,* and also coming on the omnibus to Llanfair station. Mr. Arrowsmith was a fellow passenger. Heard prisoner say he had been to Australia and America and had been lucky. Prisoner was rather drunk. Saw him show the papers. (Papers produced.) These are them. Prisoner stated that he had been home three years. Their date was May 13, 1859. Witness then said he was afraid that accused had been to the wreck. Prisoner was talking in Welsh and English. He had two rings. Told him that most likely they came from the same place. Prisoner said he had given £2 for one and £3 for the other. Mr. Arrowsmith came from Llangefni for Llanfair. Prisoner, when he got down, was followed by witness and Arrowsmith. The latter said "Here, old fellow, I think you have some strange notes about you." After a little while he delivered them up. Left prisoner at the station.

Cross-examined by Mr. Lloyd -- "He talked as if he was a lucky man from Australia or America. Mr. Arrowsmith gave witness the bills, and information was given to the police inspector at Bangor. The inspector wouldn't take the bills. Witness was going to Manchester, so he kept them in his possession until they came back. Prisoner got down at a great many inns on the road to get some drink. Heard another person say that he saw prisoner quite drunk at Menai Bridge, but he was very drunk in the omnibus."

Mr. Arrowsmith deposed – Saw prisoner

on the omnibus from Amlwch to Llanfair. Was told prisoner had some papers in his possession. After witness came down, he asked prisoner to show him the bills, and after a good deal of hesitation he brought them out. He said that he had had them in his possession some time. Witness then said "On account of the date it bears, it must have come from the *Royal Charter*", and the prisoner acknowledged it.

Cross-examined by Mr. Lloyd – "This happened at Llanfair station. Didn't see him lying drunk afterwards. Witness went to Bangor. Prisoner was very drunk."

William Williams deposed – Was porter at Llanfair station, and recollect on 27th October, prisoner came on the omnibus. Saw Mr. Arrowsmith take some papers from him. Heard Mr. Arrowsmith ask about some papers, and prisoner took some rings out of his pocket. One of the rings fell down. Mr. Arrowsmith asked again for the papers. Prisoner gave them to him. Prisoner told Mr. Arrowsmith he got them from the wreck of the *Royal Charter.* The two former witnesses went to Bangor. Didn't see prisoner after he went down the steps. He was very drunk.

Cross-examined by Mr. Lloyd – There are two ways to Beaumaris. Going through Bangor, there is a shorter distance to walk. J. Jones, police inspector, went to Llanfair about the papers, but afterwards found prisoner in his house at Beaumaris. He told witness that a man on the coach had taken the rings, and upon searching him he could not find them. Didn't search the house. He said he saw several persons get no thanks for bringing things to the Receiver, and that he wasn't to be done so.

Mr. Morgan then referred the case to the jury, who, on account of the prisoner being drunk, dismissed the case.

David Edwards, Gatehouse, Penrhos Lligwy, was brought up and charged by police inspector Owen, with having stolen a shirt and a Guernsey jacket, marked B. & N.A.R.M. and an anchor, from the wreck of the *Royal Charter.*

Inspector E. Owen said – "When I was going down to the wreck, on Saturday the 29th of October, between 7 and 8 o'clock, I saw several persons near to a creek on the shore, and I asked them what they were doing there at that time of the night. One of them gave a whistle. I examined those who came up from the shore. I afterwards met police constable No. 14 on the rocks. We watched until David Edwards and another man came up. When I examined them, I found the shirt and jacket which I now produce, in Edwards' coat pocket. I took him down to the boat and ascertained his name. I afterwards reported the case to the chief constable. I told Edwards that he would be summoned. He said he thought there would be no harm in taking them."

At this time a letter was read from the Rev. S.R. Hughes, Rector of Llanallgo, stating that he had told the accused and others to bring up any article to him that bore any mark by which it might be identified; and that the accused was a highly respectable young man, and that he had no other intention than to bring the article of clothing to him.

The case was then adjourned for a fortnight to enable Mr. Hughes to be present at the next inquiry at Llangefni.

The case of David Edwards appears to have been settled by the intervention of the Reverend Stephen Roose Hughes, as the case does not appear again in the local newspapers.

The Wreck of the "Royal Charter". A painting by Joseph Josiah Dodd. Reproduced here by kind permission of Llyfrgell Genedlaethol Cymru / The National Library of Wales. The bows are to the left, while the stern-rails can be seen just clear of the water to the right.

Sir,

It may not be uninteresting to many of your readers to know that Messrs. Gibbs, Bright, and Co., and the other authorities in charge of the coast at the scene of the late disastrous wreck of the *Royal Charter,* are now making most strenuous endeavours to raise portions of the wreck, the long expected "lump", furnished with proper gear, having arrived from Liverpool for that purpose. No doubt, many of the bodies of the unfortunate souls that have perished will therefore be recovered, and there is yet hope that some may be recognised. I think it is right to put the public on their guard with respect to rumours appearing, stating that bodies have been washed ashore at Penmaenmawr. This is wholly incorrect, that place being a great distance from Moelfre. The mistake arises from the name being confused with that of Penmon, in Anglesey, a small bay, near which bodies have been found, it being close to Moelfre. Many relatives of the poor souls lost, and who have anxiously visited the scene of the wreck, have left, unable to obtain even a relic of the clothing belonging to their relations; but, I am happy to be able to inform you that, owing to the indefatigable exertions of Captain Griffiths (the inspecting commander of the police), large quantities of articles of clothing which had been collected and secreted in the neighbouring cottages was yesterday recovered, and of which a list will now be made in order to give publicity for the purpose of identification.

I am, Sir,
yours respectfully,
HENRY S. PITCHER
Moelfre, scene of the wreck,
November 6, 1859.

CHAPTER TWELVE

The Salvage Work.

As soon as the ferocious winds had died away, salvage attempts began on and around the stricken wreck, but there were conflicting priorities for the various parties on shore. Families and friends of the passengers and crew had flocked to Moelfre, desperate to recover the bodies of their loved ones, and to bury the mortal remains in consecrated ground. Meanwhile, bodies continued to be recovered laden down with gold coins, while cheques and letters of credit were being washed away by the tide, and copper, jewellery and other valuable items were still trapped inside the hull. The painting opposite shows how the wreck now lay in relation to the shore, but which was more important - the bodies or the gold? Surely the gold could wait while the bodies were recovered and handed over to the relatives and friends gathered at Moelfre.

The following letter has been addressed to the President of the Board of Trade by Sir R.W. Bulkeley, Bart., M.P., urging more prompt measures for recovering the bodies of those who perished in the wreck of the *Royal Charter*:-

Baron Hill, Beaumaris,
Nov 13.

Sir, - you are aware that a large steamer of 2,500 tons, called the *Royal Charter*, was wrecked about three weeks ago on the coast of Anglesey, and about four hundred persons perished. The remains of eighty persons (thereabouts) have been found in the neighbourhood of the wreck and buried, the greater part of whom have been identified by their friends and relatives. I have been waited upon by the relatives of some of the sufferers to bring under your notice and to receive if possible your assistance in compelling the owners and others interested in the ship to take some more active measures than have marked their operations up to the present moment in endeavouring to free the bodies which are still supposed (by those capable of giving an opinion) to be entangled in the debris of the wreck. I need not describe the painful scenes that daily take place in the neighbourhood of the wreck between the relatives of individuals and families known to have perished, and whose remains, not having yet been discovered, are supposed to be kept under water by the position of the wreck. To the applications of these sorrowing relatives to the agents in charge of the ship, requesting them to use their apparatus to weigh up portions of the wreck with the view of releasing a number of bodies, not the slightest attention is paid; on the contrary, nothing but the most revolting indifferences to their feelings is shown. The recovery of the gold appears to be the only object of the representatives of the owners and underwriters. Whether the Board of Trade or the Admiralty have the power of insisting upon the removal of the wreck, you, sir, are the best judge; but I have thought it my duty, as a magistrate, to bring the state of things at Moelfre under your notice, and for further information, I beg to refer you to Mr. Pitcher, the eminent shipbuilder, at Northfleet, whose brother, brother's wife, and two children are among the sufferers.

I am, sir, etc.
R. WILLIAMS BULKELEY.
M.P. and J.P. for the County of Anglesey.

So who actually owned the wreck, the cargo, the bullion, or the personal effects and wealth of the passengers?

It is stated that Lord Boston, as lord of the manor of the district near which the *Royal Charter* was wrecked, has sent in a claim to all property or treasure that may be washed ashore.

Lord Boston's claim was unsuccessful, but the 'Royal Charter' was insured by the underwriters at Lloyd's, so they were now the owners of the wreck and the cargo, although not the personal property of the passengers.

A tug with divers arrived on Saturday, but there was too much sea on for them to commence operations. No more bodies had washed ashore up to Saturday. We hear that six bodies were picked up on Sunday. A bar of gold, 7½ lbs. weight, valued at nearly £300, was picked up at the wreck on Friday last, (by one of the Crew of H.M.S. Sea Mew) which proves that one box at least of the specie has been washed ashore, but as this is the only bar that has been found, it may be supposed that the box containing it might not have belonged to the bulk of specie in the specie room, which may still remain intact. It is, however, quite conjectural as to the fate of the specie, and until the divers ascertain whether the specie room has broken up or not, it is impossible to make any accurate calculations as to the chances of recovery, in whole or part.

Liverpool, Saturday. A gentleman who arrived early this morning from the wreck states that very few additional bodies had been washed ashore, and he accounts for it on the supposition that the great majority of the corpses are still confined in the body of the ship, some parts of which he believes are still entire. Divers have been dispatched to Moelfra, but our informant thinks that as a great proportion of the vessel's rigging must be entangled with the wreck, they will have some difficulty in getting inside the vessel. At low spring tides, it will be possible to obtain a footing on the wreck. Many persons continued to arrive in search of relatives and friends, and as the accommodation is exceedingly limited, much inconvenience is experienced.

North Wales Chronicle.
Saturday, October 29, 1859

Sunday. No bodies were picked up.

Monday. The divers brought up some copper, but no specie. A male body also was brought up, but so mutilated, that it could not be recognised by any of the parties present.

Tuesday. The bodies of three men were found this morning – also a sovereign and a pistol on the beach. The divers still bring up nothing but copper. We cannot but notice the hospitable kindness of the Rev. Stephen Roose Hughes, who, assisted by the ladies of his family, have with unwearied benevolence throughout the trying scenes which have been brought before them, done everything in their power to administer to the comforts and necessities of all who might have required their aid. Many of the distressed relatives of the ill-fated passengers will long remember the hospitable reception they met at Llanallgo rectory, as well as the dreadful occasion which drew them to the vicinity.

Friday. Last night, one of the divers descended down that part of the wreck where it is supposed the specie lies, and brought up a bar of gold, weighing 4 1bs; and a cash box, much crushed, containing a photograph, bearing the following address:- James Hawkins, Esq., High-street, Wells, Somersetshire. No bodies were washed ashore either last night or this morning, except a portion of a mutilated body of an infant, which was conveyed this morning to the parish church. Parties having friends on board continue to arrive, and seek admission into the Church to view the bodies which remain there to be identified, and every civility and attention is shown to them by the rector, the Rev. Mr. Hughes. That gentleman, we are told, received a guinea from Major Egerton Leigh, of Cheshire, to be distributed amongst the poor villagers, who vie with each other in rendering assistance to the poor sufferers.

North Wales Chronicle.
Saturday, November 5, 1859

Sunday. One ton and a half of copper was got up yesterday; also, a bar of gold weighing 4 lbs. Two bodies washed ashore, making a total up to this date of 54. The steamer that arrived from Liverpool yesterday, with lump fitted with requisite gear to clear away parts of the wreck, has returned today, taking all the copper recovered, about 14 tons, and the passengers and crew that remained at the wreck, with the exception of one passenger, unfit for removal, and one of the crew left behind to furnish necessary information. The lump has commenced operations over the wreck, and got up the rudder wheels, and also weighed the frame connected with the fan [*propeller*], but as it was apparently foul of the screw, it could not be got up, and had to be let go. Three more divers have arrived from London, from Lloyd's.

Monday. Seven pieces of copper got up by divers. Some silver spoons and a silver pint measure tankard picked up on the beach.

Tuesday. One body picked up afloat this morning, evidently a passenger (male), but no name on linen, or other marks to identify it. The steam tug and lump came to the wreck, and divers were down a short time, but recovered nothing, and were obliged to discontinue work in consequence of the weather.

Wednesday. Nothing done at wreck. Too much sea on. Five bodies picked up, one a female. A few small articles of plate picked up on the beach. The militia party left the wreck today.

Thursday. Nothing of any consequence recovered from the wreck today. A second tug has arrived. Four bodies picked up at the wreck, (one female, two males, and one child), in a very mutilated condition. Ten more bodies picked up in Red Wharf Bay. One body picked up in Bull Bay, (two miles the other side of Amlwch), and two picked up afloat, by fishing boats; one of these is a female, with the name of "L. M. Fenwick" marked on the stockings. It is evident the bodies are now rising from the wreck as the work of the divers proceeds, but it is almost impossible to identify any that may be washed ashore from this time.

Penmaenmawr. The headless trunk of what was once a human being was washed ashore near this place on Wednesday last. It was conveyed to Dwygyfylchi Church to await the Coroner's inquest.

North Wales Chronicle.
Saturday, November 12, 1859

Moelfra, Tuesday. The 'lumper', or lifting apparatus, for which Gibbs, Bright & Co., had sent to Liverpool in the early part of last week, arrived here on Saturday. The 'lumper' is in appearance something like a fishing smack. She has a powerful heaving machine on board which is worked from the deck, and with which large portions of the wreck are sure to be hoisted from the position in which they now lie. Some additional divers were brought from Liverpool with the lumper, and descents were made on Sunday forenoon. The divers say that the wreck lies in a very intricate and, to them, dangerous heap. They walk beneath some of the heavy machinery of the ship, and have to grope their way amidst ironwork. One of them met with a corpse on Sunday, but was unable to remove it from the mass of timber and iron in which it was entangled. The *Royal Charter* was steered with a splendid patent steering apparatus. This the divers succeeded in attaching to the chains of the lumper, and it was hauled up in an almost perfect state: a segment of the wheel being the only part broken away. The framework to which the patent-steerer was attached when it stood in its place on the ship was subsequently got up. No gold was discovered by the divers on Sunday. The bullion-room of the *Royal Charter* was about eighteen feet up from the keel. It was, as is usual in similar ships, formed out of a portion of the stern, to which an

227

iron deck, iron sides, and an iron door were attached. In this room the ingots, specie, and dust consigned to parties in this country were deposited. The gold consigned to the captain was placed in small cubical mahogany boxes, on which were affixed the seal of the captain and that of the party who committed the gold to his custody. Those boxes were deposited in the bullion room. That the bullion-room is not intact, but has been knocked to pieces, is proved beyond a doubt by the fact that fragments of the cubical mahogany boxes, with seals on them, have within the last few days been found along the beach. Nevertheless, the professional gentlemen who watch the operations of the divers are very sanguine as to the recovery of the ingots and the specie. Of the recovery of the gold dust, the same hopes are not entertained. On Sunday night there was a very heavy gale in Dulas bay. The *Fury* was obliged to seek shelter round by Moelfra, and to tow the lumper out of the same place. They both came back to the scene of the wreck on Tuesday morning, but the weather was too unfavourable to permit of the lumper being got to work. Up to that time only two bars of gold had been found; one, that which the divers brought up last week, and the other, one that had been picked up by some men of the Royal Navy, in a boat belonging to Her Majesty's steam tender *Sea Mew*. Nineteen thousand and ten plates and bars of copper, weighing about 13½ tons, have been recovered; and the total amount of money found on the beach and on the persons of the drowned who have been washed ashore is £280 13s. 3½d. On Saturday last, the police made a seizure of several bundles of clothing which some of the villagers had conveyed to their cottages. There was no article of any value amongst these clothes with the exception of a very beautiful black silk dress, which had belonged to some lady passenger. This discovery, and the fact that some photographic portraits had previously been carried by a villager to his house, and only given up when demanded by parties who had traced them, have raised suspicions in the minds of those who have lost friends with property on board.

Lloyd's Weekly Newspaper.
November 13, 1859

Saturday. Two male bodies yesterday, and two today – on one was 17s. 6d. Divers have got up a piece of the deck, close to the stern, also a beam and carline* and other pieces of iron work and some copper. Five sovereigns were found in the clay, and sent up on its being washed.

Sunday. Two male bodies, both seamen; on one was found a pawn ticket for a silver watch issued in Liverpool, in the name of Henry Hodson. Divers and lump at work. A bar of gold, about 3½ lb, got up, stuck in a piece of iron; also a few loose sovereigns and about a ton of copper.

Monday. One body – a seaman – with 6s. 2d. on his person was picked up at Moelfre. Two bodies washed ashore at Red Wharf Bay, one naked, the other a seaman, having on a duck frock, marked '106 S. Craig No 34', also a blue Guernsey frock with the letters 'L.A.N.C. & Co.' on the breast; clasp knife and key round neck. American flag and star under left arm. One body picked up ashore (male) 'James Davies, No. 3 Woodside 1858', marked on the shirt. One body washed ashore, supposed to be a Mr. Moss, a Jew. Two bodies picked up at Amlwch, very much disfigured; one had on a waist-belt, containing 13 sovereigns, 3 nuggets, and a gold ring, no mark; portemonnaie in trouser pocket with five half crowns and a florin, and four small keys in the other pocket. The divers have sent up a good deal of copper today, also some ironwork, three watches and a nugget.

Tuesday. One body picked up by boat at Moelfre, very much mutilated, nearly

* carline - a square piece of timber.

This piece of quartz measures about 3 inches across, and is embedded with golden flecks.

naked. The lump lifted a portion of the side of the wreck, and brought it ashore. Divers got up two boxes of gold weighing 56 lbs. and two bags of sovereigns, each containing about 700, and weighing about 18 lbs. each. A considerable quantity of copper got up. Wednesday. Five bodies picked up near wreck; one a female with half-mourning gown, black stockings, black cloth boots, wedding ring on finger. One (male) with 30 sovereigns, 13 shillings, 2 rings, a piece of foreign coin, a purse with a receipt marked 'Edwin Smith'. One body with 17 sovereigns in a belt, two gold rings, two breast pins (free-mason's arms on one), two pairs of earrings, and a piece of Albert chain with watch-key attached, several scraps of paper, on one of which was a wax seal, marked 'Gold RXR' One body with frock on, marked 'T. Lewis, No. 4' – on drawers, 'T. Lewis, No. 4, '53' – supposed to be the purser of the vessel,

but as there were other parties of this name on board, the doubt can only be solved by friends identifying the marks on linen. Two bodies recovered at Amlwch. One a male, with 6½ sovereigns in leather bag, with 2 oz. gold dust; portemonnaie, with 4½ sovereigns, 4 half-crowns, 4 shillings, 2 keys of boxes in pocket. The other body female, partly clothed; quality of clothes seeming to denote a first-class passenger. The divers have got up another box of gold weighing 26 lbs., and have lifted a portion of the mizzen rigging and sails in a mass, and dragged it further in shore, but could not get it completely free from the wreck. A steam-tug and lighter arrived from Liverpool with workmen on board, for the purpose of taking some of the iron plates from the wreck, for the examination of the authorities from the Board of Trade engaged in the enquiry. The three divers who arrived from Lloyds some days ago have not commenced work yet, as arrangements for their employment have not been settled.

Thursday. Three bodies recovered at Moelfre, one a female, linen marked 'Florence Davies, Nov. 30th 1857'. Two bodies - no marks on clothing, and in a very disfigured state. One body picked up floating off Amlwch, and identified as Capt. Withers, having silver snuffbox, with name on in pocket, and gold watch.

North Wales Chronicle.
Saturday, November 19, 1859

Friday, November 18. On the body of Captain Withers, picked up off Amlwch yesterday, was found £36, besides gold watch and silver snuff box, with presentation inscription on it. The two divers from London, who have been here some time, waiting in expectation of employment, were engaged today, so there will now be four divers at work. No bodies picked up today. Wind off the land, blowing strong.

Saturday. Four bodies, (two at Moelfre, and two at Red Wharf Bay.) One of these a very fine-looking man, upwards of 6 feet, stout built, features perfect, sandy hair, moustache and whiskers; no marks on body or linen. The divers down only a short time in the forenoon. Sent up 24 sovereigns, some ironwork, and 2 bales of wool.

Sunday. Picked up afloat at Moelfre, a body on which was found a pocket-book with name "Captain James Morris, 'Achilles' – Messrs. Ferguson, Runkin and Co., Bathurst, Brunswick, North America"; also photographic likeness of female and child. A male body 5ft 6in., stout built, pocket book with several letters, two knives, and silver pencil case. Name on a certificate "Henry Frederick Turner". French and other foreign letters in pocket book – Afloat off Moelfre - body of a passenger; "F. Rufford" marked on linen. Afloat off Amlwch – body of a passenger, 5ft. 6in.; with gold watch, marked inside No. 9746, H. Perrigam. Piece of paper with name "Rev J.B. McCaul, Gower Place, Gower-street, 40 Huntington-street, Darnsbury Park" – £2 10s., and a nugget in portemonnaie. Off Moelfre, body of a man about 5ft. 8in.; £1 1s. 6d. on person and certificate of competency as master (to Anthony Bolt) issued by the Lord's Committee of Privy Council for Trade. Male body, 5ft. 9in.; two gold rings in pocket, Freemason's Arms on one, other a diamond; a breast pin with miniature of a female; stamp mark on the inside of Masonic ring, "W.Z." Off Moelfre - body of a man, a passenger, with gold watch, marked inside case "James Moddell and Co. 14, Northampton-square, London." Albert chain and seal, silver watch, gold chain, and seal; mark on case "J.R.G.", a spread eagle, 12512 underneath; 3 gold rings, 2 gold studs, 4 gold lockets with wire gold chain; pair of earrings; in small purse, shape of a hat, was a fancy ornament resembling a nutmeg; a piece of newspaper marked July 1859, a dollar marked 'California gold, 1855'. Off Amlwch – a female body; wedding ring on finger, also, a gold ring with diamonds; black silk body to dress, deep crepe trimmings; black jean boots laced at the side; middle age, and stature stout, well made, and very lusty, some flesh on the face, no marks on body or linen. Male body; about 40; height 5ft. 7in.; no marks on linen; four and a half sovereigns and nine shillings in a small bag in waistcoat pocket; a small piece of writing paper, much torn and illegible; penknife in pocket; clothing, monkey jacket, two waistcoats, socks and boots. Body of a female, about 5 feet; clothing, stays, chemise, boots and black woollen stockings; wedding ring on finger. Body of a man, about 5ft. 9in.; three glass marbles in waistcoat pocket. Picked up at Pentraeth a male body; height 5ft. 8in.; pea jacket, tweed trousers, Crimea shirt, Wellington boots, waist belt, with £55 3s. 3d., two rings in pocket and a nugget. Picked up off Moelfre, body of a young man, about 5ft. 8in., face nearly perfect, black trousers, £9 2s. in his pocket. Eight other bodies were picked up, much decomposed, and no marks.

Monday. Afloat off Moelfre – male body, 5ft 7in.; blue fancy shirt, flannel drawers, and blucher boots; in pocket £44 10s. in gold, and 9s. in silver, four gold rings in a tin box, two of them with "hearts" and two plain; no marks on linen. The body of Dr. Hatch brought on shore at Moelfre; name on shirt; £150 on person; silver watch, and silver snuff box with inscription. The body of a male; black frock coat, white drill trousers, fancy yacht shirt; blucher boots; silver Geneva watch, No. 3353 inside; knife and key; no marks on linen. Two other bodies; no marks, and much decomposed. The divers were down a very short time today, and sent up nothing – too much swell on to work.

Tuesday. The body of Mr. M.W. Pitcher recovered at Amlwch, and identified by his nephew, Mr. Rich, who has attended at the wreck daily, prosecuting an anxious and sedulous search. The body of Mr. Edwin Fowler picked up at Red Wharf; a piece of a letter in pocket addressed to "Edwin Fowler, Esq., Royal Charter"; £85 on person, also silver watch, gold chain and seals. A body – no marks; a piece of silver, with a cross on it, and a representation of the Virgin Mary; foreign inscription round it, and suspended from a piece of ribbon. A body, black cloth trousers, and waistcoat, fancy shirt, gold ring on finger, £1 10s. in gold; in pocket, bunch of keys, penknife, penholder, and watch key. A body, nearly naked and much disfigured. Six bodies recovered by boats creeping near the small island close to Moelfre. Of these, one had £1 6s. in pocket, £10 10s. in belt, a gold ring with a heart on it, two small locks of hair in separate pieces of paper – marked on outside "David" and "George," also a receipt for a registered letter in Melbourne, August 24, 1859, for "William Richardson"

from "David Bell." One body, apparently a youth, about 16 or 18, clothing – check trousers, fancy shirt, and half boots. One body. Several letters in pocket book, addressed to persons in Liverpool, and a memorandum showing he left Liverpool for Melbourne on March 20th, 1859 in the *Lader;* name – John Watson, gold pencil-case and penholder, marked "J.W." silver pencil-case and an American coin; a letter, addressed to "Mr. Robert Watson, farmer, Sheep Park, Pollackstraits, by Glasgow." Two bodies – much disfigured, no marks on linen. The divers have sent up today a bag containing about 1,200 sovereigns, and 232 loose sovereigns, and some iron work.

Wednesday. Female body. Stays, chemise, drawers and cloth boots; no marks on linen; a waist belt, with £36, and one sovereign in pocket. A male body; mark on drawers "Emery," silver watch, gold guard, and £2 7s. 6d. on person. Two male bodies much decomposed; no marks. One male body; on person a bag containing £58; a Bill of Exchange on Union Bank of Australia, dated 4th July, 1859, for £60, to the order of Mr. Robert Ellison; and 1st and 3rd Bills of Exchange on same Bank, 20th August, 1859, payable to order of J.P. Ellison, for £300; and two gold rings in portemonnaie. One male body – plaid trousers, black vest, and £2 in gold, silver coin of the reign of George II, ring on finger, hands clasped. One male body – on person, two Bills of Exchange on Bank of Australasia, dated Aug. 1859, for the sum of £96 payable to order of Mr. Robert Evans, and in pockets £6 10s. One male body, Mr. John Grove (supposed) – on person a Bank Order payable in London for £140. A Victoria bank note for 52 sovereigns, two florins, one rupee, a silver watch and chain. Nothing done by divers today, too much sea on.

Thursday. One male body, 5ft 9in; grey coat, plaid vest, duck trousers, blucher boots, red scarf round the body, gold chain and key, gold ring, initials "F.S.," pocket book with address on flyleaf, "Alexander Maule, Harryton, Middlesex," identified as John Maule, by Gapper, one of the saved. One male body, gold ring in pocket; a full-rigged ship, and "Ballarat" on it. One male body; no marks; much decomposed. Divers have done nothing today – too much sea on. The steamer and lump have gone to Beaumaris for shelter.

North Wales Chronicle.
Saturday, November 26, 1859

The following is a continuation of the progress made at Moelfre to Thursday last. Friday, Nov 25. Picked up at Red Wharf – A male body, £6 10s. on person, one brooch, two rings, several small nuggets. Very much decomposed. At Red Wharf – male body, brown plaid trousers. Not identified. At Dulas – A passenger; on person, a gold watch and chain, and a receipt for rent, paid on 18th August, 1859, for No. 10, Napier-street, FitzRoy, Melbourne. Name appears to be "Lyat". At Dulas – two children, boy and girl, about three years of age. Very much mutilated. At Moelfre – a male body; on person £7 10s. in gold, and £5 in silver, and a subscription list in favour of "James Potts," represented to have been disabled by a fall at Indigo Diggings, and a free passage given in the *Royal Charter.* The list headed by Captain Taylor for 10s. Divers have done nothing today; too much sea on. A silver table spoon marked "F" picked up on the beach.

Saturday. At Moelfre – A male body, (flannel singlet, check shirt, large black whiskers), in an excellent state of preservation. Not identified. A male body – six foot, very stout, £3 2s. 6d. on person, flannel shirt, Kerseymere trousers. No marks on linen. A male body – Blue shirt, white flannel, black trousers, blue worsted stockings, flannel drawers. About 5 ft. 10 in.; slight. A male body – Dark cloth trousers, brown jacket, corduroy vest, checked fancy shirt, flannel shirt, worsted stockings, gold ring (onyx stone), an elastic belt with "Bat, Ball and Wickets," two keys in pocket, a letter on person commencing "My dear Frank," and concluding "your affectionate father, C.W. Wm. Haylard," and a small keepsake, with words "Hope is the anchor of the soul." A male body – Brown corduroy trousers, woollen drawers, red and black Guernsey frock, Crimean shirt, white flannel shirt. Height about 5 ft. 10 in. On person £70 in gold and 8s. in silver. Four gold rings, on one a double heart in a scroll, and on the others, bracketed hands holding a hoop with a heart inside; a pair of gold earrings, thistles pendant. Two portemonnaies. A male body, 6ft. 2in., very stout, drab pea jacket, Scotch plaid trousers, fancy shirt, white flannel, blue worsted stockings, cotton drawers. – No marks to identify. A youth, about 14 or 15; blue overcoat, trimmed with black braid, short blue jacket, mixture trousers – No marks – very much mutilated. Three bodies picked up near Dulas. – No marks – not identified – much mutilated. The steamer and lump returned from Beaumaris at 10.30 a.m. Divers sent up 38 sovereigns in buckets of sand, also, a small bag containing portions of gold chains, and pieces of old gold ornaments, valued at about £30.

Sunday. A male body with the following marks;- On right arm, an anchor, a woman holding a glass, two fish, initials "E.Y.", gold ring on finger, with diggers' arms. On his person was found a part of a letter addressed "For Wm. Young, Mrs. Ladd's, No.16 Mary-street, Ocean-street, Stepney, London, England." Divers sent up a bag, containing half sovereigns, weight about 156 lbs., 167 sovereigns loose, and a small bag with about half-a-pound of gold dust.

Monday. A male body, identified as Mr. J. Croome, the fourth mate. Divers sent up 252 sovereigns in buckets of sand, and a bag containing about 100.

Tuesday. Divers sent up 42 sovereigns.

Lump has lifted a portion of deck, etc. and landed it on the rocks. Wind now blowing strongly from eastward. Steamer and Lump gone to Beaumaris. A letter has been received here today by the coxswain of the lifeboat at Moelfre, from some party at the Isle of Man, dated November 25th, reporting that several bodies were washed ashore at Castletown on 24th and 25th. One female identified as Miss Davies; a gold watch on her person. Information was received here yesterday evening that a female body, identified as Mrs. Foster, was picked up at Port Ferry, north of Dundrum Bay, Ireland.

Wednesday. A male body, a young man supposed to be one of the two cabin stewards. Black cloth coat, trousers, and vest; Wellington boots. On his person – seven twenty-dollar pieces, two ten-dollar ditto, two five-dollar ditto, five sovereigns, £1 7s. 6d. in silver, ring – marked T.B., one pin, one match-box, penknife, and a bunch of keys. A male body, at Red Wharf. No marks. Not identified. Clothing – a vest, and plaid shirt. On person- £19 14s. 1d., and silver watch. Divers not at work.

Thursday. One female, identified as Mrs. Eliza M. Pitcher, from marks on stockings. Recovered by boat at Moelfre. Body of a male child, about 14. No marks. Body of a passenger, dressed in black; letter in pocket, dated 3rd August, 1859, to his cousin, Mr. Elliott, "from your affectionate cousin, Edward P. Sansom", two £5 notes, Union Bank of Australia, Nos. 5290 and 5122; and a leather waist belt, a bill of exchange, 60 days sight, on Union Bank of Australia, for £280; silver watch, pencil-case, and penholder. Body washed ashore to westward of wreck, very much mutilated. Body- about 5ft. 8in. On person, £27 0s. 6d.; bill of exchange for £5, Melbourne, 18th May, 1857, to Mrs. Sarah Scott – T.A. Walsh, manager – English, Scotch, Australia Chartered Bank; and 1st and 2nd of same tenor, to order of Mrs. S. Scott, 1859; bill of exchange, £130, 25th July, 1859, to Mr. Matthew Scott, on Bank of New South Wales, London. Five bodies – no marks. Much decomposed. One female body – much mutilated. No clothing. One male body – washed on shore at Benllech, in the parish of Llanfairmathafarneithaf; about 5ft. 3in.; blue frock, Guernsey frock, white flannel, blue trousers, flannel drawers, and sea boots. No marks – much decomposed. Divers not at work. Steamer and lump still absent at Beaumaris. Blowing hard from E.S.E. with a heavy sea on. The following is a description of the bodies cast ashore in the parish of Llanwenllwyfo, Dulas Bay, from our Llanwenllwyfo correspondent.:-

A male body, supposed to age from 40 to 45, height 5ft. 10in.; had on dark tweed vest and trousers, black silk necktie, cotton shirt, woollen singlet and drawers, brown socks and Wellington boots. No name on clothing. In a portemonnaie, in trousers' pocket, was found three Australian sovereigns, 6½d., a small nugget, and on fancy lace paper a blessing, which is as follows – "May the blessing of God await thee; may the sun of glory shine round thy bed; and may the gates of plenty - honour and happiness, be ever open to thee; may no sorrow disturb thy days; may no grief disturb thy nights; may the pillow of peace kiss thy cheek, and the pleasures of imagination attend thy dreams; and when length of years make thee tired of earthly joys, and the curtain of death gently close around thy last sleep of human existence, may the angel of God attend thy bed, and take care that the expiring lamp of life shall not receive one rude blast to hasten on its extinction" – Had on a long silver watch guard, and in a pocket was found two trunk keys, two watch keys, and two printed ballads – "The Green Lament" and "Emma and William." On the 21st. - The trunk and head of a youth, supposed age from 12 to 14, features gone; had on a fine black cloth jacket, with silk conder buttons. On the 24th – A stout-made male body, height 5ft 11in. supposed age from 45 to 50, head mutilated; had on a dark cloth vest, shepherd's plaid trousers, purple woollen shirt with white stripes, cotton woven singlet and drawers, blue Angola socks and short boots, with elastic sides. Found – A portemonnaie, containing two Australian sovereigns, five and a half English ditto, and 2s. 6d in silver, a bunch of keys and watch key, a knife, with one blade perfect. On the same day – A slight-made male body, height 5ft 8in., supposed age from 30 to 35, features gone, dark hair; clothing – dark grey Guernsey frock, white duck trousers, cotton shirt, dark woollen stockings and a pair light buttoned boots – the shirt and stockings marked "J.M." In the trousers' pocket, three keys attached to a foreign copper coin. On the 25th – The head and trunk of a male body, supposed age from 45 to 50, stout made, features gone; had on a dark brown cloth vest and purple woollen shirt, with white stripes. In the vest pocket was found a penknife. On the 26th - A stout-made male body, about 5ft. 10in. in height, supposed age from 45 to 50, full features, very dark brown hair on the head; beard and whiskers of a lighter shade; light blue eyes; small sharp nose; low forehead; had on a strong flannel shirt and drawers, such as worn by miners; a striped blue cotton shirt, mended in two places; and the remains of a fustian trousers on one leg. Found – A night dress, marked "Jane Fowler, No. 1, 1858" Also, a gentleman's shirt marked "A.C." We have received the following from our Llandudno Correspondent – The body of a man was washed ashore on the 28th ult., on the Conway side of Llandudno, and is supposed to be one of those who perished with the *Royal Charter*; the body was in a very mutilated condition from the waist upwards. Deceased had on black cloth trousers with fly front, and a pair of woollen socks on his feet, but no marks of identification. An inquest was held on the 30th and a verdict of "Found drowned" returned.

Mr. John Lester, grocer, Port St. Mary, Isle of Man, writes thus:- A young female, supposed to be one of the passengers of the *Royal Charter*, was picked up off the Quay-head, Port St. Mary, Isle of Man. When brought ashore, we examined her. There was a brooch with the centre out, supposed to contain a likeness. Her stays were cut, when a purse with clasp was found, and another inside with four sovereigns, a two shilling piece, a large coin supposed to be a dollar, a small 1½d. silver piece, and a five pound Bank of England note, which was dried and pasted on paper; the number and note are correct. There was a mourning ring on her finger on her right hand; on the outside was "In memory of," inside "Thomas Davies, obit. 26th June, 1847, and Jane, his wife, obit. 26th Feb., 1857". The writing was well worn. That is the correct inscription, as we examined it with a magnifying glass. The body was badly decomposed. Black cloth jacket, flannel petticoat, black cloth boots, good; all her appearance being of a young lady. On further examination, the initial on her stockings is "F. Davies." According to the paper, she will be Miss F. Davies, second-class passenger.

Seamen's Superstitions.

We have an illustration of the horror with which seamen regard bearing the dead on board ship in the case of the schooner *Richard*, of Preston, which entered Drogheda Harbour on Thursday with a dead body in tow, supposed to be one of the passengers of the ill-fated *Royal Charter,* and which was found floating near Holyhead. She must, therefore, have towed this body quite across the Irish Channel; and the reason for the act has certainly been the dread, or superstition, which naturally attaches itself to the mind of the sailor, who considers that to carry a dead body on shipboard is fraught with omens of evil to the ship and to the crew who navigate her.

North Wales Chronicle.
Saturday, December 3, 1859

The Royal Charter - Recovery of part of the sunken treasure. A telegram received at Lloyd's from Captain Fell, who has the superintendence of the divers and other operations on the sunken wreck of the ill-fated *Royal Charter* on behalf of the underwriters, states that they succeeded in lifting the starboard quarter of the wreck on Monday, when the divers found part of the bullion, namely 12 boxes, 12 bags and several ingots of gold. Other telegrams also received from Captain J.A. Lodge at Moelfra bay represent the amount of gold and specie found to be nearly £80,000.

Recovery of nearly £100,000 in specie. The following is a continuation of the progress made at Moelfre up to Thursday last.

Thursday. (Dec 1) Red Wharf – Body of a male, a young man, one side very much mutilated, features perfect; on the left hand an impression of a ring in Indian Ink; no clothing. Not identified. Body of a male – grey whiskers, blue striped flannel shirt, white flannel drawers, light blue stockings and blucher boots; to all appearances an old man; no marks on clothing. Not identified. Female body – small earrings in her ears, white flannel petticoat and drawers, white stockings, kid boots, small victorine round neck, stockings marked "F.R. Munroe, No. 14."

Friday. Moelfre – Male body, about twelve years of age; height about 4ft. 4 inches; face perfect, no clothing. Not identified. Female body, height 5ft. 4in.; clothing, brown jacket, trimmed with black velvet, stockings with name "F.R. Munro, No.13". Two rings – one a wedding ring. Steamers and lump absent at Beaumaris for shelter. An overcoat picked up at Red Wharf, with pocket book containing cards with the name "Mr. Francis Rufford."

Saturday. Two steamers arrived from Beaumaris. Divers sent up about 30 sovereigns in buckets of sand. – No bodies recovered.

Sunday. No bodies recovered. Divers were not at work. Blowing very hard off the land. A piece of a portrait was obtained from one of the villagers, of a young lady, recognised by Williams, Quartermaster, as being the likeness of Miss Murray, one of the passengers.

Monday. Divers employed in slinging a portion of the wreck. The lump succeeded in lifting it about 4 p.m., when the divers immediately commenced sending up boxes of gold, bars of gold, bags of sovereigns, and gold dust, to the value of about £40,000. This portion of the wreck appears to be a piece of the quarter which had fallen over the bullion, and prevented the divers seeing it. No bodies recovered.

Tuesday. Divers busily engaged in sending up specie, consisting of boxes, bars (some weighing 20 lbs. each), bags of gold dust, and a great many loose sovereigns in buckets of sand, between £50,000 and £60,000 sent up during the day. At dark, a steamer proceeded to Liverpool with the specie recovered. No bodies recovered.

Wednesday. Steamer absent at Liverpool. No divers at work. No bodies recovered.

Thursday. The steamer arrived from Liverpool last night; but too much sea on for divers to go down. No bodies recovered.

Births. On the 5th inst., at Mount-street, Bangor (prematurely), the wife of Mr. Owen Williams, (one of the survivors of the crew of the Royal Charter) of twins – boy and girl.

North Wales Chronicle.
Saturday, December 10, 1859

Friday. (Dec 9) Female body washed on shore near the wreck, about 12 years of age. No clothing on; very much disfigured - taken to Penrhos Lligwy Church. Steamer and lump still absent. Strong winds, S.E. heavy sea on.

Saturday. Steamer arrived this morning. Divers went down and sent up one bar of gold in forenoon. In the afternoon, divers busily engaged sending up boxes of gold bars, gold dust, and loose sovereigns in buckets, to the value of about £19,000. No bodies recovered.

Sunday. Divers busily employed in sending up bars of gold, gold dust and loose sovereigns to the value of about £11,000. Tug left for Beaumaris in the evening to tow lump around to the wreck. No bodies recovered.

Monday. Steamer and lump arrived this morning, but there was too much sea on for divers to work, and they returned to Beaumaris for shelter. No bodies recovered. The letters from Moelfra received on Monday report a further discovery of gold from the wreck of the *Royal Charter*, namely, 540 lbs. of gold coin, 40 ingots of gold, 286½ sovereigns, 47 rupees, 38 lbs. gold dust, five bars of gold and one cup ingot, and a piece of iron plate with part of a bar of gold, and some sovereigns driven into it, which latter, it is observed, "is a great curiosity."

Tuesday. Steamer returned from Beaumaris. Divers busily employed - sent up bars of gold, loose sovereigns, and nuggets, to the value of between £9,000 and £10,000, in the forenoon. Too much sea on in the afternoon for the divers to work. Steamer left for Beaumaris. One male body picked up at Moelfre, and identified as Isaac Lewis*

belonging to Moelfre, by having stockings marked, and initials "I.L." on the arm. One male body picked up at Moelfre – height 6 feet; clothing, part of flannel shirt, worsted stockings, with an eyelet-hole worked in top, leather belt round waist, with knife sheath attached; no marks on person or linen; very much mutilated.

Wednesday. Blowing hard from the N.N.E., heavy sea on the coast. One male body picked up afloat; height, 6ft., clothing, Crimean shirt, coloured tweed trousers and waistcoat, socks and boots, black necktie; features gone, part of pocket book, and some money found in trousers' pocket, amounting to £1 19s.; not identified, brought ashore at Moelfre

Thursday. Seven male bodies picked up. (Particulars not received)

North Wales Chronicle.
Saturday, December 17, 1859

Thursday, Dec. 15th Moelfre – Body of a male, about 5ft. 10in.; clothing – part of a white shirt, flannel, black velvet waistcoat, flannel drawers, black cloth trousers, and grey stockings; third finger on the left hand gone, having been amputated from the third joint; gold watch, with gold guard and key; seal and key in one; name on works

* Different news reports give Isaac Griffiths, Francis Lewis and Isaac Lewis as being seamen from Moelfre who were lost on the 'Royal Charter', but Captain Hughes, one of the 'Rescuers of the Wrecked' later stated that there was only one seaman from the village on board the wreck. Burial records show that Isaac Lewis, aged 21, of Ty Hen, Moelfre, was interred at Llanallgo churchyard. His father, John Lewis was a Master Mariner, and was one of the twenty-eight 'Rescuers of the Wrecked'. Note that there is a contradiction in the dates of the two reports of the recovery of his body.

An affecting account was related of one of the seamen belonging to the *Royal Charter*. His name was Lewis, a native of Moelfre, and it was said that his father resided within a stone's throw of the spot where the dreadful catastrophe occurred. The father recognised his son on the wreck, and they hailed each other in agonising terms. "Oh", cried the young man, "I have come home to die!" He then made an effort to reach the shore by means of the hawser, but was struck by a terrible sea and drowned in the presence of his father. It was stated on Saturday evening that the body had been recovered and removed to his father's house.

Liverpool Mercury. October 31, 1859.

"Finley and Field, Glasgow, 4087"; also, a silver watch – name "William Thompson, Glasgow," one nugget, breast-pin, £39 1s. in a leather purse; photographic case – likeness gone. – Not identified. Moelfre – Body of a male, about 5ft. 8in, in height, brown hair; clothing – cotton striped shirt, black coat and waistcoat, grey socks; gold top of a walking stick, with green glass stone; gold ring, with blue stone; key of a box or trunk. Moelfre – Body of a male, about 5ft. 9in, in height; clothing – tweed trousers, flannel shirt boots, stockings marked "M"; £27 4s., three nuggets, two gold rings – one marked "A.E.", in two purses on a fustian belt around waist; two small keys; left foot second toe, short – by nature. – Not identified. Llaneugrad Parish – Body of a male, about 5ft. 8in. in height; clothing – striped and Crimean shirt, miner's overboots, and woollen stockings; ring on right hand, little finger, stamped "Ballarat," with the miner's coat of arms, washed on shore. – Not identified. Llaneugrad – Body of a male, 5ft. 7in. in height; clothing - part of cloth trousers, blucher boots, and blue worsted socks; left foot crippled – what is termed a club foot; letters on right arm, marked in India ink – "T.D. and G.H." washed on shore. – Not identified. Llaneugrad – Body of a male, 5ft. 7in. in height; clothing – sea jacket, moleskin trousers, part of a shirt, blucher boots, black necktie, small trunk key, and leather strap round waist, washed on shore. – Not identified. Llaneugrad – Body of a boy, about 12 to 14 years of age; clothing – flannel shirt, shepherd plaid trousers, blucher boots, and white cotton socks, washed on shore. – Not identified. Llanddona – On the 14th inst., a male body, clothing – serge frock, flannel fustian trousers, white flannel drawers, blue stockings, and leather boots, sixpence in copper, and a knife. Benllech – on the 15th instant, a male body, clothing – corduroy trousers; initials "J.S."; serge shirt, cotton shirt, and a pair of boots; also, a male body with only a boot and sock on.

Also, picked up on the sands, washed ashore – 4 bales of wool and 4 half-bales, nearly in a sound state.

Friday. Moelfre – Tug boat and lump still absent in Beaumaris. No more bodies recovered.

Saturday. Moelfre – This morning the steamer with lump arrived from Beaumaris. Divers are busily at work. Sent up loose sovereigns about £2,000. They are now slinging some more of the after part of ironwork, to clear it away.

Sunday. Moelfre – The divers are still busily engaged – Sent up in bags and loose sovereigns, some bars of gold and gold dust, to the value of about £4,360. At noon they hauled the lump in, to endeavour to clear away some more of the after part of the ironwork. Picked up a gold watch case; inscription on the back outside – "Echappment a cylindre, arguilles quatre trous en rubis" with flourishes over inscription and under; also, a figure of a horse. No more bodies recovered.

Monday. Moelfre – The divers are still busily engaged. Sent up two bars of gold and loose sovereigns, to the value of about £825, and five rupees. The lump is at present over the wreck, with a portion of the ironwork slung, and endeavouring to weigh it. They want to clear away this ironwork, but it appears very heavy to lift. It has slipped several times. They are bringing the wool here from Red Wharf by boat, which Captain Martin is taking charge of.

Tuesday. Moelfre – The divers are still busily at work. Recovered in specie, loose sovereigns, with four bars of gold and gold dust to the value of about £2,480. The lump, in endeavouring to weigh the portion of ironwork, parted the chain. The tug had her in tow at the time, trying to drag it clear of the wreck. No more bodies recovered.

Wednesday. Moelfre – Sent up by divers – 11 sovereigns, 10 rupees, and chronometer, some pieces of iron, and a few of the deck planks. This morning, it blowing strong from the N.W., too much sea was on for the divers to work. Captain Martin intends leaving for Liverpool, having £40,000 on board the steamer, leaving the lump at Beaumaris. They have also taken the wool on board that has been picked up.

Thursday. Moelfre – Divers not at work this day. No bodies found, but a human skull found on the rocks. £30,000 was sent to Liverpool this day, making a total of £318,000 despatched from the wreck since the divers commenced their operations.

North Wales Chronicle.
Saturday, December 24, 1859

Friday, December 23rd. Nothing done at wreck today or yesterday. The steamer left for Liverpool yesterday with £40,000 on board.

Saturday, Sunday, & Monday. Nothing done.

Tuesday. Divers sent up about 350 sovereigns, and a few ounces of gold dust.

Wednesday. Too much sea on for divers to work.

Thursday. Divers sent up 25 bars of gold and sovereigns. Lump lifted a large piece of ironwork and landed it on rocks.

Distinguished Visitors in Bangor.

We understand that the celebrated Charles Dickens, accompanied by Mr. Willis, arrived at the *British Hotel* in this city on Thursday evening last, and left the following morning for Moelfre, the scene of the late wreck of the *Royal Charter*.

North Wales Chronicle.
Saturday, December 31, 1859

Saturday, Dec. 31st, 1859. Moelfre. Specie recovered yesterday in sovereigns and bars of gold is valued at about £5,700. The lump also lifted up one of the deck beams and landed it on the rocks. This morning, the divers are busily at work - Sent up a bag

containing 1,000 sovereigns, five loose sovereigns, and a few rupees. Some pieces of iron work slung and weighed by lump.

Sunday. Moelfre. Sent up by divers in loose sovereigns, dust and one bar of gold to the value of about £1,000. This morning, from the state of the weather blowing a gale, the divers are not able to work. The tug boat with lump are at anchor in Moelfre roads.

Monday. Moelfre. This morning the divers are principally engaged slinging a small portion of the side, which the lump has weighed, and landed it abreast of the beach near the tent. Nothing further done,

Tuesday. Moelfre. Divers sent up in loose sovereigns, gold dust and bars, to the value of about £1,066. At dusk yesterday evening, Captains Martin and Lodge left in the steamer for Beaumaris to forward the money obtained, by rail from Bangor to Liverpool. The steamer has just arrived from Beaumaris, It has been blowing fresh from the S.E. This morning the men that have been employed in the boats with the divers were put to work on the beach, near the quarry, raking and turning stones over, by Capt. Fell. They have found thirteen sovereigns, a half-sovereign, and three shillings; a miner's ring, with coat of arms — the cradle and bucket, also marked 'Castle Maine', and a silver spoon.

Wednesday. Moelfre. This morning, the divers are busily engaged, and have been very successful, having obtained about 15 gold bars, and a quantity of sovereigns.

Thursday. Moelfre. The amount of money recovered yesterday in loose sovereigns, bars, and gold dust is to the value of £12,000. Also, a piece of the side lifted by lump and landed on the rocks. This morning, the divers are busily engaged. Sent up one bar of gold, and sovereigns to the value of about £600. They have also slung some more iron-work. In lifting it, the chain parted.

North Wales Chronicle.
Saturday, January 7, 1860

238

MOELFRE - Accounts from Moelfre report the removal of further portions of the wreck, and the recovery of about £19,000 more gold, comprising 1,486 sovereigns, 10 oz. dust, and 106 rupees, 26 ingots and 15 pieces of ingots, in all about 8 lbs. The ingots are all identified as belonging to the Bank of Australia, the Bank of New South Wales, and the Oriental Bank.

Caernarfon & Denbigh Herald.
Saturday, January 7, 1860

Friday, Jan 6. Moelfre. Sent up by divers in loose sovereigns to the value of about £500. At dusk yesterday evening, the wind shifted round to N.E. Steamer and lump left for Beaumaris.

Saturday. Moelfre. This morning, the steamer with lump, arrived from Beaumaris. Owing to the swell, there is too much sea on for the divers to work.

Sunday. Moelfre. Since last Saturday's report, the divers sent up in loose sovereigns and gold dust to the value of about £110. This morning they are at work with the lump, endeavouring to lift some of the iron-work. No money obtained. A roll of leather hides sent up. Red Wharf Bay. A male body was picked up yesterday at Red Wharf Bay. Clothing - A blue sea jacket, black silk waistcoat, white cotton shirt, Wellington boots and plaid trousers. No marks on clothing. Height about 5 ft. 6in.; features gone, slight built. Also found on his person, a bill of exchange, very much torn, bearing, date "Bank of Australia, 24th August, 1859" for £300; Manager, Charles Caldill; second and third of the same tenor. No. 46 and 728 same tenor payable to Mr. Thom — the remainder of the name is torn and can't be made out; also a silver watch, with gold guard and gold key, a silver guard, gold ring, with digger's coat of arms - pickaxe and shovel; and a small nugget.

Monday. Moelfre. The divers are still at work, principally engaged this morning in lifting a piece of the side. Eleven sovereigns only obtained.

Tuesday. Moelfre. The portion of side the lump was about lifting yesterday was weighed and landed on the rocks. On examining part of the port side next to the run at low water, found in the clay and about it, 11½ sovereigns, a sixpence, and a penny; also a piece of a musket stock, bayonet, and the works of a small clock. This morning, the divers slung another piece of the side, and are now hauling the lump on to land it. That has been the principal work this morning. No money obtained.

Wednesday and Thursday. Moelfre. The divers have left, and all operations at the wreck are to be suspended for the next two months — the Coast Guard remaining in charge to protect the wreck. The whole amount of specie recovered is supposed to be about £330,000. It seems doubtful what the amount un-recovered really is. It is said to be from £40,000 to £70,000. It will be necessary, when operations are renewed, to have more power at work than has been hitherto employed, as the wreck must be dragged asunder, to accomplish which, three or four lumps will be required. To commence operations on that scale now, at this uncertain season, when the divers are so often unable to work, would be very costly, without holding but good prospects of a satisfactory result.

Wreck of the *Royal Charter*.

To the Editor of the North Wales Chronicle. Sir, You will oblige me by inserting this communication which I had direct with the Board of Trade. The following is a copy of my letter to the Board of Trade.

Hon. Sir,

This day, the remains of a Gentleman were found on Red Wharf Sands, in the parish of Pentraeth, Anglesey. The Coast Guard brought the corpse to me in a very mutilated state. This person had a large amount of notes on his person, they say to the amount of

£900; a valuable watch, gold ring, and three or four nuggets of gold etc. The Coast Guard have taken possession of all his property, for the purpose, as they say, of handing it over to the Board of Trade. The officers told me they cannot touch a farthing of the assets to defray any charge or cost connected with the interment, or any other pecuniary outlay however requisite and proper it may be. Under these circumstances, being Saturday night, I gave the Coast Guard candles and three shillings in money out of my own pocket, to enable them to obtain assistants to remove the body from the cart to a coach-house near the church. I have ordered the joiner to make a good, decent coffin, not a 14 shillings pauper coffin, but such a one as an ordinary farmer would be placed in. I have buried some who have had large sums of money in their pockets; and when their dear friends and relatives were informed of the fact that all their property was taken possession of, and the poor remains handed over to parish authorities to be treated in their interment as paupers, they were most sorely grieved.

I remain, Sir, yours most obediently,
Morris Hughes,
Rector of Pentraeth. Anglesey

The following is a copy of the communication received from the Board.

Sir, I am informed by the Lords of the Committee Council for Trade to acknowledge the receipt of your letter of the 7th inst. respecting the interment of a body on which was found a sum of £900 in notes and other valuables, and to inform you that my Lords are of opinion that you should have this body decently interred, and send the bill for the expenses etc. to the Receiver of Wreck at Beaumaris, who will forward it to this department for payment.

I am, Sir, your obedient servant,
James Lortil

North Wales Chronicle.
Saturday, January 14, 1860

The Whitstable and Liverpool divers have been stopped by order of the underwriters, it is believed on account of there being more gold already recovered than the amount on freight, and there being some doubt as to what is to become of the surplus, in the absence of proof as to whom it belongs.

Caernarfon & Denbigh Herald.
Saturday, January 28, 1860

The search for treasures was recommenced on the 7th inst. Mr. Smith, of Beaumaris, Receiver of Droits of Admiralty, being present overlooking the removal of large blocks of stone and rubbish. Ere an hour had elapsed after commencing, a purse with 24 sovereigns was found among the debris.

Caernarfon & Denbigh Herald.
Saturday, February 11, 1860

The men work daily at the scene of this sad catastrophe, and get twenty per cent. Two hundred and thirty sovereigns were recovered up to 12 o'clock on Tuesday last.

Caernarfon & Denbigh Herald.
Saturday, February 18, 1860

The men employed to turn the stones on the shore near to this wreck have been able to obtain the sum of 10 shillings only, since our last publication.

Caernarfon & Denbigh Herald.
Saturday, February 25, 1860

GOLD NUGGET IMBEDDED IN A PLATE OF IRON RECOVERED FROM THE WRECK OF THE " ROYAL CHARTER."

GOLD NUGGET IMBEDDED IN A PLATE OF IRON.

The fragment of iron, of which we here give a representation, is part of the unfortunate ship *Royal Charter,* wrecked on the 26th of October last, near Moelfra, Isle of Anglesea, on voyage from Melbourne to Liverpool. The mass of gold impacted in the fissure is part of an ingot of the purest quality imported, worth more than £4 an ounce. It was sent up in its present form from the wreck by divers employed in recovering the sunk treasure, who found the gold so firmly fixed that it was impossible to separate it from the iron. The remainder of the ingot, of which an engraving is also given, was found subsequently near the same spot, and has been identified, together with nearly £300,000* worth of gold of the original shipment of about £320,000. When found by the divers, the fragment of iron and wood was studded with sovereigns, the greater number of which were picked out under water before it had been found possible to release the ingot; a few, however, still remain, as will be seen. The weight of the ingot is about 211 ounces, and it is worth about £860. A great quantity of the gold dust on freight in the *Royal Charter* has also been recovered, the sand about the wreck being brought up and washed.

The total extent of treasure recovered from the wreck of the *Royal Charter* up to the 14th instant has been 23 boxes of gold, 272 bars and ingots, and 57 broken pieces of gold; 14,888 half-sovereigns, 38 lb. of gold nuggets, 275 lb. gold-dust, 496 rupees, six shillings, a gold pin, and several small articles. All the boxes, and a great many of the bars of gold, bear the marks contained in the *Royal Charter* manifest, and no doubt can be entertained of their identity. The *Royal Charter* is stated to have had 40,000 sovereigns on board. The amount of gold she had on freight was £335,000, and the passengers, it is believed, had a further sum of gold amongst them to the extent of £120,000.

Illustrated London News
January 28, 1860

Multiply by 100 to 150 to arrive at today's price of gold.

A Queen Victoria sovereign (1851) and an East India Company rupee (1840).
'I saw men picking sovereigns out of the holes and crevices of the rocks, almost as they would shellfish.' -- -- Chester Chronicle. Saturday, October 29, 1859.

Some gold was carried as small bars, some as sovereigns, and some as dust, with the latter being especially difficult to recover if the bags containing it had split open. In this case, the contents would have been scattered everywhere to perhaps make this the most valuable stretch of 'golden-sand' anywhere in the world. The recovery work was very successful at first, but the 'Law of Diminishing Returns' soon began to bite, so the underwriters decided that this was not the sort of work that they were best involved with. They quickly sold the wreck to Gibbs, Bright & Company for £1,000, an investment that was to bring considerable rewards to the Liverpool shipowners.

> The whole of this wreck has been contracted for by Messrs. Gibbs, Bright & Co., and they have consequently become the entire salvors. About sixty men are to be employed. Lumpers on sea and sheers on land and other *modi operandi* will be put into speedy operation. It is said that five months will be occupied in effectually clearing all away. The coastguard (the watchers hither-to) have all been discharged.

Caernarfon & Denbigh Herald. Saturday, March 3, 1860

Many estimates have been made of the total amount of gold being carried by the 'Royal Charter' on her final voyage, but as there was no record of the personal wealth being carried by the passengers, that figure will never be accurately known. With ownership of the 'Royal Charter' now firmly back in the hands of Gibbs, Bright & Co., a new approach was needed to that age-old problem of 'Can we make a profit?'
Yes, there was precious gold to be found, but the iron and copper that still littered the seabed could help to cover the on-going costs of the salvage operation. Gibbs, Bright & Co. would have had some idea of the sheer quantity of valuables left on the seabed, especially as the captain's bullion chest still lay entangled amongst the wreckage. This quest for the 'El Dorado' of the 'Royal Charter' was going to keep the divers, lumpers and labourers employed for many months before they were finally successful.

Even in midsummer, the underwater-visibility rarely exceeds four metres. Working here during the winter of 1859 - 1860, the divers would have experienced a total blackout.

The operations on the wreck were merely routine, that of scratching in the crevices for what could be found of the passengers' property in gold, etc., and preparing for the ultimate floating of the larger fragments into a more convenient spot for breaking up. This work, however, is not expected to be accomplished under three months. In the interim, the smaller pieces of the hull, with the masts, rigging, etc., will be secured. The iron will be conveyed to Liverpool, and the other materials will be sold at Moelfre. For floating the larger fragments, about sixty large casks, of about 300 gallons each, will be lashed to a framework made for the purpose, to which the wreck will be made fast, and this machine is calculated to support a weight of 80 tons.

Caernarfon & Denbigh Herald.
Saturday, March 10, 1860

Since our last, nothing of consequence has been carried on here. The sheers have been raised on the ledge of rocks by the side of the wreck, and large pieces of loose iron are being removed - some amounting to ten tons weight. Mr. Davies, Inspector of Police, has at present in his possession a small black pigeon, which was picked up amongst the rocks near the wreck the day of the dreadful catastrophe. It has been unable to fly ever since, having received some injury during the storm.

Caernarfon & Denbigh Herald.
Saturday, March 17, 1860

Under the able superintendence of Captains Martin and Grey, operations are being carried on daily. About 400 tons of iron have already been got from the wreck, and it is expected that on or about the 4th of May, it being low-tide, more workmen will be put on, as it is proposed to float the poop (where all the treasure lies) sometime from the 15th to 25th May.

Caernarfon & Denbigh Herald.
Saturday, April 21, 1860

It was known that the bullion was kept in the strongroom near the stern, which was the part of the wreck nearest to the cobble-covered shore-line at Porth Helaeth. From the salvor's point of view, it made sense to move those mangled remains above the low-water mark, and dismantle the ironwork by unskilled labourers in fresh-air rather than by skilled divers working in the dark, murky waters of this eastern coast of Anglesey. This seems to have been fairly successful, as a visitor to Moelfre soon reported:

> The hull and stern have been raised, and towed round the point at a few hundred yards distance from the wreck, where they have been dragged on shore to be broken up. I saw the village boys playing round them, and swimming their tiny boats in the pools close by, growing up to love the treacherous sea, in spite of wrecks and storms. Here, fixed in this broken framework, had been the wheel, and here the helmsman died at his post; underneath were the remains of the powerful screw, all bent, jagged, and broken. Looking with curious eyes at the shattered boarding outside, I made out what had once been modelled and painted upon it as an allegorical device. Neptune in his chariot, trident in hand, gliding with light wheels over the smooth waves, and the Winds going forth from his presence to discharge his auspicious bidding.
>
> The Leisure Hour, summer-time, 1860

Even re-floating part of the wreck and dragging it ashore wasn't the final answer to the problem of the missing treasure, so work continued on throughout 1860 and 1861, when Gibbs, Bright & Co. thought they had really had hit the jackpot!

> On Thursday, the diver now engaged in operations at Moelfre, the scene of the disastrous wreck of the *Royal Charter*, met with great success. The late captain's chest, containing from £40,000 to £50,000 was recovered. The circumstance was at once telegraphed to Messrs. Gibbs and Bright, Liverpool.
>
> The Times. Monday, December 2, 1861

The euphoria must have only lasted a short while, as a correction to the initial report was published only two days later.

> It was stated in our impression of Monday that a safe containing £40,000 had been recovered from the wreck of the *Royal Charter* at Moelfra, whereas the safe contained £3,000 only.
>
> The Times. Wednesday, December 4, 1861

Even the recovery of the captain's chest didn't signal the end of the salvage operations.

> It will surprise many to learn that, after the lapse of nearly four years since the melancholy wreck of the *Royal Charter* occurred, operations for the recovery of the treasure contained in it are still carried on. Messrs. Gibbs, Bright, and Co, sold the pool some time ago to a firm in Anglesea for, we believe, about £700. Whenever the weather permits, divers descend to collect the mud at the bottom, and this on being washed is found to contain gold dust and coin. Five pounds and upwards are thus recovered every week. Numerous persons visit the now celebrated village of Moelfra. Some of these are persons who were themselves saved from the wreck. One of these has lately been at much pains to cut and carry away a portion of the rock to which the heroic Maltese sailor Rogers had made fast the hawser that was the means of saving so many lives. In the Llanallgo churchyard, situated about a mile from the scene

A selection of cutlery recovered during the salvage operation of 1986.

of the wreck, a monument has been erected of stone carried chiefly from the place where the unfortunate vessel struck. On this column, a late visitor had carved with his knife these words:— "Came from Australia to see this. B. NEIL."

The Times. Monday, July 6, 1863

Over four years after the destruction of the 'Royal Charter', the hard-working divers and their support teams were still finding parts of the lost treasure.

A short time ago, the divers engaged in searching the pool where the *Royal Charter* broke up four years ago, came upon a very rich store of gold. They found in the same spot, in the course of a few days, about £1,200 in sovereigns and a bar of pure gold, weighing 9 lb., which was brought up to London this week. The treasure was far from being exhausted, when the storm came on and put a stop to the diving operations for the season. Messrs, Gibbs, Bright, and Co., the owners of the vessel, sold, about a year ago to some persons in Anglesey, all claim to the treasure found on the spot, and it is said that the speculation has already paid 300 or 400 per cent profit, although the cost of working it is very considerable.

The Times. Thursday, December 10, 1863

The divers have again commenced operations on the *Royal Charter*, and have been very lucky. They have brought up from the deep, eighty sovereigns on the 25th of this month, twenty on the 26th, and eight on the 27th.

North Wales Chronicle. Saturday, July 30, 1864

Yesterday, Hugh Williams, a farmer who bought the wreck of the *Royal Charter*, lying on the coast of Anglesea, went down in a diving suit with some gunpowder for the purpose of blasting. The powder exploded prematurely, and when taken up, Williams was quite dead.

Liverpool Mercury. Saturday, September 27, 1873

The operations continued throughout the nineteenth and twentieth centuries, with further work taking place even today.

The Victorian Divers

The aqualung, that wonderful, self-contained invention that allows us easy access to the undersea world, is a product of the latter-half of the 20th century, whereas the salvage-divers at Moelfre in the 19th century would have used the 'hard-hat' system, a technique that required fitness and strength from the diver, plus a reliable, dedicated surface-support team to operate the air-pump and keep the diver's supply-hose clear from entanglement. The author Charles Dickens visited the wreck-site in late 1859, and wrote this article for publication in 'All The Year Round' and various newspapers. Dickens seems to have a rather imaginative idea of the local conditions, as any diver who has visited the wreck will tell you that the underwater visibility is rarely good, and after a storm it becomes absolutely zero. Try to imagine yourself working in total blackness, wearing boots with soles made of lead, with extra weights hanging on your back and chest, and being surrounded by sharp plates of iron. All of this in a confined space where dozens or perhaps even hundreds of human bodies are slowly being eaten by the crabs!

WHAT DIVERS MEET WITH UNDERWATER

When the vessel has settled down on a sandy bottom, it is preserved for many months from breaking up; and its position may be much the same as it would be when floating in calm water, if it be not tilted over by any under-current drifts. The light, of course, depends a great deal on the depth, and upon the nature of the bottom; but, where there is no chalk to give a milky thickness to the water, the diver pursues his work in a kind of gloomy twilight. By the aid of this, he can see and feel his way round the ship; but when he ascends to the deck, and winds down to the principle cabins, he finds everything pitch dark, and has nothing to guide him but his hands. This is the most difficult, and yet the most frequent labour he has to encounter; the danger being that, in a large vessel, where the cabin stairs are deep, and the cabins are long and broad, he may get his air tube twisted round some unfamiliar projection, and so squeeze off his supply of life from above. In positions such as this, he requires all his nerve and self-possession, all his powers of feeling his way back in the exact road that he came. He may have got the precious casket, to which he has been directed, in his arms; but what of that if he die before he can find the stairs? The cold, helpless masses that bump against his helmet, as they float along the low roof over his head, are the decomposed corpses of those who were huddled together in the cabin when the ship went down. A few of these may be on the floor under his feet, but only when pinned down by an overturned table or a fallen chest. Their tendency is upwards – ever upwards – and the remorseless sea washes away the dead infant from its mother's arms, the dead wife from her dear husband's embrace. If the wreck be in the Channel, the small crabs are already beginning to fatten on their prey. The diver disentangles himself from this silent vessel, and ascends the welcome stairs to the deck. The treasure he has rescued is hauled up into the attendant diving boat; and he turns again to renew his work. He seldom meets with an accident under water; never, perhaps, with death; and the chief risk he runs is from getting some heavy piece of ship lumber overturned on his long train of air-pipe. Even in this case, he feels the sudden check and want of air, gropes his way back to the obstruction, removes it, signals to his companions to be raised, and reaches the boat exhausted and alarmed, but not so much as to give up his place in the trade. His earnings mostly take the form of shares in what he recovers. If fortunate, his gains may be large; if unfortunate they may be small; but no man can grudge him the highest prize it is possible for him to win.

Caernarfon & Denbigh Herald.
January 21, 1860

The equipment used by the 'hard-hat' diver changed very slowly. This is Richard Rigg and his attendants at Amlwch in around 1919, using equipment that would have been familiar to those working at Moelfre sixty years earlier. Photo courtesy of Joyce Rigg.

In the caverns deep of the ocean cold,
The diver is seeking a treasure of gold;
Risking his life for the spoils of a wreck,
Taking rich gems from the dead on her deck;
And fearful such sights to the diver must be,
Walking alone in the depths of the sea.

The Diver (The Popular Song)
Words by G. Douglas Thompson.

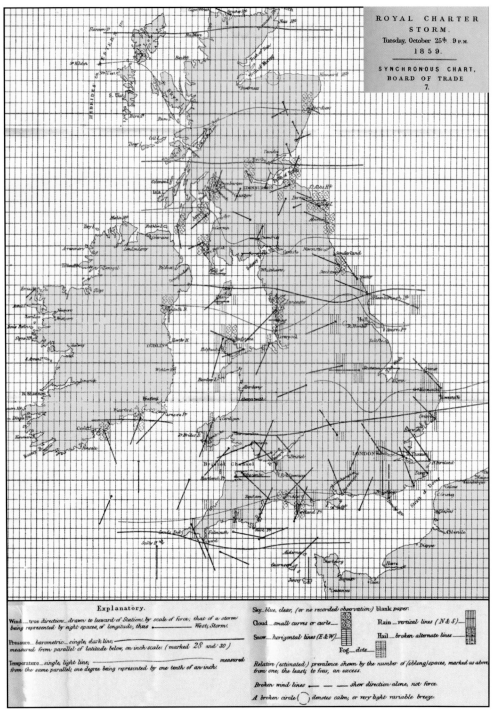

An extract from a series of weather-charts of the storm. These were produced to accompany the 'Board of Trade Wreck Returns of 1859', and were a record of the event rather than a weather-forecast. Straight lines drawn on the map indicate the strength and direction of the wind, while rain, hail, snow and fog were also shown.

CHAPTER THIRTEEN

Lessons Learned

Two profound and lasting innovations affecting the safety of mariners were to be introduced into Britain after the 'Royal Charter Storm', although the groundwork for these changes had already been done. These were:

- Weather predictions; of special importance for seafarers.
- Testing the quality of ship's anchors and anchor-chains.

Weather Reports and Storm Warnings

We now take it for granted that we can obtain reasonably accurate and up-to-date weather predictions. There are regular reports on the television and radio; we can access the internet from our computers; and we can receive a weather forecast by using our mobile telephones. The satellites orbiting around the world give us a 'birds-eye' view of the weather-fronts as they approach the British Isles, while powerful supercomputers predict how the atmosphere will behave, giving us an ability to forecast the weather that our ancestors could scarcely have imagined. Hundreds of ships and thousands of lives would have been saved if these facilities had been available during the 19th century. Vessels could have been forewarned of gales and storms so that they could seek out the nearest Harbour of Refuge such as those at Holyhead or Portland.

In the early 1850s, a method of predicting storms had been put forward by the appropriately named inventor George Merryweather, whose 'Tempest Prognosticator' was a device that relied on the theory that leeches trapped within a bottle would become agitated at the approach of a storm. Any leech that attempted to climb out of the bottle would trip a small latch to sound a warning bell, but to Merryweather's dismay, his method was not adapted for general use. The study of meteorology continued throughout the 1850s, and a clearer understanding of weather patterns was established in 1857 when the Dutch meteorologist Christophorus Buys Ballot introduced a rule that predicted the location of a low-pressure area relative to the wind direction.

Robert FitzRoy had been captain of 'H.M.S. Beagle' on that vessel's voyage of exploration from 1831 to 1836, during which time the botanist Charles Darwin first observed the biological traits that were to inspire his controversial book 'On The Origin Of Species'. During the voyage, FitzRoy had taken a special interest in weather forecasting, and had used thermometers, barometers and what were known as storm-glasses in an attempt to understand the vagaries of the weather. (Storm-glasses contained a solution which would crystallise under certain combinations of pressure and temperature.) Following his appointment as head of the Meteorological Department of the Board of Trade in 1854, FitzRoy promoted the use of barometers for mariners, and he published a series of manuals that described their correct use.

By 1859, weather reports were being printed in local newspapers such as the Liverpool Mercury, but these were reports of the past weather rather than predictions of future weather. At this time, the only way to foresee the weather was for an experienced observer to analyse the various cloud formations, rainfall-patterns and any other meteorological evidence that was available, such as that provided by a wind-vane, a barometer or a thermometer. If it was blowing a gale in Cornwall, how could anyone pass on a warning of the forthcoming danger to a ship that was passing North Wales, Scotland or anywhere else along our coastline? Radio had yet to be invented, and text messages and the internet were well over a century away.

Barometers

The principle of measuring the atmospheric pressure to give advanced warning of a change in the weather had been known for many years prior to 1859.

In the First Report of the Committee on Shipwrecks (1843), the following evidence was printed by order of the House of Commons. "I think that the neglect of the use of the barometer has led to the loss of many ships. From a want of attention to the barometer, they have either closed the land (if at sea), or have put to sea (being in harbour in safety) at improper times; and in consequence of such want of precaution, the ships have been lost owing to bad weather coming on suddenly, which might have been avoided had proper attention been paid to that very simple instrument. While alluding to the use of barometers, I may remark, that if such weather-glasses were put in charge of the Coastguard at the principal stations round the coast, so placed as to allow any one passing by to look at them, they might be the means not only of preventing ships from going to sea just before bad weather was coming on, but of preventing the great loss of life which takes place every year on our coasts owing to fishing vessels and boats going to sea when bad weather is impending. No bad weather ever comes on our coasts without timely warning being given by the barometer. The oldest seamen are often deceived by the look of the weather, but there is no instance on record of very bad weather, such as would have involved loss of life to the extent we have heard of in several years, having came on without the barometer having given timely warning. By the very small expense of an establishment of barometers, so placed as to be accessible to any fishermen, boatmen, or others on the coasts, much loss of life, as well as loss of boats, and even shipping, might be prevented.

Although aneroid barometers were available, it was the mercury-column type that was regarded as best-suited for the accurate measurement of atmospheric pressure, and there were subtle differences between those designed for use at sea or on land. It was essential that the barometers were correctly used and understood, so the Board of Trade republished their guidebook on the subject to make sure that the information was up to date and readily available. The 1859 edition of the booklet included easily-remembered rhymes that linked changes in pressure to the forthcoming weather, as well as sound advice on where to mount a barometer and how to take care of the instrument. There were tips on how to correct the barometer readings depending on the altitude above sea-level, how to interpret cloud formations, and how birds and animals would react to the forthcoming weather:

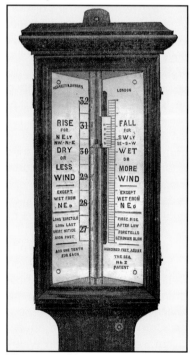

The type of barometer issued to lifeboat stations.

When sea birds fly out early, and far to seaward, moderate wind and fair weather may be expected. When they hang about the land, or over it, sometimes flying inland, expect a strong wind, with stormy weather. Also when animals seek sheltered places, instead of spreading over their usual range: when pigs carry straw to their sties; when smoke from chimneys does not ascend readily, an unfavourable change is probable.

BAROMETERS FOR LIFEBOAT STATIONS.

Public attention has frequently been called to the invaluable use of a barometer for indicating a coming storm. It not infrequently happens that a notice of a gale is given by a barometer two or three days before it actually takes place. It seems plain that with such powers placed providentially in our hands, the calamities now endured by our fishermen and coasters might in many instances be avoided. A good barometer in a public situation would warn them in time what to expect, and they could thus be frequently able to avoid the terrible consequences of storms so often at present proving fatal to them. Admiral FitzRoy, F.R.S., has compiled a useful and thoroughly practical manual for the use of a barometer, so that seafaring men of very ordinary capacity would soon become perfectly familiar with the indications of the instrument. Some time ago, Admiral FitzRoy obtained the sanction of the Board of Trade to supply some forty of our poorer fishing villages with barometers, some of which have been of great service to the fishermen. It is, however, evident that something more is absolutely required in order to make barometers generally available for our fishing and seafaring population. We are, therefore, glad to learn that this important subject is about to be taken up practically by the National Life-boat Institution. It is proposed to fix such instruments wherever found useful and practicable in conspicuous positions of the society's lifeboat houses, which are situated on most parts of the coast of the United Kingdom. To carry out effectually this plan the institution has, fortunately, the machinery at hand, for to each of its lifeboats is attached a permanent coxswain, who receives a small annual salary for his superintendence of the working part of the lifeboat establishment. It is proposed to instruct such of these men as are found capable in the indications of the barometer, so that they will act as so many storm-warners in the town or village in which they reside. It will be readily conceived what beneficial results may accrue to life and property among our hardy sea-coast population from this important step. It is a lamentable fact that at the present day the masters of our smaller coasting and fishing craft hardly ever think of consulting a barometer, if, indeed, they have an opportunity of doing so. It is estimated that a good barometer cannot be fixed to a lifeboat house under £6, so that it will require a considerable sum to carry out effectually the plan of the National Lifeboat Institution. We understand that a benevolent gentleman has presented to the institution £50, to be applied specially to the purchase of barometers for its lifeboat stations; and we cannot doubt that the public will readily make up what may be further required.

The making of the barometers has been entrusted to Messrs. Negretti and Zambra, who have already supplied forty of somewhat similar instruments to the Board of Trade for various fishing stations on the northern coast, and also a number to the British Meteorological Society for the coast of Northumberland. The object of the National Life-boat Institution will be to obtain a good instrument, and one that will not easily get out of order in travelling, or require renovating at frequent intervals; in short, a barometer that, having been once set up at a lifeboat station, will be a permanent instrument of instruction, and one that will not entail any future expense to the society. In order to meet these requirements, the makers have therefore introduced the following changes in the regular instruments, which, we think, may fairly come under the head of important improvements. The brass or ivory scales that barometers are generally furnished with are here replaced by a substantial plate of porcelain, on which the degrees and figures are prominently engraved and permanently blackened in; so that, as far as the divisions and figures are concerned, there will be no danger of their becoming faded or obliterated. This is a very important improvement, especially for an instrument that has of necessity to be placed in an exposed position, where the mariner may be able to consult it at any time, even in the middle of the night, should he wish so to do.

Illustrated London News. September 1, 1860

The Electric Telegraph

The idea that messages could be transmitted along a wire using electricity first came into being during the late 1830s, and a communications system based on this principle expanded across Britain throughout the 1840s using telegraph cables that had been laid alongside the rapidly-growing network of railway-tracks. By 1855, it was proposed to further extend the grid, with the potential of using it as an early-warning system in case of a military invasion.

A Coast Telegraph – It is contemplated to connect the whole seaboard of England, Wales and Scotland by means of a telegraph; thus, should a hostile fleet be hovering off the north of Scotland, the fact would be simultaneously known in London, Portsmouth, Plymouth, Liverpool, Greenock, and the intermediate ports. Such a means of communication will be found extremely useful in a commercial point of view, as the arrival of vessels will be reported directly their numbers are made. Submarine wires will be used to cross extensive estuaries. It is estimated that the cost of laying down the wires will be trifling, considering the extent and utility of the undertaking. The officers at coast-guard stations will be placed in charge of the telegraph.

Chester Chronicle. August 18th, 1855

By this time, the problem of running telegraph cables under the sea had been solved by the use of gutta percha, a latex from South-east Asia and Australia that allowed waterproofed wires to be laid not only across the land, but under rivers, lakes, lochs, estuaries and even the open sea. Now, and only now, could information be collected from afar, and rapidly transmitted around the country to give advanced warning to the government, seafarers and anyone else of danger, be it an invasion fleet or a storm about to hit our shores.

Observatories had already been established at Liverpool, Greenwich, Nottingham, Clifton, and other sites around the country to take recordings of the wind-strength, the wind direction, the temperature and any other data such as cloud cover. In June 1859, five months before the loss of the 'Royal Charter', FitzRoy put out a memorandum that asked for the general public to collect as much weather information as possible and add it to that already being supplied by the official sources.

In connection with this subject, a series of wind charts is in progress, and will be extended to show the simultaneous states of atmosphere over the ocean and its boundaries once a day (at least), during certain selected periods in the 12 or 14 months of special observation. During this limited interval of time a collection of various meteorological information will be gathered from every available source — from ships at sea as well as from observers on land. ...... With this memorandum are forms suitable for rather extended observations daily — but for the record or registry of wind and weather only, no specific form will be required, as the direction and character of wind, with the description of weather may follow successively, as noted thus:-

June 22, 8 a.m., N.W., fresh, 5, cloudy. (With any further useful remarks)

From time to time, monthly or quarterly, such records as may be made should be transmitted to the station from which these papers were received, whence they will be forwarded to the Board of Trade: or they may be sent direct, addressed to The Secretary of the Board of Trade, London, S.W., Meteorological, the word 'meteorological' being in the lower left hand corner. No postage need be prepaid, as they will be delivered free, being on public service.

June 22,1859.

This newspaper editorial suggested what might be done to save life and property.

A few hours' notice of a coming storm would in most cases enable seamen to be prepared for the worst. To run within a safe harbour; if no harbour be near, to stand out to the open sea would save a wreck, and one or other alternative would in most cases be adopted within that space of time. Ships within harbour could be more securely moored. Ships about to sail could defer their leaving shelter if they had warning of an approaching gale. This warning is what science now proposes to give. In the Wreck Return for 1859 Admiral FitzRoy draws attention to the fact that most of our great storms are of the nature of what scientific men have lately called Cyclones. They are, in fact, gigantic whirlwinds, often of several hundred miles diameter. But at the same time that the wind rushes furiously in a circle, the whole system has a rapid progressive motion. The centre of the Cyclone in which the *Royal Charter* was lost passed over the Eddystone Rock, over Exeter, and over Reigate. It reached the Eddystone at 3 p.m., Exeter at 4 p.m., Reigate at half-past 5 p.m. It then passed away in a north-easterly direction. At a similar rate, its circumference advanced. The Channel Fleet encountered it on the afternoon of the 25th October; it was on the morning of the 26th October that its greatest force was felt at Liverpool, and it was many hours later before it reached the east coast of Scotland. These were precious hours. How many a wreck, how many hundreds of lives would have been saved could Holyhead and Liverpool have known what was passing at Eddystone, and that what was passing there was every moment drawing near to them? Why should they not have known? We have a telegraphic system stretching from Cornwall to Inverness. In a few minutes, intelligence of the rise and progress of a gale could be transmitted from the first point at which it touched the island to all our ports. Successive intelligence would speedily give assurance of the fact, and a reasonable certainty of the extent it would affect, and of the direction and rate of its advance. The information would first be sent to London; a competent officer would then forward it to where it might be required. Such are the outlines of the plan which Admiral FitzRoy has suggested. It may be that our knowledge of the laws of storms is not yet sufficiently matured to make this scheme always successful. Some allowance, too, must be made for the influence of mistaken warnings in making seamen regardless of them for the future. Yet, taking everything into consideration, we confess we should anxiously desire that some such arrangement were forthwith carried into execution. So simple a matter as the telegraphing from every out-port any remarkable fall of the barometer, sudden change of the temperature, or other threatening of an approaching storm, with intelligence of the direction and force of the wind when it rose, could involve no serious difficulty or expense. An office in London, with two or three skilled interpreters of the signs, would, in truth, be the whole new establishment required. The local authorities of each resort of our shipping would doubtless readily make arrangements to give the speediest publicity to the notices they might receive. So easy and ready a method of at least diminishing the dangers to which our ships and mariners are exposed surely deserves an immediate trial. Within the last year, ships and cargo to the estimated value of £1,760,000 were lost upon our coasts. Sixteen hundred souls perished with the wrecks. If the method proposed were successful in saving but a few of the gallant men, of the helpless women and children, who must otherwise have gone down, it would well reward the effort. Should it save but a small percentage of the annual loss of property, should it diminish ever so little the perils of the sea, it will amply have repaid its cost.

Daily News.
June 6, 1860

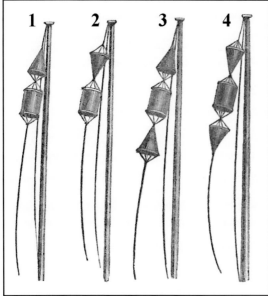

A combination of cones and drums indicated the expected direction of the forthcoming gale.

The Victorians now had the capability of recording local and national meteorological information, posting or telegraphing it to a central point, analysing that data, and then transmitting a warning of bad weather to a coastal location such as a fishing port. FitzRoy appears to have been convinced that the 'Royal Charter' would not have been lost if Captain Taylor had been given prior knowledge that strong north-easterly winds were about to overtake his vessel, with the certainty that the 'Royal Charter' would be put in peril off Anglesey. Simply putting into port at Holyhead or delaying his voyage around Anglesey would probably have saved her. FitzRoy investigated the circumstances of the disaster, and concluded that a system based on telegraphic warnings could have prevented the great loss of life and property. The British Association for the Advancement of Science had called for such a warning scheme only a few months before the loss of the 'Royal Charter', so FitzRoy presented a report to that body in 1860, and he was quickly given formal permission to issue storm warnings. The first of these lifesaving messages was made public on the 6th of February, 1861.

The problem was how to warn seafarers that such a storm was on its way, so FitzRoy promoted a system whereby cones and drums would be prominently displayed to pass on the alarm to anyone within visibility. As reported by the passengers on board the 'Royal Charter', the clipper had passed within visual distance of Holyhead, and Captain Taylor could have received such notification. These warnings could be triggered by information supplied by a local barometer, or from national gale-warnings telegraphed around the country. The method was very basic, as the number and orientation of the drums and cones could only indicate the direction from which the expected gale would blow, but at least it was the start of weather warnings that were to save thousands of mariners from drowning, and an untold number of ships from being tossed ashore or overwhelmed in bad weather.

The diagram shown above gives the following advice:

1 - Gale expected from the north.

2 - Gale expected from the south.

3 - Heavy or sudden gale from the north.

4 - Heavy or sudden gale from the south.

That method was fine on a clear day, but what about during the hours of darkness when the warnings were not visible? At night-time, lanterns were used to indicate the pattern of the cones and drums, so as to complete the round-the-clock advice to any mariner within sight of one of FitzRoy's masterpieces of ingenuity.

By the early 1860s, so much progress had been made towards producing an accurate weather-forecast that one would have thought that George Merryweather's 'Tempest Prognosticator' would have long been consigned to the history books, but there does appear to have been some truth in his theory as described in the following article:

The Leech as a Weather Glass. The following observations on a leech were made by a gentleman who kept one several years for the above purpose:- A phial of water containing a leech was kept in the lower frame of a chamber window sash, so that when I looked in the morning, I could know what would be the weather on the following day. If the weather proved serene and beautiful, the leech lies motionless at the bottom of the glass, and rolled together in a spiral form. If it rains before or after noon, it is found to have crept up to the top of its lodgings, and there remains until the weather is settled. If we are to have wind, the poor prisoner gallops through its limpid habitation with amazing swiftness and seldom rests until it begins to blow hard. If a remarkable storm of thunder and rain is to succeed, for some days before, it lodges almost continually out of the water, and discovers uneasiness in violent throes and convulsive motions. In the frost, as in clear weather, it lies at the bottom; and in snow, as in rainy weather, it pitches its dwelling upon the very mouth of the phial. The leech is kept in the eight-ounce phial, about three-fourths filled with water. In the summer the water is changed once a week, and in the winter once a fortnight.

Chester Chronicle. July 21, 1860

Hopefully, the weather forecasts of the following year relied on more than the convulsions of a few leeches scattered around the country. The first weather forecast appeared in 'The Times' newspaper on the 1st of August 1861.

General weather probable during the next two days:- North: moderate westerly wind; fine.

West: moderate westerly; fine. South: fresh westerly; fine.

That was rather less than the animated and multicoloured weather-reports that we expect today, but at least it was a start. A central office could telegraph weather information around the country, although only the larger ports would have this facility. Weather information was available to readers of 'The Times', while the smaller harbours could use their own barometer to give a local warning of approaching gales. As with many great leaps forward in technology, there had to be a snag, and in this case it was the unreliable nature of the forecasts, a problem that hasn't been fully resolved even in the 21st century. Despite many accurate forecasts and letters to the newspapers supporting FitzRoy, some of the predicted storms failed to materialise, leading to adverse comments in the newspapers, and mariners refusing to leave port when they should have been out at sea earning their living as fishermen or crew. These and other worries brought on periods of depression for Robert FitzRoy that eventually ended with his tragic suicide on the 30th of April, 1865.

FitzRoy's legacy has been a worldwide network of monitoring-stations that now communicate with each other by that successor to the Electric Telegraph, the internet; and arguably, he created the world's first successful storm warning system for mariners. The wreck of the 'Royal Charter' gave grim and tragic publicity to the lack of information on meteorological conditions, and the inability to give advanced warning of forthcoming bad weather. The disaster happened at a time when the Board of Trade was already using technological advances such as the collection of weather-data at a central point by the electric telegraph. FitzRoy's system enabled basic weather forecasts to be produced and transmitted around the country to forewarn of approaching gales and storms, and in doing so, the basis of modern weather forecasting was established.

A 'Trotman' anchor from the 'Royal Charter'. This was probably the 'stream-anchor'.

Each link in a chain was made by hand.

The anchor shown above would have been the stream-anchor, used only in calm weather or for hauling a vessel off a sandbank if she had run aground. In that situation, a lightweight anchor such as this could be lowered into the longboat and dropped in deeper water so that the ship could then be hauled out to sea. A stream-anchor was certainly not intended to hold a vessel such as the 'Royal Charter' in position during a hurricane. The main anchors, otherwise known as the bowers, were much heavier than this, with an average weight of over two and a half tons each.

The manufacture of chains was a hot, tedious and extremely physical occupation that required every link to be carefully crafted into shape by hand, when the slightest lack of concentration could result in a chain that could fail while being tested, or perhaps lead to a devastating loss of life in a shipwreck such as took place at Moelfre.

Anchors and Anchor-chains

A month after the disaster, the following letter appeared in the newspapers. Written by the underwriters at Lloyd's to the Board of Trade, they were very unhappy:

Lloyd's, London. Nov. 24, 1859

"To — O'Dowd, Esq., conducting, on behalf of the Board of Trade, the Inquiry into the Loss and Construction of the *Royal Charter,* at Liverpool.

"Sir, We, as underwriters, are severe pecuniary losers by the *Royal Charter,* and it having been stated in the public prints that her chain cables or anchors parted, and consequently that their failure was the primary cause of the catastrophe, and not having observed that an inquiry has been directed with a view to ascertain their efficiency, we respectfully suggest for your consideration that information is desirable.-

As to the diameter of link, length of each cable and weight of each; the number of anchors and weight of each respectively, including stocks; the means taken to ascertain their efficiency when purchased; the date of purchase; the price and makers's names, and why a third cable was not let go when two had parted.

(Signed by twenty-two underwriters)

In other words, the underwriters who had paid out the insurance money blamed the loss of the 'Royal Charter' on the fact that the anchor-chains had failed, so they wanted to know the exact specification of her anchors and chains, or the 'ground-tackle' as it was known. Why wasn't a third anchor let go? After all, she carried four of them, and still had two on board when she came ashore. Why weren't these deployed? It had been stated at the inquiry that the cables had parted at the hawse-holes, so was there any spare chain-cable on board once the main anchors had broken free? If not, why not? Unfortunately, the third anchor seems to have been stowed away in the hold, while the small stream-anchor was kept near the stern. These Trotman anchors were a recent innovation, so perhaps the actual design was at fault despite having won the accolade of being *'the best anchor in the world'* by an international jury in Paris.

Then the letters started flowing in to the newspapers. A seafarer who signed himself 'Circumnavigator' wanted to know why a third anchor wasn't kept ready to be instantly deployed, and advocated that vessels should be built with at least three hawse-pipes so that the three anchors could be used together. 'Circumnavigator' appears to have overlooked the fact that the 'Royal Charter' had four hawse-pipes, but simply didn't have the third and fourth anchors ready for deployment. John Trotman's reputation and business were now at stake, so he contributed the following opinion:

With a knowledge of these facts, derived from an intimate knowledge of the trade, I do not hesitate to assert my belief that scarcely one percent of the anchors and cables now made and sold to the mercantile marine would pass muster in any of Her Majesty's dockyards. In this respect, underwriters, shipowners etc. need legislative protection.

Fortunately for future seafarers, these letters started the ball rolling, and it soon became clear that Trotman's assertion was true, and that new laws were required to ensure that anchors and anchor-chains would all be manufactured and proof-tested to a certain standard. After all, Royal Navy Dockyards checked and proved the quality of Her Majesty's anchors and chains, and, in 1857, Isambard Kingdom Brunel had insisted that the anchors of the 'Great Eastern' must be tested. If this was the course taken by such a well-respected figure, why was the rest of the Merchant Marine exempt from these tests? The arguments continued, and the subject was soon to be raised in the British Parliament.

ANCHORS FOR THE "GREAT EASTERN', ANCHOR-TESTING, etc.

By Admiralty regulation all anchors and cables, before they are issued for service in the Royal Navy, must be submitted to certain proof-strains, by means of an ingeniously-contrived hydraulic apparatus, constructed for that purpose at Her Majesty's Dockyard, Woolwich. One of Trotman's anchors is here undergoing this proving process, to meet the requirements of Mr. Brunel, before it is transferred to the bows of his leviathan steam-ship *Great Eastern*. The proof of an ordinary anchor five tons weight, the largest used in the navy, is 67 tons strain; but in this instance Trotman's anchor will be proved to 105 tons.

The anchor is about to be fixed in position; the fluke is encircled by a ring, and the anchor-shackle will be attached to the lever, so that when the strain is applied there is a tearing asunder of the parts. Thus the genuineness both of material and workmanship is subjected to the severest trial the ingenuity of man could devise. The regulated strain is ascertained in an adjoining office by means of scales attached to the lever, and acted upon similarly to the well-known principle of the steelyard. Ten anchors on Trotman's plan are to be supplied to the *Great Eastern* — viz., six from 6 to 7 tons, and four of 5½ tons each. These will be carried, some at the bows, and a pair astern, to be ready for any emergency. One weighing 6 tons 19 cwt. 2 qrs. was landed last week at Liverpool, en route from Saltney Anchor Works, and caused no little sensation at that port, although the magnificent ships of the Cunard Company, Peninsular and Oriental, Collins' Transatlantic line of packets, also the *Great Britain,* the *Royal Charter*, the *Great Republic*, and the majority of the largest and finest ships now afloat, have long since been supplied with these justly celebrated anchors; the inventor of which it appears was unanimously awarded the grand medal of the first class by the International Jury at Paris in 1855, whose report asserts it "to be the best anchor in the world", and this affirms the correctness of our Government official report "of the trials of Anchors of all Nations" at Sheerness" (1852-53), under the auspices of a committee of naval officers and shipowners, appointed by the Lords Commissioners of the Admiralty, at the instance of the shipowners, underwriters at Lloyd's and United Kingdom generally.

Illustrated London News. September 19, 1857.

Suddenly, the strength and quality of anchor-chains was in the news, as shown in this article from the 'Illustrated London News' less than two months after the disaster.

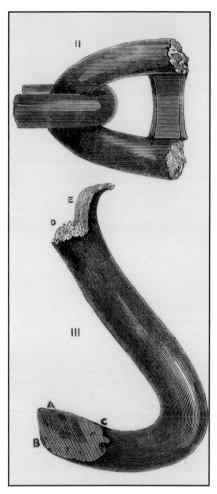

Examples of broken links.

Tests for anchor chains. By far the readiest plan for acquiring a good general idea of the imperfections both of material and workmanship to which chain cables are liable, is to pay a visit to a Government test-house, such as that at Woolwich Dockyard. In a former number, we furnished our readers with an engraving of the interior of the testing-house for anchors and of the hydraulic machinery employed there. The machinery used in testing cables is precisely similar, the only difference between the two houses being that the latter is longer than the first. The machine is a simple hydraulic press laid horizontally on the floor, worked by pumps placed in an adjoining apartment, and connected with a beam and scale, also placed in an adjoining apartment, and so arranged that every pound weight in the scale represents a pressure of one ton in the hydraulic press. Cables for Her Majesty's navy are constructed in lengths of 12½ fathoms (75 feet) each, joined together by shackles. Eight of these lengths, or 100 fathoms, make a cable; each cable being further furnished with four swivels, distributed over its entire length, in order to prevent twisting. The process of testing is very simple. The chain is brought to the test house in its separate lengths, and as each length is laid on the floor one end is made fast to a pair of strong iron "butts" and the other, by an intervening shackle, to the piston-rod of the press. The scale is then weighted according to the Admiralty regulations, which prescribe a certain "breaking strain" for every diameter of chain, and direct the cable to be tested up to two-thirds of the breaking strain. The pumps are next set to work, and the chain stretched taut, after which every one retires to the adjoining apartments, and the hydraulic press and the chain are left to fight it out alone. What a stern struggle it is, and in what a crash it sometimes ends may be gathered from the "honourable scars" which, in the shape of many a dint and trench-like scratch, adorn the stout brick walls of the test-house, as well as from a contemplation of sundry broken links which hang like trophies round the wall of the scale-room. It should be added here that an official watches the scale whilst the pumps are at work, and the moment its rising denotes that the proper amount of pressure has been attained, he rings a bell and ends the struggle. If the length of chain has sustained the pressure it is now regularly tested. Our readers are probably all aware that the links of a chain cable are made of lengths of iron rod, cut, not straight across, but in a slanting direction, and then bent round until the two ends overlap, when they are welded together. In most chains – in all large ones – a stud or stay is added to the middle of the link. In the links of chains less than one inch in diameter, the welding takes place at the end of the link, which is then said to be end-welded; larger links are joined at the side, and are said to be side-welded.

The Chain Cables and Anchors Act of 1864

The disparity between the military and civilian standards for anchors and anchor-chains was now becoming a matter of national importance. Why was there a difference between the two?

> The Select Committee of the House of Commons, appointed a short time since to inquire into the supply of anchors and cables to the merchant service, has recommended the public system of testing to be applied to anchors as well as to cables.

> Caernarfon & Denbigh Herald. April 14, 1860

Of course there was a great difference between a recommendation from a Select Committee and the actual implementation of their plan. Questions were raised as to who was going to pay for the test-facilities and the actual tests, but this telling extract from the Parliamentary debate of 1862 shows the evidence in favour of them.

> Sir James Elphinstone said he had presented a petition in favour of the proposal [*for testing anchors and chain-cables*] from the City of London signed by the representatives of 1,000,000 tons of shipping belonging to that port. The Dock Committee of Liverpool had memorialized their representative to support the motion. The town of Birkenhead was also in favour of it. He believed the only opposition to it arose from a small number of shipowners not quite as careful of the lives of men in their employment as proprietors with larger capital. The manufacturer of the cables on board the *Royal Charter* stated that they were only tested to seventy-two tons, and that if they had been tested to Admiralty proof, that was to say to twenty tons more, in all probability they would not have parted. The additional cost would have been only £1 a ton; and as the ship had thirty or thirty-five tons of cable on board, it followed that 497 human lives were lost for £35 worth of ship's cable. It was stated in a work published by General Brereton that during the great gale of November 14, 1854, in the Black Sea, according to the testimony of the merchant captains, their cables all snapped like glass at a particular period of the gale. The breaking strain was reached at that point; but of the men-of-war lying at Kazatch, not one parted her cable. Thirty transports were lost on that occasion, and the safety of the allied army imperilled solely because the merchant vessels were not supplied with cables properly tested.

The reference to the gale in the Black Sea was the situation in 1854 where numerous supply-ships including the 'Prince' had been wrecked at a critical stage of the Crimean War. See page 209. Could we really have lost that war because the anchor-chains of our merchant-ships were inadequate? Those used by the Royal Navy were subjected to more stringent tests than those for the cables of commercial vessels, and these basic precautions had saved Her Majesty's warships at a time when many British merchant ships and seamen had gone to the bottom of the sea. But this wasn't just people and property at risk - the strategic future of the British Empire was at stake because of a little cost-cutting! Did it not make sense to have legislation ensuring that the anchors and chain-cables of every ship operating under the British flag should be capable of taking the strain, even in hurricane-force winds?

Finally, the Chain Cables and Anchors Act received the Royal Assent on the 23rd of June 1864, whereby an inspector was appointed by the British Government to check that the facilities for testing anchors and anchor-chains were up to the required standard. Anchor-cables that successfully passed the test were to be stamped every five fathoms, while anchors were to be individually marked.

A section of chain, recovered from the wreck of the 'Royal Charter'.

The new legislation led to the establishment of additional testing facilities that included the Lloyd's Cambrian Chain and Anchor Testing Company. This was located alongside Henry Wood's factory at Saltney where the anchor-chains of the 'Royal Charter' had been made. It was expected that the new legislation would put an end to the problem of defective or inadequate cables, but the following letter was sent to the Board of Trade only a few years afterwards, showing that there were still major problems with the manufacturing process of these essential items of safety equipment.

Liverpool,
11th February, 1867.
Sir,

We venture to take the liberty of calling your attention to the unreliable character of certificates of the testing of chains and anchors given under the provisions of the Act of Parliament. Confining ourselves to our own experiences and beginning with the month of November, 1865, no less than seven cases have occurred of the breaking of new and duly certified chain cables in use on board steam vessels of which we are owners. In all these cases the certificates were such as would comply with the requirements of the Board of Trade surveyors. The latest of these cases, that of the screw-steamer *Donati*, which happened in the River Mersey on the 8th inst., affords means for minute inquiry into the circumstances, in the event of your considering the subject sufficiently important for such an investigation. This steamer was supplied with two cables, 150 fathoms each, of 1 9/16 inch chain. A copy of the testing certificate is enclosed herein. Both cables broke successively, almost immediately after the anchors were dropped, and while there was but little strain upon them. One of the cables had never been used before; the other had been used only once before. We may be forgiven for adding that so many cases of broken chains had not occurred to us in our previous twenty years experience as ship-owners.

We are, etc.

Lamport and Holt.

SHIPWRECK!
CHARLES DICKENS
& The Royal Charter

Charles Dickens, the famous novelist of the 19th century, visited Llanallgo and the scene of the wreck during late 1859 and early 1860, probably in search of news of the Hogarth family who were closely related to his wife. Dickens left us with a vivid description of the work that was being undertaken by the Hughes brothers in identifying and burying the bodies:

> From the church, we passed out into the churchyard. Here, there lay at that time, one hundred and forty-five bodies that had come ashore from the wreck. He had buried them, when not identified, in graves containing four each. He had numbered each body in a register describing it, and had placed a corresponding number on each coffin and over each grave. Identified bodies he had buried singly, in private graves, in another part of the church-yard.

Dickens also praised their strenuous efforts at comforting the relatives and friends of the dead:

> Down to yesterday's post outward, my clergyman alone had written one thousand and seventy five letters to relatives and friends of the lost people!

An excellent narrative of Dickens and his visit to the wreck is given in the above book. For further details, visit llyfrau-magma.co.uk

CHAPTER FOURTEEN

The Reverends S. R. Hughes and H.R. Hughes

Stephen Roose Hughes was rector of St. Gallgo's Church, Llanallgo, where the stipend was worth £135 per annum, and his brother, the Reverend Hugh Robert Hughes was rector of the nearby Penrhos Lligwy Church, where the stipend was £75 per annum. Stephen Roose Hughes lived at the rectory adjacent to St. Gallgo's Church, Llanallgo, along with his wife, Jane Anne, and his sisters-in-law, Margaret Augusta Moulsdale and Mary Hester Moulsdale. No-one could have prepared them for the horror of the aftermath of the wreck, when the area around Moelfre was besieged by relatives and friends of the dead in the hope of finding and identifying the body of a loved one, and ensuring that it was buried by the appropriate authority in accordance with the deceased person's religious beliefs. What a task that must have been, with the complex problem of recording the details of a rapidly decaying, badly-battered corpse before it could be interred. Graves that containing unidentified bodies sometimes had to be reopened so that visitors could view the remains, a rather traumatic situation that needed to be repeated time and time again. At least the efforts of the Hughes family were being recognised:

The kindness shown by Mr. and Mrs. Hughes should not go unnoticed; the services of the Rev. Mr. Hughes are very great. The corpses, as they are recovered, are all numbered in succession; and previous to the interment of those bodies which are unrecognised, Mr. Hughes commits to writing some of their most striking peculiarities for the inspection of those parties who might arrive too late.

Caernarfon & Denbigh Herald. November 5, 1859.

Sir, having lost a dear son in the late fatal wreckage of the "Royal Charter", I consider it my duty to make known to the public the Christian kindness of the Rev. Mr. Hughes, rector of Llanallgo, and his family, to all who may arrive on the spot who had lost relatives and friends. My youngest son, on reading the news of the loss of the vessel in which his dear brother was, instantly started for the spot, quite unprepared for so long a journey; but on his arrival, the Reverend gentleman kindly took him by the hand, and upon his recognizing his poor brother's body, endeavoured to soothe his grief, found him a bed, provided him with what he wanted, and on Saturday, kindly buried my lost boy, and accompanied my son on the road to meet me, blessing him at parting with him. This worthy gentleman, not only showed kindness to my son, but to every one who arrived at the scene of the wreck to look for relative or friend, his house was open. When I was there on Saturday, everyone was speaking after his exertions and kindness; indeed, every one in the neighbourhood seems to do his utmost to assist the bereaved ones. Your insertion of this will oblige, Sir.

Yours respectfully, James Walton.

Chester Chronicle. November 5, 1859

Then there was the financial burden of the cost of the coffins, the burial expenses and other incidental outlays, but donations soon flooded in, including the following:
Gibbs, Bright & Co. £50; G. Maworth, Mold. £5; Mrs. Roose. £1; Mr. Gillett. London. £1; Mr. Ed. Mellish, Surrey. £10; The congregation of St. Marks, Liverpool. £21; Lady Willoughby de Broke. £5; Mr. Trout. 10s.; Mrs. Rogers, Blackpool. £1; Edmund Swetenham, Esq., Chester. £5; The 'Tayleur Committee', Ireland. £20; Subscribed by the Irish Gentry. £21; Mrs. Abraham Howell, Welshpool. £5; Mr. Coupland, Bangor. £1; Miss Roberts, of the George Hotel, Bangor Ferry. £3; Major Egerton Lee, Chester. £1; Miss Williams, Warwick. £3; Mrs. C. Hopkins, Shropshire. £5; and Mrs. Bulkeley Allen, Manchester. £2 10s. etc.

In addition to their duties at Moelfre, the two brothers even went as far as London in their quest to obtain closure for as many of the families as possible.

The *Royal Charter*. A painful incident in connection with the wreck of this ship occurred on Saturday at Brompton Cemetery. Among the passengers lost were a whole family named Pitcher, consisting of father and mother and two children, with their nurse. Mr. Pitcher was brother of the eminent ship-builder bearing his name at Northfleet. He was formerly connected with Messrs. Dent's house in China, but had been for some years resident at Geelong, where, although only 42 years of age, he had acquired a fortune, and was returning to England for retirement. His wife was 29 years of age, and his children respectively of the ages three and one year. The eldest (a boy) was among the first to be washed on shore on the morning of the wreck, and had medical assistance been at hand his life, it is stated, might have been spared, for after being picked up the little fellow was observed to sigh and place his left hand convulsively across his breast. In such a terrible moment of excitement, however, nothing could be done for him on that bleak spot. His remains were soon recognised by one of the saved passengers, and the body, having been placed in a coffin, was taken in charge by the Rev. S.R. Hughes, the humane and highly respected incumbent of the Welsh village of Llanallgo. The body of Mrs. Pitcher came ashore at Moelfre, not far from the scene of the wreck, and, although the remains had been in the water more than a month, her features were easily recognised by comparison with a photographic portrait in the possession of her relatives. Mr. Pitcher's remains were brought ashore by a fisherman in Bull Bay, a small creek about two miles west of Amlwch, at a considerable distance from the wreck. When found the pockets of his trousers had been cut across and their contents abstracted*, and nothing being observed to lead to identification, the body was buried with two or three others, as those of persons unknown. Subsequently it was ascertained from an article of clothing that the remains must have been those of Mr. Pitcher, and the body having been exhumed, was, together with those of Mrs. Pitcher and their little boy, placed in charge of Mr. Griffiths Davies, of Bangor, who completed the necessary arrangements for their interment in one grave in the Brompton Cemetery, and brought the remains to London by the mail train on Saturday morning. The mourners assembled at the Victoria Hotel, about 1 o'clock, at which hour the coffins were brought over from the Euston Station in two hearses. Those who followed, consisting almost exclusively of relatives and friends of the deceased lady and gentleman, occupied three mourning coaches. The only strangers were the Rev. S.R. Hughes and the Rev. H.R. Hughes, brothers, and fellow labourers in the two parishes of Llanallgo and Penrhoslligwy, adjoining the scene of the wreck, of whose truly Christian virtues since the occurrence of the awful catastrophe it is impossible to speak too highly. On the arrival of the funeral cortege at the cemetery, the bodies were removed into the chapel, where the Rev. S.R. Hughes read the service appointed for the burial of the dead in an impressive manner. Each of the coffins bore a brass plate, upon which was engraved the name of the deceased person, and the date on which the body had been cast ashore from the wreck of the *Royal Charter*. The funeral was conducted as privately as possible, and none of the circumstances having been allowed to transpire in the neighbourhood, the mourners were permitted to pay the last tribute of affection to the sufferers without any molestation from the vulgar curiosity of a crowd.

North Wales Chronicle.
December 17, 1859.

* The same paper says that this was *'totally erroneous and totally devoid of truth'.*

Mrs. Hughes and her two sisters were also involved in the grim and painful task of identifying the bodies, preparing the corpses for burial, and consoling the dozens of bereaved visitors to Moelfre. One helpful letter published in the newspapers suggested that the relatively-new invention of photography could prove invaluable in ensuring that each gravestone was engraved with the correct name, but there is no record of this course of action having been taken, probably due to the scarcity and cost of a camera.

Llanallgo, Anglesey. The Late Wreck.

The attention and compassionate hospitality shown by the Misses Moulsdale, of the Rectory, to the friends and relations of the unfortunates at Moelfre, are worthy of particular notice. These ladies have been actively engaged since that awful catastrophe in accommodating and relieving those parties who come to the church for the identification of their drowned friends. Nor have their merciful services been less towards the dead bodies of the unfortunate creatures. These excellent ladies are diligently employed day and night in making shrouds and other articles for the dead, and the most marked sympathy pervades all their efforts. The kindness shown by Mr. and Mrs. Hughes should not go unnoticed; the services of the Rev. Mr. Hughes are very great. Amongst the ladies and gentlemen who have liberally contributed towards furnishing clothing for the corpses may be also mentioned, Mr. and Mrs. Williams, Tyddyn, Llanbedrgoch, Mrs. Jones, ditto, Rev. M. Hughes, Pentraeth, and Miss Roberts, of the George Hotel etc.

Caernarfon & Denbigh Herald. November 5, 1859

The task took many weeks, as bodies continued to be washed up along the shore or were recovered by boats out at sea. Stephen Roose Hughes wasn't the only clergyman giving comfort to the bereaved, as his brother was also performing a similar role in attempting to identify the deceased. Meanwhile, the salvage operation was still releasing bodies from the wreck, with the corpses of two sailors being found a whole month after the disaster.

The Rev. H.R. Hughes, of Amlwch, writes from Amlwch,

November 27, 1859.

Dear Sir,

From the peculiar striking characters in the enclosed descriptions of bodies brought up to my church on the 26th Nov., I am inclined to hope that you will be good enough to give them publicity in your next issue. The body of a sailor, about 5 feet 9 inches, having on two woollen Guernsey frocks and a pair of trousers; on the Guernsey, 'L & A.N. Co.'; devices on the right arm - the Crucifixion and a man and female; the forehead and vesture on the Crucifixion stained red. On one side of the cross the appearance of the son with a halo of red dots; on the head of the cross an imitation of the letters "I.H.S." On the left arm, a man and a female dancing, with an effort to delineate the female's dress. On the right arm were also the initials of the person's name in large letters "M.R.L." The body of a man, also a sailor, about six feet. On the lower part of the right arm, the device of a sailor and a female, the man holding a Union Jack with a streamer, the folds waving over the female's head and the end of it in her hand. On the upper part of the arm, a device of the Crucifixion, with stars surrounding the head of the cross and a large star on the side of the cross, all in Indian ink, and on the side of the left arm the letters 'H.S.', an English flag, and a mock imitation of a face.

North Wales Chronicle. December 3, 1859

The Hughes Offering and the Memorial Stone at Moelfre

People and organisations from all walks of life supported the idea of donating money to the Reverends Stephen Roose Hughes and Hugh Robert Hughes to thank them for their efforts in identifying the victims of the disaster, comforting the relatives of the bereaved and ensuring that the remains were buried according to the rituals of their faith. It was also proposed that a memorial should be erected at Llanallgo church, to be dedicated to *"the memory of those who perished in the wreck of the 'Royal Charter'"* on that fatal morning of the 26th of October, 1859.

The Hughes Offering
and Memorial Stone at Moelfre.

The powerful and inimitable pen of Charles Dickens, while depicting in No. 40 (Jan 8) of "All the Year Round" the truly awful and melancholy scene of the Wreck of the *Royal Charter*, does noble and well-deserved homage to the Rev. Messrs. Hughes, the two most Christian brother clergymen on whom, by Divine Providence, fell the duty of examining, for the purpose of identification and burial about 230 bodies of the 500 lost in the ill-fated vessel. "It became their duty", wrote a reporter on the spot "to protect all marks, clothes, or property by which each body could be identified; and, lastly, to comfort, console, satisfy, and give hospitable shelter, not only to those who had escaped the engulphing sea, but to the relatives and friends of the deceased, who, as soon as the fatal tidings had spread far and near upon the wings of the telegraph, came hastening from all parts of the Kingdom to learn tidings of the lost and loved."

The object, therefore, of this subscription is to repay those benevolent gentlemen the actual cost their arduous and well fulfilled duties have imposed upon them, adding, if possible, a small testimonial in grateful recognition of their Christian services, and to erect at the entrance to the churchyard at Moelfre, a monolith to the memory of those who perished, above 200 having been there buried. We do not despair of obtaining the required amount, feeling sure there are yet many benevolent persons of all denominations who never will allow a memorial of so truly deserving a character to pass unaided by them.

We did not think it necessary to resort to the usual course of endeavouring to form an influential committee to carry out the object required, trusting that the merits of the case would plead successfully.

Subscriptions will be thankfully received and acknowledged by Messrs. Prescott, Grote and Co., bankers, Threadneedle-street; the Commercial Bank, Henrietta-street, Covent Garden; and by ourselves; also by our nephew, Mr. Arthur Rich, 13, Wellington-street, Strand, who daily, at Moelfre during a period of six weeks, while in search for the remains of our deceased relative (Mr. Montague Pitcher, of Geelong, his wife, two infant children, and nurse), witnessed the unremitting exertions of the clergymen named.

S. Leigh Sotheby,
The Woodlands, Norwood, Surrey.

Henry Sotheby Pitcher,
Dockyard, Northfleet, Kent.

At the close of the subscription, after the remainder of the wreck of the *Royal Charter* has been brought to land and the more immediate services of the two clergymen are concluded, a sketch of the Memorial Stone now being erected at Moelfre will be forwarded to each of the contributors, together with a statement of the receipts and expenses. It is proposed to present to the Rev. S.R. Hughes two-thirds, and to the Rev. H.R. Hughes the remaining third of the balance.

The Times.
Monday, July 2, 1860.

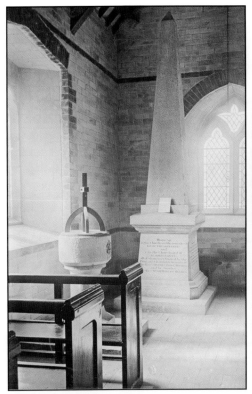

Previously placed inside Llanallgo church, the memorial now rests in the churchyard.

The appeal certainly attracted the attention of the public, despite there being other requests to support the families of the bereaved, such as the one for the dependants of the Reverend Charles Hodge.

-- the fund at Manchester for the family of the late Rev. C. Hodge, lost in the *Royal Charter*, which was commenced a month ago by Mr. Cooper, now reaches about £500.

Donations to the 'Hughes Offering' came from near and far, with 286 donations totalling £357 14s. by August, 1860, an impressive response that showed just how highly the two clergymen were held in esteem by the British public after the trauma of the previous winter. Meanwhile, the sea was still taking its toll of life around the shores of Britain, with yet another appeal that shared a page of 'The Times' alongside the list of donations to 'The Hughes Fund'. This article appeared on the 13th of August, 1860, to prove that a mariner's life was not an easy one.

An Appeal on Behalf of the Widows and Orphans of the poor Fishermen and Mariners lost during the Late Gale. The recent awful visitation of Providence in the fearfully sudden gale of the 21st of May, on the eastern shores of the kingdom, has swept into eternity 192 steady and industrious men in the prime of life, earning their livelihood by honest labour for themselves, their wives and families. The large proportion of those lost were fishermen connected with Yarmouth and Lowestoft, and the adjoining villages in Norfolk and Suffolk, and prosecuting a valuable branch of national industry. The hard-earned wages of the husbands and parents in previous fisheries had already been spent during a winter of unprecedented length and severity, and more than 76 widows and 192 children are bereaved of their natural supporters, and left in a destitute and helpless condition.

The illness and death of Stephen Roose Hughes

The inclement weather and the stress of coping with so much death and sorrow put an enormous strain on the health of Stephen Roose Hughes, so that by the middle of September 1860, the newspapers were reporting that he had fallen ill:

The *Royal Charter*. The public, and especially the friends of the 500 persons wrecked in the above ship, will be sorry to learn that the Rev. Stephen Hughes, the truly good clergyman of Llanallgo, has been confined to bed for many weeks, from a severe attack of rheumatic fever, brought on by continued exposure during the inclement winter of the past year, in the dreary bay of Moelfra. A correspondent, who called to thank the worthy clergyman for his kind attention to the wishes of the widow of the lamented Dr. Hatch, the surgeon of the *Royal Charter* whose remains are interred at Llanallgo, heard it with that regret which he feels will be participated in by a sympathising public generally.

Caernarvon and Denbigh Herald. September 15, 1860

Sadly, the health of Stephen Roose Hughes declined, and he died on the 4th of February, 1862, to be buried at Llanallgo close to the graves of many of those who perished on that terrible dawn of just over two years beforehand.

Death of the Rev. Stephen Roose Hughes. Deep regret will be felt by our readers and a widely-extended circle at the announcement in our obituary column, recording the sudden death of the Rev. Stephen Roose Hughes, the esteemed Rector of Llaneugrad and Llanallgo, at the comparatively early age of forty-seven. The lamented gentleman's name will not readily be forgotten as one of the two excellent brothers who took such an active and laborious part in the work of benevolence upon the loss of the *Royal Charter* on the Anglesey coast. The reverend gentleman's exertions in relieving the sufferings, both mental and physical, of those who survived were untiring, while he was equally indefatigable in burying the dead, and writing innumerable letters to the sorrowing friends of the deceased, entertaining those relatives who visited the scene of the disastrous wreck with an hospitality as unbounded as it was unostentatious. A more simple-hearted Christian love towards his fellow-man than that exhibited by Mr. Hughes throughout the whole of the mournful period of the wreck could not be imagined.

Caernarvon and Denbigh Herald. February 8, 1862

The situation meant that Mrs. Hughes and her sisters no longer had a home or source of income, leading to her friends appealing for assistance for them.

The sudden demise of the late much respected Rev. Stephen R. Hughes, in the very prime of life, has imposed upon society a certain, and it is to be hoped not unpleasing, duty – that of contributing to the financial exigencies of his estimable widow. Owing to the value of the Rectory being small, (about £140 per annum) it is but too clear that no provision could be made for Mrs. Hughes. A few friends who met at the funeral, the service of which was conducted by the Rev. Hugh Owen of Llanerchymedd, proposed that a committee should be formed to receive subscriptions with the view to secure a small annuity for the bereaved lady. Several gentlemen have consented to act on the committee, and Mr. Owen has kindly undertaken to act as secretary. As the necessary arrangements could not be completed so as to announce the matter by way of an advertisement in this impression, we have been requested to prepare the public for a more formal appeal. There can be no doubt that, whatever the immediate cause of it may have been, Mr. Hughes's death was hastened by over-work and exertion at the time of the disastrous wreck of the *Royal Charter*. Those who have known him for many years, have observed that he declined rapidly from the over-exertions of that period:

The grave of the Reverend Stephen Roose Hughes, at Llanallgo churchyard.

and it is to be feared that his widow is on the verge of being literally destitute. To those who bear in memory the assiduous untiring zeal of the good pastor in the case of the aforesaid wreck, no lengthened argument will be needed on behalf of his widow; for if she be left to suffer either the fierce reality or the almost equally harassing anticipation of penury, it would be a living and lasting reproach to the community.

Caernarvon and Denbigh Herald. February 15, 1862

This local appeal was quickly declined by Mrs. Hughes, and a letter to this effect appeared in the Caernarfon and Denbigh Herald a week later. However, she did write to a Mrs. Nanney on the 7th of March, 1862, in which she states:

My beloved husband's sudden death has indeed robbed me of all support. .... On the day of his death, he had been engaged all the morning in visiting his poor parishioners, and returned home to tea, happy and cheerful; in ten minutes after tea was over, when sitting in his chair by the fire, he expired without a sigh, smiling even in death!

Her plight was made public by the Reverend Hugh Nanney, who appealed for donations to be sent to himself or to a bank. Contributions soon flowed in from local and national well-wishers, with donations to this worthy cause from the Board of Trade, various insurance companies, Charles Dickens and even Lord Palmerston, the British Prime Minister. This reached over £600, with further monies being sent from Australia:

The intelligence lately received of the death of the Reverend Mr. Hughes, well known for his exertions on the occasion of the wreck of the *Royal Charter,* has created a very general sympathy for his widow and children. Without any pre-concerted plan or effort to raise subscriptions, some merchants and others have commenced voluntary collections, and the amount already succeeds £400. The publication of the list will stimulate further exertions, and I feel very little doubt a considerable contribution will be transmitted from this colony, and probably from the neighbouring colony also.

The Times. Saturday, August 16, 1862

Memorial

Porth Helaeth   Reef   'Royal

Wreck of the 'Hindlea'

The shingle-beach of Porth Helaeth, the memorial and the actual wreck-site. It is often thought that the 'Royal Charter' would have been safe had she run ashore at Porth Helaeth, but note the reef that becomes exposed at low-water to partially block the bay.

The 'Seawatch Centre' at Moelfre provides a convenient starting-point for a visit to the wreck-site, where a statue of lifeboat coxswain Dic Evans looks out over Moelfre Bay. Artefacts from the wreck, paintings and memorials are on display here, while guidebooks and further information can be obtained.

The wreckage at the foot of the cliffs near Porth Hellaeth is the remains of the motor-vessel 'Hindlea', which was wrecked here in October, 1959. Dic Evans was awarded a gold medal for his part in the rescue of her crewmen, with one silver and three bronze medals being awarded to his fellow lifeboatmen.

CHAPTER FIFTEEN

The Wreck of the 'Royal Charter', 150 Years Later.

This memorial to the disaster was erected in 1935. The arrow points to the wreck-site. The small island on the horizon is known as Ynys Dulas or Dulas Island.

W.F. Peacock wrote a book in 1860 in which he describes his visit to Moelfre in June of that year. Entitled "A Ramble to the Wreck of the 'Royal Charter'", Peacock introduced his book with this text:

> Accompany me to the scene of disaster! I have been there before, and am going again. As the shortest and most expeditious route, let us take tickets from Manchester to Bangor direct. We can then go by car or on foot to Moelfra, the little hamlet in Anglesea, within a mile of which lies all that is left of the *Royal Charter*. And, believe me, you will not readily forget your experience of the wreck, for in the memory of the oldest Welshman, such a wreck was never before known.

The cliff-top walk past the scene of the wreck forms part of the Anglesey Coastal Path, for which guidebooks are available. This a very pleasant experience on a warm, calm summer's day, but the same trek in a north-easterly gale makes you realise just how horrendous the scene was at daylight on the 26th of October, 1859.

Leave your car at the Seawatch Centre in Moelfre, and follow the path past the lifeboat station. The memorial shown above lies less than a mile to the west of Moelfre. The footpath can be difficult even in good weather, while the adjoining cliffs are extremely dangerous due to their vertical faces, loose boulders, deep pools and slippery seaweed. Take great care if you decide to venture away from the security of the footpath!

The remains of the 'Royal Charter'

Having been extensively salvaged, very little wreckage stands proud of the seabed.

This sheet of iron is covered in marine-life such as kelp, starfish and nudibranch eggs.

To fully appreciate how the 'Royal Charter' was built, visit the Seawatch Centre in Moelfre where a section of the hull has been preserved after being recovered from the wreck. See the photo on page 206. Here, you can identify the techniques used to fasten the hull-plates together using a series of iron rivets. Other broken pieces of the wreck still lie in shallow water at the base of a series of limestone ledges between Moelfre and Lligwy, about 200 metres to the west of the memorial erected in memory of those lost in the disaster. These few remnants of the clipper lie only two or three metres deep at low-water on a spring-tide, when it is possible for a diver to stand on the highest point of the wreck with his or her head in the fresh air. Amongst this maritime scrapyard, there are still a few sections of hull that remain partially intact, where divers can see how the iron plates and curved ribs were riveted together to form the outer shell of the vessel. Although the 'Royal Charter' was quite a large vessel of over 2,700 tons, it must be remembered that much of the hull was dragged ashore by the Victorian divers and salvage-workers in their quest for the gold, and that salvage-work has continued here sporadically since 1859 with the result that there is very little wreckage still remaining for divers to explore. Today, most of the remaining ironwork has been covered by a thick layer of sand and boulders to reveal very little to a visiting diver, whist any wreckage that does stand proud of the seabed is mostly hidden under a cloak of seaweed and soft corals.

Artefacts from the wreck

The crest of the Liverpool & Australia Navigation Co. features a Liver Bird, the emblem of Liverpool, and a Kangaroo to represent Australia. This piece of broken crockery was found on the wreck, and is shown here with Australian sovereigns and gold dust.

When the 'Royal Charter' was wrecked, it contained not only a treasure of gold, but a wealth of personal possessions from the middle of the 19th century, as many people were returning to England with all their worldly possessions. Many items of low value have been recovered over the last 150 years to lie dispersed among the many divers who have visited the stretch of coast to the west of Porth Helaeth at Moelfre. Some of these artefacts are on display at Anglesey museums such as Oriel Mon at Llangefni, the Seawatch Centre at Moelfre, Holyhead Maritime Museum and Amlwch Heritage Centre, while others can be seen at Liverpool Maritime Museum, where a display-cabinet holds a section of the hawser that was hauled ashore to save some of the passengers and crew.

Many hundredweights of coal were brought up from the wreck in the 1980s, proving that there was still enough fuel to keep the fires alight in the boilers, while several blocks and pulleys that operated her sails have been found in excellent condition. Cooking-pots, eating-utensils, umbrellas, propelling-pencils, letter-holders, spectacles, candlesticks, candle holders and leather boots have been some of the common finds, but care is certainly needed when opening any sealed stoneware-jars, as one was found to contain some rather smelly prunes!

Modern-day divers using an airlift, an underwater vacuum-cleaner powered by compressed air.

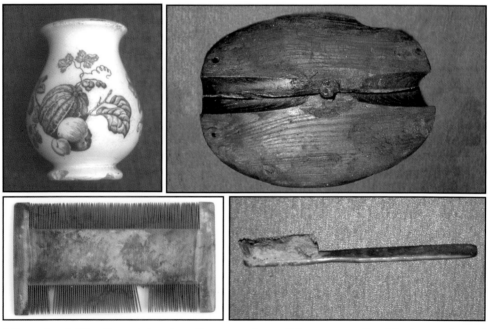

Although of little financial value, items such as this vase, pulley-block, comb and toothbrush provide a small insight into what life was like aboard the 'Royal Charter'.

Marine-life around the wreck

The wreck lies in shallow, often murky water, in an area that is not particularly renowned for its marine-life. The turbidity of the water and the lack of suitable holdfasts means that there is relatively little seaweed growing here, but there is quite a variety of fish and crustaceans, while even an occasional mammal puts in an appearance. The wildlife is particularly noticeable when divers disturb the seabed in the hope of recovering an artefact from amongst the debris. Any disturbance quickly exposes worms and other tiny creatures, to provide an easy feast for the larger animals.

Poor-cod swimming over riveted hull-plates.

A hermit-crab and a masked-crab.

Poor-cod, wrasse, tiny flounders, hermit-crabs, velvet swimming-crabs, masked-crabs, starfish, honeycomb-worms, sea-slugs and plumose anemones are easily spotted by divers, but octopus have also been sighted here, peering into any newly-excavated hole in the seabed. Seals occasionally visit the wreck, seemingly to enjoy the company of human beings. One of these mammals lay alongside a diver for many minutes, allowing him to stroke its stomach, while another seal pushed a diver out of the way in a bid to see what he was doing with an airlift. It then proceeded to play with the author's underwater metal-detector by pushing its snout firmly into the loop of the electronic unit. Further offshore, dolphins and porpoise are a common sight at Point Lynas and at Moelfre Island, where they are often seen leaping completely out of the water.

Approaching the shore-line from out at sea, a diver will find that the underwater terrain changes quite abruptly from a flat, sandy seabed to a coastline of large boulders and small, underwater cliffs. These vertical walls have a series of narrow gullies and small caves that have a sprinkling of soft corals known as *Alcyonium Digitatum,* more commonly known as *Dead-men's Fingers.* Perhaps this is a most appropriate name, given the number of people who died at this very spot.

A narrow gully, lined with dead-men's fingers.

Life and death on the 'Royal Charter'. A hermit-crab under attack by a cuttlefish.

A cuttlefish ready to attack or retreat.

Well-camouflaged cuttlefish lurk here in search of food, so divers can sometimes observe them as they launch an attack on a potential source of food such as a hermit-crab, a small crustacean that uses an empty mollusc shell for protection. Of a similar size to its attacker, the hermit-crab is easily visible at the left of the photograph above, but can you identify the cuttlefish that has changed its colour to perfectly blend in with the seabed? If not, check our website. On this occasion, the cuttlefish was seen to make at least half-a-dozen attempts to drag the hermit-crab out of its shell before it gave up and headed off in search of an easier meal. They may be only two to three inches long (5 to 8 cms), but cuttlefish certainly are formidable predators of the shallow seas.

Fossils, graffiti, and strange sounds

One of many fossils found along this coast.

Was R.W. working here in 1866?

 As already mentioned, great care must be taken by anyone venturing away from the path and onto the rocks near to the wreck-site. There are loose boulders, vertical cliffs, narrow crevices and slippery seaweed that can easily cause a broken limb or worse. Please do not add to the list of casualties. Even Alexander McKee, the author of 'The Golden Wreck', broke a leg here.

If you do visit the site, look carefully at the limestone, where you can see the fossilised skeletons of a variety of ancient creatures embedded in the rock.

As well as fossils, there is a certain amount of graffiti that has been scratched into the limestone rock, most of which seems to be people's initials and the date that they visited the site. For example, R.W. appears to have visited the site in 1866, but what was he or she doing here? A relative of one of those who died in October 1859; a salvage worker idling his time while bad weather made it impossible to work, or are these simply the initials of a curious visitor who wanted to see the final resting place of the 'Royal Charter'?

It is also possible to see where various holes have been cut into the rock, presumably as part of the salvage attempts of the 1860s when a succession of salvage companies that included Gibbs, Bright & Co. were using ropes and sheerlegs to rip the wreck apart in their quest for the gold. See the painting on page 224.

Waves crashing on the rocks on a relatively calm day.

Watching and listening to the waves as they crash onto the rocks during an easterly gale only gives a small notion of the horror that befell those aboard the 'Royal Charter' on that fateful night in October, 1859. The cracks, gullies and crevices that litter the flat strata must have broken dozens of limbs and split many a skull, as hundreds of bodies were washed to and fro in the maelstrom. Even when standing here on a calm day, the scene isn't totally peaceful. Limestone is a porous rock, and at low-tide, just the slightest swell is enough to force air up through small holes in the rock to produce a mournful wail reminiscent of deep and laboured breathing at the place where over 400 lives were lost. Standing here and listening to this naturally produced sound really does make the hairs prickle on the back of your neck. Log-on to our website at www.calgopublications.co.uk to listen to this strange and disturbing noise.

Places of interest associated with the 'Royal Charter'

The site of Cram's shipyard at Sandycroft near Chester is now largely overgrown with woodland, but a public footpath leads onto the bank of the River Dee from where the tidal-bore can be watched as this naturally formed wave makes its way upstream towards Chester on the floodtide.

Saint Gallgo's Church at Llanallgo near Moelfre was used as a temporary mortuary for the bodies that were recovered from the wreck. This is where many of the bodies were interred, and the churchyard has a memorial to those who died in the tragedy. The Reverend Stephen Roose Hughes was buried here.

The Seawatch Centre at Moelfre has a collection of artefacts from the wreck, including a length of chain and a section of hull-plates, along with personal items that have been recovered by divers. Keith Shone's superb painting of the wreck is on display, along with Sam Holland's stunning bronzes of the disaster. Books and prints are available here, giving further details of the area and the wreck.

Penrhos Lligwy Church lies within two miles of the wreck of the 'Royal Charter', and the Reverend Hugh Robert Hughes was rector of this church in 1859. According to the inscription on the memorial at Llanallgo, forty-five victims were buried here, but many of the graves are unmarked. The Hogarth family, relatives of the wife of Charles Dickens, were buried together in this churchyard.

Llaneugrad, Llanwenllwyfo, Llanddyfnan, Llanfairmathafarneithaf, Llanbedrgoch, Llanddona, Pentraeth, and Amlwch Cemeteries on Anglesey also hold the graves of people lost in the disaster.

Point Lynas Lighthouse affords a spectacular view westwards to the Skerries and eastwards to the approaches to the River Mersey. Note that the building and headland are privately owned.

Amlwch Heritage Centre at Port Amlwch has a fine display of artefacts from many of the local shipwrecks.

The Oriel Mon centre at Llangefni has a display that includes a model of the 'Royal Charter' and artefacts from the wreck.

Holyhead Maritime Museum on the seafront in Holyhead is well worth a visit, as items from many wrecks, including the 'Royal Charter', are on display there.

Liverpool Maritime Museum has a large area dedicated to those who emigrated from that port during the Victorian era, and displays a small collection of artefacts from the wreck of the 'Royal Charter' including a lifebelt and a gold ring. Of particular poignance is a small piece of the hawser that provided an escape-route for some of the survivors.

What happened to the 'Ships of Iron'?

The 'Great Britain'. Having been scuttled at Sparrow Cove in the remote Falkland Islands in the South Atlantic, one would have thought that the 'Great Britain' was destined to slowly rust away and disintegrate. To the delight of anyone with an interest in our maritime heritage, she was rescued from that fate, and returned to Bristol on the 19th of July, 1970, where she can be visited in the dry-dock that was her birthplace. Restored, but in need of constant attention, she is a prime example of an iron-built vessel from the middle of the nineteenth century.

The 'Tayleur'. The remains of the 'Tayleur' can still be explored by divers who visit the waters off Lambay Island on the east coast of Ireland, around fifteen miles north of Dublin.

The 'Great Eastern'. Having narrowly escaped the same fate as that which befell the 'Royal Charter', the 'Great Eastern' steamed out of Holyhead on the 2nd of November, 1859, for what was believed to be a much safer berth at Southampton. This proved to be an unfortunate move for Captain Harrison, who was drowned there in January, 1860, when his small boat overturned. Beset by financial problems, the maiden voyage of the 'Great Eastern' took place in 1860 with a visit to New York, but this and other transatlantic crossings proved uneconomical due to a lack of passengers, while a contract with the British Government lasted for only a single journey.

The first transatlantic telegraph cable had been laid to great acclaim in 1858, but this worked for just a short period of time before communication failed, and efforts to repair the fault were abandoned. With the ability to carry an immense amount of telegraph-cable, the 'Great Eastern' was introduced to a new career, that of creating the communications-network that was to link countries and continents around the world by thin strands of wire. This certainly wasn't the future that Brunel had envisaged for his 'Leviathan', but this task proved to be perfect for his creation, and a remedy for the financial woes of her owners. The 'Great Eastern' then spent the years 1865 to 1874 creating a network of undersea-cables that provided rapid communications across the Atlantic and Indian oceans, before her useful days were over. Laid up for many years at Milford Haven in South Wales, she was scrapped at Tranmere on the River Mersey in 1888.

'H.M.S. Megaera'. Originally designed as a man-of-war, this ship was down-rated to a troopship when tests appeared to show that an iron hull provided poor resistance to cannon-fire. As previously mentioned, it was stated in 1859 that:

> thousands of rivets are now in her bottom which can be knocked out by a common punch from the inside.

Amazingly, she was repaired on several occasions, and continued in her duties until her luck finally ran out in June 1871, when holes appeared in her hull while she was somewhere in the vast ocean between South Africa and Australia. With seawater gushing into her hull, the vessel managed to reach the remote island of St. Pauls, where she sank in shallow water.

'H.M.S. Birkenhead'. Like the 'Megaera', the 'Birkenhead' had been down-rated to act as a troopship before she was wrecked off the South African coast. With a reported treasure of 120 boxes of specie aboard, it isn't surprising that the wreck of the 'Birkenhead' has attracted the attention of several groups of salvors. Gold and silver coins have been recovered, along with regimental buttons, spoons, knife-handles and many other artefacts.

A Few Questions Answered

Was Captain Taylor drunk?

Despite an attempt to tarnish his name, all the witnesses at the inquest and the inquiry stated that he was perfectly sober. There would have been a tremendous outcry and intense legal proceedings if it had been proven that Captain Taylor was intoxicated and unable to make well-judged decisions in such a testing situation. However, this letter was published on the 15th of November, 1859, after the inquest, but while the inquiry was taking place. Given that Captain Taylor had previously been described as *'having a ruddy face, a quick, abrupt manner, and a husky utterance which naturally proclaimed him intoxicated'*, is Mr. Ferris describing the appearance of a drunken sailor, or was this how anyone would look under the intense pressure brought on by the impeding devastation of his ship, his crew and the hundreds of men, women and children who had entrusted their lives to his care? We shall never know.

THE WRECK OF THE ROYAL CHARTER – THE LATE CAPTAIN TAYLOR

Sir,

After coolly deliberating about the propriety of keeping secret what I know of Captain Taylor at the time of the wreck, and the benefit that may result to the public by my making it known, I feel it is my duty to state the following:-

About half-past three o'clock on the morning of the wreck, I passed through the second cabin into the lower saloon, and right up the stairs that led to the upper saloon. I then walked along the division between the bed-rooms and sitting-rooms, which was about a yard wide. I had only gone about eight yards along when I saw Captain Taylor coming forward to a number of young ladies and a few gentlemen that were assembled together in the sitting-room. They were quite close to where I was, being distant only about three or four feet. He seemed to me to be in a state of intoxication. I then looked sternly and coolly at him lest I should judge him wrongly, but am sorry to say the longer I gazed, I was the more convinced. I then turned to see if the young ladies observed the state the captain was in, and I believe – in fact am positively persuaded from the aspect of their countenances – that it was quite clear to them. The captain now said to them, while their eyes were riveted upon him, and a kind of wild despair flashed from their countenances, "Don't be afraid; we are not far from land – close to it; and in a short time, daylight will appear, and we shall all get ashore safely. I assure you there is no danger at all. I assure you; I assure you." These words were expressed in such a confused and inarticulate manner that no man in a state of sobriety would have uttered, his face at the same time being flushed, his eyes dim and vacant-looking, and his countenance was of a stupid, unmeaning aspect. So soon as he uttered those words, I looked at the young ladies to see if they appeared to receive his miserable consolation, but the want of confidence their countenances portrayed, together with their wild despairing look, pierced my very heart, and satisfied me on that subject. I then said to myself, what a miserable comforter, and there and then determined that it was time for me to look out for myself. The following passengers, if disposed, are as fully prepared to prove that Captain Taylor was not sober at the time of the wreck as I am:- James M'Cappin, Samuel Grenfell, Mr. Bradbury, of Manchester. Seamen – Wilson, M'Carthur, Tims and others whose names I cannot remember.

By inserting this statement, you will oblige,

yours respectfully,

Wm. JOHN FERRIS.

Mr. Ferris supported his assertion that Captain Taylor was drunk by stating that Messrs. M'Cappin, Grenfell, Bradbury, Wilson, M'Carthur, and Tims would support him, but Bradbury had written to the inquiry contradicting a rumour to the effect that he (Bradbury) had said that Captain Taylor was intoxicated on the day of the wreck.

Was there a target to arrive home within sixty days of leaving Melbourne?

No evidence of this is given in the newspapers, although Frank Fowler stated that Captain Taylor would receive a bonus if he achieved the round-trip within 150 days.

Did the 'Royal Charter' pause at Holyhead so that passengers could view the 'Great Eastern'?

No. Some of the passengers requested Captain Taylor to do so, but he refused to divert out of his normal route.

Why wasn't there a pilot on-board?

Quite simply the weather was too rough and the night too dark for a pilot-boat to rendezvous with the 'Royal Charter'. There was a hurricane blowing, and it was the night of a spring-tide and a new moon.

Why didn't the captain order the masts to be cut down to lessen the strain on the anchors?

Captain Taylor simply didn't expect the anchor-cable to fail, saying: *'I have her fast by the nose, and we may want the masts again.'* There was the risk of loose rigging becoming entangled with the propeller, and the probability that the falling masts and spars would penetrate the deck and cause injury to those below.

Why were only two anchors deployed, when the 'Royal Charter' carried four of them?

Although the 'Royal Charter' was fitted with four hawse-pipes, only two anchors were carried ready for deployment at the bow. The third anchor was stowed away in the hold, while the fourth one was kept at the stern, and was probably too light to be of much use. However, assuming that there was still a sufficient amount of chain left aboard the 'Royal Charter', these anchors might have slowed the rate of drift towards the shore and kept the vessel off the rocks until daylight, when Captain Taylor would have been in a far better position to assess the situation.

Did the anchors fail?

No. Trotman's anchors performed well; perhaps too well, as a dragging anchor would have put less sudden-strain on the anchor-chains.

Why did the anchor-cables fail?

The chains met the requirements of the mercantile marine, but their specification was less than that required by the Royal Navy. It had been suggested that they parted due to the constant snatching, as the 'Royal Charter' was driven forward by the engine but was then forced backwards as the next wave hit the vessel. The sudden strain was so great that the chains might have failed whatever their specification, but they might have remained intact had the anchors dragged.

Why were there no women or children saved?

The women and children were deliberately kept below decks in the saloon, where it was expected that they would be out of harm's way. In the expectation of being able to wade ashore, they were told to put on extra layers of clothing, but the ship's hull split apart while they were still below, flinging them into the cold sea.

Happier days. The 'Royal Charter' under sail. From a watercolour by B. Booth.

Who was Tom Tyson?

Up to the date of publication, no information has come to light as to who he was, or if and why he was on the 'Royal Charter'. Hopefully, some information will be uncovered, and this will be made available on our website.

Why was she wrecked?

The 'Royal Charter' came to grief because she was in the wrong place at the wrong time, having had no prior warning of the ferocious weather that was about to devastate much of the British Isles. A moonless night, a spring-tide, and hurricane-force winds combined to create a situation that overwhelmed the power of her steam engine and over-strained the anchor-cables so that she had no means of keeping away from a lee-shore. She grounded in darkness at low-water so that no-one could ascertain their position, but the rapidly-rising tide lifted the hull onto the rocks, where she was pounded by the waves until she split apart.

Could Captain Taylor have done more to save his ship, his passengers and his cargo?

Shipmasters of the 21st century can obtain instant and accurate information on the tides, the weather, their own position, and the location of many other resources such as the Liverpool Pilots and the rescue services. Captain Taylor had no navigation systems that gave him his exact position, no information about the forthcoming weather, and no accurate means of checking the strength and direction of the tidal-flow. All he had was a compass, a barometer, a sounding-weight, and the sharp eyes of the seamen on duty. As Captain Fell, a representative of the insurance underwriters, said at the inquest:

> I have heard the evidence given by Captain Martin, and I agree with him that Captain Taylor did all that could be done under the circumstances to save the ship.

> I should have done everything that Captain Taylor did.

What if?

Dulas Island and tower at half-tide, as seen from the shore with a zoom lens.

If the cables had snapped earlier or later, or the hurricane had blown from a slightly different direction, the 'Royal Charter' would have come ashore on a different stretch of coast to where she actually came to grief. Southwards from Point Lynas, the shoreline is rocky and inhospitable, where there was little chance of anyone being on the cliffs so early in the morning of that disastrous day, and therefore no-one to help the survivors. Closer to Moelfre, Lligwy Bay offers a gently-sloping, sandy beach, where Captain Taylor may have been correct in his assertion that they could all go on shore at daylight.

Alternatively, the vessel could have hit Dulas Island, the small rocky outcrop shown in the photograph above. Several vessels have come to grief here, with the result that a small tower was erected as a shelter for shipwrecked mariners, and the building was kept stocked with food. A plaque in front of the building is inscribed --

This tower was erected A.D. 1824 by Col. James Hughes as a beacon or place of refuge to the shipwrecked.

It is possible that more lives would have been saved if the 'Royal Charter' had hit the island, as the rocks do not rise vertically from the sea, but can you imagine five hundred survivors trying to shelter here from the hurricane as the tide rose higher?

The stony beach at Porth Helaeth lies only around two hundred metres eastwards of the wreck. The 'Royal Charter' is less likely to have broken up here, but there is a small, rocky reef that partially blocks the bay and would have caused immense damage had the clipper collided with this obstruction.

Around the village of Moelfre, the coastline is similar to that where she finally ended her days, with Moelfre Island being especially dangerous as it would have been inaccessible to the 'Rescuers of the Wrecked'.

Further eastwards, the coast is mostly rocky, except for the wide, sandy expanse of Red Wharf Bay where many ships have been beached during bad weather. One heroic rescue occurred here just five years before the tragedy of October, 1859.

Welsh Bravery. On the night of the 17th inst., it blew a fierce gale from the N.N.E., during which the sloop *Two Brothers*, of Aberystwyth, had her sails split and was driven on the sands north of Red Wharf Bay. The sea soon made a break over her, washed away the hatches, filled her with water, finally dashing her boat to pieces on the attempt being made to launch her. Taking to the rigging as their only hope, the crew lashed the apprentice boy to the masthead, and anxiously waited for the day. Despite the probability of a watery grave, nine brave fellows volunteered to rescue the shipwrecked mariners, or to perish in the attempt.

North Wales Chronicle. October 28, 1854

Revenge of the Albatross!

Myth and superstition have been a deeply embedded part of a seafarer's life since man first left the safety of dry-land, and the albatross, that beautiful sea-bird of the Southern Ocean, was well-known to mariners as an omen of ill-fortune, tragedy and death. However, they were also regarded as a precursor of good luck. Samuel Taylor Coleridge published his poem 'The Rime [*sic*] of the Ancient Mariner' in 1798, in which an albatross comes to the rescue of a ship enveloped in fog, snow and ice. With disaster looming:

> At length did cross an albatross,
> Through the fog it came.
> As if it had been a Christian soul,
> We hailed it in God's name.
>
> It ate the food it ne're had eat,
> And round and round it flew.
> The ice did split with a thunder fit,
> The helmsman steered us through.

So, they were saved by one of those magnificent birds, but to harm an albatross was to injure the restless soul of a dead seaman, and to do so was to risk the wrath of the gods of the sea.

As William Scoresby reported on the maiden voyage of the 'Royal Charter', killing an albatross was regarded as 'sport' by the ship's passengers, with several being shot, or caught on a baited line. This cruel pastime continued long after the loss of the 'Royal Charter', as depicted in this engraving from 'The 'Graphic' magazine of 1892. In Colleridge's rhyme, an albatross is killed by a bolt from a crossbow, and his words continue:

> And I had done a hellish thing,
> And it would work 'em woe:
> For all averred, I had killed the bird.
> That made the breeze to blow.
> Ah wretch! said they, the bird to slay,
> That made the breeze to blow!

For all averred, I had killed the bird.
***That* made the breeze to blow.**

On the fateful morning of the 26th of October, 1859, there was far more than just a breeze.

It blew a 'perfect hurricane!'

The final word

Edwin Fowler, his wife and two children died only a few hours away from completing their return to England. A tombstone in Llanallgo Churchyard reads:

"Beneath repose the remains of EDWIN FOWLER and of his daughters JANE & IDA EMILY, who were lost in the wreck of the *Royal Charter* from Melbourne, on the coast of Anglesea on the 26th of October, 1859. This monument has been erected to their memory and to the memory of ANNA FOWLER, the beloved wife of EDWIN FOWLER, who perished in the wreck but whose remains were not recovered, by their orphaned children FANNY LEUCRETIA & EDWIN. Also the remains of EMMA GALE, the nurse of IDA. Her body was recovered but a few paces from that of her infant charge. She was faithful unto death."

Five months after the disaster, a ring belonging to Edwin Fowler was found on the shore at Moelfre. He had worn the ring in memory of a sister who had died some time ago, and the treasured artefact was returned to his father by the Reverend Hugh Hughes. Jane Fowler Jones, a niece of Edwin Fowler wrote this poem in memory of the family:

Lines on a ring cast ashore five months after the wreck of the *Royal Charter.*

> Five moons the raging sea retained.
> Within its secret hold,
> This ring, the sad and sacred type,
> Of mourning manifold.
>
> This ring, that to a brother's love,
> A sister's death declar'd,
> Returneth, crying from the deep —
> " Woe! woe! He hath not spared !"
>
> Oh ring of mourning! ring of Fate !
> In what unfathom'd scene,
> Of horror unexplor'd and dark,
> Hast thou mute witness been ?
>
> Thou hast been where the hidden dead
> Repose beneath the sea,
> Nought fearful, or soul-harrowing,
> Is there unknown to thee.
>
> Oh sea! we bade thee not restore,
> Our jewels, or our gold;
> We ask'd of thee a greater debt,
> The lives within thy hold.
>
> In vain, in vain, oh ruthless sea !
> In vain our arms we spread,
> And prayed thee for our lov'd ones,
> Thou gavest us our dead.
>
> Yet not in vain, from thee, sad sea,
> This precious gift is riven,
> Imparting hope — to us who weep,
> That we may meet in heaven.

Bibliography

Historical data, dive-sites and shipwrecks

McKee, Alexander (1961, 1986) The Golden Wreck

Williams, Robert (2009) Shipwrecked. Charles Dickens and the 'Royal Charter'.

Hughes, John (2009) Loss Royal Charter Steam Clipper.

Hawes. G. (2005) Journey's End. St. Gallgo Church & the 'Royal Charter' Shipwreck.

Holden, Chris (2008) The Essential Underwater Guide to North Wales. Volume II

Stamp, Tom & Cordelia. (1976) William Scoresby - Arctic Scientist

Scoresby, Rev. William. (1859) Journal of a Voyage to Australia and round the World for Magnetical Research. (Republished 2005 Elibron Classics)

Cameron, Paul (1859) Variation and Deviation of the Compass Rectified.

Board of Trade (1860) Wrecks and Casualties

A & JK, (1859) Wreck of the 'Royal Charter'.

Fowler, Frank (1859) The Wreck of the 'Royal Charter'

Fowler, Frank. (1859) Dotings of a Lounger

Fowler, Frank. (1859) Southern Lights and Shadows.

Baynes, E. Neil. The Wreck of the 'Royal Charter'.

Bourke, E.J. Bound for Australia: The Loss of the Emigrant Ship 'Tayleur'.

Jones, Ivor Wynne (2000) Shipwrecks of North Wales (new revised edition).

Shears, Andy and Scott Waterman (2002) Anglesey Wrecks & Reefs (Volume 1).

Larn, Richard & Bridget (2000) Shipwreck Index - Britain, Vol. 5. W. Coast & Wales.

Stubbs, John M. An Index to Shipwrecks on the North Wales Coast 1807 - 1914.

Bennett, Tom (1995) Shipwrecks Around Anglesey.

Bennett, Tom (1987 & 1992) Shipwrecks Around Wales, Volumes 1 & 2.

Gater, Dilys (1992) Historic Shipwrecks of Wales.

Hocking, Charles (1989) Dictionary of Disasters at Sea 1824 - 1962.

Eames, Aled (1981 reprint) Ships & Seamen of Anglesey.

Skidmore, Ian (1979) Anglesey & Lleyn Shipwrecks.

Parry, Henry (1969) Wreck & Rescue on the Coast of Wales, Volume 2.

Sennett, R. (1882) The Marine Steam Engine.

Evans, Wilson P. (1978) Through the Rip. Ships & Seamen of Old Port Phillip.

Dixon J. & Pickard G. (2002) Crichton & Co. Shipbuilders Saltney & Connahs Quay.

Loney J. and Peter Stone. (2000) The Australia Run.

Howitt, William (1855) Two Years in Victoria.

Chester Chronicle, Caernarfon & Denbigh Herald.

North Wales Chronicle, Liverpool Mercury, Illustrated London News, The Times.

Lloyd's Register, Lloyd's List.

Libraries

Ynys Mon Archives, Llangefni.
Denbighshire Archives, Ruthin.
Gwynedd Archives, Caernarfon.
Flintshire Record Office, Hawarden.
Chester City Library.
Cheshire County Archives, Chester.
Liverpool Maritime Museum Library.
Liverpool City Library.

Places to visit

Llanallgo Church.
Penrhos Lligwy Church
Seawatch Centre, Moelfre, Anglesey.
Oriel Mon, Llangefni, Anglesey.
Holyhead Maritime Museum, Anglesey.
Liverpool Maritime Museum.
S.S. 'Great Britain', Bristol Docks.
'H.M.S. Warrior', Portsmouth.
St. Mary's Church, Whitby

Glossary (further details available on our website)

Aft / Abaft	Aft = At or towards the stern. Abaft = sternwards of.
Ballast	Stones or similar heavy material placed low down in a ship to improve stability.
Bilges	The lowest part of the interior of a ship. This is where the 'bilge-water' collects.
Bitts	A pair of strong, vertical posts that were used to secure the rigging or a mooring-rope.
Board of Trade	A department of the British Government.
Bulwark	Wood, iron or steel that forms a vertical barrier along the outer sides of the upper deck.
Cable	1) An anchor-chain 2) A distance of 100 fathoms or 200 yards (183 metres).
Caulking	To make a hull watertight by hammering oakum (tarred hemp or manila) into any gaps.
Cock-bill	Prepare the anchor for being lowered.
Droits (Receiver of)	The person to whom items of shipwreck should be reported.
Fathom	Six feet (approximately two metres).
Garboard strake	That part of a ship's hull adjacent to the keel.
Gibbs, Bright & Co	The owners of the 'Royal Charter' and the 'Great Britain'.
Hawse-pipe	The tube where the anchor-chain passes through a ship's hull.
Hawser	A strong, heavy rope.
Hobson's Bay	The northernmost part of Port Phillip, Australia.
Howe's System	A system of easily decreasing the amount of sail that has been set.
Keelson	Extra strengthening for a ship's hull, fitted internally to run fore and aft.
Knots	Nautical miles per hour. One nautical mile = 1.1516 statue miles. Note that some of the text in the old newspapers is somewhat confusing when using this term.
Lead / lead-line	A lead weight and line used to check the depth of water.
Lee-side	The side of a ship away from the wind.
Liverpool	A major shipping-port in north-west England.
Lloyd's	An association of insurance underwriters which has its headquarters in London.
Melbourne	A major city in Victoria, south-east Australia.
Middy / Midshipman	A non-commissioned rank at sea.
Mizzen	The after-most mast.
Neap-tide	This is when the difference between high-tide & low-tide is the least.
Orlop deck	The lowest deck on a vessel.
Pelorus	A sighting device on a compass, used for taking the relative bearing of a distant object.
Poop	A raised deck at the stern of a vessel.
Port	1) The left-hand side of a ship. 2) A harbour.
Portemonnaie	A purse.
Port Phillip	A large bay near Melbourne, Australia. See the map on page 91.
Queenstown	Cobh, a natural harbour in Southern Ireland.
Receiver of Wreck	A Government official to whom all wreckage, jetsam, etc. must be reported.
Screw	Propeller. Sometimes also referred to as a fan.
Se'nnight	An abbreviation for 'seven nights' i.e. a week
Sounding	Usually, the depth of the sea, but occasionally of water in the bilges.
Spanker	An extra sail, hoisted on the mizzen mast to take advantage of a following wind.
Spring-tide	This is when the difference between high-tide & low-tide is the greatest.
Starboard	The right-hand side of a ship.
Stay / Staying	To change the tack of a vessel by bringing the bows past the direction of the wind.
Steerage	The cheapest form of accommodation on board a vessel.
Stringer	Additional pieces of iron that run fore and aft to strengthen a hull.
Tacking	A sailing vessel cannot head directly into the wind, so has to sail at an angle to it.
Trotman	A type of anchor, designed by John Trotman.
'tween-decks	The space between two decks.
Wearing	To change the tack of a vessel by bringing the stern past the direction of the wind.
Weather-side	The side of a ship towards the wind.
Yard	1) Three feet (approx 1 metre) 2) A horizontal beam on a mast. Used for carrying the sails.